PETERSBURG, CRUCIBLE OF CULTURAL REVOLUTION

PETERSBURG, CRUCIBLE OF CULTURAL REVOLUTION

Katerina Clark

Harvard University Press
Cambridge, Massachusetts
London, England

Library of Congress Cataloging-in-Publication Data

Clark, Katerina.
Petersburg, crucible of cultural revolution / Katerina Clark.
p.   cm.
Includes bibliographical references and index.
ISBN 0-674-66335-7 (cloth)
ISBN 0-674-66336-5 (pbk.)
1. Saint Petersburg (Russia)—Intellectual life.   I. Title.
DK557.C57   1995
947'.453—dc20
95-17161
CIP

This book is dedicated to the memory of
Frantisek William Galan (1947–1991),
battered child of the Revolution,
scholar, aesthete, friend

CONTENTS

PREFACE

Any revolution occurs within a particular cultural ecosystem that delimits possible change. Ideological formations in the system act as constraints on any extrahistorical agendas the revolution's agents might have. Yet the rhetoric of "revolution" assumes that the ecosystem is malleable. The frames of reference are largely inherited, although the ones that prevail in the new conditions may not be those that were dominant under the old order.

In this book I examine this dynamic by focusing on the quest of Petersburg intellectuals to establish a quintessential revolutionary culture during the fateful years of war and revolution, 1913–1931. I ask the question how the Soviet 1920s became the Stalinist 1930s. I have tried to rethink what happened in the 1910s, 1920s, and 1930s outside the somewhat tired and Russo-centric frame of "continuity or change?" Indeed, a foundational premise of this book is that these categories are inadequate to the complexity of the subject. I argue against the assumption that in cultural history there was some sort of big bang in 1917. I also argue against the mysticism of "decade" and resist the notion that the 1920s represent a single entity that is either absolutely unlike, or some sort of precursor to, that other entity that is the 1930s. Instead, I focus on an entire series of shifts in the cultural models that occurred in the period covered, shifts involving both continuity and change.

This book, then, is a case study in the ecology of revolution. It argues that the evolution of "Stalinist" culture did not proceed in a series of radical breaks or in an unswerving line. Rather, it draws an analogy with what is called "punctuated evolution," and points out that while cultural history in the 1920s and 1930s was marked by a series of cataclysms (purges, cultural revolutions, and so on), the more formative moments tended to be not these dramatic times but the intervening years of adaptation and consolidation as the surviving flora and fauna responded to the new conditions; some came to dominate, others not, and others again generated mutations. Moreover, in the evolution of Soviet culture though the Party or the regime might be the apparent agent (cause) of the cataclysms, they are themselves not extrasystemic figures but part of that ecosystem; consequently, even as they act they are also acted upon. So often the Party was acting out models suggested in intellectuals' works. The Party and the intelligentsia were never completely separate groups, nor was either of them ever homogenous (this was true of the Party even in the darkest years of Stalinism).

Thus in this book I seek to avoid representing events in a tale that culminates in Stalinism as a culture formulated and instituted either by him personally, or by his regime generally. What historians have personalized as Stalinism was largely in evidence well before he had the power to dictate policy. Though Stalinist culture might seem to represent an abomination of the intellectuals' aspirations, it was nevertheless not the product of an act of parthenogenesis on the part of the Party leaders, nor was it merely the case that their ideas were ventriloquated through the intellectuals.

To assume that the Party made Stalinist culture and that the intellectuals did not is to participate in the same kind of either/or mentality that was characteristic of official Soviet thinking. The relationship between the two groups was much more dialogic than such accounts assume, despite the fact that they were so unequal in power terms. Consequently, in analyzing cultural evolution, a blow-by-blow account of "And then the Party ruled..." does not necessarily yield the most rewarding or profound narrative. An additional problem is that the Party did not always rule consistently. For example, the 1930s under Stalin saw several shifts of the basic cultural model, despite the fact that the leadership remained fairly stable. Arguably, these shifts reflect not merely successive whims on Stalin's part but broad cultural changes.

My intention is not to deny all the horrors and excesses of the Stalin regime. Nor is it to deny that, in the 1930s and 1940s especially, the Party leadership's overweening role in cultural politics was tremendously consequential in determining the shape of Soviet culture. But the story of its repressiveness has been told many times before. This book seeks not to contradict that account, nor to rival it (we already have some fine studies), but rather to explore other aspects of the dynamic in the interests of pointing to the vicissitudes and paradoxes of cultural evolution and adding a level of complexity to the existing paradigms of Western historiography.

Although many intellectuals resisted the Bolshevik regime and many were persecuted by it or succumbed to its pressures and became mere "hacks," still others were challenged by it and saw the overthrow of the old order as an opportunity to press for their own agendas. The single most powerful reason many non-Party intellectuals were able to find some common ground with the Party I explain in terms of a fundamental loathing for the role of the marketplace in culture, a loathing to be found among highbrows and avant-gardists alike. Hence, in many instances, intellectuals could not be characterized as merely "resisting" the regime or "collaborating" with it but were, rather, maneuvering within the spectrum of possibilities available in the name of their own revolutionary ideals. Another point of common ground frequently found between intellectual groups and the Party is what might be called "evolutionary impatience." So often revolution was, in the understanding of a given group, a form of voluntarist evolution.

In this book I do not assume that revolutions are all-powerful. Consequently, I begin in 1913, the last year before the Great War, which saw the culmination of late Imperial culture, a nodal point where one can observe traffic patterns between Russian and Soviet culture, and also between European and Russian culture. In so doing, I show that many of the "revolutionary" programs represent trends to be found across a spectrum of Western countries. To analyze these patterns comprehensively would be a mammoth task, and so I have selected a single but crucial focus for my study: the city—the phenomenon—of Petersburg/Leningrad.

Most accounts of Soviet culture in the 1920s have been about individual figures or groups, but the picture they present of its evolution has been, de facto, Moscow-centric. In the interests of obtaining a more complex account, I take the other direction and focus on Petersburg, a focus with obvious limitations, but also certain advantages.

Revolutions renegotiate center and periphery; they renegotiate hierarchies. Petersburg, as the capital, had been the center of Russia. It lost that status in 1918, and by the time the city was renamed Leningrad, in 1924, it was fast becoming ever more peripheral. Cultural evolution is not unilinear, however, and those elements that are marginal at one time may become dominant in another. Hence a cultural history of Petersburg in the revolutionary years can serve as a prism for looking at this process. As Moscow became the center of an authoritarian culture, Petersburg changed its function from seat of power to that of significant other. The various alternatives to "Moscow" culture, representing all points on the Soviet Union's political and aesthetic spectra, have tended to come out of, to be published in, or to identify with, "Petersburg," a tendency that is apparent in the period covered by this book. In other words, there was always a dialogic relationship between Moscow culture and that of Petersburg/Leningrad.

This book covers not only Petersburg culture *tout court* but also follows, with a particular focus on events in that city, this developing dialogue in the Soviet period. The dialogue, however, is not merely between intellectuals located in the two cities; it is also between old and "new" models of national identity. Ever since the city's foundation in 1703, contending accounts of "Petersburg" have played a crucial role in thinking through this identity.

A revolution is supremely an iconoclastic act, but it entails more than a rupture; in its attempt to forge a new and more authentic beginning, it must locate some prior ground for this authenticity. More often than not, the struggle for the future has worked itself out as a conflict between contending versions of the past. In modern Russia, Petersburg has been the text in which intellectuals have sought to read the past as an index to the future. The city has functioned in their imaginations as more than a mere city: it has been a mythopoeic space.

Thus my subject is not just the urban complex Petersburg/Leningrad. As intellectuals and revolutionaries worked out their common task of creating a new, revolutionary culture, questions of time, space, language, and authority became crucial in giving it shape. Petersburg was in many respects the frame of their endeavor.

PETERSBURG, CRUCIBLE OF CULTURAL REVOLUTION

INTRODUCTION: THE ECOLOGY OF REVOLUTION

This book tells the story of the Great Experiment, of that generation of intellectuals who in the 1920s sought to create a truly revolutionary culture. Many saw their dreams evaporate in repression, obtuseness, and even outright quackery so that their enthusiasm was rarely passed on to their children or grandchildren. Often their progeny became dissidents or, in the 1970s and 1980s, sought to emigrate. David Remnick in *Lenin's Tomb* discusses the family of Masha Lipman as an example of this common generational pattern. Masha was a dissident, but one of her grandfathers had been a member of RAPM (the Russian Association of Proletarian Musicians, the most militant revolutionary group of the late 1920s in that field), and his wife had been a disciple of Vs. Meyerhold and acted in his theater. As Masha describes the grandparents:

> They and their friends developed a revolutionary style even in the way they lived at home. . . . They had no dishes, no real furniture. They decided it was all too bourgeois. . . . Birthday parties, weddings and New Year's [Christmas] trees were also gotten rid of. Bourgeois. . . . They thought that traditional Russian felt boots, *valenki*, were also bourgeois, so the children walked through the slush and the snow in thin leather shoes, crying of the cold. They just mocked all traditions of the old order. So they had my mother call them by their first names and they ate their meals off of butcher paper.[1]

This rigidly ascetic code with its system of taboos extending to the most banal aspects of life, resulting even in needless cruelty to one's own children, is reminiscent of a religious sect. The avant-garde artist Pavel Filonov, along with other Russian intellectuals of this time, participated so fully in such Manichaean scenarios that during NEP (the New Economic Policy; the period during the mid-1920s when small-scale private enterprise was permitted) he would not let one of the petty capitalists spawned by the age (a nepman) so much as cross the threshold of his apartment.[2] But if so many Russian intellectuals were taken by a religious-like belief system that in its more extreme expressions resembled a sect, arguably its idols were not Marx or Lenin so much as they were some version of culture.

Much of intellectual life was driven by a version of a thirst for the sacred with a concomitant revulsion against the profane, a contest of values that can be seen in an early paradigm, the story of Christ's throwing the moneychangers out of the temple. In the modern, post-Enlightenment period, a wide range of intellectuals in the West as well as in Russia have essentially reacted against strictly secularizing tendencies and reinvested religious fervor in their version of culture as a sacred value threatened not just by the moneychangers (its commercialization) but by a more comprehensive category that might be called "the profane." This category includes market forces but essentially represents the mundane, worldly aspects of everyday life, such as seeking comfort, profit, personal advantage, and so on. Some intellectuals contended that culture should play the leading role in a religious revival, but a revival conceived outside the parameters of conventional religion and the organized church. They did, however, share with the other groups represented in this trend a repugnance for the bourgeoisie or the petty bourgeoisie as the icon of the profane. This essentially aesthetic utopianism, or quest for the sacred, coincides at key points with the more strictly economic or political criticisms of figures such as Marx, to whom some but not all of them subscribed to a degree.

Even before the Revolution in Russia, many different intellectual groups sought greater power and authority as a means of assuming a sacerdotal role in society. After the Revolution, many, but by no means all of them, devoted their lives to the cause of the Revolution's culture as a possible step toward realizing their goals; Meyerhold, the Formalist theoretician Osip Brik, and others even flirted with the Cheka (the secret police) as the force most committed to driving the moneychangers out of the temple. Others worked for the Bolshevik state with heavy hearts as an uneasy and ultimately turncoat ally in the pursuit of the millennium. (Many of them abandoned this pursuit, whether to external or internal emigration, or because they had themselves been purged or enticed into becoming Soviet "hacks.") Still others resisted the Bolsheviks from the very outset as false prophets of a purifying transformation, as a force for darkness or heresy.

The Great Experiment's master narrative, one that can be associated with the story of how Christ drove the moneychangers out of the temple, involves the repurification or resacerdotalization of space. This was a foundational myth of Soviet culture in the 1920s and 1930s (its centrality in the latter decade, a time of purging, is not far to seek). Masha Lipman's grandparents, like so many others, sought to purify even the most banal corners of their private space. But the concern with private space was essentially subsumed under the overriding concern with public space. It is in this latter concern that the trend intersects with Russia's main myth of national identity, the myth of Petersburg.

Petersburg

In 1913 Andrei Bely published his Symbolist novel *Petersburg*,[3] which opens with a playful disquisition on the existence of the city. The narrator concludes: "If Petersburg is not the capital, there is no Petersburg. It only appears to exist." He then goes on to insist that no matter how it might seem, Petersburg must exist because it appears on the map in the form of two concentric circles with a dot in the middle (the marker of the capital city), and "from precisely this mathematical dot, which has no dimension, it proclaims forcefully that it exists: from here, from this very point, surges and swarms the printed book, from this invisible point speeds the official circular."[4]

When Bely wrote his Prologue, he did not realize how serious his implied question was to become. Just a year later, after the Great War started in August 1914, Petersburg was no more in the sense that its name had been russified to Petrograd lest it be mistaken for a German name.[5] And in five years, in March 1918, the city lost its status as the Soviet capital, since it was deemed too close to the West and the sea and hence more vulnerable to attack than Moscow. The new Bolshevik city fathers in Petrograd lobbied periodically for returning the capital to their city, not, needless to say, because it had been the old Imperial capital, but on the grounds that it was the "city of the Revolution" (the new point of origins). A particularly concerted effort was made after the Civil War ended—and with it much of the danger of attack—but all their bids were in vain.

The issue of whether Petersburg exists is not, however, only about whether or not it is the nation's capital. What Bely is also alluding to in his Prologue is the sense that Petersburg at some level "exists" only as the focus of a myth of Petersburg, that is, only in books, and versions of that myth question whether the city exists as an actuality at all.

The myth of Petersburg, sometimes referred to as the Petersburg theme, has been an obsession of Russian intellectual life since at least the beginning of the nineteenth century. There is scarcely a major writer, historian, or thinker who has not examined the meaning of Petersburg. The city was founded by Peter the Great in 1703 to effect the transformation of Russia from a "rude and barbarous," semi-Asiatic country to a respected member of the concert of Europe. All interpreters set themselves the task of defining this event as an emblem for Russia's historical destiny or the identity of its culture.

The myth rests on a somewhat legendary account of the city's foundation.[6] By the will or genius of one man, Peter the Great, the boggy wilderness was transformed into a resplendent capital. When, with a system of canals, Peter tamed the waters of the Neva and drained its adjoining swampland, a city of culture arose where once there had been only desolate nature. And then, as if to proclaim the transformation from nature to culture, statues were erected in the new city, principally at points where they preside over the tamed waterways, on the Neva embankments and the canals.

This traditional account of Petersburg claiming that the town was built on an uninhabitable swamp is not entirely based in fact. Equally dubious is the myth's insistence that the fabled city emerged "suddenly."[7] But the facts of the city's foundation matter less than the function of its myth. As cultural anthropologists and historians have noted, in each major culture system a city has emerged as its emblem or paradigm, always embodying particular values, political, metaphysical, or aesthetic.[8] Generally, each culture has fastened on a particular city as the privileged subject for successive readings of itself.[9] As Clifford Geertz has remarked, "Political authority requires a cultural frame in which to define itself and advance its claims," and hence the city chosen as emblem has most often been the nation's capital.[10]

In eighteenth-century Russia, the achievement of Petersburg and the story of its foundation became the focus of legitimizing myths for the Russian empire. Peter emerged as the principal actor in the new originary myth, a myth of the magnificent city founded *ex nihilo*. The response to Petersburg was not all laudatory, however. As Geertz has pointed out, the opposition to the regnant political authority requires a "cultural frame" no less than does the authority itself and tends to articulate its case within the same frame. Together with the official foundation myth of Petersburg there developed a foundation antimyth that included virtually the same elements in the story of Petersburg's foundation as did the official myth, but reinterpreted each.

Such negative interpretations had been largely festering in oral lore, but in the early nineteenth century the antimyth assumed a major role in the written tradition. Writers identified the foundation of Petersburg in a poor, inhospitable, and dreary site as Peter's cardinal error, the moment that symbolized how he turned Russia from her natural course; they lambasted the city as "founded on tears and bones."[11]

In 1833 Aleksandr Pushkin, Russia's most famous poet, published a long poem entitled *The Bronze Horseman* (Mednyy vsadnik, a reference to the famous equestrian statue to Peter the Great erected by Catherine) incorporating many of the clichés from both the positive and the negative versions of the myth. The poem concerns an actual event, the disastrous flood of 1824, generally regarded as the most severe of all the recurrent floods to which Petersburg has been subject.

The poem opens with a laudatory preamble, written in the style of the occasional ode, in which Pushkin praises the great builder of Petersburg and his "creation" and, by implication, the great line. After this, however, Pushkin shifts both genre and tone to treat the flood in a fictive account of a poor clerk, Evgeny, whose fiancée is drowned when raging waters engulf the island in the Neva where she lives. Evgeny is driven insane and challenges the statue of the bronze horseman, who proceeds to gallop after him through the deserted squares of Petersburg; in the end, Evgeny is so reduced by hunger and exhaustion that he dies.

The poem has been widely interpreted as an attack on autocracy. Another common interpretation has to do with Peter's role in opening up Russia to the West and its toll on native traditions and citizenry. Both interpretations see as the center of the poem the confrontation between the oppressive tsar and the raging Neva as a figure for the "elemental" masses who periodically rise up against his repression.

The Bronze Horseman, locus classicus of the Petersburg myth, has launched a thousand creative works (poems, films, plays, paintings, and so on), including Bely's *Petersburg*. Although Pushkin was far from the first to rework the myth, with his poem the myth cohered and the equestrian statue became the city's *genius loci*.[12] Since *The Bronze Horseman* appeared, its tropes have become standard for the Petersburg theme, but they are continually being reaccentuated. Many of the landmarks in this process are among the best-known works of Russian literature; Petersburg has ranged in meaning from a phantasmagoric and unreal city in a Gogol or a Dostoevsky tale to, in modernist works of the early twentieth century, the raw materials of a meta-literature that explores the role of art and the artist, and the problematic nature of consciousness.

One might think that the Revolution would have killed off this already overused theme. After all, it overthrew the hated autocratic order; moreover, in its wake the capital and bureaucracy were moved to Moscow. But in fact this was not so.

By 1918 Petersburg no longer existed either in name or as those circles around a dot on the map which proclaim it to be the capital. Yet it has persisted in Russian culture to this day as an idea, an ethos, an ideal, and above all as a language of clichés that Russians have deployed in debating the country's way forward. Although in the 1920s Moscow became ever more powerful politically, it was not until the 1930s that a cogent Soviet myth of Moscow emerged and the first great Muscovite novel of the Soviet period, M. Bulgakov's *The Master and Margarita,* was written (final draft version 1938–1940). Even then the myth of Petersburg continued to captivate the imagination and to generate new interpretations in response to a changing reality. To this day, its principal terms have proved tenacious as frames for the inevitable identity search conducted in literature, theater, and film after the cataclysmic upheaval of revolution.[13]

Some versions of this myth might have questioned whether Petersburg exists, but an even greater illusion is that it is a unique myth. It seems quite derivative in many of its clichés (for example, "the city founded on bones and tears" is but a variant of the myth of the building of the pyramids or of Versailles). Russian writers found many of their "Petersburg" tropes among those that Balzac, Hugo, and others applied to Paris.[14] Also, the representation of Petersburg as phantasmagoric came not just because of its peculiar history and geography but also because Russian writers wanted to inscribe E. T. A. Hoffman into a Russian reality and fastened upon Petersburg as the most grateful site for this.

The Petersburg myth is essentially a variant of the myth of the center and as such is very comparable with the myth of Paris. There are elements that make this particular version distinctive, however, not the least of which is that there exists another claimant for the title capital, Moscow, the one superseded when Petersburg was founded. Each of the two capitals has functioned as the symbol for rival interpretations of the national identity.

In the old days, as Lewis Mumford and others have remarked, a city was seen as a simulacrum of the heavens.[15] Petersburg was originally conceived as a seat of power, and also a city of science and culture. As such, with its statues and grid of broad avenues and canals, it was deliberately contrasted with obscurantist, medieval Moscow, a city of narrow, winding lanes and onion domes. In other words, it was built in the image of a new belief system. Petersburg, as anti-Moscow, was always considered more secular and cosmopolitan. This was an important element in those interpretations of the myth that saw the city's very existence as illusory. Yet, in actuality, the city was the most insistent reality of a highly centralized state. To see it as a phantom-like mirage is to deny the kingdom of necessity.

In the nineteenth century Petersburg was, for all its statues and canals, a paradigm of the industrializing city. By the middle of the century the statues were anachronistic, like the medieval parts of Paris or London in the mercantilist era. As Petersburg industrialized, a huge population growth exacerbated the already dramatic divisions of class and education and was accompanied by the predictable gamut of social problems (poor public health, prostitution, housing, and so on). When Russians wrote about urban problems they often used elements from the myth of Petersburg as their frame. This is evident in Dostoevsky's *Crime and Punishment* when the narrator dwells on the horrors of the Haymarket district, which is situated just behind grand buildings of the city's center.

In the 1910s and 1920s, many intellectuals used tropes from the myth of Petersburg in interpreting the meaning of revolution for Russia. Some saw the city as standing for all that was retrograde in the old Russia, as a constraining, stagnant, or polluted space, a scab that obscured or putrified the purest or most vital expressions of culture and therefore had to be removed.[16] For others, by contrast, Petersburg became the symbolic site of humanistic culture, of a quasi-religious value system that many believed should become the basis of a new social order. After 1917, some enjoined the state to realize these "Petersburgian" ideals, the more naive of them contending that it could be done by reviving the very architecture and culture of the city. Others, however, saw no such role for the Soviet state but, on the contrary, regarded the spirit of Petersburg as something that had to be kept alive in the face of Soviet barbarism.

In 1920 Osip Mandelshtam pronounced, "We shall gather again in Petersburg," suggesting that though a dark cloud had obscured the sun of the Great Tradition, "we," its torchbearers in the Soviet night, might triumph yet. Petersburg became the locus, actual or symbolic, of certain segments of the intelligentsia who saw themselves as not implicated in the regime's culture and who declared themselves bards of Petersburg. The clichés of the myth had become so standardized that they could be used as a code. Now frequently focused on a cult of past intellectual giants associated with the city (such as Pushkin), they were used as a sort of Aesopian language for discussing the fate and role of the intellectual in Soviet Russia. The cult of Petersburg substantially underwrote the poetry of Anna Akhmatova and of her disciples, who formed a "Petersburg school" that continues to this day and includes such names as A. Kushner, E. Rein, and Joseph Brodsky.[17] Thus there is some logic in the fact that in the initial years of Mikhail Gorbachev's glasnost Petersburg culture rose up to prevail over the discredited Brezhnevian culture and Akhmatova became an idol for the young and *mater dolorosa* of Stalinist oppression.

The subject of this book, however, is not the Petersburg myth per se and its many transformations over time, but rather the ecology of Russian revolutionary culture. The myth of Petersburg played an important role in this because it was a myth about transformation whose frames of reference had resonance in the historical moment.

It might be said that Stalinist culture was formed at least in part as the myth of Petersburg (the main secular myth of Russian national identity) was married to Marxism, but this would be a very crude and mechanistic account of a much more subtly calibrated dynamic. Neither Marxism-Leninism nor the myth of Petersburg was a static, hermetic system, and both participated in a larger European intellectual force field. This is evident in the case of Bely's novel.

As Bely's disquisition about the dot on the map playfully proclaims, his Petersburg is both a symbol and a city. It is the place where the city as a historical entity gives intimations of other possibilities. The novel is set at a moment early in the twentieth century when worker unrest seems about to explode in revolution; phantom-like hordes advance toward the capital's center, preserve of the upper class, and their rumblings carry across as the sound "oo-oo-oo." In the city itself, the grandeur of the facades and statues is deceptive; on closer inspection, they are crumbling and decaying. The canals seethe with bacilli unseen by the naked eye while the veneer of European culture acquired by the Imperial elite who frequent the city's grand buildings conceals a fundamentally Asian interior. The ticking of a time bomb in a can of sardines intended for a political assassination punctuates the narrative, suggesting an impending explosion when the makers of those inchoate sounds penetrate the city's center. But the ticking bomb does double duty as a figure for mind expansion; Bely projects a scenario whereby, as the victim's head explodes, his mind soars beyond the limits of his skull to reach the astral, resolving the dialectic of the inner and the outer, of appearance and essence.

Thomas Mann's *Death in Venice*, published just two years earlier, suggests a similar scenario. Venice is in his account no less a city of illusion than Petersburg. The novella's central conceit for multiple contrasts of veneer and actuality is the facade of the Grand Canal, which is, on closer inspection, crumbling; to go behind it is to descend into a maze of ever darker and seamier alleys. In Mann's city, too, disease (cholera) lurks everywhere unseen and to drink the water is to invite a death that is figured as both grotesque in its naturalistic inventory and paradoxically alluring. The protagonist even hears the same sound, "oo-oo-oo," as was heard by his upper-class counterparts in Bely's *Petersburg*. But here it is not the sound of revolution but the vocative ending of the name of his obsession, the boy Tadzio. Its sound is borne up to him from the shore as "Tadziu-u-u" by a mysterious wind from the East bearing the Dionysiac, that other reality lurking behind the grand facades of Venice and the pretense of respectability maintained by the tourists.[18]

Obviously, the differences between these two works, diminished in my schematicized account, amount to more than the import of the sound "oo-oo-oo" heard by their respective protagonists. Yet even this difference is not as great as it might seem. Bely's sound of impending revolution ("oo-oo-oo"), like Mann's mysterious wind from the East, essentially augurs the possibility of liberation from the time-space of actuality. In Bely it bears witness to his identity as a sometime Symbolist, a member of a school that proclaims its preference for realiora over realia, but who at the time he wrote the novel was often translating this into terms provided by his current obsession, anthroposophy (hence his periodic invocations of the astral). Simultaneously, the sound motif bears nostalgic witness to Bely's enthusiasm for the 1905 revolution in Russia, which occurred immediately after the time of the novel. As for Mann's novella, the Nietzschean frame of reference (Dionysian / Apollonian) is not far to seek. But the impulse that underwrites both works is broader in its frame of reference than any single literary movement or influence.

The similarities between these two works are not a function of influence but attest to the way both catch common concerns and prejudices of the time and organize them using a very basic set of oppositions. The opposition grand buildings and statues versus fetid waters informs the symbolic systems of much European literature of the nineteenth century about the city (in novels of Balzac and Hugo, for example). In the case of Petersburg such a choice of imagery is hardly surprising since for much of the nineteenth century the city lacked a proper sewage system and its canals functioned both as sewers and as sources of water, with inevitable consequences for public health.[19] Thus in Dostoevsky's *Crime and Punishment* a cluster of motifs having to do with canals and with the opposition pure and impure water is crucial to the symbolic system.

The opposition does not derive just from literary conventions or from pressing real-life problems. Several theorists have in recent years explored a broader context for it. One of the most comprehensive schemata is provided in Peter Stallybrass and Allon White's *The Politics and Poetics of Transgression,* in which they give the opposition a place in a general model for what they call the "popular Imaginary," that is, the axiological model that in theory underwrites popular and even highbrow attitudes. Their basic opposition is high versus low, or hegemonic and canonical versus noncanonical, but they adduce an entire series of homologous oppositions that figure high and low in specific realms. Among them, "sewers versus grand buildings" plays a prominent role as the opposition within the symbolic space of the city. Parallel to that opposition are high and low in class terms, high and low in the body—roughly the higher bodily strata versus all those unmentionable orifices and protuberances in the lower—and high and low in language, that is, the classical or standard educated language versus the unruly vernacular and scatology.[20]

Clearly such binaries are overly spatialized and essentialized. They do not allow for the considerable ambivalence in attitudes toward the two poles, an ambivalence that was particularly marked early in the twentieth century and that can be seen in Mann's and Bely's novels. For example, the lower orders have often been regarded as Stallybrass and White insist they are in the popular Imaginary, as the Great Unwashed, that is, in terms of filth and disease, and therefore also of contamination and danger. Yet the general thrust of many of the "isms" dominating intellectual life at the time, and of so-called Modernism in particular, was a perverse reversal or confusion of the spatial and temporal hierarchies that Stallybrass and White associate with the popular Imaginary but that it might also be said Europeans had generally inherited from the Enlightenment. So often what is underground, or what lurks in the dark, fetid recesses of the mind, is considered more fundamental and essential than what is in plain view.

The canals are the point of greatest ambivalence on the symbolic map of the city and hence natural choices as figures in modernistic fiction. On the one hand, they are fetid waters, unacknowledged sewers, and as such suggest sex, disease, flux, decay, and corruption. In the myth of Petersburg, they also suggest the masses—those forces Peter thought he had tamed in building his city but that reassert themselves in a raging fury. On the other hand, they are an integral part of the grand design for taming nature and imposing order on the city; they are of a piece with the statues and grand facades that line them and as such represent culture—the high.

Such hierarchies are only constructs. That other construct, the myth of Petersburg, is in a sense only a narrativized and localized embodiment of a similar register of oppositions. The October Revolution translated the potential of the myth into the sphere of politics, promising to reverse the ratio of high and low, of center and periphery.

The interesting question for the purposes of this book is what happens when there is an inversion in the hierarchy of class—as allegedly occurred in Russia after 1917. Are all the other binaries so much in sync that they follow suit? This is a problem for anyone seeking to essentialize class divisions, and particularly pertinent for anyone seeking to adduce a model for culture in a postrevolutionary society.

If all these oppositions were truly in sync, then when low became high in the social order in theory there would be analogous reversals in the symbolic systems and canons of culture. Initially this might have seemed to be the case. After the February Revolution in 1917, and again after October, there was a flurry of iconoclasm as enthusiasts set about tearing down the statues. This is depicted in Sergei Eisenstein's film *October* (1927), which opens with an emblematic scene as the Lilliputian "folk" bring down a massive statue of the tsar, a moment that is recapitulated parodically as all manner of bric-a-brac and statues from the Winter Palace are destroyed by derisive montage. The actual storming of the Winter Palace is represented as a lava-like flow of the masses streaming to engulf it (as it were, the sewers and canals flooding the statues).

The tearing down of statues is largely a symbolic gesture. A fundamental inversion of the hegemonic hierarchies is much more difficult to attain. Reversal of the sociopolitical or economic status quo does not necessarily bring about corresponding reversals in other hierarchies (such as the bodily or, particularly pertinent to this book, the aesthetic or linguistic). Those who occupy a low position on the socioeconomic hierarchy are, if elevated for some reason, not always eager to jettison the cultural baggage of their former superiors.

Any renegotiation of the ratio of center and periphery (canonical and non-canonical) takes place within the existing language, as cultural revolution can only occur within a given ecosystem. Consequently, this book rejects the notion that Soviet culture was formed in the 1920s and 1930s as the Party advanced, Bronze Horseman–like, upon an unsuspecting intelligentsia, imposing upon it an abomination of culture called socialist realism; there was no absolute agency in the evolution of Soviet culture.

Fernand Braudel, among others, has argued against concentrating in historical studies on those dramatic and volatile "events" that chronicle surface change (such as, in this instance, Party decrees). Such events, he argues, are themselves constrained by structures and narratives present at a more profound level and observable over a much longer period of time (what he calls *longue durée*), the parameters, as it were, of a given culture system. Thus, if one looks only at the surface one sees only what is active at a particular time, oblivious to the currents and countercurrents that may be dormant, as well as to the hierarchy of elements informing surface events.[21] By studying a given society or culture system over a long period of time one may observe the successive cycles and intercycles within which the dominant narratives of the culture are played out.

The Bolshevik Revolution and its aftermath, those events in which Russia attempted to overcome history, were worked out within a pre-existing cultural system in which the myth of Petersburg enjoyed a dominant presence among the master narratives. The myth proved particularly tenacious after the Revolution not just because long-established myths die hard, but because it was a myth of radical transformation and modernization centered on a city.

The issue of urbanization, which has always been at the heart of the Petersburg myth, was made particularly urgent after the Bolshevik Revolution. Marx and Engels, children of nineteenth-century Europe, in their *Communist Manifesto* virtually equate Communism with overcoming the "idiocy of village life" by transforming society using the model of the modern city, a program that became central in Lenin's and especially Stalin's appropriations of their mentors' writings. This had particular resonance for Petersburg both as the capital of Russian science and as a focus of ongoing debates about modernization. In the twentieth century, even before the Revolution, the city served for many as the emblem of a total transformation to a post-traditionalist society. Those pursuing the Bolshevik experiment frequently articulated their aims using elements from the myth, which was even incorporated into Stalinist rhetoric, as we shall see.

The myth of Petersburg is itself about how a transformation in space stood in for a transformation in time. The extraordinary time lag between Russia at the beginning of the eighteenth century and its more advanced rival powers in Europe (it had never had a Renaissance, and so on) was overcome "suddenly" when Peter created the new capital. Time was surmounted, but space, as if in compensation, acquired enormous importance.

After 1917, the successive phases of cultural evolution were each marked by a distinctive model or master narrative informing official pageantry, literature, film, theater, and so forth. As the ensuing chapters will show, each of these master narratives attempts to figure the October Revolution (as the paradigm of national identity) in a distinctive model of space and time. Most frequently, time is collapsed in some way and greater emphasis is given to space.

In this respect, Bolshevik Russia was not unique. In several other cultural movements of the twentieth century there has been an analogous foregrounding or even sacralization of space and de-emphasis on time. One should note, for example, that in Braudel a temporal model is figured spatially (in order to find *longue durée,* you must dig deeper into the "depths"[22]).

The Nietzschean, or post-Enlightenment, transvaluation of values was frequently conceptualized in a different sense of space. Most often some Manichaean, binary pattern was adduced, a binary formed around the opposition polluted space (sewers, swamps) and pure space. Thus much cultural endeavor was informed by a rejection of the impure space and a quest for a pure one, as it were, a secularized version of the Christian dichotomy of heaven and hell but now with contamination rather than scorching fire characterizing the cautionary space. Transformation was represented as salvation from pollution. A contrast was drawn between the surface as the here and now, and some purified, authentic, other space. Different groups figured this model differently; some sought to dig down into or to divine some more fundamental reality *below,* others to transcend by moving *above* this reality, and still others to go *beyond* it. What is essential in all such scenarios is the thirst for a break between the two spaces, or at the very least a conviction that the difference between them is absolute.

Bely's *Petersburg* and Mann's *Death in Venice* typify this trend in that they are about not just cities but the problem of pollution and inauthenticity. Mann and Bely essentially challenge the old Enlightenment values by showing how the established (high / low) binaries have broken down (the grand buildings and statues crumble, are a ghostly veneer,and so on). They seek the more authentic, a culture that is not fundamentally polluted. The myth of Petersburg, like Marxist theory, was, however, originally a narrative of the Enlightenment; it enacts the way Peter overcame the hold of the Orthodox Church, the "swamp" of obscurantism and stagnation, so that Russia went from mud to marble. The city had now become problematical (polluted, inauthentic), thus a new or revised narrative, a narrative of repurification, was needed. Repurification, however, presupposes a repurifier.

Marxism-Leninism, as an account of how some people, or more specifically the vanguard, can intervene consciously in the course of history, potentially intersects with the myth of Petersburg with its all-powerful hero, Peter. Peter is the icon of absolute break, of the triumph of intention over habit. He is a political Christ who liberates the spirit from desuetude, who reclaims the city for authenticity.

Such absolute breaks are problematical for most versions of evolutionary theory, but not for Marx. In a footnote approximately half way through Volume I of *Capital,* he announces that he is trying to do for the history of economic relations what Darwin did for natural history.[23] Although Marx's *Capital* and Darwin's then recently published *On the Origin of Species,* two materially based macro-histories, are comparable in many respects, there is a fundamental difference. Darwin in *The Origin of Species* invokes the maxim *natura non fecit saltum* (nature makes no leaps) so frequently that it emerges as one of the first principles of his evolutionary theory—doubtless a reason for his using a Latin expression. Subsequent evolutionary theory has modified Darwin's position, but without ever approaching the extremism of Marx, for whom "leaps"—revolutions—are the nodal moments of history, the engines of sociopolitico-cultural evolution. Indeed, it might be argued that the centrality of all kinds of genetic quackery in the history of Stalinist intellectual abuses (Trofim Lysenko, Ivan Michurin) was precisely because Russia was a fertile place for the kind of evolutionary impatience implicit in Marx's theoretical writings. At any rate, in this aspect the myth of Petersburg lent itself to templating onto Marx's theory; Lenin could become the great acrobat of history. But it is important to note that around the time of the Revolution similar tropes also became popular in avant-garde and Formalist theory and practice, especially in the theater. A circus technique, the *salto mortale* (as it were, the ultimate leap), functioned in theoretical writings and performances as an icon of the new epistemology, a marker of impatience with physical time (see Chapter 3).

The temptation to assume absolute agency for extraordinary figures was not, then, exclusive to the Bolshevik leadership. It can also be seen in the intelligentsia. In the twentieth century, as European culture generally became more preoccupied with intellectuals, the Russian intelligentsia began to arrogate to themselves the two central roles in the Petersburg myth as crystallized in *The Bronze Horseman:* they became either absolute transformers (like Peter) or absolutely repressed (like Evgeny)—or both, since martyrdom legitimizes and enhances radical gestures.

It should be added that not one of these striking tendencies in the Bolshevik appropriation of Marxism was necessarily caused by the dominance of the myth of Petersburg in the intellectual landscape. It would be more accurate to say that there was a dialogic relationship between intellectual traditions (and this one *a fortiori*) and Marxism that led to new inflections and to a foregrounding of specific elements in both discourses. Moreover, the myth did not have any timeless identity or special agency of its own.

Thus there was not a break between the myth, to be found at some kind of deep structural level, and mere events on the surface; myths are themselves events that are constantly occurring. Braudel and many others have hypostatized and reified these distinctions to the point where they participate in the same kind of romance of the two absolutely separate places that we see as endemic to Modernism. The two places are not separate, but together form a single cultural ecosystem. It is in the constant interaction between such master narratives (or myths) and events—and between myths and events in the Russian arena and those in Europe, or even America—that Stalinist culture emerged.

Of relevance here are some recent Western interpretations of fascism, such as Zeev Sternhell's *The Birth of Fascist Ideology*, which reject the notion that fascism arose as an aberration or temporary (if ugly) blip on the screen of Europe. Sternhell argues that "before it became a political force it was a cultural phenomenon. The growth of fascism would not have been possible without the revolt against the Enlightenment and the French Revolution which swept across Europe at the end of the nineteenth century and beginning of the twentieth." He sees fascism as the "product of the antimaterialistic and anti-rationalistic revision of Marxism" synthesized with "organic nationalism." The fascists, in his account, adopted the economic aspect of liberalism—market forces and private property—but completely denied its philosophical principles. Stalinism is different from fascism in that it does reject the market and severely limits private property, distinctions that cannot be immaterial. The applicability of "organic nationalism" here is also problematical; as will become clear over the course of this book, in the case of most of the cultural trends in late Imperial and Soviet Russia, including the Stalinist, the issue of cultural identity (Russian? European? international? Soviet? Imperial?) was a fraught one. Nevertheless, Sternhell's analysis of fascism is suggestive for the case of Stalinism because, like fascism, Stalinism represents an extreme manifestation of a much broader and more comprehensive cultural phenomenon with, paradoxical as it might seem, antimaterialist proclivities.[24] Stalinism is analogous to fascism in this respect, but not identical with it.

Many of those Russian idealists who were actively committed to revolutionary culture shared a set of prejudices and agendas commonly found among European intellectuals of the late nineteenth and early twentieth centuries that can be accommodated under the rubric Romantic Anticapitalism (both Bely and, especially, Mann fall into this category to some extent[25]). Its prejudices and agendas, which many Russian intellectuals brought with them in 1917, were worked through in the somewhat singular conditions of a Communist revolution in Russia and its aftermath. Although few of the agendas were realized in anything like their original conception, they proved one of the critical factors determining the contours of Stalinist culture.

Russian Intellectuals and Romantic Anticapitalism

The term Romantic Anticapitalism was originally used by Lukács in an essay of 1931 about Dostoevsky to denigrate some right-wing intellectuals.[26] More recently, however, it has been used by scholars such as Michel Löwy to categorize an extremely broad range of intellectuals, principally, but not exclusively, leftists, and ranging from conservatives to Marxist intellectuals such as Walter Benjamin and even Lukács himself, but including Max Weber, Ferdinand Tönnies, Georg Simmel, Ernst Bloch, and some cultural movements such as Expressionism and Surrealism. Two gatherings of intellectuals are important in its history—Max Weber's Heidelberg Circle, which met between 1906 and 1918 and included many of the above among its members, and the Frankfurt School.[27] In other words, its epicenters in the 1910s and 1920s were the leftist intellectual circles of Wilhelminian and Weimar Germany, though they do not begin to define its geographical or intellectual range. But then Romantic Anticapitalism is not so much an ism or a movement as a formula for accounting for a large variety of thinkers and movements with certain common concerns.

Romantic Anticapitalists might somewhat loosely be defined as those who foreground three points in the standard critique of capitalism: alienation, individualism, and the commodification, or market model, of culture. Their stance becomes not just anticapitalist but specifically "romantic" in the degree to which it rejects them and proposes an alternative model of society.

All isms are suspect, but Romantic Anticapitalism, in which two disparate categories—anticapitalist and romantic—are hitched together almost for oxymoronic effect, is particularly so. Too many movements and thinkers can be housed under this rubric. Some have attempted to break down the various versions into a typology, but they risk the danger of overschematization. Essentially there are two major variables within this ism. The first is the extent to which in a given instance the romantic-like pole is the dominant one, and the second is the extent to which the anticapitalist is. At each extreme one finds trends where the copulative has essentially come unstuck and the other pole has faded from view completely.

While Romantic Anticapitalism is generally articulated as a social critique, it cannot be demarcated from aesthetic utopianism. The critique of capitalist society often evinced an antipathy toward its commodification of culture—which was seen as undermining true aesthetic values—and this position can readily translate into a defense of High Culture. Hence in the Petersburg journal *Apollo* (Apollon), a mouthpiece in the 1910s for highbrow intellectuals with elitist proclivities, one frequently finds a pointed contrast between "humdrum reality" *(seraya zhizn')* and beauty.

The attempts of the Romantic Anticapitalists to flee humdrum reality frequently involved absolutizing one or the other pole in the hierarchies of high and low, generally to the exclusion or denigration of the other pole, but certainly to the exclusion of the possibility that any middle ground between the two could be entertained. What is "fled," or resolutely renounced, the middle ground between the poles of high and low, is in effect ordinary reality. Versions of the idealized low include the masses (the quest for the authentic was sometimes played out in terms of class), but also the subterranean aspect of the self as in the Dionysiac, the Unconscious or dream. Thus in Mann's Venice the object of the protagonist's obsession, Tadzio, is both a Greek statue and a Hermes who beckons to that realm where the *comme il faut* no longer obtains (including conformist sexual morality); rarely is he the middle-class boy in a sailor's suit.

The mark of the true Romantic Anticapitalist is not just the impulse to flee the profane, but a critique of capitalist society as well. This critique generally focuses on alienation and the loss of a sense of unity. The critique of individualism, allegedly a scourge endemic to bourgeois society, frequently led to a form of utopianism in the sense of some dream of a society where all were truly one, a sort of secular religion of the one, whether achieved by reviving some version of the precapitalist world (the most common prescription) or in a Dionysiac frenzy, or in a revolution that smashed class divisions.

The single point of most common ground is a rejection of the market and of the commercializing forces of culture. In some versions, the basic objection to capitalist society was directed at the marketplace in its more figurative sense of the middle point between hierarchies where different values jostle, some to prosper, others not. Romantic Anticapitalists were objecting, as it were, to fluctuating currencies for elements used in verbal, visual, or aural communication, to allowing hierarchies to float at the stock exchange. Ultimately, this position undermines communication in the sense that it denies to all forms of communication the aspect of currency or commerce. One example would be that central doctrine of several Russian Futurist writers' regenerated verbal aesthetic, the "self-valuable word," the word that has no currency outside itself. In practice, this often meant that the word was all sound with no dictionary potential.

This position represents the ultimate in the flight from the profane—a flight away from meaning itself, or at any rate away from conventional meanings. One is left with the "oo-oo-oo" of a Bely or a Mann. The unsullied collages of sound were not to be mired by the slough of any this-worldly referent. Some poets experimented with poems made up entirely of vowel sounds.[28] "Oo-oo-oo" is the sound of the absolute.

Such positions did not take the avant-garde off the Romantic Anticapitalist map because most were also specifically anticapitalist. This fact helps explain why, for instance, many French Surrealists clung to their Communist Party with such zeal even after it no longer saw much use for them, why so many Expressionists joined the Communist revolutions in Munich and Berlin, and why Ilya Ehrenburg, the experimental novelist and habitué of Parisian bohemia in the 1920s, was able in reasonable conscience to serve the xenophobic Stalinist regime during the Cold War by penning the most blistering attacks on the West. A major motive was in each instance a fundamental loathing of capitalism and its perceived effects on culture.

Although the term Romantic Anticapitalism seems so broad in its referents and shaky in terms of its ability to define a clear trend or movement, it is nevertheless useful here because it shows how a broad range of intellectuals warring among themselves in many respects could find common cause. It also helps find the points of common interest between the Bolsheviks and a wide range of intellectual groups, enabling them to become bedfellows after the Revolution, if at times strange ones. Of course not all Russian intellectuals were opposed to capitalism, but those giving capitalism (as distinct from modernization) a central role in their schemes for Russia's improvement were far from legion and tended to be based in Moscow rather than Petersburg; the best-known examples are the Riabushinsky Circle (which advocated a curious amalgam of capitalism and Old Believer tradition) and the controversial liberal Petr Struve.[29]

In Europe, the antipathy toward capitalism generated among many a sense of pan-European common cause and led to several de facto alliances of intellectuals crossing national boundaries, such as that between the French and the Czech leftists between the wars. In the case of Russia, the Romantic Anticapitalists were largely linked to a loose Central European alliance, centered in Germany for most of the 1920s and embracing leftist intellectuals such as Lukács, Benjamin, and Bertolt Brecht, and also Expressionism, which had a particularly strong impact in Leningrad. During the course of that decade, many Europeans joined the Communist movement and some were drawn to Moscow.[30] But the traffic was far from one way, and the Romantic Anticapitalists of Central Europe, many of them non-Marxist, remained major influences on their Russian counterparts for all the formative years of Soviet culture.

Various intellectuals might have gravitated to some form of Marxism to satisfy their anticapitalist zeal, but surely Marx himself was much more hardheaded with his economistic analyses of power than these would-be epigones. What could provide a better cold shower for a romantic than those three volumes of *Capital?* Let us embrace the people of the satanic mills, Marx enjoined, sweat, grit, and all. Let us ground our theories not in those airy categories of the superstructure, but in economic and power realities. Let us call exploitation by its name.

And yet, even as Marx threw down the gauntlet to the illusions of the intelligentsia of his age, his own theories were not free of the potential for illusion. An obvious point of possible romanticism is the heroic billing Marx accords the proletariat. Similarly, the more leftist among the Romantic Anticapitalists, rather than revile the masses as the Great Unwashed, have idealized them. In some of their writings, proletarians emerge as projections of the ideal intellectuals, more purely devoted to the life of the mind than any actual intellectuals.[31] Others, by contrast, do not portray them as lovers of high culture, but idealize them for their alleged resistance to it, for safeguarding the low. According to such accounts (to be found even today in simplistic appropriations of Mikhail Bakhtin's theory of carnival) the lower orders are by nature rebels and revelers, and thus the only ones who can help regain humanity's lost unity; the bourgeoisie are labeled repressed and repressive, and proletarians are said to reject instinctively bourgeois conformism.

Whether, then, the masses were projected as ideal versions of the low, or of the high, they were not seen as degraded (filthy and so on). But as a consequence the rhetoric of filth and contamination was transferred to two other sociological categories, the upper and, particularly, the lower middle classes. In so much literature by Romantic Anticapitalists, bad taste, commercialism, conformism, repressiveness—the entire gamut of the bad in culture—are laid at the feet of the petty shopkeeper (*lavochnik*) as icon of the petty bourgeoisie. One sees this among German leftists as well, but attacks on the mentality and culture of the petty shopkeeper are also a feature of Bolshevik rhetoric.[32]

Both the upper and the lower middle classes have contaminated culture, but the source of such contamination is the market. The "canals" of commerce seethe with bacilli that the unsuspecting do not see (flux by another name). To commodify art is to threaten the cultural gene pool; in discussing how to guard its purity intellectuals frequently confounded cultural purity with biological purity. The metaphors of prostitution or the house of ill repute were favorites for condemning commercialized (inauthentic) culture.

This was a pan-European trend but it gained particular currency among Soviet intellectuals as the ultimate rationale for the Soviet state. To jump forward in time, even after the Soviet Union under Gorbachev was liberated from its last shackles of Stalinist dogmatism, the suspicion of the market proved more tenacious among intellectuals than any espousal of specifically Communist ideals.[33] This market phobia was the cement of Soviet culture.

In prerevolutionary Russia, intellectuals were haunted by the way mass commercial culture—what was sometimes called an "Augean stable" of virtually insurmountable filth—was constantly being dumped on society by the bourgeoisie, the class most clearly implicated in the market. It would obviously take a Herculean figure, or some god, to clean it all out. In many Russian revolutionary scenarios the proletariat emerge as the group whose very function is not so much to serve as production-fodder as to repurify the world by driving out the market. But at the same time, with a certain amount of casuistry many leftist intellectuals argued that the proletariat, who would normally see more truly than any other class the dangers all around, have been blinded temporarily by those iniquitous commercializing forces and cannot see the bacilli polluting the precious bodily fluids of culture.

Enter the intellectuals as temporary guardians, saviors of fallen women, surrogate gods. They have not been so blinded and in this crisis situation can fend off the menacing commercializing hordes. But as gods their prototype will be not Hercules but Hermes, the messenger between two worlds and hence the god of communication.

So many of the Romantic Anticapitalists and other intellectual groups of the early twentieth century exhibited what I refer to as a "Hermes complex," which by another name could be called guild megalomania. They advanced their own group as "messengers" to mediate between the world of truth (aesthetic or political) and the world of actuality, where people are afflicted by blindness—a version of Plato's Myth of the Cave in *The Republic*. Some German political theoreticians called this a "temporary dictatorship of trust" whereby the masses should accede to the will of the educated "temporarily."[34] Lenin called it a "vanguard of the proletariat" whereby the few who were truly enlightened politically ("conscious") should guide the less enlightened masses of the proletariat to their own hegemony.[35] The avant-garde and many other groups saw themselves as ahead of their time and hence able to lead others to a future place-time. But even the guardians of the Great Tradition of high culture often saw themselves as mediators between their version of a great place-time and the present; in Petersburg, a local movement for regenerating society by bringing Greek drama to the people, the Nietzschean project, founded a journal that was actually called *Hermes* (Germes).

Where, then, might a revolution fit into this scenario? A revolution would mean giving power to Hermes (the intelligentsia / vanguard) to unbind the prisoners who can see only the shadow world so that they might experience the true forms. It is at base a revolution in epistemology. Thus the identification of political and epistemological revolution in Bely through the metaphor of the sardine-tin time bomb is no mere expedient born of aesthetic purposes (trying to represent as many ideas as possible with the one metaphor), but reflects a marked trend to obscure the distinctions between the political and the aesthetic, making possible alliances with, and even commitments to, the Communist movement.

It is at this point that the most fundamental differences emerge between the Marxist-Leninist position and that of other Romantic Anticapitalists. Marx and Lenin saw a socioeconomic revolution as a precondition of any spiritual revolution; most non-Marxist anticapitalists (and some Bolshevik intellectuals) insisted that this sequence had to be played in reverse.

In many of its manifestations, then, the Hermes role might be seen as serving the masses. But it might also be interpreted as an unacknowledged reach for power.

Fritz K. Ringer in *The Decline of the Mandarins* discusses this kind of reach to power among intellectuals in turn-of-the-century Germany and extending into the Weimar period. He identifies a sort of window of opportunity for intellectuals, the period when the power of the aristocracy was in decline as the nation drew away from a primarily agrarian level of economic organization but full industrialization had not yet been achieved. In this period when hereditary titles based on landholding were no longer guarantees of status in society and the ownership of significant amounts of liquid capital was not yet acknowledged as entitling such status, intellectuals tried to constitute a nobility of the educated to supersede the "merely traditional" ruling class. Moreover, they were not interested in mere social status, in just serving the state as specialists, but sought to form an aristocracy of the intellect (or spirit) that would lead the nation.[36]

If the dynamic is seen in these terms, the real class struggle was between the would-be aristocrats of culture and the aristocrats of capital; indeed, that between the proletariat and the bourgeoisie, which intellectuals were wont to represent in their writings as a tussle to the death, merely obscures this.

Ringer's analysis focuses on academics in Germany but in Russia it would apply more broadly. Early in the twentieth century one sees a shift in the nature and composition of the Russian intelligentsia in response to a historical moment analogous to the one Ringer describes in Germany. No longer was it the characteristic pattern for creative intellectuals to be sons of the nobility (as during Pushkin's time), or déclassé graduates of the seminaries (as in the second half of the nineteenth century). The age of dilettantism was ending as the intelligentsia evolved into a caste with a sense of ongoing generations in a line that intermarried with increasing frequency. As is often remarked, many of the leading writers of the period around the Revolution, such as A. Blok, B. Pasternak, M. Tsvetaeva, and Bely himself, were children of professors (or in Tsvetaeva's case a museum director), while in art and architecture the Benois dynasty (see Chapter 2) was a formidable presence.[37]

For dynastic intellectuals, the historical moment ushered in by the October Revolution might seem to have been particularly opportune. The landed nobility and the rentier-mercantilist class were routed, and the New Class had not yet become so entrenched that the intelligentsia had to be coopted into it or suffer the consequences if they remained aloof. By another ongoing historical dynamic, however—modernization and the democratization of education—their newly won sense of dynastic succession was to meet a challenge from below. With the ever broader spread of education through the populace, and, as a concomitant of modernization, a shift of emphasis in determining status in intellectual fields to professional qualifications (which in Russia became increasingly marked in the 1910s), the intelligentsia as a group was being desacralized. Positions within its traditional bailiwick became available to those who advanced through a standardized educational route.

Intellectuals resisted the trend to specialization by advancing models for intellectual life (most often from the past) in which the different branches of their activity were united in a special place—an academy, or a Gesamtkunstwerk, or a Bauhaus.[38] Those who could participate in several different intellectual fields were particularly prized. In other words, though for different reasons, the intelligentsia were resisting divisions of labor within their world as were the Marxists within society at large.

In this context, the Hermes agenda might be viewed as a preemptive strike. The sardine-tin time bomb was ticking away. Thus in the specific case of the journal *Hermes*, a cynic might analyze its altruistic mission in terms of a last fling by those who have benefited from the old education system built around expertise in the classics before the shift to a more pragmatically and democratically oriented system of secondary and tertiary education robs them of their special status.[39]

But the cynics would also be wrong. Conviction was the stronger emotion. It is all very well for us with our ex post facto perspectives to impute self-serving or caste-preserving motives to what intellectuals attempted in Russia circa 1917. What many of them undertook was the Great Experiment: not a flight to some better place, not a *voyage autour de mon livre*, but a transformation in place. They attempted to transform a Russia trailing its alleged peers, Britain, France, and Germany, in most indices of political, economic, and cultural development into a society that would be a beacon for the rest of the world in all three—to accomplish a "Petersburg" on an even grander scale. They believed they could achieve this through work on the cultural front. The most zealous spared no efforts for the cause. Many of them later paid for these efforts with their lives.

The Quest for a New Culture

Many of those Russians who in the 1910s and 1920s sought to realize a culture that might transform society were looking for a medium that was the purest and the most authentic: the purest movement, sound, language, or organization of space. It was felt that by finding (or recovering) this distilled essence of culture, society would be able to transcend the profane and regain its lost wholeness. Thus the prescriptions were for a kind of revolution—a radical transformation—whether or not they were conceived within the framework of political revolution.

The ritualization of space was a common denominator of all prescriptions for realizing this goal. Consequently, in the 1910s and 1920s architecture and theater (or, more broadly, the performing arts) emerged as the sites most commonly chosen for factories of the perfect. This may seem unexpected given that the official culture of the 1930s, socialist realism, is most often associated with literature. In socialist realist literature, however, symbolic space is even more fundamental than the ritualized biography that structures the master plot.[40]

In this book, then, I analyze the changing models for a sacralized space. The book is arranged in approximate chronological order, while seeking to avoid the implication that it charts a linear development from 1913 to the

1930s. Hence it essentially comprises a series of essays each of which covers a phenomenon characteristic of a particular time in the overall span—the exception being the first, which looks at the avant-garde during the entire period covered as a sort of frame for the subsequent chapters. In this way, the book gives some sense of the tortured political, sociological, and institutional history of Petersburg's intellectual life in these years but does so largely as a setting for its central theme, the intellectuals' quest to find the quintessential revolutionary culture. In charting this, I touch on most branches of cultural activity: painting, music, architecture, film, linguistics, opera, ballet, official pageantry, history, literary theory, and literature itself, although I do not pretend to cover them all in great detail; indeed, I do not profess to encompass all the cultural life in Petersburg during these years or all its political and institutional history. I do not even give center stage to many of the cultural giants from this time, such as Velemir Khlebnikov, Mandelshtam, and Bakhtin. Their very singularity, the mark of their stature, makes them less grateful subjects as examples of general trends. Also, as the focus of endeavor shifted in Russia to a culture appropriate for the masses (a shift that can be perceived even before 1917), the agendas of avant-gardists such as Khlebnikov and Kasimir Malevich proved less viable, as did the kind of high culture that presupposed a classical or higher education, such as the poetry of Mandelshtam or the novels of Konstantin Vaginov. Such figures therefore assume much more peripheral positions in this book than their intrinsic merits would warrant. Because the trans-sense language of Khlebnikov and the nonrepresentational art (Suprematism) of Malevich also represent limit cases in the quest for a purified culture, however, they have been taken as the subject of the book's opening chapter and then reappear periodically in its narrative as a kind of bench mark against which other trends are measured.

The book's "heroes," Sergei Ernestovich Radlov (1892–1958), Adrian Ivanovich Piotrovsky (1898–1938), and other cultural activists of the 1920s, do not leap to the minds of many, not even to experts on the culture of that decade. They were scions of the Petersburg intellectual elite and continued throughout the 1920s to be active players in the city's intellectual life. Yet they played leading roles in the transformation of Petrograd / Leningrad culture, from elitist and highbrow to mass and agitational, retaining their identities as distinctive players even as their work reflected, successively, all the phases and *volte-face* of that most volatile of decades. This book is not *about* these figures, but as their careers keep resurfacing in the narrative they provide case studies in the twists and ironies in the formation of Soviet culture which illustrate my general point that its evolution was far from unilinear.

The examples of Piotrovsky and Radlov are adduced for the way they challenge some common assumptions about the provenance of Soviet culture. In particular, they raise questions about how alien official Soviet culture was to both the work of the non-Marxist European avant-garde and the high intelligentsia. Their original training was as classical scholars and translators and they belonged by birth and association to the cultural elite of Petersburg. They were never Party members, and they never abandoned their identity as intellectuals. Even in the 1930s when Piotrovsky was the artistic director of Lenfilm, the body that produced the canonical socialist realist film *Chapaev*, he would come to work early to put in some time on the classics before turning to his administrative work.

Not surprisingly, Piotrovsky and Radlov brought much of the baggage of the cultural elite with them when they went to work for the Revolution, which they saw as a means for realizing their ideals. They exemplify that broad category of intellectuals who believed they could play a role as Hermes figures. In a sense, they represent an Enlightenment heresy; they saw themselves as cultural ecologists who were ahead of their time because, they believed, they had divined the formulae that might transform Man. As with Mandelshtam, Bakhtin, and many of the finest minds of their generation, their university training in the classics gave them, more than a set of skills, ideals that fired their future work. Radlov and Piotrovsky, like many others of this period in the grip of a "Greek" ideal, wished to revive what they saw as the ethos of the old polis. Unlike Mandelshtam, who interpreted the classical ideals differently, they were prepared to work as cultural bureaucrats for the new state.[41] Thus they are representative of that broad and variegated category of intellectuals (by no means all of them influenced by classical ideals) that, out of idealism, mediated between the world of intellectuals and state institutions. Consciously or unconsciously, they recognized that in order to achieve a radical transformation some kind of state intervention or sponsorship was necessary.

Much of Western historiography has seen the evolution of Soviet culture in terms of a battle between the avant-garde, as the force most committed to transforming culture, and traditionalists who sought to set the clock back rather than forward. This was a battle that began well before the Revolution (seen in, for instance, the exchanges from 1912 to 1917 between Alexandr Benois and various Futurist groups); in the Soviet period the traditionalists ultimately triumphed at the cost of the avant-garde (or, as in Boris Groys's recent revisionist book, vice versa).[42] The avant-garde have thus played a central role in Western paradigms of Soviet cultural history as valiant fighters against Stalinist entropic forces. This scenario is valid, but also inadequate. The avant-garde was far from unitary and the fates of individual avant-gardists have no necessary bearing on the extent to which their agendas influenced the subsequent shape of Soviet culture. More important, the opposition avant-garde / traditionalist was not as absolute as avant-gardist rhetoric claimed. This is well demonstrated in the cases of Meyerhold, Radlov, Piotrovsky, the Leningrad Formalists, and many other figures treated in this book who identified with avant-gardism but were also in many senses traditionalists. Indeed, an important reason for their centrality in the book is that they stand at the center of a host of dialogues (the Party / the intellectuals, the intellectuals / the masses, Western European cultural trends / native traditions), including that dialogue between would-be avant-gardists and traditionalists.

Much more fundamental in the formation of Soviet culture than the opposition between avant-gardists and traditionalists was another dichotomy that might be called monumentalist versus iconoclast.

Any revolution draws heightened attention to meaning, but there are several possible ways meaning is figured. Paul Ricoeur in *Freud and Philosophy* has explored for the case of biblical hermeneutics two diametrically opposed ways meaning can be prosecuted—either by deepening truth and elucidating it more fully, or by tearing away the masks of false interpretation that have overgrown the text—demystification—to reveal more authentic meaning in a new interpretation. Ricoeur does not lament this polarity, but on the contrary sees it as "the truest expression of our 'modernity.'" He continues: "The situation in which language today finds itself comprises this double possibility . . . on the one hand, purify discourse of its excrescences, liquidate the idols, go from drunkenness to sobriety, realize our state of poverty once and for all; on the other hand, use the most 'nihilistic,' destructive, iconoclastic movement so as to *let speak* what *once*, what each time, was *said*, when meaning appeared anew, when meaning was at its fullest. Hermeneutics seems to me to be animated by this double motivation. . . ."[43]

Arguably, the quest for a revolutionary culture was also animated by the tension between these two hermeneutic poles. Marxism was originally conceived as an act of demystification, of tearing off the masks of false consciousness, but the more it became institutionalized, the more the other pole, affirmation, figured in interpretation.

Versions of both poles can be found among the programs for a new culture: on the one hand, the impulse to monumental gestures of affirmation, to write the true or the beautiful more clearly and in bolder strokes than had been done before (hence totalizing schemes, gigantomania, a proclivity for "mysteries" in the movement for a mass theater, novels as Manichaean epics, and so on) and, on the other, an iconoclastic, demystifying gesture that not only tears off the masks of the old, rejecting all the cant and ossified conventions, but in its quest for a more authentic culture advances the non- or a-canonical, the parodic, the eccentric, unsystematic, "peripheral," or even trivial. The two poles are obviously not absolute since such binaries as monumental/iconoclastic and canonical/noncanonical themselves depend on the "situatedness" of the person who pronounces them so. Today's noncanonical may become tomorrow's doxa, thus psychoanalysis, which Ricoeur identifies with the demystifying pole, has over time become institutionalized in the West and is even now being subjected to its own demystification. Moreover, the two poles are interdependent (monumentalizing schemes depend on iconoclastic acts for their realization). What is important here is that in all the movements that sought to create a new, revolutionary culture, one can find a tension between the two poles.

The defining gesture in the cultural history of the 1930s is not the killing of the avant-garde per se, but the attempt at censoring out the iconoclastic, demystifying pole, leaving a more purely ritualized and sacralized culture such that cultural artifacts became acts of affirmation. This statist culture could have been presided over by the avant-garde in its most monumentalizing avatars (as in Mussolini's Italy), but was in fact generally not.

In the initial years of this study, the tension between the monumentalist and the iconoclastic poles found its expression in rival scenarios of cultural transformation figured spatially. Returning to the two models of revolution presented in Bely's *Petersburg*, revolution occurs when the workers who live in the outer suburbs invade the center, the realm of the privileged, but it also occurs as an explosion eliminating the center and hurtling the detritus out beyond its confines. Is revolution, then, a centripetal or a centrifugal event? In Marxist-Leninist analysis it was primarily centripetal; the socioeconomic periphery should take over the center. In prerevolutionary Russia there was a whole range of people who saw the panacea for the profane not in a revolution, nor even in rituals of revolution, but in terms of elevating the intelligentsia to a greater status and consolidating the center—pure culture—unsullied by commerce and secured by norms. In 1913 they formed the aesthetic majority.

To an extremely vocal minority, however, revolution appealed as an explosion of a limiting conceptual frame (sardine tin / skull) that would simultaneously be an explosion of class constraints ensuring humanity's transformation. Marx in *Capital* once used a similar figure for revolution when he described the end of the capitalist system in terms of its "integument" *(Hülle)* being "burst asunder."[44] In Marx, this was a peripheral trope for revolution. The more extravagant Russian fantasists, however, gave a central role to such tropes because they saw revolution as a centrifugal movement out toward an entirely different realm.

1

REVOLUTION AS REVELATION: THE AVANT-GARDE

In the 1910s and 1920s a sort of international avant-garde emerged, one that spanned all of Europe and to some extent the Atlantic Ocean as well. This was not a single and unified group, but a somewhat peripatetic and inchoate collection of individuals who floated over the map of Europe from country to country and city to city with Paris as their most frequent symbolic base. Characteristically, in the early period especially, a number of individual avant-gardists from different countries and backgrounds would find themselves in a particular town, and for a brief period they would arrange exhibitions and theatrical happenings, issue some manifestoes, and publish a journal or two before the constant comings and goings of the conspirators, the chronic bickering and divisions, took their toll and brought the moment to an end. But once dispersed, its members would soon participate in other such brief flowerings, perhaps in another town and with a somewhat different configuration of participants.

The Russian avant-garde were largely part of this inchoate group, though some cultural patriots resisted all implication in it. The tyranny of distance limited their participation to some extent in the prewar years; the war itself, then the Western blockade of Soviet Russia from 1918–1920, and other barriers set up by the tensions in the 1920s between the new regime and the West also frustrated their attempts at contact with their European counterparts. Nevertheless, most Russian avant-gardists shared a sense of common cause with them and fought to maintain contact as much as possible.[1]

This sense of common cause does not suggest that a single motivation or set of beliefs could characterize so fiercely individualistic a group. On the contrary, for every general trend to be found among certain avant-gardists, the very opposite can also be found among others. One can, however, isolate a particular core of beliefs that were characteristic of a range of individuals and movements and that were to play a significant role in the evolution of revolutionary culture.[2]

Perceptual Millenarianism

Many avant-gardists, particularly but not exclusively in Russia, were in the thrall of "revolution," but they interpreted it as essentially the acquisition of a "new vision" (novoye zreniye). This new vision was in their account a precondition, not an end result, of any fundamental political or social revolution. The avant-garde ideologues claimed that through their art modern, bourgeois, conventional man with his tired assumptions might be jolted out of his epistemological rut and helped to "see" and therefore "be" anew, an idiosyncratic version of Romantic Anticapitalism.

For this position I am coining the term "perceptual millenarianism"—the belief that the millennium could only be reached through a new vision. Walter Benjamin discusses something like perceptual millenarianism in his essay on the Surrealists where he notes their yearning for a kind of "profane illumination" that he contrasts with, and also sees as a substitute for, the mystical epiphanies of Catholicism.[3] The essay is entitled "Surrealism: The Last Snapshot of the European Intelligentsia," suggesting a broader frame of reference. The quest for a kind of profane illumination was at the heart not only of the Surrealists' mission but of many other factions and individuals in this heroic age of the avant-garde. For this reason, the present chapter confounds chronological and geographical distinctions, moving back and forth from Russia to Western Europe, from the prerevolutionary period to the late 1920s or the initial postrevolutionary years, all in the service of elucidating an ethos that largely resisted such changes and distinctions.

One reason perceptual millenarianism was generally impervious to the barrier of the Russian Revolution was that for its enthusiasts profane illumination was the stuff of revolution, of a revolution in consciousness, which was to them the essential one. For the millenarians, revolution was revelation, but a secular form of revelation.

Most European avant-gardists were captivated by the notion of revolution or at least attracted to some political movement that promised a radical transformation of society, an end to the hegemony of bourgeois, mercantilist culture, and greater social equality. Hence alternative, though less common, allegiances were to anarchism or Italian fascism. In the early days even many Italian Futurists, who have been more or less written off politically as fascists, were leftists or anarcho-syndicalists.

In Russia, the religious-like fervor and rhetoric of avant-garde projects were particularly marked, possibly because Russia was one of the last great theocracies in Europe and, the apparently more secular Revolution of 1917 notwithstanding, it had taken that society longer to secularize. Yet not all avant-gardists in Russia in the 1910s and 1920s could be categorized as perceptual millenarians. Indeed, the term does not even define a particular group or movement. Rather, it pinpoints an ethos and a set of prejudices to be found among many European groups in the 1910s and 1920s, but most classically in the work of those avant-gardists who from late 1912 through early 1914 came together in Petersburg.

In the 1910s, the Russian avant-garde had operated very loosely on a Moscow-Petrograd axis but were gloriously decentered, split, and embattled. In late 1912 and early 1913, however, several leading Futurists from Moscow, such as Kasimir Malevich, Vladimir Mayakovsky, Aleksey Kruchënykh, and Vladimir Tatlin, joined the Union of Youth (Soyuz molodëzhi), which had been founded in Petersburg in 1910 and was led by figures such as Mikhail Matyushin but also included Velemir Khlebnikov. The frail merger lasted only until December 1913, but, thanks in part to a wealthy patron, L. Zheverzheyev, it generated some of the most famous works of Russian Futurism.[4]

Around this time the Russians wearied of merely following the latest ism from Paris and launched a "campaign against Paris," with the intention of capturing the lead with their own *outrance*. Vociferously declaring their independence from French Cubism and Italian Futurism (also launched in Paris), they worked up new isms that they claimed to be not merely more radical than those of Paris, but the ultimate in avant-gardism. The tone was essentially set in December 1912 when leading Futurists issued their foundational manifesto, "A Slap in the Face of Public Taste," with its call to heave Pushkin and other writers of the Great Tradition off the "steamship of modernity" (again, purification of space). Leaders of the Union of Youth, including Khlebnikov, Kruchënykh, and Matyushin, followed this up with a series of manifestoes and anthologies that established the theory and practice of trans-sense poetry *(zaum)* and other literary and artistic techniques designed to take avant-gardism beyond any point reached thus far.[5]

Such techniques were to provide the royal road to a new vision. But the most coherent general formulation of the avant-garde's theory is to be found not in such Futurist tracts, which tended to be allusive and frequently alogical, but in the earliest writings of the Futurists' eager ally, the future Formalist Viktor Shklovsky. Russian Formalism in some senses began with a lecture by Shklovsky entitled "The Place of Futurism in the History of Language," delivered when he was still a young student, on December 23, 1913, at the Stray Dog Cabaret, a center of theatrical experimentation.

A later essay by Shklovsky that makes similar points, "Art as Technique" (Iskusstvo kak priyëm, 1915–1916), the de facto manifesto of early Formalism, contains a quintessential account of the first premise of perceptual millenarianism. Here Shklovsky quotes a passage from Tolstoy's diary of 1897 in which the writer remarks how it is often the case that with a routine task such as dusting the room one cannot recall whether one has dusted the divan or not. If one has dusted it but forgotten about it, it is as if the act had not occurred, so little has it impinged on one's consciousness. Indeed, Tolstoy concludes, "If for many people an entire complex life passes by unconsciously, it is as if this life had not been." Shklovsky goes on to say that "art exists in order to recover the sense of life, in order to feel objects, to make the stone stoney" (not coincidentally, perhaps, *Stone* [Kamen'] was the title of Mandelshtam's first collection of verse, published in 1913).[6] Shklovsky, like the Futurist artists and so many other avant-gardists of his time, gives the ability to "see" an object or word absolute priority. He draws a distinction between "seeing" *(videniye)* and "recognizing" *(uznavaniye)*, the latter being what happens when a word or object has been routinized: "Once objects have been perceived several times one begins to perceive them by recognition: an object stands before us, we know about it, but we do not see it."[7] He labels such a predicament "automatization" *(avtomatizatsiya)*, and he provides a solution for it, a technique he calls "making strange" or "defamiliarization" *(ostraneniye)*. This technique involves taking things out of their context as a means of seeing them and "using an impeded *[zatrudnënnaya]* form that increases the degree of difficulty and the length of perception, for the process of perception in art is self-valuable and must be prolonged; *art is a means for experiencing the making* [delan'ye] *of an object, and what is made* [sdelannoye] *in art is not important*."[8]

In this essay Shklovsky focuses particularly on defamiliarization in language. He decries the way conventional meanings and usage have become so automatized that they no longer have any resonance. One can combat this by combining words in an unexpected and perhaps even jarring way, and in their combination draw attention to the words themselves, bringing about, as suggested by the title of his essay of 1914 based on the foundational address at the cabaret, "The Resurrection of the Word."[9] By such incongruous, or clashing, juxtapositions of words or word units (phrases, sentences, or even entire plot morphemes), the author draws attention to the very process of making a creative artifact and in this way heightens the reader's consciousness of words and the creative act. Moreover, Shklovsky contends, new meanings are thereby created and, as a corollary, new possibilities for reality are presented to the beholder. Thus, although his formulation was one of the more secular and analytical of the perceptual millenarianist position, we see here the common project to overcome the ordinary and banal and attain a level of experience that is more intense and more authentic.

The scenario Shklovsky outlines here, *mutatis mutandis,* underwrote much Russian avant-garde creative endeavor both before and after the Revolution. One can recognize it in, for instance, the theory of montage as outlined in the late 1920s by Eisenstein (who was originally Meyerhold's pupil), at the heart of which is the juxtaposition, both within and between frames and shots, of radically contrasting material resulting in what he variously describes as "clashes," "collisions," and even "explosions." With such explosions, and by certain other montage techniques, such as setting up contrasting rhythms within and between shots, Eisenstein claimed that the audience would not be lulled into passivity, as is usually the effect of watching a movie, but would be forced to attend to what was happening on the screen; in their efforts to comprehend it, they would attain a new revolutionary consciousness.[10]

Thus Eisenstein in his essays on montage was constructing a new film aesthetic with an allegedly ineluctable connection to Marxist-Leninist dialectic. Here we see how epistemological and political revolutions were identified among perceptual millenarians. But in such formulations, in effect, the Kantian revolution in philosophy was taken up and extended.[11] This revolution had entailed a shift of focus from reality to the perception of reality. Kant argued that insofar as we cannot perceive the thing in itself, what we do "see" is a construction. The avant-garde radicalized this position in what was, de facto, a crude appropriation of Kant's views inasmuch as their work was implicitly based on an assumption that since we do not see the thing in itself, it is available for reconstruction. A version of Kantianism was adopted by the new philosophy and aesthetics in which the models were often given *pre*scriptive rather than *de*scriptive force.

As can be seen in the case of Eisenstein's theories of montage, perceptual millenarianism can in no way be identified with the Union of Youth merger, nor did it evaporate as a trend with either the merger's dissolution in late 1913 or the Union's in early 1914. Given the itinerant nature of the avant-garde, even the contention that the Union of Youth or, worse still, perceptual millenarianism itself, was a Petersburg, or even a Russian, phenomenon has to be an act of literalism or casuistry. Similar prejudices can be found in many avant-garde groups in Europe and America in the 1910s and 1920s, and for that matter among non-avant-gardists as well. They are particularly characteristic, for instance, of Dada; there is a minor link here in that the Russian Futurist Ilya Zdanevich (a.k.a. Iliazde), who had, *inter alia*, organized some theatrical events in Petersburg in 1915, gave a reading of Russian trans-sense poetry at a Dada evening in Paris in 1923.[12]

The perceptual millenarian ethos particularly informs the Suprematist movement in art, promulgated by Malevich at an exhibition of 1915 and developed further in the postrevolutionary period while he was based (1919–1921) at the Popular Art School in Vitebsk (at the time a common place of retreat for intellectuals from civil war–torn Petrograd), where he formed the association UNOVIS (an acronym for the Affirmers [*utverditeli*] of the New Art), with branches in several major Soviet cities.

The principal focus of this movement for a new vision might seem to be the verbal and visual arts. Yet another medium—performance—was a dominant force in the avant-garde's conception of both. The new vision was not to be won by passive contemplation; accounts of it included some dimension of action—the stuff of revolution. It is important to note that when Shklovsky in "Art as Technique" defines "defamiliarization" he uses *routinized action* as a trope for *verbal* routinization. Also, the various prescriptions for *zaum* poetry emphasize the sound potential of such verse, thus implying performance; in some accounts, the word emerges as an actor in its own right.[13] The bread and butter of avant-garde movements from the 1910s and 1920s—manifestoes, manifesto-like works, theater, *épatage* in the art exhibitions—all have a dominant performative element.

Marjorie Perloff, in her book on the pre–World War I avant-garde, has defined their paradigmatic gesture as collage; related gestures include framing or confusing figure and ground, the canonical and noncanonical.[14] Such definitions are clearly analogous to Shklovsky's defamiliarization or to Eisenstein's montage inasmuch as, whichever way the paradigmatic gesture is defined—collage, montage, breaking or confusing the frame, and so on— it involves placement or juxtaposition with the aim of confounding borders and hierarchies. One has to place the like against the unlike in order to "see" anew; one has to cause a violent movement such as an "explosion"; or one has to (or the artifact has to) move in time or space for a radically new epistemological experience to be possible.

Epistemological transgression (confusing seemingly unbridgeable cognitive or discursive boundaries) was the dominant aim of all these movements that saw such a crossing as the road to any new vision. Often, however, epistemological transgression was figured as, or conflated with, sexual or political (revolutionary) transgression. This is most clear not in a text by a Russian avant-gardist, nor in a prerevolutionary text, but in *Nadja,* a novel published in 1928 by the French Surrealist André Breton.

In *Nadja,* the narrator wanders around Paris in the late afternoon, buys a copy of a book by Trotsky, and then encounters workers streaming out onto the streets at the end of a day's work. As he "unconsciously watch[es] their faces, their clothes, and their way of walking," he concludes: "No, it is not yet these who would be ready to make the Revolution." The narrator walks on and crosses an intersection. Then he "suddenly" sees a "young, poorly dressed woman." His attention is drawn to her eyes, which are made up in an unusual way, but are above all such as "I had never seen." The woman smiles, "but quite mysteriously and somehow *knowingly.*" This stranger is Nadja, who is to become the enigmatic object of his erotic obsession-cum-existential / aesthetic quest.[15]

We tend to dismiss the Surrealists' invocation of Trotsky and revolution, together with their ultimately abortive attempts at joining the Communist Party, as a kind of leftist infantilism, an aberration in Surrealism and not part of its essence. Yet among so many avant-gardists, especially those of the 1910s and 1920s, one finds that same combination of commitment to a radical political movement and aesthetic iconoclasm. In *Nadja,* this allegiance to a leftist revolution is not merely prominent on the surface of the novel, but is powerfully present in its subtext as well. Most of the places in Paris where the narrator has an overpowering sense that something momentous or inexplicably painful will occur have associations with revolution.[16]

Benjamin called the Surrealists "adoptive children of the revolution,"[17] and they were subjected to the sort of ambiguous status that too often comes with that relationship. As adoptive children, they were also of a different bloodline. One would have a hard time recognizing the iron maiden of revolutionary commitment in Nadja. She is a sometime prostitute, an immigrant girl who otherwise supports herself through menial tasks. Unaccountably, she is also attracted by the same writings as are the Surrealists. But is this really "unaccountable"? Nadja's pedigree, for all her lower-class identity, clearly derives from Baudelaire more than from Marx.

Nadja is elevated above the status of tawdry figure from the demimonde not just because of her exotic allure but also because of the intensity of her gaze. Her most crucial characteristic is that she perceives the world differently from the way it is perceived by others; she seems to have powers of clairvoyance, to be able to make connections between trivial details and occurrences from ostensibly different epistemological series. She also hallucinates and does not always distinguish between that which "is" in conventional reality and that which "is" as seen from within.

In the lengthy first part of *Nadja*, before the narrator encounters the alluring object of his obsession, he essentially outlines for the reader the nature of his project. Nadja is sought before she appears "suddenly." The narrator begins with a project to investigate, during his strolls around Paris, "things which, reaching me in unexpected ways," seem to be "at the mercy of chance . . . [and which] admit me to an almost forbidden world [note the spatial transgression] of sudden parallels, petrifying coincidences, and . . . facts that may belong to the order of pure observation, but that on each occasion present all the appearances of a signal, without our being able to say precisely which signal."[18] Breton describes these "experiences" as "flashes of light that would make you see, really *see*, if only they were not so much quicker than all the rest."[19]

For such avant-gardists, this profane illumination was the stuff of revolution, of a revolution in consciousness that was to them the essential one. They believed they should make that leap, see the sudden flash of light, and be changed. Or, at second best, they, like the narrator of *Nadja*, should follow someone else who can make, or has made, that leap, and try to acquire some of the light by osmosis.

Of course Russia with its Revolution of 1917 had already, allegedly, made such a leap on a national scale. Once that revolution occurred, the Russian avant-garde, more than any other non-Party group (actually, some of them were Party members), supported it, and the Revolution—as it were, a trump card the Russians could play in their "campaign against Paris"—became a beacon for many of the avant-garde in Europe. At more or less the same time as Breton wrote *Nadja*, in the late 1920s, Mayakovsky and others were traveling to Paris emphasizing the links between French Surrealism and the Soviet avant-garde, while Malevich traveled to the Bauhaus in Germany where El Lissitzky, his erstwhile disciple from Vitebsk, was established; Malevich brought with him color charts done by his coterie in Leningrad that were the fruit of the experimental work on perception. Slightly earlier, in the years immediately following the Revolution, Russian Futurists, who after 1917 preferred to be called "left artists," served as propagandists and cultural bureaucrats of the state, while German Expressionists such as Ernst Toller were involved in the Munich Communist government, and Dada's Richard Huelsenbeck served as Commissar of Fine Arts in Berlin after its short-lived revolution of 1918. Symptomatically, in the early years after the Revolution the avant-garde of Russia sought to found an artistic International (analogous to, but not connected with, the Communist International) and proposed that embassies for art be opened in the different countries, thus implying that art was a country unto itself.

This aim also implies a separation of art and state, although in Russia initially the two were not seen as in conflict. As time wore on, however, many avant-gardists became more ambivalent toward the new state. Their writings began to reflect a much more complicated and enigmatic attitude toward the Communist Revolution than is evident in *Nadja*. After all, Communism was not for them an alternative to the temporal power, but had the misfortune to be the name of that power itself. Moreover, highly formulaic ways of expressing enthusiasm for a Communist state were already becoming the expected norm.

This more mediated response to the Revolution can be seen in an approximate Russian analogue to Breton's *Nadja*, two novels published in 1929 and 1931 by the Leningrad writer Veniamin Kaverin, *The Troublemaker, or Nights on Vasilevsky Island* (Skandalist ili vechera na Vasil'yevskom ostrove) and *Artist Unknown* (Khudozhnik neizvesten). In both, as in *Nadja*, an intellectual of letters—identified with the author himself—follows a mysterious and potentially crazy acquaintance all around the city, drawn by the belief that he may thus learn to "see" a reality of an entirely different order from the conventional one, and to which his subject seems to have unique access.

There are substantial differences between Kaverin's novels and Breton's *Nadja*. For example, not only is there no sign of Trotsky in Kaverin (hardly surprising given that Trotsky had been ousted from power in 1926), but in the more puritanical political climate of the Soviet late 1920s the object of epistemological quest stands for bohemian eccentricity rather than sexual transgression.[20] As with *Nadja*, however, the motif of revolution is ever present in cryptic allusions to revolutionary moments and figures (here, as in *Nadja*, primarily of French revolutions); in *The Troublemaker*, for example, the most intense experience of the observer figure, the student Nagin, in trying to follow his enigmatic seer around Leningrad occurs as the two stand on the icy Neva between the Lieutenant Schmidt Bridge (a name associated with Russia's revolution of 1905) and Equality Bridge (associated with the French Revolution) and are cut off from the city by mist.[21]

Of Kaverin's two novels, *Artist Unknown* contains the most sustained and idealized account of the visionary eccentric who becomes the object of an aesthetic-cum-epistemological quest. I say idealized advisedly, even though the visionary, the artist Arkhimedov, is represented as a quixotic and totally inept figure. At the end of the novel, Arkhimedov seems defeated by the forces of the new age; his wife has committed suicide and he has fallen into such a state of madness that his child has been taken from him. Yet in an epilogue we are given the following account of a picture by an "artist unknown," whom the reader assumes to have been Arkhimedov:

> . . . This could have been achieved only by someone who with all the freedom of genial talent strode through the barriers set up by timidity and constraints. . . . His mixing of the high with the trivial, of everyday detail with a profound sense of the times is of an order that cannot be learned at the feet of other masters, living or dead. Only an artist's eye [zreniye] boldly orienting itself around material others consider contingent [sluchaynyy] or banal could resolve to return like this to a childlike perception of things. . . . One would have to have been smashed to death to paint such a thing . . .[22]

Both of Kaverin's novels are also *romans à clef* of his own intellectual set. These figures who "truly see" are based on particular idols of the author's milieu, although Kaverin in representing them used caricature, inversion, and other forms of distortion. The subject in *The Troublemaker* is E. Polivanov, a noted linguist originally from the Formalist circle who in the late 1920s was the only prominent linguist to attack the theories of N. Marr (see Chapter 9). In *Artist Unknown,* the subject represents a conflation of Petersburg avant-gardists from the perceptual millenarians' pantheon, the poet Velemir Khlebnikov and the artist Pavel Filonov, and to some extent also Kaverin's own mentor (and relation by marriage), the Formalist theoretician Yury Tynyanov.[23] In short, Arkhimedov is a composite representation of the ideals of his set; the novel is a rather curious—and devious—form of iconography.

Even in the above quotation from *Artist Unknown* there is an emphasis on the necessity for shattering as a precondition for creating anew and on having a Nietzschean "courage" to transgress boundaries. Such convictions were by no means confined to Kaverin. Nor were they just a phenomenon of the late 1920s. They can be seen as a central credo of the Union of Youth merger, one most clearly present in that milestone of Russian avant-gardism, the 1913 production of *Victory over the Sun.*

Victory over the Sun

Nineteen thirteen, the annus mirabilis of Russia's avant-garde, culminated in two theatrical productions that some have seen as an orgiastic effort after which the Petersburg-Moscow merger was spent and disbanded.[24] From December 2–5 in Petersburg the Union of Youth sponsored Russian Futurism's first two theatrical ventures, Vladimir Mayakovsky's *Vladimir Maya-kovsky: A Tragedy* (Vladimir Mayakovskiy: Tragediya) and *Victory over the Sun* (Pobeda nad solntsem), a joint effort by Kruchënykh, Khlebnikov, Malevich, and Matyushin.[25]

Recent Western productions of these plays, especially Mayakovsky's, have frequently interpreted them as absurdist proto-Pinter. Yet with "A Tragedy" as the subtitle of Mayakovsky's work and "An Opera" as the subtitle of *Victory over the Sun*, one should not overlook the extent to which both were written in the context of the Nietzschean / Wagnerian movement.[26] This was especially true of *Victory*, which with its "strongman" characters and rhetoric of "daring" can be read as a Nietzschean parable.

Victory over the Sun contains not so much a coherent plot as a series of events that are interconnected to some extent at the level of action but more by allegory or "associative chains." The main events in the play illustrate its title: a time traveler arrives at an unidentified time and place, reporting that he has wandered through all the ages and in the thirty-fifth century the people are waging a battle against the sun; some characters then capture the sun. The inhabitants of this unnamed place thus live in a world without the sun and in a dwelling where the windows are arranged alogically and all look inward (when the sun was pulled down it was not destroyed, but rather redirected *inward*, so often the locus of the new vision). At the end of the play, an aviator crashes, but only laughs at this and sings a "military song" consisting almost entirely of consonants.[27] These vaguely related events are interspersed with scenes of struggle and violence, including military action, duels, and suicides.

It is hardly surprising that the play should have a leitmotif of combat because a major theme is confronting and confounding one order of reality with another. This theme is enacted at all levels, from language to the play's major metaphor of victory over the "sun." According to Mikhail Matyushin, the composer of the "opera," the sun stands for the "sun of cheap appearances."[28] It stands for the conventional sense of reality, for existing scientific systems, and for sterile rationality; after the sun is captured, an unidentified character remarks, in an obvious reversal of Galileo's famous pronouncement about the earth's moving: "You know, the earth does not move," whereupon those at the scene report, "We tore out the sun with its fresh roots / They were thick and smelled of arithmetic."[29]

The play is thus a parable about overcoming the limitations of received science, in that sense a further development of the charge of Dostoevsky's narrator in *Notes from the Underground* that "two plus two" must equal "five." For the Russian and European avant-garde, this was a typical theme.

So much of their work starts with the premise that the old science has been superseded in the work of scientists such as Georg Riemann and Nikolai Lobachevsky.[30] Lobachevsky, a nineteenth-century Russian mathematician, was a favorite not just of the Russian avant-garde but of Dada as well; his work establishing that parallel lines *could* meet (contrary to Euclid's eleventh "axiom") had particular appeal because it showed how one could overcome a seemingly unbridgeable boundary—that between two lines that should forever maintain a stipulated distance from each other.[31] Many avant-gardists, particularly in Russia and France, were absolutely opposed to all closed scientific systems (such as that of Euclid), which they saw as akin to that "wall" which Dostoevsky's narrator in *Notes from the Underground* insists must be challenged, no matter how illogical and even painful and self-destructive it might be. In their place they sought totally new scientific systems in which "contingency," "chance," and the seemingly trivial— that which is irrelevant or nonsystematic according to the established systems—might become the central "scientific" principles. Accordingly, Dadaists generated a series of new principles for a science of systematic aberrancy, such as "chance selection," *hasard objectif,* and *geste gratuit.* Dada artists such as Marcel Duchamp and Kurt Schwitters (with his *Merz*) reified contingency in their works of art by declaring bits of trivia (newsprint, debris, and even dust) randomly or haphazardly collected to be the work of art itself.

Thus in *Victory over the Sun* "science" is interpreted in a rather extended sense to mean the old (conventional) epistemology and axiology. Within those systems, language and visual representations were the most fundamental for members of the Union of Youth. Artists and writers tried to conceive a new language that would be constructed on a system quite antithetical to that of conventional language, and frequently random; they delighted in all examples of linguistic singularity and aberrance. Thus, more figuratively, *Victory* is a parable about overcoming the limitations of conventional systems of meaning and of the aesthetic. But it is simultaneously an object lesson with its extensive use of *zaum* (as in the "military song" that consists entirely of consonants).

The sets and costumes by Kasimir Malevich were, analogously, intended to confound conventional systems, in this instance of visual representation. One particular backdrop has been claimed to represent proto-Suprematism, his avant-gardist movement in art (first proclaimed in 1915) which purports to represent a *nec plus ultra* in that it has renounced all ties between art and representation. Instead, quasi-geometric shapes (squares, rhomboids, crosses, circles, triangles) painted in a limited register of colors were placed in seemingly random patterns on a painted background (the backdrop in question makes gestures toward the "black square" that was to become one of the signatures of Malevich's Suprematism).

Victory over the Sun is not just an attack against received science and linguistic conventions but also more directly a Nietzschean parable about "victory" over the Apollonian, which is in its very name associated with Apollo, the sun god. Nietzsche in *The Birth of Tragedy* identifies the Apollonian in terms of the *principium individuationis,* or principle of individuation, that is, in terms of the individual's sense of boundedness, which is shattered in Dionysian frenzy.[32] The general mission of the various artists associated with the Union of Youth in Petersburg at this time was to shatter the precise and unerring logic of line and contour that Nietzsche associated with the Apollonian. They sought to transgress or confuse all manner of set bounds. Thus in the backdrops for *Victory* Malevich incorporated musical notes to symbolize the way the barrier between the musical and the visual had been flouted in this "opera."

This tendency is particularly marked in the writings of Malevich, who liked to define Suprematism in terms of exploding boundaries and creating new forms out of the pieces. In an article of 1917 entitled "The Theater," recalling the effect of Matyushin's atonal music at the performance of *Victory over the Sun,* he wrote: "Matyushin's sound smashed to pieces the crust of the old music . . . while the words and word-letters of Aleksey Kruchënykh [the librettist] turned the stock [*veshchevoye*] word to dust. The facade was shattered and in the same moment the wail of the consciousness of the old brain was shattered as well. . . ."[33] Here we find a formulation similar to Bely's central trope in *Petersburg* of the assassination explosion that shatters the skull, used by Bely as a figure for mind expansion, or Marx's trope for the end of the capitalist system as the "integument" bursting asunder.

Bely's and Malevich's referring to the brain in formulations that are otherwise analogous to Marx's is symptomatic of the fact that the avant-garde, unlike most Marxists, generally gave priority to some kind of spiritual revolution. Many of them sought true authenticity in absolute otherness, though it remained elusive. For example, a favorite technique of the Surrealists was automatic writing, writing often attempted immediately upon awakening in an effort to obscure the boundary between the conscious and the subconscious. Potentially, automatic writing (and *zaum*) could be a kind of speaking in tongues, yet somehow the veil of the culturally conditioned was never ripped off and their allegedly unfettered and spontaneous verbal compositions came out in complete sentences.

As this example shows, a fundamental problem for such varieties of avant-gardism is that nothing can be random or noncanonical except in relation to that which is fixed. This is particularly apparent in the use of the alleged *zaum* in *Victory over the Sun*. The play seems to alternate between *zaum* and outright proclamation. Moreover, even in the use of *zaum*, although there is much "madness," there is also clearly method. The method consists in part in the fact that the authors have used a perfectly methodical system for the "deformation" of conventional verbal and even plot material (putting unusual suffixes on recognizable roots, substituting a word that rhymes with the original one, and so on). The text is constantly walking a thin line between semantic iconoclasm and proclamation. In Khlebnikov's Prologue, a virtual Sargossa Sea of neologisms, the audience has no difficulty grasping the most fundamental tenets of perceptual millenarianism as he readily deciphers the neologisms in statements proclaiming that those with a new vision will lead and transform ("sozertseben est' vozhdeben" and "sozertsavel' est' preobrazhavel' ").

Victory over the Sun is written as a textbook of semantic iconoclasm. At base, however, it opposes meaning for the purpose of substituting other meaning. Paradoxically, in order for the practitioners of *zaum* to demonstrate how they have flouted conventional usages, they are often obliged to use the most familiar and mundane as points of orientation. Frequently, commonplaces or well-known quotations are invoked at inappropriate moments or with substantial changes; for instance, "All's well that begins well" is used at the beginning of the first act and also in the play's closing line. Similarly, Pushkin's title and the opening line from his famous poem of 1836, "I have erected a monument to myself...," is invoked in the play unacknowledged, but is debased by the use of the more prosaic verb "I have put up *[postavil]*" rather than "erected *[vozdvig]*." Moreover, the character making this claim is lying down—and hence far from a vertical position—and talking of suicide rather than immortality.

The Pushkin (mis)quotation comes from a poem in which the poet makes his greatest claim for the significance of his own writing, metaphorized as a monument erected to himself but "not made by hands." It also alludes to an earlier poem, Horace's *Exegi monumentum*. As is typical for this play, then, the theme of art is invoked in a context where it is not explicit. The Pushkin figure in this scene is parodied as a cowardly buffoon, inept in the face of a canon attack by Futurist forces *(budetlyane)*. Then, following the canon attack, comes the extravagant remark, attributed extremely vaguely, "I am without continuation and imitation."[34]

The implication, then, is that the kind of art being showcased in this production represents not just an attempt to decenter existing meaning, an exercise in cognitive estrangement, but an attempt to discover a unique meaning, to find an irreducible specificum. The meaning of *zaum* is to get out of a discourse in which you have the rational possibility of generalizing; not to get out of language for its own sake, but to achieve a perception of a unique meaning. Most visions are comprehensive, general, and in that sense utopian; this is a vision of the particular. These perceptual millenarians seek an art that reaches even beyond the intrinsic state of the aesthetic; they seek something so absolutely in itself that it has gone beyond self-valuableness (aestheticism) to another and more radical degree of in-itselfness.

Despite such iconoclastic bravado, many avant-gardists laid some claim to science as a legitimating authority (hence the Russians' need to invite Shklovsky, a young scholar of literature and language, to pronounce on their work). In this respect, the avant-garde seem to find common cause with the Bolsheviks.

In the writings of both groups science emerges as the emblem of revolution. One of Leninism's greatest claims to superiority was its promise to establish a kingdom of science and advanced technology where before, under the tsars, there had been a kingdom of obscurantism, a major factor in Russia's backwardness compared with Western Europe. However, Lenin's understanding of science differed from that of the Russian avant-garde; he essentially favored the old science and, in famous polemics with members of his own party, insisted that the world is not "constructed" but has palpable—material—existence.[35] In their account of science the avant-garde were generally less systematic than he was, as can be appreciated in the fact that even Kaverin (a disciple of the Formalists), when he called for a more rigorous and scientific approach to literary theory and practice, adduced the work of E. T. A. Hoffman as a model.[36]

Perceptual millenarians presented themselves as occupying a kind of liminal position between art and science. Hence their task of achieving profane illumination, an essentially aesthetic experience that leads to a new way of knowing. They often represented their artistic projects as "experiments," or conducted experiments themselves as if no less justified in doing so than scientists. Indeed, Duchamp insisted not merely that the new artist is like a scientist, but that in his work he would surpass even the most pathbreaking scientist. In this conviction he conducted systematic experiments with chance. In Leningrad after the Revolution, the coterie of Malevich, Matyushin, and Filonov pursued their activity as artists by conducting "scientific" experiments on perception of color and light. In their more extravagant formulations, they contended that the artists, as those with the "keener vision" who can more readily perceive new meanings and new systems behind that which is ostensibly "contingent" and inconsequential, will, rather than the scientists per se, be the ones to lead humankind to epistemological revolution. In order to do so, however, they must train their eyes to see or, as in Breton's *Nadja* or Kaverin's novels, move around in order to have chance occurrences impinge on their consciousness. In training themselves to become open to contingency, they must overcome the limitations in perception that have been culturally conditioned.

One limitation that particularly concerned the Petersburg perceptual millenarians was the fact that individuals cannot simultaneously see all 360 degrees. The solution they proposed was a heightened intuition (such as is attained in *Victory over the Sun* when the sun is not vanquished in the "victorious" struggle but brought to reside within). This problem was addressed in an article Matyushin published in May 1923 in the leading Leningrad cultural journal, the *Life of Art* (Zhizn' iskusstva), to introduce his new movement, *Zorved* (roughly, "see-know"). Zorved proposed overcoming normal human limitations in perception by heightening the artist's capacities until there is "a physiological change in the previous method of perception," introducing for the first time the observation and experience of the "rear plane" that was hitherto hidden, of all that space that, hitherto, was *outside the human sphere due to inadequacies of experience.*" "New data" from the experimental work of the Zorved group, Matyushin continues, "have revealed the influence of space, light, color, and form on brain centers through the back of the head *[zatylok]*," "clearly establish[ing] a sensitivity to space to be found in the visual centers located in the rear *[zatylochnyy]* section of the brain. In this way a great power of spatial apprehension has suddenly been opened up to man . . . the most valuable gift for both man and the artist is knowledge of the spatial. . . ."[37] It was commented at the time that Matyushin's theories in this article represent a version of the "fourth dimension" for art, but by this dimension is not meant Einsteinian theory.[38] When in 1913 Matyushin published Albert Gleizes and Jean Metzinger's *Du cubisme* in Russian translation, he interspersed sections of it with quotations from P. D. Ouspensky's *Tertium organum* (1911), a key text for these perceptual millenarians that viewed the "fourth dimension" in a mystical or theosophical framework.[39]

Thus the perceptual millenarians, as those who claimed that they could give man new vision, represent a limit case of the Hermes complex. Their role as the privileged few who could go beyond the conventional systems and "really see" conferred on them a sort of nobility of gnosis (generally referred to as Intuition). The practitioners of *zaum* might be seen as paradigmatic Hermes figures, mediating between a language no one speaks and a language everyone speaks.

The problem, however, is that were one to come back from a truly different reality, one would be unable to describe it in terms recognizable to those who had not been there—perhaps one could only act it out or try to render it not in words but in the more expressive medium of sound. Arguably, this was one reason for the attraction of *zaum* with its incantatory potential.

Naming was in general very important to the avant-garde. Consider, for example, their proclivity for renaming themselves (well-known examples include Tristan Tzara and Velemir Khlebnikov). This convention suggests that when a new self has been constructed a new name is in order (not coincidentally, perhaps, this practice was also popular among the Bolshevik leaders). Thus avant-gardism is an Adamic ideology, a form of paradisiac hermeneutics.

At the same time, names play an important role in the avant-garde's paradoxical, self-ironizing underside (an aspect not shared by the Bolsheviks), its salutary antidote to the heavy mystical / religious and self-aggrandizing tendencies. Thus, though Dada's leaders kept rehearsing how they discovered the movement's name, they also stressed that the name was gratuitous (it was allegedly found randomly in a dictionary and is in any case from the realm of baby talk). Similarly, Duchamp and Man Ray gave many of their works of art fatuous names that involved punning, challenging artistic canons, and playing with sexual crossing and linguistic hybridicity.

Naming and renaming have to do with the Hermes role assumed by a perceptual millenarian. It might be argued that the basic device of the avant-garde manifesto, the catalogue of names, is a favorite not only because of its incantatory-cum-performance value, but also because, given that the essence of their movement is so radically other that it cannot be conveyed directly, they try to capture it by maneuvering within a series of paradoxical juxtapositions of nouns. Kruchënykh in his canonical account of *zaum* talks in terms of seeing both "here" and "there."[40] Thus *zaum* is a concept that centrally entails a journey. Perceptual millenarianism involves, metaphorically at least, getting away, going beyond, going to a place or time that is not of this world in the sense that its "reality" is not of this world's systems.

The Myth of the Journey to Atlantis

In 1922 Yury Annenkov noted in an article in the Leningrad journal *The Life of Art* that the three latest rages among the intelligentsia were Einstein, Oswald Spengler—and a novel by the French writer Pierre Benoit called

Atlantis (Atlantide, or Atlantida in Russian).[41] What an unholy trinity—the leading scientist of the age, a gloomy philosopher of history, and a novel about fatal attraction! *Atlantis* is an improbable tale of exotic adventure and mystery in the vast, unexplored reaches of the Saharan desert, where the characters stumble upon the lost city of Atlantis, which is presided over by a bewitching queen, Antinea; the price to pay for one glorious night with her is to die and be embalmed so that one can be displayed as a trophy in one of her opulent marble halls. But Antinea rules a kingdom that is not merely "lost"; it is the (unknown) center of alternative science, of that body of knowledge that for centuries has been marginalized or proscribed; it is the place that functions as symbolic worthy antagonist of the contemporary European world. As in *Nadja*, sexual transgression, epistemological transgression, and to some extent political transgression are conflated, but the enabling trope is a journey to a totally other place.

Thus this unholy trinity—Benoit, Einstein, and Spengler—stands at the intersection of the exotic journey (Benoit), the abolition of conventional concepts of space and time (Einstein),[42] and millennial expectation (Spengler). That point of intersection marks an attempt at epistemological iconoclasm that typified avant-garde extremism.

A first premise of the avant-garde was the destruction of time and space as they were then understood. Indeed, *The Founding and Manifesto of Italian Futurism* proclaims: "Time and Space died yesterday." Of the two, the destruction of time is the most apparent. There is not a great deal about the future in this manifesto, nor indeed in most other such manifestoes of the avant-garde. And as for the past, Italian Futurism and many of its Russian counterparts called for incendiarism, for torching or dynamiting it, as the only way to destroy the cult of the past *(passéisme)*, while Dada claimed it had no past or future but was "ageless." Similarly, the avant-garde tended to reject linear or cyclical models of time (and therefore of narrative), favoring epiphanic or fragmentary structures. Thus in a sense Futurism is a misnomer and "presentism" would be a more accurate name for these kinds of movements, although even that is imprecise. There is no "present" as a point in time, for nothing can be more than process (hence, for example, Shklovsky in "Art as Technique" privileges "experiencing the making *[delan'ye]* of an object" over "what is made *[sdelannoye]*").

So often, in consequence, the work of the avant-garde became a kind of metaphysical or metaphorical journey, a journey that sought to transcend time and thereby "find" a new order of space. Malevich frequently insisted that "my new [Suprematist] art does not belong to the world exclusively. Earth has been rejected as a home . . ."; in man's consciousness he is drawn into space and experiences a pull to "cut loose from the terrestrial globe." "I can't wait to hear that breaking off [*razryv*]," he would say. "When will we take off?"[43] It is perhaps not surprising, then, that perceptual millenarianism in Russia coincided with a time of great interest in utopian fiction shading into science fiction fantasy literature.

The possibility of seeing a new world *elsewhere*, which the prerevolutionary avant-garde erected into a radical epistemology, was, then, at that time far from their obsession alone. A similar impulse informed the popular press and fiction of the day. One can, for example, sense it by looking at the journal *Argus*, a periodical particularly representative of the times. *Argus* was first published in 1913, at the height of prerevolutionary avant-garde activity. It attracted some highbrow readers (several noted writers published there[44]) but generally aimed for a broader audience. Its title refers of course to Argus with his one hundred eyes, which could, as the journal's subtitle proclaims, "see everything" (*vsë vizhu*). But the name also suggests the possibility of the argonauts, especially since most of the articles and photos in the journal were devoted to accounts of exotic travel, of far-flung and primitive peoples, of flight, ballooning, or exploration (in 1913 it published as a supplement the journals of Captain Scott's expedition to the Antarctic of 1910–1913). Another favorite was firsthand accounts of extraordinary visual experiences; one such gem, an article entitled "What the Blind Journalist Saw," provides a utopian vision of the future.[45] *Argus* also had a section titled, as if in paraphrase of Kruchënykh's claim for *zaum*, "Both Here and There," which contained somewhat popularized tales of "believe it or not." This fare was accompanied by Gothic short stories embellished with illustrations of skulls and such, and adventure romances set in exotic climes à la Rider Haggard (or Benoit).

Such publications did not merely supplement the work of the avant-garde. The avant-garde themselves, in their writings from both before and after the Revolution, frequently invoked moments from science fiction, especially from H. G. Wells and Jules Verne, as symbolizing a radically different order of experience that ordinary folk—earthlings—would find alien, incomprehensible, and perhaps even frightening. Thus in *Victory over the Sun*, for example, one of the characters is "the time traveler" in the manner of Wells's *The Time Machine*. But the most often appropriated motif from science fiction was "Ullya, Ullya [we are] the Martians," a version of the Martians' call in Wells's *War of the Worlds* as they made their inexorable advance on a terrorized London. This phrase was used by the Russian Futurists as a sort of war cry heralding their own advance with that which was radically new and which threatened to destroy the old completely:

Khlebnikov used it in 1916 in "The Trumpet of the Martians," and Shklovsky picked it up in his opening sally for a programmatic article of 1919 entitled "On the Art of the Revolution" (and elsewhere).[46]

In fiction of exotic adventure travel, such as Benoit's *Atlantis*, the essential characteristic of the traveler-protagonist's destination (Mars, in space, in the desert) is less crucial than that it should be absolutely cut off from all else. Very frequently at the center of this new world there is, as in Benoit's novel, a femme fatale, a version of Rider Haggard's She who stands for the spirit of the new place. She is the icon for "there," for "Atlantis," for desire, for the journey beyond the mind (*za-um*). "Atlantis" (Mars, and so on) is not a place but a symbol.

Yet in Russia elements from the myth of Petersburg are often incorporated into this kind of literature, perhaps because that myth is associated simultaneously with the rigid and centralized as well as with radical change. This can be seen even in *Victory over the Sun*. Although the setting in the thirty-fifth century represents both anywhere and no place, the authors implicitly invoke patterns of contrast recognizably associated with the myth of Petersburg. For instance, a random remark by one of the characters about how the place where they are ("here") is the opposite of what obtains on "the islands"[47] suggests the pattern of contrast that is fundamental to Bely's *Petersburg*. This character reverses the meaning of these poles in Bely's novel, however; in *Victory*, the central location stands for the chaotic and the islands for the ordered.

It might seem that the aim of the journey to Atlantis is to discover Atlantis, to attain a new time and place. But just as Heinrich Schliemann's discovering Troy destroyed the myth of Troy, the discovery of Atlantis would no doubt also strip "Atlantis" of its magic and mystery.

The journey to Atlantis cannot be a journey to a place that is *found*. Modern historians such as Paul Carter who write about the great explorers have begun to emphasize the distinction between "discovering" a place and "exploring." When you are traveling the names you give to what you perceive en route are never definite statements of arrival (hence the gesturing with catalogues of names in an effort to interpret for those who have not taken that route). Such places always point to what V. S. Naipaul has called "the enigma of arrival."[48] The whole function of Atlantis is to serve as a beacon for setting out on the journey, but its purpose is to occasion exploration and not discovery.

At the end of Breton's *Nadja*, the heroine is institutionalized in a mental hospital. The narrator rants about this, pointing out that such an institutionalization was the fate of three heroes from the Surrealist pantheon:

Baudelaire, de Sade, and Nietzsche.[49] Yet he appears to do nothing to help Nadja, who fades from his purview. Some have viewed this as evidence of the essential male chauvinism of the avant-garde or of an unacknowledged elitism whereby such lower-class exotics can be consumed and spat out when no longer of interest. But it might also be argued that the narrator, the questing Surrealist, cannot follow Nadja to that end, her end, which is totally beyond the systems of this world.

In a lengthy footnote toward the end of the book the narrator relates how one day as he was driving Nadja around she covered his head with hers in a passionate clinch and then put her foot over his on the accelerator. He confesses that he was unable to take this moment, to hurtle on to his death in an access of passion, claiming that he did not love Nadja enough.[50]

This exercise in situational ethics highlights a major dilemma for the perceptual millenarians. Perhaps that is why it was coyly hidden in a footnote. In the vertigo of the earlier years of the avant-garde, many flirted with the idea of pressing down on that accelerator and reaching true otherness: "Lâchez tout!" was a slogan of Dada, an instruction from ballooning to cut all the strings so that the balloon can fly up from earth, but which might also be read more literally as "Leave everything [behind]," and is comparable to Malevich's "When will we take off?" cited earlier.

This is the ultimate project of the avant-garde, and they flirt with it like the narrator in *Nadja,* but leave before they reach any "Atlantis," or mythical destination to be sought but never found. Thus the aim was not ultimately to go right out of this world. You cannot "lâcher tout" or you will end up with a language no one speaks. The first-person narrator (or, in the case of a Duchamp or a Schwitters, the "creator"/namer of a reified contingency) provided a travel diary of his journey. But most often the narrator journeyed as a *sputnik,* or co-traveler, of the putative visionary, returning "here" before his journey took him beyond the chartable.

The enigma of arrival is akin to the ambiguity of revolution, an event that is meant both to destroy and to create. Malevich had advocated destroying boundaries and then putting together the new out of the shards of the old. But unless you smash the new bounds, you merely get a new fixity, what Yevgeny Zamyatin in a famous essay of 1923 called "entropy."[51] Recall here that Hermes, a patron of hermeneutics, is also the saint of thieves and heralds. He is a go-between but also a trickster. The messages he carries with him have to be interpreted; hence allegory, enigma, pun, parable, and paradox are avant-garde favorites. It is often difficult—or inappropriate?—to decide whether, when a Malevich, for example, writes of his art journeying like planets through space, this is to be taken literally or as a trope.

Such vagueness, however, was scarcely appropriate in that other enterprise in which most Russian avant-gardists were also *sputniki,* the Revolution. Both the perceptual millenarians and the Bolsheviks sought revolution, but both claimed a special, elite function for themselves that was legitimated by alleged access to a "consciousness," whether that consciousness was political (Marxism-Leninism) or aesthetic (the "keen eye" [*zor'kiy glaz*]).

When D. Shterenberg, the first head of the Art Section (IZO) within the Commissariat of Enlightenment[52] (Narkompros) of the new government, wrote a major report on the "theoretical principles" for the new State Free Art Studios (SVOMAS), the institutional backbone of a reformed program of tertiary art education, he asserted that the aim of such places was to help the underprivileged, who would fill the studios and acquire a new vision. Consequently, he continued, "the organ of sight" would "play a decisive role" in their artistic training. "The cultivated and keen [*zor'kiy*] eye can open up a world of phenomena in nature that is still infinitely vast yet remains closed for the majority of people. Thanks to this organ and their capacities for invention, artists have given these phenomena concrete reflection in works of art. But even the works of art themselves can be understood completely only by a highly cultivated eye." It is unrealistic to expect that their worker and peasant students could immediately find the "true path," however, and hence for the present the SVOMAS can teach them only the "craft of art." Ultimately, they would be able to produce "creative people who follow the one and only effective [*tselesoobraznyy*] method."[53] Implicit in this somewhat self-serving proclamation of first principles, then, is a hierarchy in people based on the quality of the "eye," a hierarchy that has not been overcome by the Revolution and the setting up of the SVOMAS themselves. It is analogous to the hierarchy in "consciousness" of Marxism-Leninism, and, like it, implies training in, and gradual progress toward, such a consciousness.

After the Civil War the Suprematist movement UNOVIS petered out in most cities, but in Petrograd Malevich, along with other leading artists of a perceptual millenarian orientation such as Matyushin and Filonov, found a base for most of the rest of the 1920s in a Leningrad art institute (see Chapter 5), where they spread their ideals and conducted experimental work on color and perception together with their disciples.

Seen from this perspective, the Revolution of 1917 marks no border, no break in cultural trends. There was bound to be change as such a movement which, as Irving Howe has remarked, is always in danger of becoming solipsistic encounters the triumph of another that preaches the collective existence.[54] How could the kind of radical individuation and cult of contingency that so many perceptual millenarians espoused be reconciled with the aims of a mass revolution, their frequent, intense dedication to such a cause notwithstanding?

Initially, perceptual millenarianism was a dominant trend among Russian avant-gardists. But many of them had begun to rethink their position even before the Revolution. The shift is exemplified in Mayakovsky's declaration "A Drop of Tar" of 1915 in which he announces the death of Futurism as an "idea of the elect." Futurism, he claims, has now gone beyond its first, iconoclastic phase: "Don't be amazed if in our hands instead of rattles you will find the designs of an architect."[55] After Constructivism emerged around 1920, many who had previously taken a perceptual millenarianist position joined that movement, which was centered in Moscow. It came to dominate Soviet architecture, photography, avant-garde film, and set design, and was also a significant, if more minor, force in literature. A core of intellectuals based largely in Leningrad, however, were still guided by the ideals of perceptual millenarianism and effectively carried its flag through the late 1920s and even the 1930s, when such a position became much more difficult to espouse.[56] These included Malevich, Matyushin, Filonov, and their followers, the followers of Khlebnikov, and also some leading Formalists and a group of writers and students associated with them (such as Kaverin). Although they cannot be identified as a group, they shared certain fiercely held common values.

The Constructivists believed that a new man and a new consciousness could be created less by individual acts of perception than by establishing a totally new aesthetic-cum-material environment: buildings, clothing, utensils, and even the organization of one's basic day should be completely restructured, as should such obviously aesthetic objects as theater, film, and art. The new man would be formed, they believed, if one applied "scientific" laws to man's behavior patterns at home and in the workplace so that in his every movement he might live the maximally rationalized and simultaneously collectivized and aestheticized existence: key values for them were hygiene, regularity, efficiency, and utility.

In other words, while Shklovsky and the perceptual millenarians deplored routinized action and designed their entire aesthetic system with the aim of counteracting it, the Constructivists, on the contrary, sought to perfect just such routinized action.[57] This is one of the paradoxes of the avant-garde.

But there are other paradoxes to be found in the case of perceptual millenarianism. On the one hand, it stands for all that was to prove most threatening to Stalinist culture, yet, on the other, the myth of perceptual millenarianism itself can be seen as providing narrative norms used in much of the writing and ritual occasioned by the Stalinist cult of personality (see the Epilogue). One should not conclude, however, that the avant-gardist figures discussed here were the secret legislators of that cult. For a start, perceptual millenarianism was far from confined to the avant-garde; indeed, in the initial postrevolutionary years, a time of general millennial expectation, it is to be found in a wide range of cultural expressions.

A case in point would be the work of Boris Pilnyak, "the first celebrity of early Soviet literature."[58] His most famous novel, *The Naked Year* (Golyy god), was the main Russian literary hit of 1922, the year of Einstein, Spengler, and Benoit. *The Naked Year,* which is about 1919, a year of chaos, famine, and civil war in Russia, in some senses picks up where Bely's *Petersburg* left off; although its setting is provincial Russia, its framework is the myth of Petersburg and it chronicles the time after those turbulent forces gathering on the islands ("oo-oo-oo") have taken over the capital.[59] Pilnyak takes what might loosely be described as a Scythian position, that is, the position of a literary movement in which Bely was a leader—but to which Pilnyak had no formal connection—and which was active between 1916 and 1924 and centered in Tsarskoye selo, outside Petrograd. Most of its leaders were sons of professors, making this yet another case in which the scions of the intellectual elite become infatuated with the primitive. The Scythians were fierce nomadic tribes that left Central Asia in the 8–7th centuries B.C. and established an empire between the Don and Dnieper Rivers. The movement sought to revive what it took to be the spirit of these Scythians, which was characterized in the foreword to their first miscellany (published in the spring of 1917, between that year's two revolutions) as "eternal readiness to revolt" against—yet again—"petty philistinism [meshchanstvo]": "It is he, the world-wide philistine . . . who is now destroying . . . art in aestheticism, science in scholastics, life in stagnation, revolutions in petty reformism."[60]

Essentially, then, Scythianism involves marrying Romantic Anticapitalism to one of the myths of Russian particularity (its essentially Asian identity making it freer and more expansive than the dry and repressed "logical" Europeans). Pilnyak, in several lyrical passages in *The Naked Year,* identifies the possibility of being able to "see, really *see*" with liberating oneself from society, from its materialism and even its laws to gallop across the steppe, wild and free. Although this is the iconic image of the Scythian, here he identifies it with a pagan sect, a common variant. Thus Pilnyak provides another version of the "seer" who is an outsider or marginal in society, comparable with those in *Nadja* or *Artist Unknown,* but in this instance a primitive child of nature.[61]

Pilnyak's heroes declare the mandatory scorn for material possessions or comfort: to see is all. "[I long] to renounce possessions," one of his characters cries in inspired frenzy, "to renounce time, to possess nothing, to neither desire, nor to have regrets, just to live in order to see,"[62] while another goes further: "Let the trains stop running in Russia [a symbol for technological progress] . . . We must learn . . . just to look, to belong to no one and go on farther and farther, to get beyond both joy and suffering."[63]

Here we see the kind of zeal for a rigid purification of space already noted in the Introduction in the example of Masha Lipman's grandparents. The technological utopia of many Futurists is explicitly rejected, and the model for a purified space is sought in examples from the past. Yet in this novel Pilnyak uses many experimental techniques aimed at undermining linear narrative and even stable identity of character, time, and place. The opposition avant-gardist / Retrospectivist is, then, full of holes. Indeed, one half of the Union of Youth merger in 1913 came from Hylea, a group that in their very name identified themselves with a version of a Scythian identity.

In *The Naked Year* we see a common pattern whereby this zeal for purification is married to a scenario involving a journey at breakneck speed to radical otherness. The subject is to hurtle on ever faster. But once time has been overcome, space becomes the dominant dimension. Indeed, most artistic movements of this time tended to foreground one of two things: either accelerated speed and dramatic gestures of iconoclasm or an idealized space.

2

IMPERIAL PETERSBURG, 1913

Nineteen thirteen, the last year before the Great War, was an extraordinary time for the arts in Petersburg. Bely's novel *Petersburg* appeared. Mandelshtam published his first cycle of poems, *Stone*. And the Russian seasons in Paris, a Petersburg export organized by the enterprising Sergey Diaghilev since 1909, saw their apotheosis when the Ballets Russes presented Stravinsky's *The Rite of Spring* danced by the legendary Vaslav Nijinsky. *The Rite* provoked one of those *succès de scandale* that are *de rigueur* in Paris if a work is to be deemed avant-garde, and the music could not be heard above the din of an outraged audience.

In Petersburg itself, 1913 was also a year of high drama, manifestoes, and scandals, especially centered around the Futurists. In November a group of Futurists toured the country shocking the public with the ever more *outré*. They declared that all the world was becoming one huge city and nature would soon be obsolete, which would make the poetry of nature obsolete, too; hence the emergence of nonreferential (trans-sense) verse. The Futurist salvoes were met with impassioned denunciations and accusations, especially from self-appointed guardians of Russian culture; so charged was the atmosphere that when a crazed man named Balashov slashed Repin's painting of Ivan the Terrible, some of their opponents argued that the Futurists were responsible.

Nineteen thirteen was notable in Petersburg not just as an incredible year in the arts but also as the three-hundredth anniversary of the Romanov dynasty. The climactic moment of the anniversary celebration was the Jubilee day, February 21 (March 6 new style),[1] when a triumphal procession of the tsar and his family proceeded from the Winter Palace along Nevsky Prospect, the legendary main thoroughfare, to the Kazan Cathedral for a solemnizing mass.[2]

The entire processional route was lined with lavish decorations. The most monumental of these were placed on the Winter Palace and the Admiralty building opposite, which were adorned by huge double-headed eagles and portraits of famous tsars in the Romanov line. The side facade of the Admiralty was draped in imperial purple with a coat of arms covering its entire length, topped by a crown about fourteen feet in diameter. These decorations were all in place by nine o'clock the night before the procession. At ten, however, a fierce wind came up and destroyed all the decorations on the Admiralty. It blew down Nevsky all the next day as well, wreaking further havoc with the decorations.[3]

It does not take much imagination to see heavy symbolism in this destruction of the largest decorations for the Jubilee, emblems of imperial might placed by the very seat of power, the Winter Palace, where in 1917 the final storm would rage, tearing down the last vestiges of the old order. In literature, revolution was most often likened to some elemental force; in Bely's prophetic *Petersburg* (1913), as already noted, the sound of the wind, "oo-oo-oo," carried intimations of the gathering mass uprising, while in the most famous literary celebration of the October Revolution, Aleksandr Blok's poem "The Twelve" (Dvenadtsat', 1917–1918), it is represented as a raging snowstorm.

The winds of revolution were indeed blowing in 1913. Even as the Imperial family traveled around the country attending endless ceremonies reaffirming their enduring power, worker unrest was increasing and becoming more organized. By April 4, preparations in Petersburg for huge strikes and demonstrations to mark May Day were already so advanced that the police began mass arrests in anticipation and closed down several revolutionary presses, including the Bolshevik *Pravda* and *Zvezda*.[4]

A wind or some other natural catastrophe such as a flood is most often used as a metaphor for revolution because it suggests a force that is elemental and irresistible. Analogously, when Russian creative intellectuals wanted "to take Paris by storm" they often conceived their project in terms of the pagan (as with Stravinsky's *Rite of Spring*), or of that which is "Asian," that is, something that confounds European systems and aesthetic expectations, is wild, daring, and erotic. The latter was a common interpretation of another item from 1913's Russian season, Nijinsky's legendary performance of the virtuoso "Polovtsian Dances" from Borodin's opera *Prince Igor*; a proud Petersburger reported back to readers of the *Stock Exchange Gazette* (Birzhevye vedomosti) that "all of Paris . . . was captivated in the most elemental way [stikhiyno] by the primitive power of the frenzied dance of the steppe nomads who were dressed with an 'Asian-daring' gaudiness [aziatski-derzkoy pëstrotoy]."[5]

This claim, however accurate, encapsulates one popular version from that time of what Russian culture represents. It combines a Nietzschean predilection for Dionysian frenzy with the sense, common among Russians early in the twentieth century, of Russia's singularity and her essentially "Asiatic" identity, which made her a potentially healthy antidote to staid and effete Europe. Indeed, versions of this can be found even in statements by some Russian Futurists.[6]

Not all intellectuals sought an "Asian-daring" cultural identity. As the performers for the Russian season were leaving Petersburg that year, Fyodor Chaliapin told the excited throng that had come to see them off that he was leaving with great pleasure because "however much I might love my native land . . . there one can breathe true 'European' air."[7] Those who sought out Europe were looking not necessarily to its actuality or current vogues but rather to what they perceived as a greater commitment to culture and innovation and also a less oppressive state presence—hence the air there is "true" as contrasted with autocratic Russia, where it is "unbreathable."

Petersburg may have been the cultural capital of Russia in 1913 but it was also the center of its civil service. The Imperial Chamber controlled the main opera and ballet theaters, and would-be innovators were subject to not only political but also aesthetic censorship. This was particularly frustrating for the Mariinsky Theater (called the Kirov between 1934 and 1991), whose troupes provided the virtuosi Anna Pavlova and Nijinsky, the innovative choreographer Mikhail Fokine, and most of the others who dazzled Paris in 1913. Thus when Diaghilev took the "Polovtsian Dances" to Paris he was not really exporting Petersburg art in the sense that at that time the dances— first introduced in Paris in 1909—were banned in staid Petersburg and *Prince Igor* had to be performed there without them.

In Petersburg, 1913 was the high point of an age when large sections of the town's educated classes were obsessed by a desire to shine as Europeans. A variety of intellectuals found the air of the capital unbreathable and looked to Europe for its purification. Europe had for them become both a yardstick against which Russia should be measured and a panacea for her ills. For them, the antonym of "Europe" was "provincialism" or "ignorance." Many argued that it was time to "break down the ghetto of Russian culture" and finally enter "the family of European peoples."[8] But if Europe was an ideal, America was a sort of bogeyman, the land of pure commercialism, of arrivistes and of a degraded popular culture (frequently identified with the latest Petersburg craze for the roller-skating rink).[9] It is important to note here the Manichaean hierarchy of space, the concern with purification, and the phobia of the commercial—that common pattern among Russian intellectuals that was to play a decisive role in Soviet cultural history.

The apparent contradiction between the "Asian-daring" or pagan fare of the Russian season and the idealization of Europe among its star performers was not so fundamental as it might seem. Both orientations essentially identify a symbolic locus in space and time as a focus of aspirations to found a new, secular culture. The Futurists, for example, gave both Asian and European accounts of their iconoclastic stance: they were an Asian or pagan force assailing the stultifying conventions of European Christian civilization, which was, as Spengler was even at this time formulating, spent and in decline, or they were the voice of the new technological age more fully realized in Europe that would extirpate what Marx had called "the idiocy of village life" with its Christian "obscurantism" and fill the landscape in its stead with smokestacks and other cathedrals of the post-Christian city.

The two avant-garde trends that emerged in Petersburg circa 1913, transsense verbal art and Suprematism, also entail purification—in this instance of mundane referentiality. Yet neither was to play a significant role in the formation of Stalinist culture. Much more determining of the ultimate shape of that culture was another formula for aesthetic transformation proposed by many of the Futurists' antagonists in Petersburg. This formula, widely supported among the educated classes, sought the revival of a distinctly Petersburgian Neoclassical style in art and architecture that had seen its apogée under Alexander I in the early nineteenth century in an Empire style (so named for the Napoleonic original on which it was partly modeled) or Alexandrine style, or Empire Alexandrine style. The style had been in decline ever since Alexander's reign and recent vogues for Russian national revival, eclecticism, and *style moderne* (more or less art nouveau) threatened even further decline.

The revival of interest in Old Petersburg, a movement referred to here as Preservationism,[10] was not an innocent gesture that merely reflected a predilection for antiquarian styles. This was especially not so given that the current tsar, Nicholas II, like his father Alexander III, had shown active distaste for the Empire style and even for Petersburg itself, preferring Moscow and other provincial cities and the Russian architectural styles of the seventeenth century. Some have argued that Alexander and Nicholas's preferences for Moscow over Petersburg and for styles of the seventeenth century over those of the eighteenth and early nineteenth are also preferences for what they saw as an uncomplicatedly autocratic Russia in which the tsar enjoyed the enthusiastic loyalty of his subjects, allegedly the Russia of the seventeenth century before it was Europeanized by Petersburg's founder, Peter the Great.[11] Thus, for instance, Alexander III had insisted that the Cathedral of the Savior of the Blood in Petersburg, erected on the site where his father had been assassinated in 1881, be styled after the period of the seventeenth-century Muscovy tsars, resulting in a near copy of St. Basil's cathedral in Moscow. Most Petersburgers were appalled by its gaudiness and found its general style absolutely out of keeping with its surroundings.

The battle of the styles (Empire versus national revival), closely related as it was to the issue of which tsar or period should provide the national model, was at least in part a battle over issues of national identity and governance. Thus in Petersburg the Jubilee decorations were strictly in keeping with the Empire-style architecture while in the rest of the country they were mostly in Russian national style; analogously, in many instances the busts and bas reliefs placed along the Petersburg route started their series of great tsars with Peter, ignoring Mikhail Romanov, whose ascension in the seventeenth century was ostensibly being celebrated.

As has been recognized by numerous theoreticians, form is value and value is the stuff of politics.[12] In the movement for reviving the Empire style one finds a curious example of that aesthetic absolutization of space that was so characteristic of groups in this period who sought some radical transformation in the name of, or through, culture. The Preservationists believed that the authentic essence of beauty had been established in the classical era, and their panacea for lapse and decline was to fill space with its pure forms, a position in this respect not so remote from the aspirations of such avant-garde movements as Suprematism and Constructivism. A crucial difference, of course, was that the Preservationists valued historical precedents while the Futurists wanted such precedents "thrown off." In the case of Preservationism, the transformation entailed, paradoxical as it might seem, not iconoclasm but preservation. But the paradoxical formula "transformation as preservation" inescapably led to its equally paradoxical corollary "preservation as transformation," for the Preservationists sought to implement their aesthetic ideals on a monumental scale—that is, totally. (Analogously, the Futurists in 1913 had promised a new age when "the city" would fill the landscape completely.)

The Revival of Empire Style

The movement for a revival of Neoclassical Petersburg was part of a general trend early in the twentieth century for rethinking the meaning of Petersburg, and with it, national identity. The transcoding of the various clichés associated with the myth of Petersburg that occurred then should not be regarded exclusively within the hermetic series of art or literature, for it was in its own way a political gesture. The foundation of the city had in most of the literature of the nineteenth century been represented as Peter's great blunder. Now it received much more ambivalent treatment. On the one hand, a cult of Peter emerged qua founder of Petersburg, the nation's greatest achievement. On the other, one of the negative interpretations of the founding of Petersburg was preserved from the standard nineteenth-century version—the notion of Petersburg as wrought by an absolutist monarch and at the cost of the oppression and suffering of the people, now generally represented in terms of persecution of intellectuals.

An influential proponent of the new positive interpretation was Alexandr Benois, a leader of a group associated with the journal *World of Art*. His essay "Painterly Petersburg," published there in 1902, played an important role in the transvaluation of the meaning of the city. Benois's point of departure in this article is that Petersburg should no longer be scorned by artists as a subject for painting. He called for a renaissance of Petersburg art that would, he believed, lead to a renaissance of art in general. In establishing his point, Benois went over the clichéd criticisms of Petersburg to be found in nineteenth-century literature—that it was built on marshes, was unhealthy, "fantastic," and so on—and counterposed each with a positive interpretation. Responding to the usual charge that the city was alien to native Russian traditions, he asserted that it was high time for Russians to get out of their "Slavophile nappies" and stop being afraid of showing the European side of Russian life.[13] Although, he admitted, most of the major buildings and town planning of Petersburg had been done by architects from Europe, this did not mean that it was, as usually claimed, a derivative architecture. Rather, the country had left its mark on the work of these Europeans. Consequently, Petersburg architecture was unique within the Neoclassical tradition and as such was worthy of European admiration.[14]

The cult of "Old Petersburg" grew into a movement. A group of artists including K. Somov, M. Dobuzhinsky, and A. Benois's nephew E. E. Lanceray, together with a number of architects and specialists on architecture such as I. V. Zholtovsky, I. A. Fomin, V. A. Shchuko, V. Ya. Kurbatov, and Georgy Lukomsky, formed the core of the movement, which gathered strength over the next two decades. They became a dominant presence on the cultural horizon of Petersburg, organizing their own exhibitions and public lectures and enjoying de facto control of the line on culture in the liberal press, where articles on Old Petersburg appeared with predictable regularity. They also launched their own journals, in most of which Benois had editorial control. Besides the *World of Art*, Benois founded *Art Treasures of Russia* (Khudozhestvennye sokrovishcha Rossii) in 1901, which he edited until 1903, and between 1907 and 1916 he co-edited *Bygone Years* (Starye gody), a magazine specifically devoted to Old Petersburg.

The Preservationists also acquired ever greater power through their empire of institutions. They assumed leading roles in the Society of Architect-Artists, organizing under its auspices a Commission for the Study of Old Petersburg, and in 1909 they achieved their aim of establishing a Museum of Old Petersburg, which was opened to the public in 1912. In 1911, the Society sponsored an Exhibition of Architecture and the Applied Arts, which put on view extensive plans, models, documents, and historical paintings of Old Petersburg, many of them from private collections, giving the public a much fuller sense of the development of classical Petersburg than had been remotely possible before. Also in 1911, Benois became vice-president of the new St. Petersburg Society for the Protection and Preservation of Russian Monuments of Art and Antiquity, the most powerful focus of the lobby that continued its activities even in the initial years of Bolshevik rule, under the sponsorship of its Commissariat of Enlightenment.

By 1913, its apotheosis year, the revival movement had become so entrenched in mainstream Petersburg culture that scarcely a day passed without some item in the press devoted to it. The movement's mouthpiece, *Bygone Years*, was the most popular magazine of the time.[15]

The proselytizers for Old Petersburg were not so much concerned with the functionality of the buildings as with their external appearance. In the exhibition catalogues, books, articles, and artwork inspired by this movement, a body of characteristic vocabulary and attitudes emerged; the terms "ensemble," "facade," "panorama," "harmony," and "the integrated whole" keep recurring as self-evident values exemplified in Petersburg's Neoclassical buildings (these same epithets were used in the liberal press to describe the decorations on the procession route for the Romanov Jubilee[16]).

The Preservationists essentially wanted to create a static, monumental landscape.[17] In a move reminiscent of the paradigm of Christ's chasing the moneychangers out of the temple, Benois and others constantly stressed the need for spatial purification, to create great squares or other vast, uncluttered spaces around the major buildings; in 1913 the Society passed a resolution that the area around the Kazan Cathedral be cleared of street stalls (those accursed *lavochki* of the petty traders), which destroyed the "panorama" of the building.[18]

So wedded were the Preservationists to their aesthetic that a building's value consisted for them in its ability to lend itself to being painted in a certain style. Little wonder their Society was called "of Architect-Artists"; the order of the two professions in its title implies priority for art over architecture. Thus the leading article in the official book for the 1911 exhibition praises Thomas de Thomon, the architect who designed the Petersburg Stock Exchange, for his project for a mausoleum that was "more like a picture than a design."[19] In the Preservationists' conception, however, the two purposes were essentially combined. While architecture was to look like art, conversely, much of the art inspired by this movement and created principally by members of the Society or of the World of Art group makes Petersburg's buildings and urban scapes look more like architectural models than lived-in spaces (some called them "architectural landscape artists"[20]). In A. P. Ostroumova-Lebedeva's painting *Kryukov Canal* (1910), for instance, there are no humans and the canal is unruffled by the wind.

The obverse of static, harmonious, and an integrated whole would be what happens when the peaceful "ensemble" *is* ruffled by the wind (as were the decorations for the 1913 Jubilee). Disorder, as Benois made clear in "Painterly Petersburg," was anathema to his ideals. He contrasted the "elemental force of the old lady [Moscow]" with Petersburg's "Roman severe [zhestkiy] spirit" of "order" (a strange attitude in a modernist, to be discussed later).[21] The epithets he and his fellow Preservationists most often used to describe the buildings they praised were "simple," "severe" (strogiy), "austere" (surovyy), "restrained" (vyderzhannyy), and "lucid" (svetlyy).

The writings of the Preservationists idealize not only the classical landmarks of Petersburg, such as the Admiralty and the Stock Exchange, but also their architects. There is a marked tendency to represent them as having sacrificed themselves in the supreme effort of designing and overseeing construction of their genial buildings so that they are totally spent thereafter.[22] Even more striking is the tendency to isomorphy in the depiction of the architects and their buildings; the architects are "stern," "restrained," "strict," and "simple," as are their buildings.[23]

Such epithets are fairly standard in writing about Neoclassicism and are implied in its classic formulation from Johann Joachim Winckelmann: "noble simplicity and calm grandeur" ("eine edle Einfalt und eine stille Grösse"). Other standard characterizations of Neoclassical architecture include: "sober clarity and archaic purity"; "firm, unequivocal contours"; a simplified color scheme or none at all (a marker of their absolute opposition to the nexus of values encapsulated in "an Asiatic-daring gaudiness"); "calm"; and "noble."[24] These iconic qualities have specific significance in the Russian context, where the small details of language are even more likely than is generally the case to indicate large-scale cultural prejudices.[25] Their being cited as values in Preservationist literature signified in itself a revalorization of those associated with the myth of Petersburg; in nineteenth-century versions "order," "strictness," and so on were indicators of soullessness, emptiness, constraint, and the alien.

What began around 1902 as a movement for the revival of classical Petersburg developed over time into a much more ambitious and comprehensive cultural movement. A landmark in this progression was the formation in 1909 of a new journal, *Apollo (Apollon)*. The *World of Art* had ceased publication in 1904, but many of its core contributors and editors, including Benois, worked on *Apollo,* which became a mouthpiece for the Preservationist position in art, the theater, and literature.[26] The continuity of personnel is deceptive, however. *Apollo*'s "world of art" was more inclusive than that of its predecessor, for it espoused a new conception of "classical" form. The models chosen expanded its canon beyond familiar Greek or Neoclassical sources to include examples from a variety of times and places in European history. The journal also shifted its account of the "classical" from styles to values.

By 1913 the kind of Neoclassicism most often espoused did not just entail going back to a certain point in time, or even, as Benois and others preferred to put it, reviving the informing aesthetic principles of an earlier movement while developing them further in the modern age. Georgy Lukomsky, one of Preservationism's most ardent proselytizers, described the movement's aims in an article of 1913 in terms of leading to a "clearly formulated new world view [mirosozertsaniye]."[27]

The lead article in the book published by the Society of Architect-Artists on the occasion of their exhibition of 1911 includes an illustration depicting visionary architecture of eclectic Egyptian and classical origin, below which is printed an inscription from Gogol: "Can it be that the age of architecture is gone forever? Can it be that we will no longer be graced by greatness or genius?"[28]

The Preservationists longed to usher in an age of architecture. By this they meant not just a time when great buildings would be erected, but a utopian aestheticism when people's entire visual environment would be controlled and there would be, as Lukomsky defined the essence of Petersburg architecture in an article of 1913, an "overall harmonious interconnectedness of all its component parts."[29]

This aspiration was a version of the post-Enlightenment quest for a form of the sacred vested in some aesthetic. The sought-after "age" would see the flowering not just of architecture but of a whole complex of arts and other fields that organize the spatial environment and the objects within it. Architecture would be the queen, and the other fields would be subordinated to it. Preservationists liked to draw analogies with the time of Palladio (whose buildings inspired much of Neoclassical Petersburg), when all the arts were subordinated to the will of the architect.[30]

Not all factions in Petersburg cultural life subscribed to this idea that the architect should be hegemon, but architecture, or more particularly architectonics, the way a work of art is put together, became for many groups the central metaphor for creativity. For example, the poetry and theoretical work of Acmeism, a movement that emerged around 1912, was informed by the ideal of an art that was static, eternal, and crafted the way the artisan constructs a building. By 1913 *Apollo* had become the de facto organ of the Acmeist movement and printed several manifesto-like works by its leaders.[31] Among these were poems by Mandelshtam that focus on famous architectural monuments, singling out in each that quality of "overall harmonious interconnectedness of all the component parts." But even the ostensible opponents of any kind of Retrospectivism such as the Futurists (the principal bugbears of Benois) had begun to proclaim that what is important in a work of art is not the "what" (the subject depicted) but the "how" (the way it is put together).[32]

Preservationists spoke wistfully of "the good fortune that any architect dreams of having—to be able to create huge architectural complexes."[33] As early as 1908 Alexandr Benois's older brother Leontiy, an architect from the family dynasty, unsuccessfully urged the Petersburg city council to develop a comprehensive plan for the city to restore its unity; in 1916 he renewed the campaign against "lack of system" in the city. But slightly earlier, in 1911 and 1912, his fellow Preservationists Fomin and Lukomsky had become agitators for a "new Petersburg" in which giant Neoclassical complexes would mark the city; only two were attempted, the most ambitious being a new suburb in Neoclassical style that Fomin planned for Golodai Island. At its center was to be a vast square from which radiated streets. Fomin's conception is reminiscent of Bath, but even more than that the square replicates on a grander scale the Palace Square itself.[34]

Thus the Preservationists had a distinctly utopian streak, but the underside of utopianism is dictatorship by an elite. Preservationism, its purist aesthetic stance notwithstanding, was also about power and control. In order for "the architects" to realize an aesthetic utopianism, they needed not just "empty spaces" but also the means for actualizing their grand schemes, usually by finding some powerful patron or client. It was frequently said that only the control of a great man can realize such aims. Lukomsky in a 1913 article pointed out that in order to create the great "ensembles" of the "new Petersburg" what was needed was a "single will" and a "center."[35]

In actuality, the movement for the preservation of Old Petersburg depended to a large extent on the patronage of the Imperial family and the upper nobility.[36] Several of the names that regularly published in *Apollo* were prefixed by baron or *knyaz'* (prince or duke). The 1911 exhibition of historical material related to old Petersburg would have been impoverished had members of the Imperial family and the upper nobility not generously lent material from their private collections. In the catalogue for the exhibition the enabling role of each successive tsar is described with great enthusiasm while the buildings are often described in terms of their regal bearing (*tsarstvenno-velichavyy*).[37]

The question arises, is this homage a result of the Preservationists' dependence on Imperial patronage, or does it reflect a natural alliance, as is suggested in the fact that Fomin seems to have drawn his inspiration for town planning from the focal point of Russian monarchical power? It would be difficult to provide an unequivocal answer to this question. It should not be assumed that the Preservationists were all monarchists. Around the time of the 1905 revolution, several of them, including M. Dobuzhinsky and Benois's nephew Lanceray (but not Benois himself), contributed antitsarist lampoons to the satirical magazines *Adskaya pochta, Zritel'*, and *Zhupel*. Preservationists also found advantage for architecture in autocracy. For instance, L. Rudnitsky in the lead article of the exhibition's catalogue talks of how the court's control in architectural matters under Alexander I made it possible to achieve a "unity of impressions," and he lamented the decline since then into a more "individualistic" situation in architecture. He also contrasted unfavorably the chaotic development of the traditional Russian town with the situation in Petersburg, where everything was subjected to the control of a Buildings Commission (Komissiya stroyeniy).[38]

Rather than being either for or against the monarchy itself, the Preservationists favored the powerful autocrat because they recognized that such a concentration of temporal power was essential to realizing their own aims. Although their monarch, Nicholas II, was far from obliging in his architectural policies, other members of the Imperial family supported them.

The movement to revive Empire style in Petersburg can be read as an instructive chapter in the story of the intellectuals' "reach for power" at about this time. The Preservationists sought greater control over the way the arts were administered in the state. During the 1910s, they began to find common cause with a number of other groups within Petersburg with whom they seized the moment after the February Revolution and formed a lobby for a ministry of the arts. The composition of the leadership that presided over their successive meetings varied a little, but the hard core generally included representatives of Acmeism, *Apollo*, the World of Art (an association of artists that took its name from the journal and included many Preservationists), the Society of Architect-Artists, and leading names in music and the performing arts such as Chaliapin and Vs. Meyerhold, and Maksim Gorky. The group also elected a body to press for safeguarding the nation's cultural treasures (sometimes referred to as the Gorky Commission).[39] The aims of the ministry were to release the arts from subordination to the Imperial Chamber and to give them an enhanced position within society with more funding, freeing them from overdependence on market forces. The issue of the ministry divided the intelligentsia because some factions, such as the avant-garde, were for greater autonomy for art, but most favored more control and paternalism, hoping that the administration of the arts would be run by authority figures from within their own ranks.

Most Russian mandarin intellectuals of this time sought to justify the huge and privileged role in society that they wanted to arrogate to themselves in terms of cultural myths. The majority of these myths involved points of reference in the past. The Neoclassical revival and the cult of Petersburg, though undoubtedly reflecting widespread tastes and prejudices, must also be analyzed in this broader context.

Neoclassicism and the Lobby for a Secular, Post-Autocratic Culture

Neoclassicism is far from a watertight concept and covers a range of trends to be found in different countries at different times. Some sort of a classical revival has been a perennial of European cultural history since at least the Renaissance, and more recently in America and other countries of the colonial diaspora as well. But Neoclassicism has, in its many expressions, been larger than a movement for a classical revival in the arts, which it also incorporated. An obvious reason for the popularity of classical revivals has been the need, whether consciously felt or not, to legitimize a given political or aesthetic movement. The more a regime has been in need of legitimization and aggrandizement, the more likely it has been to appropriate Neoclassical architecture and symbols, as has been seen in the well-known examples of the French Revolution, the Napoleonic regime, Stalinist Russia, and fascist Europe.

The Neoclassical revival in Petersburg early in the twentieth century can be associated with one of the dominant strains in the movement that found its canonical expression in late-eighteenth-century France, that Neoclassicism which in art is most associated with Jacques-Louis David. His painting *The Oath of the Horatii* (1784–1785) is generally taken as the beginning of a Neoclassicism that came to dominate during the French Revolution and continued, if in somewhat distorted form, in the Empire style of the Napoleonic years, progenitor of Russia's Empire style that flourished under Alexander I.

Thus this strain is associated with a revolution—the French Revolution. Indeed, David played a considerable role in the revolutionary government, serving not only as de facto official artist and organizer of the mass festivals, but also as an active political leader. But there is no necessary connection. The French Neoclassical artists reacted variously to the Revolution itself; while some, such as David, were attracted passionately to it and even to its terror, others, such as the architect Thomon, joined the monarchist diaspora (he ended up in Petersburg).[40]

These French artists regarded their work as "revolutionary," but in a different sense from that of most political revolutionaries. They were offended by the tastes of the aristocratic and monied classes. However, the logic of their position entailed not the overthrow of the privileged classes but their moral / aesthetic reformation. They rejected previously regnant styles such as rococo as frivolous and self-indulgent, as mere ornament or entertainment to gratify the whims of an idle aristocracy of sybarites; their own art was by implication the more authentic.

The Neoclassical revival of early-twentieth-century Russia was informed by a similar rejection of the tastes of the monied classes, characterized by Benois in "Painterly Petersburg" as that "infectious . . . illness that has befallen modern society: the spirit of easy money and the glitter of the *café chantant [kafeshantannogo bleska]*."[41]

At a general level, then, this movement can be seen as a variety of Romantic Anticapitalism. Its purist avatars did not share the antirationalist proclivities that so often characterized Anticapitalism, however. Indeed, some have characterized the French Neoclassicists as a sort of artistic arm of their Enlightenment; they had strong links with the *philosophes,* particularly with such figures as Diderot and Rousseau. The Russian Preservationists, like the French and several other Neoclassical movements, had a commitment to order, the mind, and "science"—and most of them to secularism as well. Like the French, they sought to unify the arts and sciences as a classical ideal[42] and to collect and systematize knowledge (one of the *philosophes'* greatest causes was the Encyclopedia).

In this respect, the Preservationists can be seen as a particular expression of a marked trend among Russian intellectuals at this time—one not exclusively associated with Petersburg—toward looking at systematization, rationalization, and a greater role for culture and science as key items in an agenda of social transformation. These figures and groups were to be found primarily among liberal intellectuals, the mainstream (many of the leaders of the liberal parties were professors or former professors[43]), but also among Bolsheviks and other leftists. Comparable attitudes were also to be found in Germany at this time. For example, Weber's introduction to *The Protestant Ethic* of 1920 is informed by a similar nexus of values, including the notion that a proclivity for systematization is a "European" trait.

Many Russian intellectuals in the liberal movement shared a faith that science and culture could potentially transform society. Here one might cite the geochemist Vladimir I. Vernadsky and his circle whose members contributed considerably to the leadership ranks of the Kadet Party. They believed that the "antediluvian" state with its "anarchic" organization and arbitrary exercise of power was holding the country back and should be progressively phased out in favor of a constitutional democracy. To this end, they proposed a package of reforms that were designed to rationalize government and the legal system, and to reform educational and cultural life, giving intellectuals more autonomy, expanding the tertiary system, and raising educational standards.[44] Their drive to rationalize society has to be seen in the context of the fledgling emergence around 1913 of Russian sociology—the science of society— featuring figures such as the Petersburger Pitirim Sorokin, whose first book appeared that year.[45]

Vernadsky was also involved in a venture that essentially attempted to arrogate some of the state's administrative functions to intellectuals. Under his initiative, in 1915 the Academy of Sciences founded KEPS, The Commission for the Study of the National Productive Forces. This title was a little disingenuous in that the intention of KEPS was not merely to "study" the productive forces, but also to plan for a more effective mobilization of them than the tsarist government had as yet achieved (initially, KEPS was intended to find ways of averting the disaster caused when Russia found herself at war with Germany, the chief supplier of her technology).

The liberal intelligentsia wanted to curb or obviate the arbitrary exercise of power on the part of the monarch and, generally, of the Orthodox Church as well. To that end, many intellectuals lobbied for the adoption of the Julian calendar, which would synchronize Russia with the West, a move of symbolic as well as practical value, but their efforts were frustrated by the Holy Synod, who branded the Western calendar "papist."[46]

Faith in science and culture was by no means confined to liberals. Petersburg cultural journals from around 1913 are full of articles about how science and reason married to culture might provide the magic formula for political reform and democratization in Russia.[47] One of the most active advocates of this marriage was the Bolshevik fellow-traveler Maksim Gorky. After he returned to Petersburg from exile in 1913, Gorky delivered public lectures on this topic and organized a society of scholars and intellectuals, the Free Association for the Advancement and Development of the Positive Sciences (SARRPN, its leaders included Vernadsky), which was aimed at fostering scientific research and utilizing its findings in the hope of spurring Russia's growth and propelling her into something closer to European norms. In 1915, he founded the journal The *Chronicle* (Letopis'), which attempted to bring together leading scientists (such as K. A. Timiryazev and Ivan Pavlov) and other intellectuals (Vladimir Mayakovsky, Sergei Esenin, and others) in the cause of raising the scientific and cultural consciousness of Russia.

The mandarins of prerevolutionary Russia dreamed of founding some version of the academy or of a "city of science" that would function as a cauldron of the new order (frequently somewhat on the order of Bacon's *The New Atlantis*). The Academy of Sciences had already been in existence for almost two hundred years, but it was generally rejected as a model because it was seen as too academic and did not embrace a sufficiently broad spectrum of intellectual activity. They wanted something closer to an elite forum that would debate—and very possibly legislate on—the key issues of the nation. Vernadsky and Gorky toyed with different versions of the city of science. Benois, for his part, like David before him in revolutionary France, sought to revamp the Academy of the Arts (another of those institutions laboring under the yoke of the Imperial administration) as a headquarters for the "architect-artist" from which he could lead the nation by designing huge ensembles that would bring the environment "into [an aesthetic] order, into a system."[48]

A great deal of the activity of Russian intellectuals in these years can be subsumed under the headings "encyclopedism" or "a cult of systematization and classification." The programs of Alexander Bogdanov, a Bolshevik and chief theoretician of the Proletcult (an organization founded in 1917 and dedicated to fostering proletarian culture), come to mind particularly. Between 1913 and 1929 he worked to adduce a system of systems, or "tektology." He also advocated producing an encyclopedia for the proletariat and used the metaphor of the "engineer-architect" for the intellectual leading society, anticipating a key metaphor of the Constructivist movement. As Bogdanov's career demonstrates, these ideals and efforts did not disappear after the Revolution; indeed, the years 1918–1921 saw rampant encyclopedism, with Gorky one of its principal promoters (see Chapter 4).

Thus the movement for a Neoclassical revival in Russia was not just a matter of aesthetic taste, but more a particular expression of a recognizable nexus of values that informs many Neoclassical movements but was also more broadly found in Russia at this time. The movement assumed a rational human nature and sought an ordered, regulated society whose art and architecture represented aesthetic counterparts of the architectonically integrated whole that is society. In order to streamline and regulate human activity, and in order to abstract the beautiful from other possible aesthetic expressions, one must pare away all that seems incidental, contingent, merely whimsical, or ornamental, leaving only the essential essences.[49] It is in establishing such criteria that the classical model plays its crucial role: antiquity was deemed to have established most perfectly the dividing line between essential and inessential.

Neoclassicism is at base a historicism oriented toward the establishment of norms that enact certain values. As such, it does not have any necessary connection with either ancient Greece or Rome, though there is a certain inevitability about the selection of the two as points of reference, given their unchallenged status in the Europeans' account of themselves. Some other contemporary movements imputed entirely different meanings to "Greece," while others found Neoclassical values in different aesthetic traditions. Thus, for instance, Mandelshtam in his architectural poems of 1913 celebrates similar values in homages to three buildings, each of which represents a separate tradition: Hagia Sophia for the Byzantine, Notre Dame for the Gothic, and the Petersburg Admiralty for the (Neo)classical.

Those who sought a Neoclassical revival might, then, seem to be resisting change. But the movement can also be seen in a broader context that essentially has to do with modernization and increasing state, as distinct from autocratic, control and regulation. In this context, one is struck by the applicability of Ernst Gellner's recent theoretical writings on the rise of nationalism to the Russian historical moment. Gellner has argued that nationalism does not "arise" to impose on the populace a standard account of themselves (of the nation) but that the sequence goes in reverse: with modernization, the uneducated and largely rural masses begin to acquire a standard "high culture" (that of the educated) as a necessary condition for their becoming actors in the new society. They then change from a situation in which they define themselves by local identities and speak local dialects to attaining a trans-local identity and language that come from high culture though they are frequently attributed to the low. This includes a constructed or abstracted identity for the nation and its citizens.[50] What Gellner is really talking about is modernization as standardization. He has largely established that there is a coincidence between the two events (modernization and the rise of nationalism), but not that the connection is always a necessary one.

During the 1910s, the modernization of Russia was the cause that attracted the greatest consensus among the educated populace of the capital. But many of those who sought a more rationalized society articulated their goals in terms of reviving the spirit of Peter's-burg. In their redaction of the Petersburg myth, Peter and his city became twin symbolic heroes. They functioned as emblems rather than necessarily representing historical realities. In the liberal press of 1913 the time of Peter in Petersburg was a positive obsession and journalists contrived to provide historical precedents from it for a host of contemporary events, extending to such unlikely subjects as Easter and May Day.[51] The prominence of such articles reflects not only the antiquarian interests of their readership but also a shared ideological program. A highly selective account of Peter is advanced; he is remembered as the Europeanizer who founded the first secular intellectual institutions in Russia.[52]

Modernization was no less central in the Bolsheviks' agenda of proletarian revolution. This became clear when, soon after gaining power, Lenin revamped his account of Marxism to fit an agenda of modernization. In 1920 he announced the slogan "Communism Equals Socialism Plus the Electrification of the Entire Countryside," which essentially means "Communism Equals Standardizing Cultural and Social Identity" plus "Modernization as Industrialization" as two oxen hitched to the same yoke. Unlike Gellner, however, Lenin was not observing or predicting a process; he wanted to press the pace of change. When Stalin came to power he tried to modernize by fiat. What might otherwise have been a result of this process of modernization—cultural and linguistic standardization—his ideologues saw, as we shall see, not as an effect but as an instrument of modernization. There is even the potential to see some of Lenin's agendas as expressions of a belated *Aufklärung*. For example, in his account in *State and Revolution* of the way the state will "wither away," he foresees that oppressive state organs will be replaced by bodies and individuals whose function is to rationalize and systematize the business of production and distribution within society.[53]

This is not intended to imply an equation between Lenin—or even those who held a touching faith in the transformative potential of "science," such as Vernadsky or Gorky—and those who lobbied for a Neoclassical revival.

Although Lenin's aesthetic tastes were conservative (as were, for the most part, those of Vernadsky and Gorky), his position is radically different from that of the Neoclassicists in that he gave absolute priority to *practice,* to politics and affairs, whereas for the Petersburg Neoclassicists of the 1910s aesthetic values had absolute precedence even over considerations of utility. This trend reached an extreme in articles published in the journal *Apollo,* especially as Russia went through the two revolutions of 1917 and the Preservationists set themselves up as watchdogs to guard cultural treasures against the forces of revolution (Benois took an extreme position, maintaining that the Revolution should exclude all artistically valuable sites from its sphere of operations).[54]

The Preservationists, like so many in that broad category Romantic Anticapitalists, were effectively looking to some prebourgeois model for the role of the artist in society. Many were attracted to ancient Rome or Greece, which fit the centralizing ideals of the movement. But a more frequently invoked precedent was the time of Louis XIV, whose court was held by many to be an emblem of good taste. One of the many associations sought in the title Apollo was that the motif dominated the decor of Louis's Versailles (many of the classical Russian ballets from the turn of the century also paid homage to Versailles).[55] It should be noted, however, that Louis's court also represented the centralized, absolutist state that was combatting local feudal loyalties and a different style of politics;[56] Preservationism was not just about taste but also about national aggrandizement and centralization, values no less important in Stalinism.

Any monarchist leanings among the Preservationists declined after the February Revolution in 1917. They welcomed the overthrow of the old order in which many of them had in some senses been implicated, but did so in terms of its having failed its mandate to provide an aesthetic aristocracy. It was said that Nicholas II, the deposed tsar, had truly reprehensible, "petty bourgeois taste."[57] Thus he was, by implication, a sort of usurper to the title tsar in that his taste befitted a lower social station; in this respect, he was sometimes contrasted with the positive example of Louis XIV.[58]

The February Revolution, imperfect as it was, seemed to promise the triumph of "Petersburg," that is, the triumph of the ideal of a more European and secular society that would seek to regulate everything rationally and to observe due process, a society in which the arts would play a central role, civic virtue would be extolled, and science would flourish. But the new government continued the unpopular war and failed to redress glaring inequalities. This led some intellectuals to part company with the liberals who gained power. Even Benois was alienated and left the liberal journal *Sp*

(Rech'), to which he had contributed a weekly column since 1908; for a time he joined Gorky's *New Life* (Novaya zhizn'), a socialist outlet.[59] Nevertheless, the ideals of the February Revolution appealed to most intellectuals and they were reluctant to accept October. Yet, as we shall see, in the initial years of Bolshevik power many of the same figures who led the lobby for a ministry of the arts also played a prominent role in bodies set up in Petrograd by Narkompros.

Intellectual aristocrats as agents of Bolshevik cultural policy? How could those who yearned for an aesthetic aristocracy serve the cause of mass culture for the Great Unwashed? Actually, in the countdown to 1917 many in the *Apollo* set shifted their position and began to talk with increasing frequency of their mission to bring culture to the masses; to this end, they attempted to set up a "palace of culture" in Petrograd.[60] At some gatherings organized for the masses Preservationists clashed with Futurists, with both sides claiming the right to save the workers' souls with their cultural offerings.[61]

It should be pointed out that canonical Neoclassicism is associated with the move to spread enlightenment to the masses. It ushered in an age when great public libraries, art galleries, and museums were founded; in many instances the projects were even initiated by Neoclassical artists. Thus the movement presided over a period when culture was passing from the preserve of the aristocracy to the public domain.

One should not, then, conclude that the movement for a Neoclassical revival represents only a lobby for turning back the clock and resurrecting a dated architectural or aesthetic style. It is not even true that Benois and his fellow Preservationists were monomaniacally pursuing this retrograde aim. With such strong links to the World of Art, the group responsible for introducing Aubrey Beardsley, Gauguin, and Cézanne to the Russian public at the turn of the century, the Preservationists themselves were not rigidly committed to allowing only an art that represented a revival of old forms. Indeed, some members of their set (for example, M. Dobuzhinsky) represented Petersburg in their art more in terms of the opposite interpretation— as the site of phantasmagoria and repression.

This ambivalence is characteristic of Neoclassicist movements. For all the insistence on purity of line (or perhaps precisely because of the utopian rigidity), Neoclassicism rarely appeared in pure, unalloyed form. It is, for instance, difficult to disentangle the Neoclassicism of late-eighteenth and early-nineteenth-century Europe from Romanticism, a movement to which it might seem fundamentally opposed. And in the late nineteenth and early twentieth centuries it is equally difficult to extricate the Hellenic revival—as an example of Neoclassicism—from Nietzscheanism and other such movements that reveled in excess. The stance of some of those who lobbied for a Neoclassical revival, such as Benois, shaded in practice into Modernism. Others, like Gorky, who can be associated with its ideals (indeed Gorky's later account of socialist realism is often called classical) were professed "realists." Still others, arguably, practiced the ultimate of Neoclassicisms, a Neoclassicism of pure forms known as Suprematism or "nonobjective art," thus in a sense continuing the line from the utopian architecture of Etienne Louis Boullée and Claude Nicholas Ledoux (the latter, incidentally, was Thomon's mentor).

The example of the Preservationists has been adduced here because it raises questions about the provenance of the somewhat singular variety of culture that emerged in the 1930s as "Stalinist." In many respects, this was a bowdlerized version of what the Preservationists sought. Yet, as was also true in the case of the Preservationist movement, its aims of achieving a standardized, "high" culture eluded realization. But even before the Bolsheviks came to power other intellectuals whose prerevolutionary stance can be linked with Retrospectivism and the lobby for a ministry of the arts saw radical rather than conservative potential in such a movement. A prime example would be the theater director Vsevolod Meyerhold.

3

MASQUERADE

On Saturday, February 25, 1917, a new production of M. Lermontov's play *Masquerade* (Maskarad, 1835) opened at the Imperial Alexandrinsky Theater. The play—very approximately a Russian *Othello* in that it is a tragedy in which the hero is tricked into believing his wife is unfaithful to him and learns his mistake only after he has killed her—was originally meant to be staged for the one-hundredth anniversary of Lermontov's birth, in October 1914, but bureaucratic problems and the outbreak of World War I in August of that year led to a series of postponements. The premiere's ultimate timing in February 1917 enabled it to coincide with another anniversary: the occasion was used to mark the twenty-fifth jubilee in the Alexandrinsky of Yury Yuriev, a famous classic actor who played the leading role in the production. By the time the audience poured out of the theater at 2 A.M., shots could already be heard on Nevsky Prospect. The February Revolution had begun.[1]

Obviously, this coincidence of events invites dramatic interpretations, but the production of *Masquerade* was also seen as a historic landmark for reasons not connected with the February Revolution. It is recognized as a milestone in the career of its director, Vsevolod Meyerhold (1874–1940). Thus the fact that Sergei Eisenstein attended this premiere (while still an engineering student in Petrograd) has the status of an iconic moment in his biographies. [2] The production is also famous for Meyerhold's collaboration on its opulent sets with an artist from the World of Art, Aleksander Golovin. Together they stylized Imperial Petersburg of the 1830s after one of the principal metaphors for the city—the "Northern Venice." In a time of disastrous war and concomitant misery, when the "bankruptcy" of Imperial Russia was all too evident, the theater had spent thirty thousand gold rubles on the staging. The empire was going out in grand style—Empire style, to be exact.

The extravagance of these sets and the perception that they celebrated an odious Imperial Russia made the production one of the many highly controversial acts of Meyerhold's career. During the course of the year he drew away from such lavish sets to use ever sparer stage settings and ever more grotesque representations of Imperial Russia. As memoirists are fond of noting, a prime example of this new trend, his production of *The Death of Tarelkin* from the Sukhovo-Kobylin trilogy, premiered "on the eve of [the] October [Revolution]."[3]

In actuality, these two coincidences did not occur quite as neatly as commentators would have it. The February Revolution grew out of disturbances in the capital city that had been gathering momentum before February 25. Thus "February" did not have a precise originary moment, the equivalent of the salvo from the battleship *Aurora* that was the signal to start "October." Moreover, the premiere of *The Death of Tarelkin* occurred not "on the eve of October," but a day earlier (on October 23). The need to identify these two productions with the Russian landmarks of political revolution—indeed, to see them as having occurred, in Ivan Turgenev's resonant phrase, "on the eve"—is symptomatic of the extent to which intellectuals saw theatrical revolution as the midwife of the political. It also shows the leading role that the movement for theatrical reform played in contemporary conceptions of cultural revolution, and Meyerhold's special status as a leader in that movement.

Thus the production of *Masquerade* was both exultantly *retrospectivist* and insistently *prospectivist*. Begun in 1912,[4] it represents a belated flowering of prewar (Imperial) culture swept along by contingent forces into a different historical moment, as well as a salvo at the "Winter Palace" of the old cultural order. As such, it illustrates the point that 1917 represents no mystical dividing line between tsarist and revolutionary culture. But it also provides a paradigm for identifying the dominant thrust of all cultural trends of the years just before and after the Revolution.

For many intellectuals, theater provided the charter myth of revolution, not theater up on a stage that an audience watched passively, but theater as a construct for a totalizing experience. Throughout Europe, theater was queen of the arts, but that was not coincidental. Interest in the theater was not merely voguish, but tied to a larger view of the world as a theatrical possibility. In the Russia of the 1920s, the work of leading theoreticians and directors of the theater continued to function, as it had for the past decade, as a major frame of reference for conceiving revolutionary culture.

In the years leading up to the Revolution, Russia was a principal player in a pan-European movement for the reformation of the theater and the performing arts. This movement had become a focus of avant-garde activity and of would-be social reformers as well. Its major theoreticians—such as Gordon Craig, Georg Fuchs, Adolphe Appia, Romain Rolland, Max Reinhardt, Tommaso Marinetti, Isadora Duncan, and Emile Jaques-Dalcroze, not to mention Rousseau, Wagner, and Nietzsche, on whose shoulders many of these figures stood—represent a variety of positions. There was sufficient common ground between them, however, that, for the purposes of this book, one may refer to the various supporters of this new wave in the theater, Russian and non-Russian, as the "theater activists," a term that suggests the way the political and the aesthetic were conflated in their mission.

Petersburg was a center of this movement. Almost all the major figures in it visited the city at least once over the first two decades of the twentieth century, often staging model productions there, while their writings were published in Russian translation. By 1913 it was Max Reinhardt who had become the most modish of them. Fashionable theaters in Petersburg vied with one another to entice Reinhardt himself, or failing that one of his assistants, to come and direct a production in their theater.[5] New-wave Russian theater had become very fashionable in Europe, too, with "Russian weeks" in Berlin, Vienna, and Munich;[6] Petersburg was exporting to Paris not only Diaghilev's Russian seasons but her directorial expertise as well.[7] Even Stanislavsky's troupe was in demand.

In Russia, however, theater activists were by then contending that Stanislavsky represented not the new and innovative but the stale and old. The years since 1907 had seen a shift in thinking about the theater and the way plays should be staged. As elsewhere, this shift was felt in a reaction against the prevailing "realist" approach, which the theater activists associated with the nineteenth century and saw as reaching its apotheosis in Stanislavsky's productions.[8]

The theater activists contended that an important factor in the decline of their art into dull respectability was that the modern stage rode roughshod over the traditional organization of theatrical space. They bemoaned the fact that the theater of the day was a box in which the privileged classes were cooped up, backs straight, away from the masses and the hurly-burly of life itself. They also decried the way certain features of the internal organization of the theater, such as the footlights and the proscenium, created a gulf between the actors on the stage and the audience; many urged that the theater be taken out into the streets and squares, where it could regain its role in the life of the city—or that at the very least the architecture of the theater be reorganized so that actors and audience might be closer to each other and even intermingle.[9] Reinhardt's formula—one that was to be very influential in the initial postrevolutionary years—was to stage Shakespeare and *Oedipus* in a circus. Meyerhold, however, contented himself for the time being with reorganizing the interior of the Alexandrinsky by getting rid of the curtain, footlights, and prompting booth and having the actors act on a proscenium jutting out into the auditorium, leaving the rear stage largely the realm of the sets.

Stanislavsky had wanted to institute a fictive "fourth wall" in the theater so that the actor might be enclosed in a simulation of reality, but the theater activists wanted to break down such walls; many of them contended that in so doing they could break out of an elitist culture. The constraining "box" of the theater was their analogue to Bely's sardine tin or skull (see the Introduction), and hence to break out of its physical constraints would be to break out of conventional (realist) epistemology. This movement, then, extends in its aims and implications far beyond the sphere of theater reform.

Why would Meyerhold have chosen as his vehicle for a revolutionary approach to the theater a play that is from the classic repertoire set during the era of greatest autocratic oppression, Nicolaevan Russia, and that concerns the life of an idle upper aristocracy (card games, masked balls, intrigues over love and honor)? All this seems a far cry from the productions he staged after joining the Party in 1918 and particularly after he moved to Moscow in the fall of 1920 to direct the Theatrical Department (TEO) of the Commissariat of Enlightenment, launching his new career with a call for a "theatrical October," a theater adequate to the revolutionary moment. For these later productions he had Red Army troops parade around the audience and eager young men in leather jackets on motorcycles charge up to the stage to deliver the latest news from the Civil War front; when one of them announced the fall of Perekop to the Red Army in a crucial battle, the entire audience stood to sing the "Internationale." But it might be argued that though such postrevolutionary productions were more blatantly about political revolution than the major prerevolutionary productions, which all depicted aristocratic society and used highly stylized, Retrospectivist sets,[10] these differences were more superficial than they might seem.

Meyerhold's work on *Masquerade,* no less than his productions after 1920, can be seen as an exemplum of revolutionary culture as many conceived it at the time. The production was to be a showcase for his kind of new theater. In the theory and practice of this new theater that he and others were working out in the 1910s, one can see a sort of synapse between the theories of political and aesthetic revolution. Yet the twin gods who presided over the breakout from the Stanislavskian theater were not Marx and Lenin but Nietzsche and Wagner.

Nietzsche, Wagner, and Marx

Nietzsche and Wagner were particular obsessions of Russian intellectuals from all over the political and aesthetic spectra from the 1890s through the first two decades of the twentieth century.[11] The two German theorists did not, of course, create the dominant cultural trends of prerevolutionary Russia. To begin with, the question of "influence" is a very fraught one. In any case it is misleading to equate the two with a slash (Nietzschean / Wagnerian) since, after initial enthusiasm for each other's theories, they had fallen out. But as Nietzsche's and Wagner's ideas reached Russian soil they had inevitably been refracted through a Russian prism; indeed, the Russian translations of their works are notoriously inaccurate.

Nietzschean / Wagnerian can be used as a convenient cipher for discussing a particular broad-ranging trend because so much cultural activity can be accommodated under that umbrella. It is a construct, admittedly, but one at least in part created by Russian intellectuals of the time who chose to ignore the crucial distinctions between the two thinkers. What concerns us here as Nietzschean / Wagnerian will be less that overworked binary of the Dionysian and Apollonian—although if it was overworked anywhere it was in Russia—than the implications of their theories for theatrical reform. Essentially, one can find in Nietzsche and Wagner a set of narrative norms and also an inventory of categories structured by these narratives which, in the years immediately preceding and following the Revolution in Russia, inform agendas of the various factions—Bolshevik, revolutionary, avant-garde, and even reactionary.

Nietzsche and Wagner advocated several specific reforms in the theater that were similar to those of the theater activists, such as revamping its physical arrangement to minimize the demarcation between actors and audience.[12] But for them, as for most other gurus of this movement, these modifications were not self-valuable. Their central project was the regeneration not just of the performing arts but of culture itself. Both believed the royal road to its regeneration led through the theater and from there to the regeneration of mankind.

Here we are at the point of intersection between political and aesthetic revolution. But what we see is not just a case of theoreticians from the sphere of culture with illusions of grandeur poaching on the territory of political and social theorists. Arguably, key political and social theorists of the

Russian Revolution conceived their programs using categories and scenarios sufficiently similar to those of Nietzsche, Wagner, and those of analogous persuasion to make possible the great joint-stock company of political
radicals and intellectual idealists who forged the Great Experiment of
October.

Western commentators on Nietzsche in Russia like to point out that 1898,
the year the first Russian translation of a Nietzsche text was published
(*Zarathustra*), was also the year the World of Art organization was founded;
with Benois and Diaghilev among its leaders, this moment was a landmark
in Russian cultural history, and many scholars date the Silver Age from its
inception. But 1898 was also the year the Russian Social Democratic Workers
Party was formed, that is, the Marxist party that was to spawn the Bolshevik
Communist Party.[13]

Clearly, Russian Marxism grew up in tandem with Nietzscheanism (and
with Wagnerism, too). But problematical though all emphasis on coincidence must be in cultural history, one is compelled to point out a further and
earlier coincidence that potentially has great bearing on the Russian movement for theatrical reform on the eve of October: the time when Wagner
penned two texts that are among the most seminal for theater activists, *Art
and Revolution* and *The Art-Work of the Future*, both of 1849, was approximately the time when Marx produced his *Communist Manifesto* (1848) and
also a work that will be of greater importance to this book, his *Eighteenth
Brumaire of Louis Bonaparte* (1851–1852), which Lenin pronounced the more
incisive of the two in his seminal text *State and Revolution* (1917).[14] The two
Wagnerian texts were written in a flush of enthusiasm after the author stood
at the revolutionary barricades of Dresden in 1848 (together with Bakunin,
which is one reason he was adopted by Russian Marxists). *The Eighteenth
Brumaire*, by contrast, was written in response to the French postrevolutionary reaction of 1848–1851 leading to the restoration of the Napoleonic
empire. This is a political tract, whereas Wagner's works are more concerned with aesthetic questions. Yet these texts, antithetical in many ways,
are closer than one might first suspect.

Marx's *Eighteenth Brumaire* begins with his famous salvo: "Hegel remarks
somewhere that all facts and personages of great importance in world history occur, as it were, twice. He forgot to add: the first time as tragedy, the
second as farce." Marx has, then, essentially redirected the focus of Hegel's
discourse. In a treatise dedicated to elaborating further a philosophy of history, Marx presents a highly detailed, if partial, chronology of the political
events taking place over a small time span (what Nietzsche decried in *The
Uses and Abuses of History* as "micrology"). He rescues his account from

some academic dust heap because the implications he adduces from these events are consistently subordinated, as in the above quotation, to the dominant trope of the theater. Wagner's texts, similarly, are grounded in a highly politicized account of historical progress, but they foreground a critique of culture that is figured as a sort of tale of the knight in shining armor who can save all; that knight is a purified "drama." Nietzsche began his career with *The Birth of Tragedy,* which, though published in 1872, twenty-three years after the Wagnerian texts were written, in many respects elaborates the themes of Wagner, particularly that of the saving potential of a purified drama. This text was, together with *Zarathustra,* to have the greatest impact in Russia.

Marx in his account of the Brumaire episode, like Wagner and Nietzsche in their ostensibly aesthetic tracts, advances changes within the theater as a synechdoche for reforms in society at large. But if the synechdoche in Marx can be said to be only a rhetorical flourish (a position that is open to question), in the build-up and aftermath of the Revolution in Russia what the synechdoche possibly only rhetoricizes was taken more literally and the theater was seen as a space for social transformation. As will be shown, the revolutionary mass spectacle institutionalized a set of prejudices that are already working in these texts of Nietzsche, Wagner, and Marx.

All three thinkers, Marx, Wagner, and Nietzsche, share a horror of the alienation they perceive in modern society. This is hardly remarkable, since that revulsion might be described as a common denominator of most Western intellectuals in the nineteenth and twentieth centuries. But, arguably, Russian Marxists, Wagnerians, and Nietzscheans all succumbed to the temptation of theatrical space in seeking remedies for this alienation. Within the theater one can engineer the interworking of previously unsynchronized—alienated—sectors of people, and many began to think one could use it as a basis for affecting social space as well. These thinkers tended to template theatrical space onto social space and to identify what they saw as a fall from a lost unity in the theater as the original cause of alienation.

Nietzsche and Wagner locate this fall within the sphere of culture and specifically in terms of a fall from Aeschylus as the high point of Greek drama. Wagner also insisted that such a fall occurred when and because all the arts lost their unity and became separate. In its general outlines, his account reads as a more aestheticized version of the tract by Marx, who discusses the fall in terms of the shift from a unified community to one with a division of labor alienating man from man.

All three propose remedies for this loss of wholeness. Marx's seem quite different from those of Nietzsche and Wagner in that he prescribes political-cum-economic revolution while their remedies are confined to the arts. But in *The Eighteenth Brumaire* Marx couches his account in theatrical terms, suggesting that one of the problems in the current historical moment is that the proletariat have been swept to the back of the "stage," implying that when they emerge to retake center stage the genre of world history might change from "farce" to that preferred genre of all three thinkers, tragedy.[15] Thus the dynamic of center and periphery, of hegemonic and subordinated, is figured using the trope of the theater.

Nietzsche and Wagner have a different solution and suggest that the drama will be saved by reuniting "sister" (Wagner's term) arts that were previously melded in the drama but have been cloven asunder. Their frame of reference, however, is not confined to the drama, or even to culture. They propose that the theater take its cue from the acting traditions of classical times whereby, allegedly, the actor transcended his individual self, breaking down the barrier between himself and his audience so that both attained a new sense of identity as at one with all others, or, in other words, a sort of millenarian psychology.[16]

In Nietzsche, this scenario is closely tied to his division into the Apollonian and Dionysian. Central to the Apollonian is boundedness and definition, the *principium individuationis*, which is at the same time its virtue and its limitation (man cannot reach beyond his own boundedness), while the Dionysian knows no boundaries. Thus the chorus in the Greek tragedy, as an expression of the Dionysian, enables both actor and spectator to break out of their limited horizon and fuse with others. Transgression of psychophysical boundaries—which are at the same time metaphysical or epistemological—is thus a synechdochal means for overcoming the problem of alienation, class divisions, and so forth for realizing the political agenda. Hence revamping theatrical space, breaking down its borders, and theatrical conventions—restoring "music" and the tragic chorus—were seen as the way to effect a fundamental political and social revolution.

Nietzsche and Wagner's account of how alienation is overcome shades over into, but is not identical with, Marxism-Leninism's insistence that citizens transcend their individualistic identities and attain a collective identity. Wagner in *The Art-Work of the Future* even insists that what he meant could not be known by any other name than "Communism" (though this initial enthusiasm for Communism faded out in his later writings).

Russian intellectuals such as Vyacheslav Ivanov who took Nietzsche's or (initially) Wagner's theories on the theater as their point of departure frequently articulated this scenario in terms of an ecstatic rite that would impart to all present a profound sense of community or *sobornost'*. The term *sobornost'* has particular resonance in Russian Orthodoxy, where it is a technical term generally translated as "collegiality," "communality," or "concil-iarism" and has to do with the allegedly democratic relationship between church members. In the various intellectual movements of the early twen-tieth century that sought to rethink Orthodoxy outside the formally consti-tuted church, *sobornost'* characteristically assumed a central role. Initially in Nietzsche and Wagner the return to beloved Hellas is figured as a flight to the pre-Christian, but not all Russian theater activists felt constrained to eliminate Christianity from their accounts of a "Greek" revival. However, most theater activists, whether or not they gave their accounts such religious or mystical coloration, insisted that the crucial move for the theater was to democratize, to include the masses, thereby breaking down distinctions of class and occupation. They explored the potential of several historical prece-dents for the "mass" theater—Greek drama, the medieval mystery play, the Italian popular tradition of the *commedia dell'arte,* and a Russian variant of it, the *balagan* (fairground theater).

Most commonly, taking their cue from Nietzsche, Wagner, and others, zealots advocated a return to Greece. So many of the big names in the pan-European movement for theatrical reform looked to open-air Greek drama in its huge amphitheater as the ultimate model and began to rival one another in the size of the new amphitheaters they were setting up; when Isadora Duncan visited Petersburg in 1913, she declared that she had to rush back to Paris to establish hers.[17] This transnational trend had its nation-alistic underside; a cynic might say that Nietzsche's entire tract was an elab-orate superstructure made to posit a line between "Greece," the originary moment in Europeans' account of themselves, and the "German spirit." Some Petersburg intellectuals, in turn, appropriated Nietzsche's agenda of a "yet-impending rebirth of Hellenic antiquity"[18] and conflated it with ver-sions of Russian messianism in prophesying an imminent "Third Renais-sance" in Russia whereby the spirit of ancient Hellas, recaptured in the Renaissance, would soon see its third, final, and greatest flowering in their city.

Such schemes were meant to usher in a society of the liberated masses or lower classes. In the countdown to 1917, the conception of what the new the-ater might be was becoming ever more democratic; "We must democratize the theater!" was a slogan heard with greater frequency.[19] However, one finds in the writings of those influenced by Nietzschean and Wagnerian models no less casuistry about what a theater of the masses might mean than can be found in those of their mentors; theater activists lambasted those who interpreted the concept too literally as "vulgarizers."[20] As we know, however, terms such as "masses" and "people" are all too vague, and there is significant ambiguity in all three thinkers' accounts of them.

Wagner, for instance, identifies the "folk" as the group that can revivify the drama and hence society, but sometimes the "folk" are clearly the toiling masses while at others they are defined as those who divine the essences of nature.

A similar ambiguity can be found in Marx's account of the lower classes even though he shifted the focus from the "folk" to the proletariat (he used *Volk,* too). This ambiguity is particularly marked in *The Eighteenth Brumaire,* in which the proletariat is divided up into true proletarians and false ones. The "true" proletariat are defined as the producers, but in a swift move they can be transformed into the "creators." Marx also adduces a second category, the *Lumpenproletariat,* or riffraff proletariat. This category comprises those who try to scrounge a living at the margins as ragpickers, organ grinders, prostitutes, and the like—in other words, they operate in the market, albeit on a small scale and often reprehensibly (this category also includes Louis Napoleon himself). In enumerating the sorts of professions that fall into this category, Marx slips into the middle of the list the *literati.*[21] Thus the proletariat emerge as the only true intellectuals and revolutionaries, while actual intellectuals are either bourgeois hirelings or *Lumpenproletariat.* In the *Communist Manifesto,* Marx holds out the hope that the proletariat will be transformed from drudges and drones to creators, but allows that as yet they are still mere drudges.

This proclivity for idealizing the proletarians' intellectual leanings was intensified later by Bolshevik theorists of proletarian culture, in whose writings, as in Nietzsche and Wagner, the masses emerge as the only authentic aesthetic subjects who truly yearn for Beethoven and Shakespeare (and among the Russian theorists Pushkin as well).[22] Additionally, Nietzsche and Wagner show a distinct bias against academic types and "arid" theory,[23] a bias that dovetails well with the Marxist predilection for praxis.

In Nietzsche and Wagner, what democratization really amounts to is impressing onto the many the template of the solitary "soul genii," as Wagner calls them, or the "untimely"—*Unzeitgemässe,* as Nietzsche was to call them. These genii allegedly embody or intuit the spirit of the folk / masses. Essentially, then, there is to be a single template or biography for all and yet among them some emerge as privileged creators (the paradox of elitist populism); democratization means less giving a role to the Great Unwashed than a mystique of universal community. The theater, refined to a universal art once music's role in it is restored, is commissioned with providing the medium for this spectacular conversion.

In this respect, the pattern projected is not unlike that found in Marx. All three theories have at their heart a myth of a Promethean man who brings a new consciousness to save the world.[24] Ostensibly democratic, such theories are incipiently elitist inasmuch as they advance a hierarchy in "consciousness." Wagner places particular emphasis on the contrast between the "conscious" and the "unconscious" or "involuntary" *(unwillkürlich)*. Marx was less elitist, but an analogous model can be found in Lenin's doctrine of the vanguard (those more advanced in political consciousness and hence in a sense *unzeitgemässe*). Although in these scenarios provision is made for some intermediate stages, generally they entail a sort of death-defying leap from the one to the many, from the singular and solitary hero or isolated group to the universal, no less—a kind of utopian recapitulation.

Both Nietzsche and Wagner looked not only to democratize society but also to cleanse it of commercialism. Part of the appeal of Greek culture for them was that in the polis the artist was allegedly not dependent on any mercantile patron; his patron was the state and his products were "civic" or "public" art.

The one thing that united most of the different factions among the prerevolutionary theater activists was a scorn for the commercial theater. They sought to ban not only the commercial element in culture per se (the profit motive and cultural exploitation), but also those genres, institutions, and styles that they viewed as owing their genesis to the profit motive. The icon of commercialism was for them the *café chantant*, as it was for so many cultural visionaries at that time, including Benois, whose capsule characterization in "Painterly Petersburg" of what is wrong with modern culture invokes the *café chantant* but makes no reference to architecture.[25]

There was a strong puritanical streak in these attacks. Nietzsche and Wagner set the model by accusing the commercial theater of being a form of prostitution while Georg Fuchs, one of the movement's chief European mentors, spoke of the "sexual, foul-smelling atmosphere" of this culture;[26] this equation with sexual pollution also underwrote the choice of similes used by Russian theater activists in condemning commercial enterprises.[27]

The abhorrence of the market can be seen as a version of the flight from the profane. The impulse is expressed most strongly in Nietzsche, who talks of the nausea *(Ekel)* occasioned by everyday reality.[28] But the inherent escapism also had its dark potential. "Beneath the pure, clear skies of Hellas *[Ellady]*" was a refrain of articles on theater and ballet in the 1910s. Such "clear skies," of course, represent not only that boundless blue of Greece, envy of all Petersburgers condemned to grey and cold, but also the hygienic, noncommercial environment where true art and knowledge can be pursued. They sought a "pure, clear sky" unsullied by factory smoke or the sewer or foul, sexual smells. The Russian word for "clear and pure" has as its root *chist-*, which is also the root for the word meaning a purge *(chistka)*. The "clear sky" is also the sky of a *tabula rasa* from which mundane particularity, including the particularity of Hellas itself, has been "cleared." It is perhaps no accident that the romance with ancient Greece flourished at the time when the fledgling science of eugenics was about to take its first steps in Russia.[29]

The Bolsheviks shared this vision of a renewed, universal society to which has been restored that purity lost in the incursions of the barbaric, commercializing hordes. This common purpose led many of the theater activists to make common cause with them. When, after the October Revolution, Meyerhold addressed members of the Imperial Mariinsky Theater who refused to cooperate with the new regime, he tried to win them over with the prospect that they would become the spearhead of a "theater of the entire world,"[30] essentially conflating in this rhetoric a revolutionary political agenda with a specific agenda of aesthetic revolution.

It may seem hard to reconcile the intensely ideological culture we associate with Bolshevism with the theories of Nietzsche and Wagner. In recent scholarship, accounts of Nietzsche seem to have gone beyond his discussion of the Superman and his cult of Greek tragedy. When his name is mentioned it is usually in the context of the fundamentally metaphorical nature of language and the destabilization of essentialism. These interpretations of Nietzsche from the 1980s and 1990s did not escape intellectuals of this earlier time, but they drew different conclusions and saw them as recipes for revolution. Many of the same insights underwriting that overused term Postmodernism are precisely what authorized the theatrical model adopted by the willing volunteers from the Russian intelligentsia who worked to develop a new revolutionary culture. A key insight for them was that the theater is *ipso facto* conditional construction.

In Russia, the two banner terms under which a massive overhaul of the theater was undertaken were *uslovnost'* and *teatral'nost'*. *Teatral'nost'* translates fairly readily as "theatricality," a term not unknown among Western theater theoreticians and especially popular in the 1960s among figures such as Richard Shechner, but *uslovnost'* eludes satisfactory translation. Variously rendered as "conditionality," "artificiality," "stylization," or "conventionality," *uslovnost'* essentially entails a recognition of the impossibility of mimesis, of reflecting, representing, or recreating "reality" in the theater—or for that matter in any art form—and of the consequent necessity for "conventions." The task of the theater director or theoretician was seen as one of devising or perfecting conventions to maximize that essential quality of theatricality that, allegedly, the bourgeois theater (and Stanislavsky particularly) had contrived to deny its public.

Although Nietzsche is one of the most unsystematic thinkers, about this time Russian intellectuals were drawn to the challenge of systematizing what they had adduced from the writings of gurus such as Wagner and him. In Russia there had been a reaction against Nietzsche around 1908, when many of his former epigones such as Vyacheslav Ivanov began to attack his theories. But in the "post-Nietzschean" phase defining elements of Nietzscheanism remained, just as in Postmodernism one can find defining elements of Modernism. In both instances, they have been reaccented.

It was not only Nietzscheanism and Wagnerism that had undergone such a shift, but the whole movement for Retrospectivism. By the 1910s there was a sense that Retrospectivism was not enough in itself, that no single model from the past was adequate to the problems of the contemporary theater or culture. The search for past models was an attempt to elucidate principles and criteria rather than normative practices. We have already seen this trend in the case of the Preservationists, the Acmeists, and the *Apollo* set, but it was represented more broadly.[31]

As an aspect of this trend, theater activists tried to adduce an architectonics of the theater, a science of theatricality and *uslovnost'*. Thus, although the defining thrust of this movement was to break out of existing bounds and conventions (the thrust of revolution) the movement was generally far from anarchic. On the contrary, each faction was working out its own highly codified system. Each insisted on a total overhaul of the theater (not just of theatrical space) and sought to institute new principles for all its elements: sets, acting, music, lighting, script, directing, and architecture.

In Petersburg, those bent on investigating this science set up a series of experimental studios and summer or underground theaters. Some of these places did not merely investigate the theater arts, but sought ways to make the theater the crucible of a classless society. Such experimental theater studios were conceived in a synechdochal relationship vis-à-vis the society in which they operated. The loci of the most famous European directors of the new movement to renovate the theater, places such as Wagner's Bayreuth, Oberammergau, Dalcroze's Hellerau, and Reinhardt's and Fuchs's theaters in Munich and Berlin, became as it were topocosms of a new secular culture. Nietzsche had been offended by Bayreuth, which he saw as all too implicated in national imperialism. In the analysis of the leading Russian Wagnerians, the opera house there had become the preserve of the *haute bourgeoisie* and hence had been false to Wagner's original conception.[32] The way was open for the true theater to appear in Russia and regenerate that society, and through it the world.

Yet those who sought this regeneration were in actuality focusing on perfecting *uslovnost'*. How could any concept that can translate as "artificiality," "stylization," or "conventionality" have much to do with radical social reform? I would argue that *uslovnost'*, or more specifically the move to transcend actuality, particularity, and brute materiality, characterizes not just a particular branch of the movement for theatrical reform; it is a fundamental principle of this time, something comparable to, although not identical with, the Nietzschean call for wresting values from their conventional systems.

Meyerhold and the Science of Theatricality

In describing how this project of a revolutionary, total, and yet *uslovnyy* culture was prosecuted, I am going to look principally at Meyerhold's work. Meyerhold suggests himself because not only was he the leading director and theoretician of the 1920s, but some of his disciples ran most of the revolutionary mass spectacles, while another of them, Sergei Eisenstein, went on from apprenticeship in Meyerhold's Moscow studio to become the leading Soviet film director. Moreover, he combines in his profile certain elements that are crucial for this study—cultural revolutionary, theatrical reformer, and avant-gardist.

At the beginning of 1913 Meyerhold published an anthology of his essays entitled *On Theater* (O teatre) comprising recent writings published elsewhere and also a new essay, "The Fairground Tent" (Balagan). This collection, and especially the latter article, was intended to articulate the basic principles of theater as Meyerhold had reconceived them in his recent work. The book's appearance was followed by the founding of a new Meyerhold studio on Borodinskaya Street in late 1913[33] that attracted professional actors and theater students who came to work with the master and his cohorts as they attempted to investigate these principles further in their experimental work. The studio generated a new journal, *The Love of Three Oranges* (Lyubov' k trëm apel'sinam), subtitled *The Journal of Doctor Dapertutto*, which began appearing in 1914.

Out of this studio and journal emerged many of the figures who were to play leading roles in the revolutionary theater of Petrograd / Leningrad in the 1920s, especially after Meyerhold himself left the city in mid-1919. Three of them were to be particularly prominent: Vladimir Nikolaevich Soloviev (1887–1941), a close associate of Meyerhold's in his work on the *commedia dell'arte* who was to carry faith in that medium through the 1920s, long after Meyerhold had relegated it to a more peripheral position in his theories, and two young enthusiasts who will become central figures in this book but were then essentially starting their careers, Sergei Radlov and Adrian Piotrovsky.

Meyerhold's production of *Masquerade* was intended to be a milestone in this movement to adduce an architectonics of the theater. Few critics saw it as such at the time. In fact most fastened on the opulent sets and condemned the production for pandering to commercialism and the forces of cultural hegemony. The sets and props offended for the additional reason that they emphasized the Venetian motif, suggesting a grand genealogy for Petersburg, and thus for its tsar. After all, the Italian Futurists had singled out Venice as a model of the *passéisme* they so deplored. In other words, the sets seemed to confirm the insinuation of recent caricatures of Meyerhold that represented him as the erstwhile experimental director who had grown fat as an employee of the Imperial bureaucracy.[34]

Yet Meyerhold's own colleagues hailed the production as an exemplum of *uslovnost'*, with the Lermontov text providing a rich mine for theatricality.[35] Such contradictory accounts of the stature of the production are echoed in its very make-up. Indubitably, the production was the child of the studio on Borodinskaya, yet the acting and sets were done by professionals of the Imperial theater and artists from outside the studio. Hence the production's status in the history of this particular movement for theater reform is ambiguous, which some saw as its fatal flaw. Soloviev complains in a review he wrote for *Apollo* that the staging is magnificent in terms of the direction but that the actors are not up to it. One problem he notes is that they still feel bound to subordinate their acting to the laws of psychological motivation—read, "Stanislavsky," or, as Nietzsche preferred to put it, they opt for "the death leap of the bourgeois theater."[36]

Another criticism Soloviev makes is that the actors in *Masquerade* do not know how to read the lines of their script, which are in verse form; they think that stressing its rhyme is enough, ignoring not only its rhythm but also the caesura.[37] This seems a minor criticism by comparison with the volley against the Stanislavskian system, and unexpected from a proto-avant-gardist. At the time, however, the criticism was far from minor in its implicit frame of reference.

The relationship on stage between word, music (or sound and rhythm), and dance (or gesture or bodily movement) had become the critical focus of the theater activists. It was, in other words, the Nietzschean—or more particularly the Wagnerian—frame of reference that dominated the theoretical explorations and practical work of the theater activists in the 1910s.[38] Most wrested the basic Wagnerian terms from their mystical narrative in which such elements as "sound" (or tone—*Ton*), "dance," and "poetry" are metamorphosed into characters in a Promethean saga. Theater activists sought to investigate the actual interrelation of such categories—the architectonics—

and thereby to forge a science of the theater; V. N. Soloviev tried to represent his collaborative experimental work with Meyerhold in algebraic terms.[39] They sought to crack the code of theatricality so successfully that the findings could be universally applicable, to adduce a universal grammar of theater.

Underlying the most radical experiments in the theater at this time was the impulse to get away from language, which always carried with it the possibility of difference and hierarchy—two taboos of truly democratic revolution—and to plunge into a prelinguistic world of what Nietzsche had called "music." The Nietzschean / Wagnerian model was for a theatrical form in which music was to play a dominant role, whether as the element prior to the verbal text holding out the promise of a universal language (as in Nietzsche[40]) or as a crucial element in the preferred genre, the "musical drama" (as in Wagner).

The central place accorded music in the cultural hierarchies of the 1910s is evident in the fact that the *café chantant* was so anathema then. In actuality, the cinema represented a far greater threat to the theater because of its great commercial success, and there was no dearth of articles in highbrow journals discussing this threat. But the *café chantant* provided musical spectacle and thus it most closely rivaled what the theater activists sought to do (while film, which as yet had no sound track, was in no position to do this).

The question of the relationship between word and music did not only concern theater reformers but underwrote exploratory work in many fields of culture at this time. Thus, for instance, many poets and scholars turned their attention to questions of prosody. Sergei Radlov proved one of the most zealous in attempting to recuperate the "spirit of music," and in 1916 he presented to the Society for the Lovers of the Word (a group that emerged under *Apollo*'s patronage and included poets and philologists) new translations of Greek dramas now rendered in Russian for the first time in their original Greek trimeter form, which was quite alien to Russian prosody.[41] This somewhat quixotic gesture represents an extreme implementation of the belief that rhythm (or music) is prior to the actual words and hence any rendition that merely attempts to translate the words themselves is a mistranslation.

The recurrent concern of Petersburg articles in the 1910s about the theater was some program to reorient it from the dominance of the literary text to such nonverbal forms as gesture, sound, pantomime, and dance.[42] These programs were not necessarily Wagnerian per se. Wagner was himself critical of pantomime and also allowed the verbal text an honorable role in his musical drama. But in the 1910s the campaign against the verbal text reached such extremes that some, following the lead of Georg Fuchs, whose *Revolution in the Theater* was published in Russian translation in 1911, and who advocated a theater without words, based their productions instead on the rhythmic movement of the human body.[43] Few Petersburgers took such an extreme position but some proposed that words be kept from the stage as a temporary measure while the theater sought to correct the distortions they caused.[44]

There were other contemporary gurus of this movement, such as the free-spirited Isadora Duncan, but also the more earnest Swiss Emile Jaques-Dalcroze. The main fare of the Dalcroze school was rhythmic exercises to music or, at their most expansive, "allegorical spectacles" at which a singularly limited repertoire of rhythmic movements to music was meant to convey a range of moods and events.[45]

The reverberations of this new interest in choreographing bodily movement to music and rhythm extended beyond the walls of the theater. Dalcroze was particularly interested in the effects of rhythm as a "regulator" on the psyches of those trained by his methods. He believed that such training would "ensure accuracy [*tochnost'*], ease, and success in work."[46] Such claims impressed the idealist brothers Dom when they were setting up a model garden city for German workers at Hellerau; they invited Dalcroze to move his headquarters there so that their workers might have "rhythmic education."[47] Dalcroze's Petersburg disciple, Prince Sergey Volkonsky, was impressed too. He believed that in the work of Dalcroze (and his predecessor F. A. Delsarte) the whole question of the interrelation between movement, sound, and rhythm had been put on a "scientific basis" for the first time, promising a more "hygienic world."[48]

In an article of 1912 Volkonsky describes his visit to the Dalcroze school at Hellerau to see a performance of their spectacle *Orpheus,* which was performed without costumes or sets, but also without words. In their place was a combination of singing and rhythmic dancing while a choir sang variations on the words "Do, ray, me, fa, so" to their corresponding notes.[49]

Needless to say, Meyerhold did not identify with any of this sanitized and wooden "musical theater." To him pace was all, not such ponderousness, and he was opposed to melodeclamation and "rhythmic reading."[50] "Play," "entertainment," "improvisation" and even "caprice" he nominated as the magic wands to be waved over the theater to save it from its current torpor; didacticism, improving messages, and "rhetoric" were anathema to him—though, like Wagner, whom he often cited in *On the Theater,* Meyerhold did not seek to abolish the verbal text completely.[51]

Yet, as Meyerhold acknowledges in *On the Theater,* his latest ideas developed out of the direction indicated by Dalcroze and Duncan in their pioneering work.[52] In "The Fairground Tent" he asks: "When will they write on the tablet of laws for the theater that *the word in the theater is no more than a decoration on the canvas of movement?"*[53] At a public debate on the theater in December 1913 he pronounced most crucial for the actor the mastery of techniques for bodily movement and of rhythm, declaring that the "actor who has not prepared his body" is "not worthy to go on stage."[54] By then the studio on Borodinskaya had been founded, where his class ("Movement on the Stage") began the work that would culminate in his theory of Biomechanics.[55]

Meyerhold, like Dalcroze, identified bodily rhythm as the organizing focus of theatrical production to which all gestures, physical or vocal, should be subordinated.[56] In consequence, he stressed musical abilities as a prime criterion for admission to his studio, and he maintained that dance skills are essential for an actor as well.[57] In all his productions of the 1910s, which were intended to be exempla of the *uslovnyy* theater, some musical form, such as a casual dance rhythm or a melodic walk, functioned as the dominant element defining individual scenes or characters; not merely their bodily and vocal gestures, but even the deployment of props and so forth were subordinated to it. This privileging of musical form may be seen as the ultimate in *uslovnost',* a flight from verbal literalism *(doslovnost').*

Meyerhold's proto-biomechanics with their emphasis on subordinating all to a rhythm other than the organic (resulting often in somewhat contorted or jerky movements) can be seen as an attempt to impose a system other than the conventional, quotidian one as a key to reordering the world. Bodily movement is, after all, the most basic human activity, thus the focus on it as the key is a kind of dream of ab-originality. Some believed that such fundamental reform in the theater might provide a formula for redoing society itself; as it were, if one reorders the base of bases, one will reap a fundamentally renovated superstructure. This is a particularly tempting scenario because it involves a less overwhelming task than tackling the world economy and sociopolitical order—a Goliath for the Soviet David. Around the time of the Revolution, it was not just Meyerhold and other cultural reformers who sought to orchestrate bodily rhythms according to some system, thus transcending the natural order; indeed, in Petersburg both the physiologist A. A. Ukhtomsky and the efficiency expert A. Gastev were experimenting with bodily movement in the workplace as the key to transforming productivity and even workers' psyches.

The emphasis on rhythm and musical form, and the corresponding de-emphasis on language, is in a sense also a gesture toward the kind of utopian, totalizing culture that might be universally applicable. It is the dream of a pre-Babelian state where everyone speaks the same language and there are no differences.

We might seem here to be identifying the paradigm of the age to which all of the arts subscribed. Music, or an overriding scheme for systematic inter-connectedness (architectonics), would appear to be the trope that links the architect-artists (Goethe in that overused quotation defined architecture as "frozen music") with the poets and theater reformers of the 1910s. Indeed, it might seem on the face of things that Benois and Meyerhold could find a lot of common cause. Both were interested in architecture as well as theater; both looked to the court of Louis XIV as a cultural apogee; Meyerhold styl-ized several of his productions using conventions of that time.[58] Doubtless one element that appealed to both was the way in which life at Versailles was ritualized as theater, with everyone having an assigned role.

Yet the two were in fundamental disagreement, disagreement more basic than, for instance, Meyerhold's calling for "movement" while Benois advo-cated static grandeur and panorama. Benois wrote several crusty and nega-tive reviews of Meyerhold's theories and productions, while Meyerhold opened his manifesto-like article "The Fairground Tent" with a lengthy sally against Benois's cult of the mystery.

Fundamental differences between them can be seen in the way Meyerhold identifies "the fairground tent" and the strolling player or *cabotin* as the essence of theatricality. To him, theatricality means popular theater, puppet plays, strolling players, and especially the *commedia dell'arte.* These are all subcanonical theatrical genres, although that fact in itself should not deter a Benois, who himself designed the sets for the premiere of Stravinsky's *Petrushka* for the Paris Russian season of 1911. Also, in 1913 the Petersburg Preservationists attempted to revive the annual spring tradition of setting up "popular entertainments" on Mars Field replete with "fairground tents."[59] But Meyerhold did not envisage reviving the theater of the fair-ground tent as Preservationism, as filling in a blank in the panorama of Old Petersburg.

As well as being popular attractions, the fairground theaters were com-mercial ventures like the sideshows. As such, they were the direct ante-cedents of the cinema, which effectively swept them out of business. But Meyerhold was not as repelled as were Wagner, Benois, and so many others by the specter of the popular lowbrow theater with its "sexual, foul-smelling atmosphere." On the contrary, he identified the variety theater, the music hall, and so forth as the new home of the *cabotin* after he had been chased from the legitimate theater.[60] Like Marinetti in his "Foundation and Manifesto of the Italian Futurist Theater," published in Russian translation in 1914, Meyerhold looked to lowbrow genres, including the *café chantant* and the circus, to revivify the stage[61] (incidentally, Marinetti was one of the few outsiders taken to visit the studio on Borodinskaya, in 1914).[62] To Meyerhold, the "leaps" of the acrobats, the "jokes" of the clowns, the skill of the juggler, and the thrill of the *salto mortale* were the stuff of true theater.[63]

Thus though Benois dismissed Meyerhold's new work as a "more bombastic version of the fare of the fairground tent," which was his way of damning Meyerhold for slipping below the standards of high culture, for Meyerhold that characterization was high praise. "The theater of the fairground tent is eternal," he asserted, meaning of course what he discerned as its essence, the very spirit of theatricality.[64] To him, in the fairground tent and the *commedia dell'arte*, if they be true to their essence, the actor will "transport his audience into the world of invention, amusing him all the while by dazzling him with virtuoso displays of technique [bleskom svoikh tekhnicheskikh priyëmov]."[65]

This characterization sounds all too reminiscent of Russian Formalist writings. One is particularly reminded of the centrality of play with devices in Shklovsky's classic account of early Formalist theory, "Art as Technique" (1915–1916, published in 1917), written even as preparations for the production of *Masquerade* were under way.[66] In Shklovsky's conception, as in Meyerhold's, the stature of the writer / creator was a function of the extent to which he could dazzle or surprise his reader or audience with displays of finesse through digressions, improvisations, and other tricks of the repertoire. In his early postrevolutionary articles he drew parallels between these techniques in literature and those of the *commedia*, the circus, and other such performance-oriented theatrical traditions.[67] Moreover, these articles appeared in the main Petrograd cultural newspaper of those years, the *Life of Art*, virtually alternating with theoretical or programmatic statements by activists (such as Radlov) working for a revolutionary "people's theater" that was likewise oriented toward dazzling displays of technique involving bodily movement (see Chapter 4).[68] Shklovsky also subscribed to the banner term of the theatrical reformers—*uslovnost'*.[69]

Indeed, the agendas for theatrical reform were closely tied in with those of the avant-garde and the Formalists, and also of many other groups that looked to some kind of cultural revolution in that their specific programs sought a kind of *uslovnost'* in the sense of remaking the given, the conventional, and the quotidian. For example, the ideal of divining the pure essence of theater (*teatral'nost'* or *teatr kak takovoy*) could be seen as analogous to the aims of the Formalist movement, trans-sense, and Suprematism, which likewise sought to catch the essence of, respectively, the verbal and visual arts. Not coincidentally, all three movements dabbled in the theater, and the Formalists in particular drew heavily on the vocabulary of the theater activists in their early literary analyses.[70]

The Formalists with their demand for a "resurrection of the word" might seem to have been out of step with an age bent on toppling the verbal text from its pedestal in the theater. Yet their emphasis on competence in the formal qualities of the artwork and downplaying of content can be seen as analogous to the theater activists' interest in the architectonics of sound, movement, and language on stage—the Wagnerian project. It is symptomatic of a general return of interest to formal questions; even Volkonsky identified rhythm as "form," while Soloviev's main criticism of the actors' inadequacies in *Masquerade* was that "our Russian actors are very much against anything smacking of 'form.' "[71]

Meyerhold, the Formalists, and many avant-gardists gave a central role in their theories to techniques for juxtaposing polar opposites (for example, high and low), a widespread strategy among all avant-gardist groups. Meyerhold describes some of these techniques as "attractions," or in other words as scenic pyrotechnics analogous to the star turn in a circus or a dizzying ride at the fun fair (two definitions contained in the literal meaning of the Russian word "attractions," or *attraktsiony*). Here he also anticipates "The Montage of Attractions" (1923), that famous essay of his future disciple, Sergei Eisenstein, who was in the audience in 1917 for *Masquerade*. Such attractions were used to shake the beholders out of what Shklovsky called their "automatized" perceptions; Shklovsky termed his version of such techniques "defamiliarization" (*ostraneniye*); Eisenstein called his "montage"; and Meyerhold referred to his as "the grotesque."[72] But they all represent versions of the belief that truth is to be established by demystification.

Here we see how alien Meyerhold's approach must have seemed to a Benois who looked to a preservation of the traditions of high art, to static grandeur and unruffled panoramas—to harmony. Meyerhold's constitutive principle was the unharmonious, yet he was far from advocating free expression and unstructured anarchy. On the contrary, he called for precisely measured choreography. As he said pointedly, in the *commedia*, and even in Dionysian rites, improvisation is never unstructured or (*pace* Nietzsche) open-ended, but is kept within the parameters of highly conventionalized traditions; there are no "random elements" (*sluchaynosti*).[73] Likewise, for Eisenstein the essence of montage was strict rhythm and precise cutting (timing) as much as it was "contrasts."

Meyerhold in his final sentence of "The Fairground Tent" characterizes that theater's essence almost oxymoronically as "dissonance elevated to the harmoniously beautiful," a distinctly post-Nietzschean sentiment.[74] Dissonance is, however, no absolute quality; it must be defined against the conventions of consonance. One can see a similar proclivity for contrariness in Formalist theory (especially that of Shklovsky), which pays particular attention to exceptions to the ostensible form used, rather than to the form itself (for example, omitted stresses in verse, digressions that retard or frustrate the unfolding of the plot). Essentially, the Formalists were exploring systematic nonsystem (although Shklovsky at the end of "Art as Technique" spoke of the impossibility of systematizing aberration). Meyerhold, analogously, wanted systematic improvisation, systematic grotesqueness, and so on. He advocated a kind of dissonance as the new harmony.

The approaches of figures such as Meyerhold and Shklovsky can be read as a response to the Nietzschean call to *re*order and *re*vitalize as an aesthetic agenda of revolution. As yet, however, their "revolution" was conceived almost exclusively in aesthetic terms (though with reverberations beyond the aesthetic). Thus after the February Revolution Meyerhold was more or less able to make common cause with the highly aesthetic *Apollo* set and join in their lobby for a ministry of the arts.

Masquerade and the Mask

For Meyerhold, then, the principal vehicle or demonstration model for this revolutionary aesthetic agenda was, incongruous as it might seem, a production of that old chestnut of the classic repertoire, Lermontov's *Masquerade*, a production in which, moreover, the stylized sets placed him in the Preservationist camp. This fact raises the whole question of trajectories. We see here a Meyerhold with close links to both the *Apollo* set and the avant-garde, two groups that in the years 1912–1913 had emerged as absolute antagonists. (Benois through his regular column for the liberal paper *Speech* [Rech'] functioned as antagonist *en titre* of the Russian Futurists.) After the Revolution, however, the kaleidoscope shifted a little: Meyerhold identified himself as a revolutionary activist-cum-avant-gardist while many in the *Apollo* set established their repugnance for the culture of the Revolution. The quirks of the trajectory are even more striking in the case of Radlov, who was associated with Meyerhold in this prerevolutionary period, but was possibly even more implicated in Acmeism (he was an aspiring poet and close to Akhmatova). As late as July 1917 in a letter to Akhmatova Radlov expresses his angst at the confused political situation and uncertainty about the future, suggesting that he did not anticipate the path he was to take after "October."[75]

The choice of *Masquerade* as a vehicle for *uslovnost'* was, however, neither a Preservationist gesture nor an arbitrary selection. In "The Fairground Tent" Meyerhold identifies what the actor must do on stage with "going to a masquerade ball"—the term used in Russian, *maskarad*, is the title of the play itself. He also defines the essence of theatricality (cum fairground tent, cum *commedia dell'arte*) as a "theater of masks."[76] This emphasis on the mask was typical of theater activists throughout Europe at this time (Gordon Craig gave the name the *Mask* to the journal he ran between 1908 and 1929 that was a focus of the movement). Indeed, this equation has its own logic since not only are masks (or rather half masks) an integral element in the *commedia*, but the mask might be called the very signature of *uslovnost'*—that which both signals and enables the cut-off between reality and theater. It also functions as a prop for "play" (improvisation).

The mask also has its philosophical dimension. It focuses the question what is real and what is illusory—a question raised by the very title of Lermontov's play. Both Nietzsche and Wagner insisted that everyday reality was an illusion: Wagner contended that it was art's task to strip it away to reveal the essential inner depths of the soul, while Nietzsche emphasized the project of freeing the revivifying Dionysian forces. Both believed that the mythopoeic and eternal must be saved from the dulling veneer of the quotidian; when the transformative powers of the aesthetic or the Dionysian are unleashed, reality assumes the status of the mask or veneer, the *Schein*. Thus, when the Revolution began, led by a party that promised to institute the kingdom of historical materialism, many in cultural life were exploring the notion that causality and external reality are mere masks and illusions.

Masks were particularly in vogue in the culture of that time, but the meaning of the mask varied. Some gave the mask pride of place in a program of aristocratic aestheticism. There was considerable interest in such historical precedents as the status quo–affirming masques of the court of Louis XIV and the aristocratic masked balls of Venice at its height—as well as in their local avatars, the masques of Pavlovsk (held during the time of Alexander I).[77] In Petersburg around 1913 society ball matron and aesthete alike sought to revive this bygone glory. For others, however, the mask offered the promise of a revival of the low, of the "fairground tent," conceived not literalistically but more in terms of what Bakhtin was later to call "carnival." Meyerhold identified himself as among them and in his account of the mask stressed its potential for ambivalence and the parodic.[78]

The parodic / grotesque element was a sort of fifth column in Meyerhold's work as director of the Imperial theater, a hallmark of his other directorial persona, Doctor Dapertutto (an alias from Hoffman Meyerhold used for the experimental work he did outside his sphere of duties in the Imperial theater). Many among the upper-class audience essentially came to *Masquerade* and its predecessors to gasp at the extravagant Golovin sets and did not "see" the parodic aspects of these Meyerhold productions.

Masquerade uses the mask, yet in some senses it attempts to tear off the masks of a false consciousness that was both political and aesthetic. Thus, for instance, those controversial sets were conceived as a veneer "mask"-ing the decay of Nicolaevan Russia. The production was also intended to be an object lesson in demystifying the masks of allegory and developing a new science of the theater that exposed any pretentious or mystical illusions the audience might entertain. In this, Meyerhold was at cross purposes with the dominant trends; whether the new theater was conceived as a Greek tragedy or a mystery, most contended that it should maintain a solemn and elevated tone and present a "heroic" drama on some "monumental" scale.[79] But in his work of the 1910s he sought to undermine such agendas by constantly drawing attention to the theater's essential constructedness. For instance, in an earlier production of A. Blok's *The Puppeteer* (Balaganchik, 1906), he had actors go through a window on the set, thus piercing, and therefore revealing, the painted paper representing the panes and the sky beyond.

In Meyerhold's theater, actors were to wear masks in the service of taking off those more metaphorical masks of delusion, a version of that key Shklovskian program of "laying bare the device" ("obnazheniye priyëma"). Yet tearing off the masks was also a recurrent strategy of Marx (see, for instance, *The Eighteenth Brumaire*). By the Stalin era, it was to reappear as a crude slogan vindicating repression.

Here we are at the heart of an ambivalence that hung over the would-be revolutionaries, Marxists and theater activists alike. Did they conceive revolution in terms of some scenario of tearing off the masks, of attaining a higher consciousness that superseded that of class, station, lineage, and occupation (something like what Marcel Mauss in his article "A Category of the Human Mind" calls the personage or role),[80] or were they looking to give everyone a role in a perfectly choreographed (conflictless, ritualized—utopian) society? Were citizens to break out of the "mask" of class and station, occupation, and even heredity and religion so that in Communist society individuals would not be mere subfunctions of their places on the grid of the division of labor and class? Then they would be able to change roles—occupations and so forth—which are a modern analogue to changing tribe or totem in traditional society. In this way they would become conscious beings, overcoming the problem of alienation (of inauthenticity) and reaching up in a Hegelian scenario of ever higher degrees of political (or self-) consciousness. Or were citizens in the new society to be subfunctions of some aesthetic grid (a mask), a higher-order version of the way their identity is structured in traditional society? Or would this even be possible given that such a grid is always in danger of being corroded by self-consciousness?

Hence in *The Eighteenth Brumaire* Marx is not just using the theater as a master metaphor. Theater (ritualization), mask, and role lie at the heart of the problematic he airs. The true revolution might be a matter not just of one class gaining hegemony over another, but of crossing over to a new paradigm of identity; all citizens might attain a postalienation, "authentic" identity.

Nineteen thirteen, according to Akhmatova's *Poem without a Hero* (Poema bez geroya), was a time when all of Petersburg was cavorting in masks. In this long poem, the year 1913 is represented as a nodal moment in a cautionary tale of intelligentsia folly; the perpetual carnival of masked happenings has its underside of suicides, an unheeded portent of the nightmares to come. The poem was begun many years later on the eve of the war (1940), and completed only in 1962. Thus her account of 1913 was given from the perspective of the intervening purges, though both the vogue for masks and the veritable epidemic of suicides are borne out by a reading of the press of the time.

Akhmatova saw the mask as iconic of 1913. It obscured the view of the "real twentieth century," which by her account began not in 1910 (as for Virginia Woolf and others), but in the year immediately after 1913—in 1914, when Russia entered what was for her a disastrous war. One might disagree with Akhmatova and say that in 1914 the Russian intelligentsia took off the mask of the theatrical frolic only to don military costumes. Indeed, many did not see military action but were able to serve in relatively undemanding posts in the capital, so undemanding, in fact, that they were still able to carry on many of their intellectual activities. In a sense, the greatest problem for them was the widespread withdrawal of funds from culture in favor of the war effort, causing deprivation and forcing many of their projects to be postponed (such as *Masquerade*).[81] They did not fall on Flanders Field along with Rupert Brooke and the flower of English youth; their movements were not decimated by death as were those of the avant-garde of France and Italy. The Revolution and the Civil War were to be their major traumatic experiences that would overshadow that of the world war.

On February 25, 1917, the intelligentsia's flight from the profane was about to be halted by the intrusion of an insistent reality. "The masquerade" was drawing to a close, though there would be a respite. The February Revolution, which gave the country many of the liberal reforms the intellectuals had long sought (such as freedom of belief), captivated their imagination, and figures like Meyerhold spent much of it organizing "masques"—outdoor festivals—in support of such civic causes as war bonds. But then would come October, which would take them from their sandbox revolution to a real revolution in which they would confront the Great Unwashed. The hour for removing the masks was at hand.

4

THEATER AND REVOLUTION IN THE NEW REPUBLIC

In November 1918 for the first anniversary of the Bolshevik Revolution the central streets and squares of Petrograd were decorated by artists. The focal point, the Palace Square, was assigned to the avant-garde artist Natan Altman, who draped it with gigantic festoons of red cloth on which were printed revolutionary slogans. Among them one taken from the communist movement's hymn, the "Internationale," stood out: "HE WHO WAS NAUGHT SHALL BE ALL."

This is of course the meaning of revolution: turning the power structure on its end to bring the powerless to power. But what were its implications for intellectuals? Potentially, it suggested overturning the personnel or the values that dominated cultural life. Could the intellectuals ever be party to implementing this slogan literally, since that would mean total self-effacement? In the actual resolution of the question as to who or what would dominate in postrevolutionary culture, much depended on how the issue of power and patronage was resolved. After the February Revolution, Petrograd intellectuals had agitated for a ministry of the arts essentially as a move to give them more autonomy, status, and funding, making them less dependent on either an abhorred market or a constrictive Imperial Chamber and Imperial Academy of the Arts. After October, the possibility of an enlightened private sponsor fell away as property was confiscated, many fled abroad, and before long privately owned cultural institutions were nationalized. Yet despite the usual laments about Bolshevik repressiveness, in many respects Petrograd intellectuals were able to run their own show during War Communism (that is, the period stretching from 1918 to early 1921 that was dominated by the Civil War, the foreign Intervention, and the Blockade).

In Petrograd this opportunity was, paradoxically, due in no small measure to the city's recent calamities. A severe economic crisis, unusually harsh winters, supply problems, and a civil war led to a spectacular depopulation of the city, particularly among Party members and workers. Moreover, when the capital moved to Moscow in March 1918 a large number of senior Party and government officials moved with it.

Many intellectuals fled from Petrograd in those turbulent times, most seeking havens in the south, where conditions were less severe and it seemed there was less danger. Others were simply hostile toward the Revolution and refused to work in its cultural institutions, or they got by with minimal contact by undertaking translations. But many of those who remained accommodated to the new order and their new patrons.

For most, the ideological adjustments to be made were less arduous than they were to be later. An important consequence of this emptying out of the city of workers and senior Party people was that there were few left who had the time or the inclination, in these extreme times of civil war, to oversee the development of a proletarian or revolutionary culture. Moreover, the administration of culture was low on the list of Party priorities. Symptomatically, sections of the Commissariat of Enlightenment (Narkompros), including its head, Anatoly Lunacharsky, were among the last pockets of the central government to be transferred from Petrograd. In fact, between the Civil War and the recurrent transportation crises, even after the cultural sections of Narkompros moved their headquarters to Moscow, for some time several of their Petrograd branches were officially or de facto autonomous or equal to their counterparts in the Moscow headquarters.[1] Also, it was difficult to persuade Party members to work in cultural administration. The characteristic pattern was for the wife of some prominent figure to oversee cultural life for the Party; these included wives of Party leaders, such as N. Krupskaya (Lenin's wife) and O. Kameneva (Kamenev's wife and Trotsky's sister). Zlata Lilina, the wife of Grigory Zinoviev, the head of the Petrograd Soviet, also worked in culture, primarily on education.

This meant that the Petrograd intelligentsia were in a better position to conduct their own affairs. Cultural bodies there were largely run by enthusiasts from within the non-Party intelligentsia who served as intermediaries between Party, military or state officials, and the intelligentsia at large. Few Party members played a major role in the actual administration of culture. A major exception was M. F. Andreeva, Gorky's common-law wife who became the single most powerful figure in Petrograd theater. Andreeva was hardly the conventional Party member, however. Of noble origins, she was the daughter of a former director at the Alexandrinsky Imperial Theater and herself an actress who had worked at the Moscow Arts Theater (MKhAT), a background that facilitated her appointment in October 1918 as head of

PTO, the municipal theatrical department, which meant that she not only controlled what happened in Petrograd's theaters but played a major role in the staging of the famous mass spectacles of 1920.

Gorky himself was initially a vehement public opponent of Bolshevik policies, but after his reconciliation with Lenin in September 1918 he began to play such an extensive role as intelligentsia patron that he could be called with some justification a Soviet Lorenzo the Magnificent.[2] He ran a veritable court from his Petrograd house, a court to which many an intellectual would come as petitioner or protégé, and where the more favored were housed. In addition, he founded a series of new institutions that enabled Petrograd intellectuals to continue working—and many even literally to survive. The most famous of these is the House of Arts (Dom iskusstv, founded in 1919), which played a critical role in fostering new literary movements such as the Serapion Brothers (see Chapter 7).[3] Also, as early as September 1918 he established the publishing house World Literature (Vsemirnaya literatura) as an autonomous department of Narkompros that gave several hundred otherwise destitute scholars and writers employment, often as translators. Under his patronage, the intelligentsia were sustained, and with relative autonomy. The figures who dominated their cultural events were for the most part those who had been prominent before the Revolution or their protégés.

Where, then, was the great bouleversement? In some senses, it had not yet occurred. Intellectuals were not so much "working for the Bolsheviks" as working under the general auspices of one of their own number (even Lunacharsky had been, and continued to be, active in non-Party intellectual life). They had been freed from both the conservative autocratic regime and crass commercialism, but most were not enthusiastic about working for the Bolsheviks per se; indeed, when the latter called a meeting with Petrograd intellectuals in December 1917 it was poorly attended. Many were, however, attracted by the possibility the Revolution offered to try out their particular agendas for cultural regeneration. But the question remained: Which new values—orientations, styles, groups, and even branches of art—would prevail?

Initial answers proved deceptive. For example, after the Revolution the avant-garde artists shifted roles from roués who defined themselves through *épatage* to establishment figures. As such, they dominated state-funded official art in providing decorations for revolutionary anniversaries, agitational posters, and so forth. And they were rewarded with institutional power. One of the first cultural departments established in Narkompros, the Fine Arts Department or, IZO (Izobrazitel'noye iskusstvo, founded on

February 6, 1918), was headed by avant-gardists almost exclusively. Under their leadership, the Academy of Arts was abolished and in October 1918 the first SVOMAS studios were founded in Petrograd. The studios were open to all with the intention of redressing the elitism of the old Academy by helping the formerly underprivileged obtain places there so that they might acquire the new vision.

Thus when Altman, one of those who subscribed to the idea of the new vision, decorated the Palace Square, he was determined to enact revolution in his very art. He sought to "counterpose" that Empire style "ensemble" with "a new beauty of the victorious people."[4] Needless to say, the decorations by Altman and company drew fire from Preservationists—and from the Proletcult—who complained of their "contempt for architecture," for the "majestic facades" of Petersburg; the avant-garde would (allegedly) have done better had they followed Shchuko, a Preservationist who, in his decorations for the Taurides Palace, used primarily greenery and flags, the formula for the Tercentenary celebrations of 1913.[5]

The broad spectrum of cultural activists offended by Altman's decorations lobbied to try to prevent the avant-garde artists from participating in the next major revolutionary celebration, May 1, 1919.[6] The power struggle that ensued was at least in part between IZO and official theatrical bodies. The theatrical bodies prevailed, and Andreeva, a determined opponent of the avant-garde, was made one of the heads of a new committee formed to organize revolutionary celebrations. From then on, their theatrical component became more important than the decorations.

Many of the avant-garde became so disaffected that they left Petrograd for Moscow. There a new avant-garde movement, Constructivism, developed as a postrevolutionary mutation from Futurism. Even the early prominence of the avant-garde in the administration of Soviet culture was far from unchallenged; when in February 1918 the avant-garde got their power base in IZO, the Preservationists got theirs in another new Narkompros department, the Department for Museums and the Preservation of the Historical Heritage (Otdel muzeyev i okhrany stariny)—under Alexandr Benois.

It was not only avant-garde art that became a diminished presence in the city; its musical life and ballet were decimated by emigrations. After the October Revolution, the Ballets Russes and many of the avant-garde composers (Stravinsky and later Prokofiev), together with prominent musicians, those whose art could be appreciated by audiences who did not know Russian, opted to live in the West, where conditions and commercial opportunities were better. Such an option did not realistically exist for the theater. The experimental theater emerged from its marginalized position in cellars and dachas and stepped into the breach to lead the intelligentsia's initial efforts at forging a revolutionary culture. As for the former Imperial theaters, their change of name to State theaters did not affect them radically.[7] Most of their administrators and artists at first resisted the new order, but after an administrative purge they resigned themselves to their new masters[8] and continued serving the public with *Aida* and *Rigoletto* while Petrograd was in turmoil all around.[9]

Theater as the Cradle of Soviet Culture

The conservatism of the academic theaters notwithstanding, the stage was to play a major role in the cultural life of revolutionary Russia. So many theater activists had been champing at the bit to find opportunities to implement their agendas for transforming man via theater. After October, finally, the government was committed to more or less the same cause.

Most Bolshevik leaders were impressed by the theater's potential for education and propaganda.[10] The majority of the populace in those days was illiterate, especially the peasants, whose support would be crucial if the Bolsheviks were to win the war, but one did not have to be literate to understand a play's message. The task of spreading literacy and popularizing the Bolshevik cause among the civilian masses was largely assigned to the Red Army and Navy, and to the Department of Extra-Mural Education (Vneshkol'noye obrazovaniye), headed by Lenin's wife, Krupskaya, who had great faith in the power of the theater.[11] Lenin himself favored film as the best medium for agitation, but he made his famous statement on this in 1923; in these early years there was a chronic shortage of film and projectors so that the theater as a cheaper and more realistic option dominated agitational work. The statistics speak for themselves: by October 1, 1920, the army had organized 1,415 theaters but only 250 cinemas.[12]

The First National Conference on Extra-Mural Education, convened early in 1919 as the first major forum on how to remedy the backwardness of the masses, resolved that the theater was such a vital instrument for education that it should be included in the general system of education and also be made a centerpiece for the arts, the medium that would incorporate all others.[13] With a massive state investment, the theater became in effect the cradle of the cultural life of the new Soviet republic. Thus many intellectuals were drawn into its orbit, whether as writers, scholars, directors, actors, set designers, or administrators. Activities with no ostensible connection to the theater, such as Petrograd's Free Philosophical Academy (Volfila), were often housed and funded under the umbrella of one of the bodies set up by the state to organize theatrical work.[14]

Actually, the theater had been queen from virtually the very beginning of Soviet power,[15] and several other factors conspired to give it a dominant role. For one, theater was also the rage throughout Europe, where even the avant-garde were turning to that medium.[16] And in Soviet Russia Lunacharsky, the Commissar of Enlightenment, had himself worked as a theater critic while in exile in Paris and was an aspiring playwright: several of his plays were dutifully produced during this period.

The Civil War was in general a time when oral forms of culture dominated the written, and the theater was in a sense merely one of the more elaborate of them. At all levels of culture, from Party oratory to highbrow institutions, great emphasis was placed on oral performance.[17] Reliance on nonwritten communication was in any event a necessity given not only the widespread illiteracy but also a chronic paper shortage.[18] Writers depended largely on public and private readings of their works in order to disseminate them— the age favored genres such as poetry and short stories, which were best suited to declamation.

Thus the movement for theatrical renovation got an impetus from the Revolution. Whether by purse strings or by inspiration, however, it shifted its orientation from a relatively hermetic remodeling within the theater— energies were now more consistently directed outward at theatricalizing "life" (as had been attempted only sporadically before in places like Dalcroze's Hellerau).

One of the most articulate and flamboyant ideologues of a comprehensive transformation through theater was Nikolai Evreinov, Meyerhold's chief rival as leader of the experimental theater in Petersburg / Petrograd. In his *Theater as Such* (Teatr kak takovoy, 1912), Evreinov maintains that from the earliest times man has been motivated by an "instinct to transform himself," by a drive to make himself other, and thus transcend the banal self.[19] One can see this even in the most primitive savage who dresses himself in feathers and paint, not, Evreinov holds, for utilitarian or aesthetic reasons, but to make another self.[20]

Theatricality and assuming roles are to Evreinov, then, by no means confined to the theater, but are an important element in life (as theorists such as Irving Goffman have since worked out in greater detail). Evreinov developed this theme even further in his later book *Theater for Oneself [or Itself]* (Teatr dlya sebya, vols. 1–3, 1915–1917), in which he calls for the elimination of the theater on the stage and asks for the creation of theater in everyday life. In this book he insists that individuals should not trust the professional theater for a vicarious thrill derived from the performance of others, but should perform themselves. All people should call on their innate theatrical instincts and consciously develop roles and dramas for themselves, subject only to their own desires and fantasies. They should, Evreinov concludes, become actors, directors, and playwrights in their own lives. Hence Evreinov advanced the slogan, "Let every minute of our life be theater."[21]

How prophetic Evreinov was to be! Although drawing parallels between theater and revolution or theater and war often results in a cliché, when talking of the Russia of 1917–1921 the temptation is too great. In the chaos and turmoil that followed the February and October revolutions, rare was the individual who was to continue performing his old roles. Some people adopted dramatic roles as agents of revolution or counterrevolution, others escaped the grim times in theater, while still others were forced by those times to assume roles that were tragi-comic or grotesque. Most realized another of Evreinov's slogans: "The main thing is to become other and do something other."[22] A characteristic form of theater under War Communism was the drama circle, the group of amateurs, be they workers, sailors, librarians, or just neighbors, who came together to act in plays. In Petrograd the drama circles were very popular and began to "multiply like infusoria."[23]

Although the theatrical craze had this spontaneous element, it was also highly organized. In Petrograd, the way theatrical life was ordered was complex and changed over time. There were five main bodies that ran it: first, TEO, the Theater Department of Narkompros; second, PTO, the theater and entertainment section of the so-called Northern Commune, or Petrograd City Soviet, which was responsible for the majority of city theaters and places of entertainment (which by 1920 numbered forty);[24] third, the Narkompros Department of Extra-Mural Education, which was combined in November 1920 with ROSTA and other agitational bodies to form Politprosvet, or "Political Enlightenment" (again under Krupskaya), a body far from as singularly agitational in its activities as the title might imply;[25] fourth, bodies set up by the Petrograd Military Command and the Baltic Fleet to organize agitational and theatrical work among their men; and fifth, the (semiautonomous) Proletcult.[26] Space does not permit here a proper account of the administration of theater policy through these five bodies. But they were not mutually exclusive in the sense that certain figures played leading roles in more than one of them, though they did have separate jurisdictions and to some extent separate profiles.

What is striking about the composition of the various committees set up by such bodies is that in these early years they reveal a distinctly highbrow rather than Party or worker bias. This trend was particularly marked in TEO, which functioned, in effect, as one of the Petrograd intelligentsia's first postrevolutionary homes. Many of the figures who sat on its committees (such as Blok and F. Zelinsky) were either the sons of scholars or scholars in their own right. TEO sponsored a range of organizations which went on to develop their own independent existence and which, in toto, represented a spectrum of the Petrograd highbrow intelligentsia—making it much more representative than the spectrum offered by the leadership of IZO, for instance, TEO's main rival as the cradle of Soviet culture.

Many of the activists who ran the revolutionary theater in Petrograd were not particularly Bolshevik. They could probably be identified more with the ethos of the February than the October Revolution. Many of them, including Blok and even Lunacharsky, had worked on cultural bodies set up under the Provisional Government; Gorky and Andreeva had headed the administration of Petrograd municipal theaters under the city Duma.[27] Several of those active in TEO, including Gorky, left Soviet Russia later, while others, such as Blok, were Left Socialist Revolutionary rather than Bolshevik in orientation.[28]

Normally one would assume that a theater run by the intelligentsia would be doomed at the box office, especially in such hard times. But the theater under War Communism was artificially maintained at the very time it might otherwise have collapsed under dire conditions.[29] The show could still go on, for it was subsidized by some government agency.

Lunacharsky had been arguing for at least two decades that the theater should be accessible to the masses,[30] and he was delighted to be able to enforce those policies himself. With free performances and subsidized tickets, his government attempted to bring the lower classes into the theater on a large scale. There was an official policy that ultimately all the seats should be free, and this policy was achieved to a greater extent in Petrograd than anywhere else. The aim was to squeeze out the private theaters by unfair competition, and the town Soviet was paying for this. Large blocks of seats in the theaters were allocated to enterprises, trade unions, or the military to distribute.[31] Later, the price of theater tickets was reduced progressively until, in early 1921 (that is, on the eve of NEP), it amounted to just a few kopecks.[32]

Thus the theater activists were freed from box office concerns in their efforts to reform the theater. However, these subsidies came with the understanding that the activists were, like the government, committed to serving and educating the masses. Fortunately, at this stage the Party was more interested in fostering mass culture and agitation than in anything rigidly proletarian. Thus most of those who agitated for cultural change, Party, government, and intellectuals alike, could find common cause in the campaign for a "people's," or "mass" *(narodnyy)*, theater.

The People's Theater

For much of the 1920s the movement for a "people's theater" spearheaded the campaign to transform bourgeois culture into a socialist or proletarian culture. A theater of mass participation was a project that both intellectuals and the Party carried in their knapsacks as they entered the battlefield of revolution. It flourished particularly in the two periods of revolutionary extremism (which essentially flank the decade), the times of greatest common cause between government cultural policies and intellectual schemes. In the first of the periods, War Communism, the movement dominated cultural life in Petrograd.

It was never clearly established what that rubric meant, however. The term "people's" *(narodnyy)* has a wide range of meanings and connotations. It can mean "popular," "mass," "folk," and even "national" or "state." Thus it lends itself to appropriation by persons from all points on the political spectrum. Even if the term is given a more democratic interpretation as meaning "of the people," the question immediately arises: Who are they? Are they the proletariat? the peasantry? the disadvantaged? the uneducated masses? or all citizens? And then again does it mean for the people, for their education and enlightenment, or even just for their enjoyment? Or does it mean by and of the people? Will the proletariat gain not just political but also cultural hegemony?

In those heady and confused years of War Communism, all manner of interpretations of the term were de facto accepted, but few advocated giving the proletariat very real power in legislating the new culture. In part, this was because of the historical moment when the Bolsheviks needed all the support they could get and were committed to encouraging the professionally trained bourgeois specialist *(spets)* to work for their government.[33] But Lenin himself in *State and Revolution,* his major treatise on postrevolutionary society on which he was still working at the time of the Revolution, had been vague about which version of "the people" would enjoy hegemony after the Revolution. Society is divided into two groups, to be sure: oppressors and oppressed, and the oppressors are the bourgeoisie and their stooges, but the oppressed, who are to take power after a revolution, are characterized in various ways, including as the "majority of the population," the "workers and peasants," and "those lowest on the social scale, the oppressed and exploited." In some contexts, Lenin equates "proletariat" and *narod*, while in others he differentiates between them.[34]

In truth, the movement for a people's theater was not in itself a response to the Bolshevik Revolution and had generally not been conceived rigidly in class terms. As was so frequently the case, what happened under the rubric "people's theater" in postrevolutionary Russia represents the intensification of trends that began in Europe, were marked in Russia before the Revolution, but flourished under War Communism with Bolshevik patronage. Late in the nineteenth century under the banner of the people's theater idealists in Paris, Brussels, Vienna, and Berlin tried to bring the theater to the people by offering them free tickets or subsidized subscriptions to good theaters, or by founding theaters in working-class neighborhoods or workers' clubs. The movement reached Russia early in the twentieth century in institutions such as P. P. Gaydeburov and N. F. Skarskaya's Traveling Mass Theater (Peredvizhnyy obshchedostupnoy teatr Gaydeburova i Skarskoy), founded in Petersburg in 1903. Lunacharsky's efforts to provide Soviet workers with subsidized tickets can be seen as an example of this trend.[35]

Another broadly accepted account of the term (discussed in Chapter 3) was that it meant the theater should be democratized by breaking down the gulf between the actors on the stage and the audience by changing its physical organization. As it happens, these principles suited the reduced circumstances of postrevolutionary Russia. Indeed, in the profusion of street theater troupes that appeared in the Revolution's wake it was often difficult to tell whether a given troupe was performing on a street corner in order to serve a principle, or because its members had been reduced by unemployment and need to becoming buskers.[36] The exigencies of the times had a similar effect on state-funded theaters. Given the chronic shortages of all commodities, it was fairly inevitable that the "new" theater was going to have to be fairly stripped down and ad hoc. Plays were often produced in the open air (especially those performed at the front), under canvas, or on a makeshift "stage" with only the most rudimentary of sets and possibly without make-up.

Thus most agreed that a people's theater meant serving a more democratic audience in a less artificial setting. But it wasn't so clear how to translate the new theater's aims into the specific context of a Bolshevik revolution. There was less consensus on what the repertoire or aesthetic of the people's theater should be.

One solution would have been to write an entirely new repertoire of plays, but as it happens this was an era when dramaturgy was at a low point. Assorted official bodies in Petrograd ran competitions for new plays in the hope of stimulating the drama with enticing prizes, but the quality of the entries was invariably poor and the judges sometimes decided that they could not give any awards.[37] Typical of the plays from this period was *The Bricklayer* (Kamenshchik, 1918) by the Proletcult activist Pavel Bessalko. Written in praise of the new age of technology and proletarian hegemony, it concerns the wife of an architect who, predictably, becomes disaffected with her bourgeois husband and runs off with a bricklayer to join the revolutionary movement—to her greater fulfillment, no doubt, but not to the satisfaction of critics, who found the plot poorly motivated and the play terribly dull.[38] Thus the issue became one of what existing plays would be staged, and in what manner.

One common interpretation, associated with Andreeva, Gorky, Blok, and most of those who sat on the various repertoire committees set up in Petrograd at this time, was essentially that the people's theater should mean the transformation of the theater into the gymnasium (privileged, classical secondary school) of the Great Unwashed, who had been deprived of this kind of education by the inequalities of the tsarist regime. Such *Kulturträger* made the theater the central focus of a range of activities aimed at redressing this wrong (others included symphony concerts, public lectures, and literary readings).[39] Lunacharsky and Gorky looked to the theater as a good place to teach history and called for several different cycles of historical plays to be written on, for example, the history of culture, the great epochs of scientific invention, and the genesis of the great religions of the world.[40]

Such projects are reminiscent of the eighteenth-century French mania for encyclopedism. A similar ethos can be seen in many of the projects sponsored by TEO, a body whose members seemed to be reaching out via "theater," broadly conceived, to found an entirely new cultural program. Thus, for instance, they sought to set up a theatrical university and produce a theatrical encyclopedia. They also launched an ambitious program for publishing annotated critical editions of a large number of Russian and foreign plays, a project closely tied to the World Literature publishing house Gorky had founded—one of many examples where the Petrograd TEO embraced the interlocking world of the city's intellectual life.[41]

Cultural enlighteners like Gorky favored uplifting, highbrow fare for the theater. He, Lunacharsky, and others advocated that the cornerstone of the new theater be either tragedy or melodrama—melodrama, that is, in its old sense of high drama interspersed with musical renditions.[42]

Gorky, Blok, and Andreeva, aided by Lunacharsky for as long as he remained in Petrograd in 1918, set out to stage the great classics of world drama for mass audiences. Their program for the people's theater merged with a local initiative attempted, yet again, before the Revolution (around 1914), and which was led by Andreeva (together with others, such as the singer Chaliapin and the classic actor Yu. Yuriev, who had played the leading role in Meyerhold's *Masquerade*). These leaders advanced the slogan "Back to the Classics!" as they called for a theater of classical tragedy, high comedy, and romantic drama that would stage plays devoted to historical subjects. An attempt was made after the February Revolution, in May 1917, to start this venture, but it was only after the October Revolution that their campaign bore fruit. In May 1918 Yuriev staged *Oedipus Rex* in the Chinizelli Circus, and, in August, Shakespeare's *Macbeth*. Then, early in 1919, this group was able to open a new, state-sponsored theater, the Bolshoi Drama Theater (whose board included Andreeva and was ultimately presided over by Blok).[43] The government had also financed a series of free performances of recognized classics for worker audiences, starting with a production of Gogol's *Inspector General* in January 1919.

The repertoire advocated by these lovers of classical drama included Shakespeare, Schiller, Victor Hugo, Aeschylus, and Aristophanes.[44] In other words, proponents singled out the more stirring among the various dramas that might be set for study in a gymnasium schoolroom, hoping to cast the pearls of the old culture before the underprivileged. It might have been intended that class divisions be broken down thereby, but the grand gesture in effect also represented a cultural dictatorship by the scholar caste.

Although this movement back to the classics had very powerful sponsors in Andreeva, Gorky, and Lunacharsky, arguably it did not represent the dominant response to the task of defining in practice what a revolutionary people's theater should be. This response was no less highbrow in the repertoire it sought to stage, but its account of itself was tinged with Wagnerian or, especially, Nietzschean vocabulary.

A range of theaters, individuals, and groups saw the people's theater not so much as an institution for the lower classes as an ambience in which all classes could commune in harmony; as actors and audience intermingled, they might have the ecstatic or mystical experiences of a Dionysian rite.

In the initial postrevolutionary years, this orientation was strongly represented in the Department of Extra-Mural Education, the department that was most directly mandated to help enlighten the Great Unwashed and that was also in the initial years to be one of the most important in formulating policy for the theater. At its first All-Russian Congress, held in Moscow in May 1919, which stressed the central role to be played by the theater in educational and agitational work, the keynote address on the theater was given by the Symbolist poet Vyacheslav Ivanov, who in prerevolutionary

Petersburg had been a leading interpreter of Nietzsche (his "tower" apartment had been a focal salon for modernist endeavors) but was at this point head of the Historico-Theoretical Section of TEO. In language similar to his earlier writings but also anticipating some later Stalinist rhetoric, he urged his audience to take the Soviet theater out of the "paltry" *(malyy)* art that was being produced today, to overcome the art of yesterday, class art, and produce something that was "great and universal *[vsenarodnyy]*." Later all the delegates were taken to see a performance of Wagner's *Valkyrie*, preceded by an introductory lecture in which Ivanov quoted liberally from Nietzsche's tract on tragedy and called for *sobornost'* in art.[45]

If such events seem a little unexpected for the platform of a proletarian revolution, it might be helpful to point out their timing. In May 1919 the power struggle over who should run the revolutionary mass festivals had just been resolved with the avant-garde excluded, and Lenin in his speech to this same Congress on Extra-Mural Education attacked the avant-garde. Hence the Nietzschean/Wagnerians profited from a power vacuum and emerged to prominence as the line of least resistance. The interest such directors had in founding a new religious consciousness is not, however, as far from the official view of the new theater as one might suppose. Lunacharsky himself, in a prerevolutionary article entitled "Socialism and Art" (1908), in which he outlines his conception of a new peoples' theater, praises Wagner's "Art and Revolution" and calls for a "collective production of a tragedy that should raise [the participants'] souls to a state of religious ecstasy." The theater of the future should be a "free religious cult," closely linked to the new religion of socialism; hence theaters would be "turned into temples and temples into theaters."[46] By 1917, the quasi-religious aspects of his cultural program had become muted, but they had not disappeared.[47]

In revolutionary Petrograd, a similar position was taken by the head of the Theatrical Department within the Institute for Extra-Mural Education, P. P. Gaydeburov, a veteran of the prerevolutionary movement for a peoples' theater who during the years of War Communism was at the height of his success (as was his Traveling Mass Theater). Gaydeburov sat on several PTO and TEO committees and trained Red Army soldiers for theatrical productions. His speeches and writings were influential at this time, particularly his *People's Theater* (Narodnyy teatr), published in 1918 but comprising articles written and largely published before the Revolution. As this fact suggests, Gaydeburov's understanding of people's theater in Soviet Russia was virtually unaltered from his prerevolutionary position; it was to seek "an art for all [vsenarodnoye] based on a shared [vsenarodnoye] religious consciousness."[48]

The prominence afforded leading Neo-Nietzscheans from the prerevolutionary period, such as Ivanov and Gaydeburov, in the movement for a peoples' theater was to prove short lived, but they are important figures in the story of how, later, a more rigidly proletarian, Soviet agitational theater emerged in Petrograd. Many of those who pioneered such theaters took on the work after an initial postrevolutionary apprenticeship in Gaydeburov's theater, or escorted their students to it as a model.[49] Others began their theatrical careers in a Proletcult studio run by A. A. Mgebrov, another theater activist prominent before the Revolution who had worked with Evreinov and Meyerhold; his studio was the first to press its services to tour the front for the Red Army, but his account of the revolutionary theater was tinged with Nietzschean vocabulary.[50] By the end of War Communism, most of these directors' epigones had parted company with their masters, and before many more years had elapsed the Revolution spat their masters out and closed their theaters down. Nevertheless, the hands of Nietzsche and Wagner had not withered entirely. Individuals from a younger generation no less in their thrall—and here I have in mind particularly Radlov and Piotrovsky—were to weather all the successive political moments of the 1920s to emerge as the most consistently dominant figures of the decade in the revolutionary and agitational theater of Petrograd / Leningrad. In the work of these figures, Nietzscheanism and Wagnerism are conflated not with highbrow benevolence, as in the case of Gaydeburov, but with a version of avant-garde experimentalism.

Much of the work and ethos most characteristic of the theater in postrevolutionary Russia was an outcome of the experimental and theoretical work of Meyerhold and his disciples in prerevolutionary Petersburg, or by the coterie of Evreinov. Most of those who were to become major names in the revolutionary theater of the 1920s (such as Radlov) had some prerevolutionary association with both. However, neither Meyerhold nor Evreinov was himself destined to become a leading figure in the Petrograd revolutionary theater.

The most exciting time in civil war Soviet theater was the period from 1919 through the spring and summer of 1920, when the open-air mass spectacles were staged in Petrograd. But during this precise time Meyerhold was in the south of Russia, and Evreinov was in Tiflis. Evreinov returned to Petrograd after a three-year absence in September 1920, that is, at the very time Lunacharsky invited Meyerhold to Moscow to head TEO. Evreinov was initially feted, given his own theater, and appointed head of the consortium of directors planning the famous reenactment of the storming of the Winter Palace, thus stealing much of the glory for an enterprise already under way.[51] Yet of the two coteries, in Leningrad that of Meyerhold was, despite his permanent departure from the city, to be the dominant one; crucial factors proved to be his tenure in 1918–1919 as deputy head of the Petrograd TEO, which, though brief, enabled him to set up a number of institutions that had a major impact on the evolution of the city's revolutionary theater, and his early acceptance of Soviet power.

The Revolution gave Meyerhold an opportunity to resolve his split directorial persona as Dr. Dapertutto of the experimental theater and Meyerhold, a director of the Imperial theaters. He abandoned the Imperial theaters in 1918 to concentrate all his energies on producing a new avant-garde theater for the state. After he was appointed head of the entire TEO in September 1920 this commitment intensified and he called for a theater at one with the October Revolution, a "theatrical October." Meyerhold always insisted that theatricality could not be compromised for any cause, however, and even in early 1921 he was still insisting on the primacy of form over content, something that exacerbated his problems with Lunacharsky and precipitated his demise as head of TEO shortly thereafter.[52]

This reversal of fortunes gave Meyerhold less bureaucratic power to dictate the direction Soviet theater should take. However, the theater Meyerhold set up in Moscow in late 1920, the Theater of the RSFSR (later named the Meyerhold Theater—Teatr imeni Meyerkhol'da, or TiM), became a yardstick and trendsetter for revolutionary theater. Its innovative productions attracted the greatest attention in theatrical journals in Moscow and Leningrad so that he came to dominate the Soviet theater in the 1920s de facto as he no longer could *de jure*. His work in the Moscow theater essentially picked up where it left off when he was obliged in 1919 to leave Petrograd for health reasons; Meyerhold's Moscow "theatrical October" began in Petrograd.[53] Moreover, he remained a presence in the Leningrad theater throughout the 1920s, bringing the Moscow troupe there for a whole month every year to show his latest productions and also debate his theories with his old interlocutors.

Meyerhold's most seminal act during his brief tenure at the Petrograd TEO was to found, in June 1918, the Courses in the Mastery of Staging (Kursy masterstva stsenicheskikh postanovok), established under the auspices of TEO.[54] These Courses were essentially a new home for the Meyerhold camp, a revival of the studio on Borodinskaya (most of the old names regathered there), and yet there were marked shifts in its orientation as compared with the old studio. An explicit aim of the Courses was to get for the theater "new forces from the democratic masses" to train instructors who might lead the burgeoning drama groups among the masses. This represented a break with the prerevolutionary de facto elitism of the Meyerhold camp (few outsiders had been admitted to the studio on Borodinskaya), as did the understanding of those involved that their productions would be more ideologically inspired. In most other respects, however, the Courses represented a continuation of Meyerhold's prerevolutionary studio in that they stressed improvisation and the acting styles of the *commedia dell'arte*, and their announced first principle was "to recognize 'theater' as an autonomous artistic activity and to insist that everything in the theater be subordinated to a single set [*yedinym*] of theatrical laws."[55]

These Courses proved to be a springboard for disciples such as Piotrovsky, Soloviev, and Radlov, who all taught there. After Meyerhold's departure, the position of director of the Courses was assumed by Radlov, who had joined the staff in November 1918.[56] These three also made their own mark by setting up a series of experimental theaters that sought to become models for the people's theater.[57] The last and most successful of these was the People's Comedy Theater (Teatr narodnoy komedii), founded in late 1919, which was run by Radlov and Soloviev, and in which Piotrovsky also periodically played a role as author or director of a given production.

Part of the considerable popularity of the People's Comedy Theater must be ascribed to the verve of its approach. Figures such as Richard Shechner (and Meyerhold) draw a distinction between "drama," or the inert text, and "theater," or performance,[58] but never has that distinction been so glaringly apparent as in postrevolutionary Russia. Among the avant-garde of the day, values like dynamism and pace were *de rigueur*,[59] and the bottom line in evaluating any work of art or theatrical production was its value as "spectacle" (*zrelishche*).[60] But at the hands of the Meyerholdians a crucial addition to this troika was "play." Indeed, Meyerhold was able to capitalize on his position in the Petrograd TEO to found a journal of that title (*Igra*) whose avowed philosophy was that one could revolutionize education by the use of theater as play.[61]

The People's Comedy Theater exemplified these values. Rather than search for new plays, they tended to restage the old or to put together sketches based on the tritest of plots. Plays were redone to streamline them, to alter or emphasize their ideological message, and to reduce their ponderous verbalizing and increase the potential for movement and caper. On Radlov's initiative, the theater invited a group of circus professionals (primarily acrobats and clowns) to join forces with them in staging a series of plays using the principle of improvisation but in which the audience was to be attracted by the actors' comic antics and daredevil feats—those revolutionary saltos.[62]

The supporters of the People's Comedy Theater claimed for it a respectable pedigree in a European tradition of the people's theater; parallels were frequently drawn with the theater in Shakespeare's day or the *commedia dell'arte*.[63] The theater also owed much to Meyerhold's investigations of bodily movement on stage. But the players' work could equally well be seen as influenced by the Italian Futurist theater, which used the precise nexus of techniques for which the People's Comedy Theater was famous: circus performers, improvisation, short skits, techniques of the cabaret and music hall, and de-emphasizing the verbal text.[64]

Two other versions of the people's theater tried in civil war Petrograd that could lay a more convincing claim to a pedigree in folk traditions were also fostered by Meyerhold. The first of these was attempts made under the auspices of the Courses at staging new redactions of plays from the Russian folk, or *narodnyy*, theater, the potential of which had attracted the attention of Meyerhold and avant-gardists before the Revolution who were drawn to the particular combination one finds in these plays of drama and tragedy relieved by pantomime and comic intermedia with pithy folk repartee.[65]

The avant-garde wanted to appropriate the conventions of the folk theater for developing an experimental theater that would be at the same time revolutionary and serving the masses. The difficulty of combining these three versions of the people's theater was demonstrated earlier in the famous production of Mayakovsky's *Mystery-Bouffe* (Misteriya-buff, 1917–1918), a hybrid of folk drama and avant-garde experimentalism directed at the service of the revolutionary cause. This play was staged for the first anniversary of the Revolution and directed by Meyerhold himself, who was then still in Petrograd.

Mayakovsky's *Mystery-Bouffe* became for the Futurist camp a *cause célèbre*. It was their postrevolutionary attempt at conquering the theater and represents a considerable accommodation on their part to the demand for a revolutionary, mass culture (gone was the trans-sense language of *Victory over the Sun*).[66] The play was destined to become instead a symbol of the persecution of "left art," as the erstwhile Futurists had come to label their movement, the perennial (contested) charge being that it was unintelligible to the workers; in Petrograd the chief opponent was Andreeva, once again, and her power was a factor precipitating Mayakovsky's move to Moscow in 1919.[67]

Mystery-Bouffe was intended to introduce its untutored (mass) audience to the rationale behind the Revolution. The plot is based not on any of the existing Russian folk dramas but rather on the biblical legend of Noah's ark, which it conflates with the convention for representing the Revolution in terms of some natural cataclysm (a relatively bloodless trope for spatial purification). As with productions of the People's Comedy Theater, in *Mystery-Bouffe* cardinal values of the studio on Borodinskaya—pace, improvisation, the *commedia*, theatricality—were married to the cause of agitation and education.

In a way, much of the prerevolutionary theater had become like the colorful revolutionary poster. Dramas were simplified, pared down, and protagonists caricatured—sometimes to the point of crudity—in order for the message to be immediately accessible to mass audiences. Productions had little complexity, subtlety, or exploration of characters' inner lives. Here we find points of similarity with those who favored the fare of the Bolshoi Drama Theater; their spokesmen, such as Gorky and Lunacharsky, insisted that the theater should dispense with all "half tones" in favor of a clearly delineated black and white.[68]

The theater activists—avant-gardists, Nietzscheans, and highbrow zealots—wanted such simplification as a necessary gesture to unsophisticated audiences, yet their own sense of the world was at this time fairly Manichaean. They saw the much hated rentier-mercantilist class and bourgeoisie in terms comparable with the grossly caricatured "cleans," members of the oppressing classes in *Mystery-Bouffe* who were sketched as circles to look distinctly bloated, ridiculous, and incapable of purposeful action. It was perfectly predictable that during the period of iconoclastic fervor marking the aftermath of a revolution antibourgeois themes would be the predominant fare of all the theaters. This was a topic on which theater activists could happily produce plays that their patrons (the state) would generally finance.

The theater activists were opposed to the bourgeois, commercial theater not just because it entailed the dread market per se, but also because of the alleged lulling effect of its fare on the audience. Lunacharsky, and many other figures who controlled theater life in Petrograd (such as Gorky, Andreeva, and Blok), railed against the commercial theater as one that inclined its audience to decadence, inactivity, or pessimism[69] (shades of Plato's attack in *The Republic* on the kinds of poetry that inspire inertia, but also reminiscent of influential contemporary European thinkers such as Romain Rolland[70]). Consequently, it should be a theater of action and heroism above all.

The Bolsheviks shared with the majority of intellectuals this distaste for the cultural fare of commercial enterprises. In 1918 Kameneva, then head of the Theater Section of Narkompros, claimed with a certain naive faith that if only Narkompros worked up a "healthy repertoire," then "our competition would force the private theaters to follow suit."[71] In actuality, the commercial theaters of Petrograd were jolted more by harsh economic realities than by any competition from a "healthy repertoire." During the turmoil of 1917–1919, one after the other they began to close down because they were not making enough money. The state gave them a nudge with a 500 percent tax on theater profits that it imposed in 1918 rather than nationalize the theaters (they were nationalized anyway in 1919). But when a commercial theater closed down, usually PTO would send in a newly formed experimental theater or studio to take over the premises.[72]

Many cultural zealots, on seeing the private sector among theaters, the press, and so on so badly battered, seized their moment to demand what amounted to the eradication of commercial, lowbrow culture. Spokesmen at a Petrograd Proletcult conference of 1918, for instance, called for the abolition of all "boulevard" literature and of "the yellow press."[73] Others fingered that old *bête noire* of the theater activists, the *café chantant*.

Fortunately for the theater activists the combination of harsh economic conditions and government policies forced many a *café chantant* to close down.[74] The phantom of the cabaret and the *café chantant* resurfaced whenever conditions favored them, however, attracting not only good audiences but also opera singers and assorted other servants of high culture who were reproached in the press for demeaning themselves by moonlighting in such places.[75] It was as if the highbrow intellectuals wanted to eradicate a more successful rival for public attention.

Western commentators have focused on the Bolshevik state's repression of intellectuals. But during War Communism, while the Bolsheviks approached the issue of whether to nationalize commercial cultural institutions quite gingerly and debated the issue among themselves, several spokesmen for non-Bolshevik intelligentsia positions—particularly from the avant-garde—urged total intolerance for cultural approaches other than their own.[76]

Typical of this trend would be Adrian Piotrovsky's article "Dictatorship," published in October of 1920.[77] Piotrovsky opens with a preamble reminiscent of Lenin's famous essay of 1905 "Party Organization and Party Literature." Like Lenin, he dismisses those who quake at any infringement of creative freedom, arguing in this case that a lack of state control will only give full rein to the "petty shopkeeper" *(lavochnik)* and "man on the street" *(obyvatel')*. The article is rife with intellectual elitism as he goes on to contend that the problem with the petty shopkeeper is that he is very "superficially educated." One senses deliberate stylization after Lenin, once again, in his further contention that "either the proletariat will make art, or it will be made by the petty shopkeepers." The proletariat are as yet too weak to make their own art, and hence, in a familiar move, those who are less "superficially educated" have to step in to "show another way by force"; Soviet Russia must perforce have a "repressive policy in the arts" ("politika khudozestvennogo nasiliya"). "Let the theaters be empty," Piotrovsky asserts, "Let the philistines stay at home."[78] Here, then, we see guild megalomania melded with Bolshevik repressiveness and its doctrine of the vanguard, but the catalyst is idealism.

Certainly not all intellectuals in Petrograd were demanding a cultural dictatorship. Many favored unlimited cultural freedom. Under War Communism, however, the theater in Petrograd was run largely by would-be enlightened despots who sought to impose their highbrow or avant-garde tastes on the culture of the city.

Significantly, within the theatrical world many of the people demanding a dictatorship were themselves actual or proto-scholars who were at the same time active in the theater. This trend is particularly marked among that new generation of Meyerhold's disciples who succeeded him in Petrograd in running the Courses for the Mastery of Staging and in the experimental theater. Several of them were the sons of prominent academics who had themselves begun preparing for an academic career; they were inspired to work both for the revolutionary experimental theater and as cultural bureaucrats, but they did not abandon their scholarly interests, even though the demands of the Revolution and the cause of the new theater often led them to some fairly unscholarly pursuits. A good example would be Konstantin Derzhavin, the son of the Slavist N. S. Derzhavin. Konstantin himself later went on to be a professor at Leningrad University, but during War Communism he worked (from 1918–1920) as Secretary to the Council of TEO, and also in a series of experimental theaters where he could on occasion be seen doubling for the famous circus acrobat Serge (A. Aleksandrov).

This pattern is amply illustrated in the biographies of Piotrovsky and Radlov. Both were professors' sons: Piotrovsky was the illegitimate son of the leading classicist F. Zelinsky, and Radlov the son of a scholar of idealist and classical philosophy, Ernest L. Radlov. They—especially Radlov—moved in the highest intelligentsia circles. Radlov was married to Anna Radlova, who at that time rivaled Akhmatova for the title best female poet in Petrograd (M. Kuzmin thought Radlova the better of the two, and Akhmatova was apparently so threatened by Radlova that she would not read on the same platform[79]), while his brother N. E. Radlov was, even before the Revolution, a prominent art critic. Moreover, the artist who throughout the 1920s generally designed the sets for Radlov's productions, Valentina Khodasevich, was the adoring niece of the poet Vladislav Khodasevich, who emigrated in 1921; thanks to his connection with Gorky in emigration, Valentina was able to flit back and forth to Europe for most of the 1920s and participate in the theatrical world there, too (at one point she designed sets for Luigi Pirandello).

Piotrovsky and Radlov were not just habitués of the best intelligentsia circles; they were serious scholars in their own right. Before the Revolution both had, in addition to their association with Meyerhold, been pupils and disciples of Zelinsky himself. As such, they produced scholarly translations of classical plays and worked toward their production, activities they pursued no less ardently after the Revolution.[80] In 1919 Piotrovsky in his incarnation as classical scholar was a member of the Petrograd Formalist group OPOYaZ.[81] Yet he was also the zealot who had written the article "Dictatorship." Moreover, the two occupied a series of administrative posts in government bodies set up to oversee propagandistic cultural work, both in the civilian sector and in the Red Army and the Baltic Fleet.[82]

Plato in his *Republic* had recommended that society be governed by philosopher-kings, with their positions secured by the guardians. The theater activists of postrevolutionary Petrograd had an uncannily comparable vision for the future role they would play in society. Evreinov, Piotrovsky, and others began to talk of instituting a theatocracy.[83] But by implication this theatocracy would be led by scholar-dramatists, scholar-directors, and scholar-bureaucrats (such as Evreinov, Remizov, Radlov, Piotrovsky, and even Lunacharsky, who fits this category since he published both plays and scholarly articles). Yet they claimed for themselves the right to legislate cultural taste on behalf of the masses and in the name of the Revolution, to dictate and repress if need be, though dictatorship for Piotrovsky as a classical scholar did not have the black connotations it has in our postfascist era. Although they went through all sorts of contortions to introduce a popular, mass theater (right down to co-opting circus acrobats for theater work), they were in many respects trying to turn the clock back culturally rather than forward.

The theater activists did allow popular genres into the revolutionary theater, such as the Russian folk theater and the *commedia dell'arte,* which derives in part from the ludic popular tradition—the Roman Atellanae—and in part from classic literature. This kind of people's theater no longer represented vital popular theater, however. In the prerevolutionary years Blok and others had begun to champion the theater of the fairground tent at the very moment its popularity had gone into sharp decline in the fairground itself.

To give them their due, the theater activists were caught in a paradoxical situation. On the one hand, they wanted to revolutionize the theater and bring it closer to the masses and popular theater forms. On the other hand, they sought to eradicate the commercial theater and all vogues representing the misguided taste of the as yet not fully enlightened masses, a move that brought them perilously close to stemming the tide of theatrical evolution.

This paradox was by no means unique to the theater. The first premise of revolution is that the present is so bad it must be annihilated, and consequently its models tend to come from the past. Thus a revolution is both radical and conservative. This can be seen best in the case of another expression of the people's theater, the mass spectacle, the genre that sought to provide historical paradigms for the new age.

5

PETROGRAD: RITUAL CAPITAL
OF REVOLUTIONARY RUSSIA

In culture, there are no absolute beginnings, even when revolutions invested with messianic presumptions take place. The art that follows a revolution and that we, in retrospect, say defines it, is really a selection and elaboration of pre-existing tendencies. Nowhere is this more apparent than in the mass spectacle in revolutionary Petrograd, in those dramatic pageants staged in the city to mark the festival days of a newly instituted revolutionary ("red") calendar.

The Mass Spectacle

On November 8, 1920, at ten in the evening on the vast Palace Square in Petrograd there began what was billed as the biggest mass spectacle of all time, a re-enactment of the storming of the Winter Palace. The re-enactment was staged in celebration of the third anniversary of the Revolution, and it was directed by Nikolai Evreinov.[1] Its cast of six thousand was made up largely of members of the army and navy drama circles and even authentic army units, but it also included professional actors, ballet dancers, circus performers, and drama students. An audience of one hundred thousand is said to have gasped with dismay and cheered with delight as the fortunes of the Bolshevik faction fell and then rose again in the course of a spectacle intended to evoke strong reactions with its overwhelming scale and dramatic special effects.[2]

The spectacle opened at a point after the February Revolution of 1917 when Alexander Kerensky, the head of the Provisional Government, was at the height of his power. The Government and its supporters, the liberal bourgeoisie, huddled in interminable meetings, while the oppressed masses were in disarray. As the spectacle progressed this situation was reversed, with the supporters of the Provisional Government becoming more and more flustered while the masses, by contrast, became ever more organized and decisive, eventually forming themselves into armed detachments. Then came the October Revolution itself. Onto the square came rumbling real armored cars along with thousands of actual soldiers and sailors, converging from all corners for the final storming of the Winter Palace. The members of the Provisional Government were by now panic-stricken, and the audience was treated to a comic interlude as the circus stars who played these roles gave free reign to buffoonery and acrobatics in representing their flight before the advancing Bolsheviks. The one group that remained firm was the Women's Death Battalion, which paraded with a banner declaring, "We will win through to the Dardanelles!" a claim belied by their appearing "like characters from an operetta."

As the climax approached, Evreinov as director turned more and more to special auditory and visual effects. Fifty windows in the upper story of the palace were suddenly illuminated, and in them spectators could see a shadow play of tussling silhouettes. Shots were fired from the battleship *Aurora,* still anchored at the position from which it had fired the shot that signaled the start of the October Revolution. For two or three minutes all other sound was silenced as machine guns crackled, rifles fired, and the artillery thundered. Then, to signal the victory, a rocket was sent up, and all became silent. The pathetic figure of Kerensky was seen scurrying off dressed in women's clothing. The event broke up after a stupendous finale with a mass rendering of the "Internationale," a fireworks display, and a military parade.[3]

The Storming of the Winter Palace, with its huge cast and audience, represented the culmination of the movement for a truly mass theater, the crowning achievement of the year 1920, which saw five mass spectacles in Petrograd, all of them open-air performances like *The Storming of the Winter Palace* with casts and audiences numbering in the thousands. Petrograd was not the only city to stage mass spectacles after the Revolution, nor even the first. Many provincial cities also performed them—as, of course, did Moscow.[4] But all experts are agreed that in scale, in panache, and in the frequency with which they were produced, Petrograd's performances outdid those of all other cities. It was the ritual capital of revolutionary Russia.

Why was this role not assumed by Moscow? In fact, Moscow planned some ambitious mass festivals involving Meyerhold and others that would have rivaled those of Petrograd, but they were never realized.[5] One reason may be the fact that while Moscow might be the capital, Petrograd was the place of origin for the Revolution and could thus claim more right than any other city to hold ritual commemorations of that event. Moreover, that claim was one of the few left that might give the city status in the new society. Hence an ambitious Zinoviev (head of its Soviet and Party Committee) was probably more motivated than even his Moscow counterparts to see that such massive events were realized in his city. Petrograd was also the center of an intelligentsia infatuated by the dream of Nietzsche and others for out-door rituals of togetherness. The mass spectacle became the focus of their endeavors to smash that "sardine tin" of aesthetic-cum-social constraints; their rituals of transgression were to provide the sympathetic magic that would transform society itself.

Each of the successive spectacles of 1920 outdid its predecessors in the sheer scale of its outdoor arena and in the numbers in its cast and audience, but *The Storming of the Winter Palace* surpassed them all.[6] Evreinov, no stranger to hyperbole, boasted at the time that this mass spectacle, like the Revolution itself, had been of an unprecedented scale that would secure for it a unique place in the history of theater.[7]

The spectacles of 1920 provide, to invoke the title of Lenin's tract on Tolstoy, "a mirror of the Russian Revolution." In the story of their staging can be traced some of the contradictions between the theory and the practice of revolution, and above all the problem of how to involve in one harmo-nious "performance" (or revolution) three crucial but somehow disparate groups: the Party or state, intellectuals, and the masses.

Our image of these famous events is largely of spontaneous, iconoclastic rituals, of joyous mass celebrations of the overthrow of the old order. Such a perception of the mass spectacles has given them a special status in our imaginations as a high point of the initial years after the Revolution, a time of revolutionary idealism and millennial fervor. And this perception is not without foundation.

During the first year or so after the Revolution, there was a frenzy of cultural iconoclasm. The past was to be destroyed to make way for the new era. "Only he is a Communist," the poet Mayakovsky declared in 1918, "who has burned his bridges against defeat," and "To destroy is to create, for in destroying we overcome our past."[8] Art and culture were to be both liberated and democratized by taking them out "onto the streets," and the streets themselves, the squares and even the buildings around them, were all to be repainted.[9]

The focus of the movement to bring art "to the streets" was the theater. Its chief ideologue was Platon Kerzhentsev, a theorist of the Proletcult and national head of the telegraph agency responsible for making most of the famous Soviet revolutionary posters (ROSTA). His *Creative Theater,* with its thesis "the new art will grow outside the walls of the theater," became a sort of little red book of this movement.[10]

While Kerzhentsev in *The Creative Theater* reiterated many of the common-places of the pan-European movement for a theater of mass participation, he also gave them a utopian coloration with his theory of the "eternal studio." The new theater should, he contended, follow the "principle of amateurism."[11] Its mainstay should be the nonprofessional actors from the working classes. But although these actors should be trained and forever perfect their art, they must never become fully formed professionals, for if they did they would lose their closeness to the masses.[12] Kerzhentsev also wanted to see the division between the players and their passive spectators abolished. He predicted that in the future a member of the audience might say not "I am going to see something" but rather "I am going to participate in something."[13]

If you abstract the class bias of Kerzhentsev's theories, you find here a vision of eternal liminality and intermingling of all. In this respect, Kerzhentsev's theories are reminiscent of those of Bakhtin in his theoretical writings of the 1930s, particularly in the Rabelais book, where he discusses the notion of carnival.

Bakhtin's predilection for carnival arises out of his obsessive concern for a breakdown of borders of all kinds, a predilection very characteristic of the distinctive millenarian culture of the initial postrevolutionary years. One of the first characterizations of carnival that he provides in *Rabelais and His World* is formulated in terms of the breakdown of distinctions between stage and audience.[14] In the same formulation, Bakhtin also draws an absolute distinction between carnival and theater on the basis of universality of participation, that ideal which was so important to Kerzhentsev, too: "Carnival does not know footlights in the sense that it does not acknowledge any distinction between actors and spectators. . . . Carnival is not a spectacle seen by the people; they live in it, and everyone participates because its very idea embraces all the people."[15]

Thus for many intellectuals after the Revolution, a focus of their dreams of breaking down the boundaries between educated and uneducated, rich and poor, nation and nation, and even man and man was the carnival or mass festival in which "everyone participates" in what Kerzhentsev described as "pure joy and unrestrained merriment."[16]

But this was all in theory; the practice was somewhat other. There were, it is true, several attempts to organize some "folk carnival" (*narodnaya radost'*) on revolutionary holidays with dancing, sideshows, mummers, masks, games, and songs, but in reality neither the powers that be nor the intellectuals themselves could be content with just unfocused liminality; something more educative was required.[17] Thus the high point of the revolutionary festival became an improving theatrical production, a mass spectacle. Yet the mass spectacle was by no means viewed by theater activists as simply a propaganda vehicle; it was the apotheosis of the theater of mass participation, the ultimate in cultural iconoclasm and democratization. Adrian Piotrovsky, one of its principal directors, saw the spectacle as the ideal school for its participants, the "crowning achievement" of revolutionary cultural work which, in the "transformed" world it presented, would give the participants a "window into the future."[18] What we want, he said, is "not dressing in costume, but a transformation." ("Ne pereryazhivaniya a pererozhdeniye [rebirth!]").[19] Thus those who were directing these spectacles saw their task as not just one of putting on plays or pageants, but of making citizens. Performance was to be participation in the life of the new society.

The mass spectacles were to recapitulate or define the form of revolution. But at the same time this revolution was to be in sync with a revolution in the consciousness of the participants themselves, a revolution both aesthetic and political-cum-social. As the first such spectacle was being prepared in Petrograd, Kerzhentsev came to conduct a series of lectures explaining these ambitious aims. He delivered the lectures to a packed audience gathered in the Proletcult and including most of the principal future directors of these spectacles (Piotrovsky was particularly prominent in the debates).[20] The first of the Petrograd mass spectacles of 1920, *The Mystery of Liberated Labor* (directed by Yu. Annenkov, A. Kugel, and S. Maslovskaya), was performed for May Day on the steps of the Stock Exchange.

The Mystery of Liberated Labor presented a generalized account of the progression through the ages to the socialist utopia. The setting was dominated by a huge backdrop placed on the upper platform, above the Exchange stairs, depicting a medieval castle with large golden doors closed by a hanging lock that was meant to bar the way to the Kingdom of Freedom. According to the libretto, after a fanfare, the performance opens with a procession of various members of the exploiting classes and their retainers (such as Napoleon, a Chinese mandarin, a plantation owner, the Emperor of Byzantium, and assorted merchants) who proceed to a banquet table on the upper platform where they feast and are entertained by musicians and ballet dancers. A group of slaves in chains enter, their backs bent by their hard lives, and begin their labors at the bottom of the stairs. The two groups continue their respective occupations in a dramatic contrast of "parallel play." But suddenly, when there is a lull in the drunken bacchanalia on the upper platform, the slaves are able to hear the strains of a "heavenly music" issuing from the Kingdom of Freedom. They begin to rumble, and, successively, groups of rebels attempt to defeat their masters and reach the Kingdom of Freedom, taking the spectacle in rapid succession through a series of famous revolutions, starting with the Spartacus Revolt of 73 B.C. and culminating in the canonical revolutionary moments of the modern era: the French Revolution, the Paris Commune, and the two Russian revolutions of 1917. The victory in each uprising is short-lived as the oppressors soon exert their might to quash it. Even the great October Revolution is soon threatened by a foreign intervention and civil war. In the latter instance, however, the masses' resolve is stronger then ever before; under Bolshevik guidance, echelons of the Red Army are formed. The rebellious crowd grows ecstatic as more and more troops waving red banners appear until, in the end, the sea of red overwhelms their oppressors; the sealed gates open and all the actors freeze in an "ecstasy of victory." In the final act, the backdrop of the castle falls away to reveal a representation of the Kingdom of Freedom, in the center of which stands a huge "tree of freedom" decked out with red ribbons. The soldiers beat their weapons into plowshares and other implements of peacetime labor, and then all the peoples of the earth mingle together around the tree in a joyous round dance, and festivals of many ethnic groups are celebrated. The "mystery" is brought to a triumphal close with fireworks and a mass singing of the "Internationale."[21]

Even in this sketchy account of the libretto, one can see how several disparate agendas for theater or revolution came together. For instance, the depiction of the exploited classes as slaves echoes Lenin's general paradigm of revolution in his most recent treatise, *State and Revolution* (1917), whereby the "slaves" smash the apparatus of state oppression and drive the monied classes and their henchmen from power. At the same time, the dance around the tree at the end realizes Rousseau's iconic account of true theater (a favorite of theorists of the people's theater) figured in terms of the citizens' dancing around a pole,[22] or more specifically recapitulates the dance around the Liberty Tree, which was a core element in the festivals of the French Revolution (this particular spectacle was the one most indebted to precedents from that source).[23] But the spectacle also seems to provide a literal translation of a scenario in Nietzsche's *Birth of Tragedy* whereby the world of "appearance" and "measure" is penetrated by ever more alluring and "ecstatic tones" of "reawakened tragic music" until "the enchanted gate that leads into the Hellenic magic mountain" (which even Goethe and Schiller could not breach) opens suddenly of its own accord.[24]

Thus those who produced *The Mystery of Liberated Labor*, as with the other mass spectacles of 1920, tried to create a genealogy for the new state but inscribed it into narratives—not all of which were concerned with political revolution—that had captivated the imagination of intellectuals. In these mass spectacles they tried to overcome not only the confines of the conventional theater in their staging (in the open air) but also the confines of spatial borders and historical time.

The Mystery of Liberated Labor, though quite singular in many respects, follows a general structure to be found in all five of the mass spectacles of 1920. Each depicted a historical progression that began at a different point in time, but that charted the progressive triumph of some subjugated, oppressed group (the toilers) over its oppressors, the ruling classes, disregarding the differences between countries and historical periods. The central figure for revolution was movement in space rather than time, however. The binary opposition (oppressed / oppressors) was always represented spatially, with each group having its assigned area: for the two spectacles staged at the Stock Exchange the oppressed occupied the area at the bottom of the steps, their oppressors the top, while for *The Storming of the Winter Palace,* following a convention of many earlier revolutionary dramas of mass participation held indoors,[25] the oppressors (the Provisional Government and their ilk) occupied a specially constructed stage situated, appropriately enough, on the right-hand side of the Palace Square, while the oppressed masses and Bolsheviks occupied another on the left. Each mass spectacle also utilized a third, intermediate area (a bridge, a corridor, or a flight of steps between the two spaces) where the two parties in conflict met for their tussles. The moment of triumph for the oppressed was represented by their permanent occupation of the space of their oppressors.

Here we find a major difference between the Russian spectacles and those of the French Revolution. Most of the recent analysts of the French spectacles have stressed that their locus was the free and open space outside of town. Even when there was a progression through town, generally the classic sites were avoided. There was a distinct bucolic element in the choreography (emphasis on plants and greenery, on fecundity and the life cycle) as a guarantee of liberation from oppression. But in the major Russian mass spectacles the very sites chosen (the Palace Square, the Stock Exchange) were homologous with the ritual enacted, and they proclaimed that the new regime had occupied the central sites of hegemonic forces, the government and the rentier-mercantilist classes.[26]

Thus the mass spectacle essentially involved a ritual enactment of transgression, of that crossing of borders that Bakhtin had so loved and Bely and so many others hungered for. Whether choreographed as a vertical or a horizontal progression, the transgression was of the low onto the territory of the high. This same move became a paradigm of revolutionary epiphany for much of Soviet culture to come. Its impact can be seen particularly in films. For instance, in Eisenstein's *The Battleship Potemkin* (1925) the famous massacre on the Odessa steps was arguably a parody of the movement of the oppressed classes up the stairs of the Petrograd Stock Exchange in *The Mystery of Liberated Labor* (and the later spectacle *For A World Commune*).[27] Indeed, the entire film can be analyzed in terms of the conventions of the mass spectacle and its binary structure.[28]

The progress of the revolutionary movement was represented not just in spatial terms; in general it was motivated more on a symbolic level than by laws of historical causation. After all, the mass spectacle was a pageant and did not, as in a drama, have much scope for reasoned dialogue (which could in any case not be carried far enough in the open air), although it was not just practical considerations that mitigated against extensive verbalizing in this intensely anti-logocentric time. The symbols used were primarily visual and auditory. For instance, the spread of the red flag, handed from worker to worker, or passed on like a baton from revolutionary movement to revolutionary movement, became the principal motivation for the growth of revolutionary consciousness.

The basic division into oppressors and oppressed in these spectacles was not just into two sets of spatial, visual, and auditory symbols, but also into two dramatic modes. The representation of the oppressed was initially realistic, although the oppression was exaggerated to heighten the pathos, but it became ever more elevated as the spectacle progressed. For scenes involving the oppressors, however, the mode was satiric or grotesque. In them, the audience was usually entertained by buffoonery, especially when the ruling classes made their inept attempts at resisting the rebels. For such scenes, directors used the techniques of the *commedia dell'arte* and the circus. In other words, they followed the tradition of the prerevolutionary experimental theater of Meyerhold or Evreinov, which many of the directors of the mass spectacles had themselves continued in the early postrevolutionary years.[29]

The heavy stylization and exacting demands of *commedia dell'arte* acting meant that the binary extended to a total division among participants in a mass spectacle. Those playing the oppressors were professional actors, ballet dancers, or circus people, while the oppressed were the semitrained masses from the worker or army drama circles, or even completely untrained enlisted men. Those playing the oppressors had more individual roles, were more lively and entertaining, had elaborate costumes, and even on occasion wore papier-mâché masks.[30] Those playing the oppressed, by contrast, tended to act only in group scenes, usually wore just ragged, grey costumes or drab military uniforms (their color derived from their red flags), and were never made up. Thus, even though the representatives of the oppressor classes were, so to speak, the bad guys, and had to be unceremoniously defeated and evicted from the stage at the end, if one compares the two groups from the point of view of theatricality the bad guys were the privileged ones—the reverse of the pattern in Mayakovsky's *Mystery-Bouffe*. These mass spectacles were meant to be homogenizing rituals, yet in a way they enacted the very differences between the cultured and the uncultured that they were intended to transcend.

This basic opposition in the spectacle amounts to more than just a matter of mode. It reflects the spectacles' dual function as both a celebration of iconoclasm and a ritual legitimization of the status quo. Most mass spectacles began as a celebration of the destruction of the old order. Indeed, one could view their satiric and grotesque sections as a sort of ritual purging on the part of the intelligentsia of the old mercantilist-rentier culture they so despised.

When, however, in the mass spectacle the boundaries between low and high in the social order were transgressed, there was no comparable transgression in the area of culture. On the country, the clash between the positive and the negative camps was played out in terms of high and low musical taste; that the exploiters opted for the low (or poorly executed) was the surest sign that they should be supplanted. The class war was conventionally represented as a duel in music: for *The Mystery of Liberated Labor,* the oppressed classes' signature tune was Chopin's funeral march, while for their oppressors it was gypsy music, but the "heavenly" music issuing from the Kingdom of Freedom was Wagner's "Lohengrin," which ultimately triumphed over the gypsy music; for *The Storming of the Winter Palace* there was a duel between the "Marseillaise" (used to represent the Provisional Government), which was played progressively out of tune, and the "Internationale," which drowned out the sounds of the "Marseillaise" in the end.

The highbrow prejudices that inform these spectacles are most strongly felt in *The Mystery of Liberated Labor,* where the group of what the libretto calls "oppressors from all times and all peoples" are depicted from the point of view of an intellectual puritan. The libretto stipulates that various among them should be overweight, drunken, and show signs of "debauchery, depravity, and lechery." Prominent among the oppressors is the so-called king of the Stock Exchange, whose face shows an "intellectual obtuseness and naked greed" and out of whose coat pocket there sticks a large bottle of spirits. The group feasts away in a drunken bacchanalia, for they are anyway indifferent to the heavenly music coming from the Kingdom of Freedom. Their tastes are low-to-middlebrow and oriented toward entertainment rather than culture; they prefer gypsy music (Viennese waltzes in *For a World Commune*) to Chopin and Wagner! Their retinue of retainers, characterized as "parasites and unprincipled servants of capital," a group comparable with that of the Lumpenproletariat in Marx's *Eighteenth Brumaire* in which are lumped "the artist, scholar, priest, soldier, sailor, prostitute, entertainer, musician, magician, and satirist," pamper to the oppressors' execrable cultural tastes, which are quintessentially expressed as they "dance around the throne of the bourgeois in a servile cancan"—the fare of the *café chantant* and the dance particularly despised by Wagner.[31] We see here that equation of sexual transgression and cultural impurity that was so frequently part of the intellectuals' call to arms against mercantilist culture.

This modal binarism meant that the spectacle accommodated both sides of an important division among theater activists before the Revolution— those who, like Meyerhold, wanted grotesque theater and those who saw the regenerated theater as providing monumental and mystical rites— "mysteries," as in the title of the first mass spectacle. The iconoclastic or purging function weakened as a given spectacle progressed, however, and the second function—that of affirming the status quo—took the ascendant. An important dividing line occurred at the moment the Red Army first appeared on stage, a moment generally accompanied by the lighting up of a red star on high or in the East and other such symbolic fanfare.

By the finale, the spectacle's most ritualized moment, all traces of the satiric or grotesque had disappeared and the tone ascended into one of elation. Fireworks were ignited and an attempt was made to break down the gulf between actor and spectator in a mass rendering of the "Internationale," generally by audience and actors together. Often there was a military parade as well, with the troops mingling with the audience by marching among them. The best-achieved example of the bonding military parade is to be found in the fourth of the five mass spectacles, an abridged version of *For a World Commune*. This one was sponsored by the Army Reserves and was staged before new recruits in a natural amphitheater at their base in Krasnoselsk, outside Petrograd, the aim being to prepare the recruits by means of this "audio-visual aid" for their imminent military operations against the Polish. Since the audience was made up entirely of the military, its members joined the soldier-actors for the parade at the finale, leaving no one among the spectators. Then truly could Kerzhentsev have claimed that the audience could say not "I came to see the spectacle," but "I went to participate in the spectacle."

But how much like a "carnival" was this kind of mass spectacle? To what extent do these occasions really represent spontaneous iconoclastic rituals or joyous mass celebrations? René Fülöp-Miller in his contemporaneous account of these spectacles has described them in fact in quite the opposite terms—as joyless events, totally mechanical in their execution, and in which the impersonal mass has triumphed.[32]

In reality, these spectacles were neither particularly spontaneous nor totally joyless and mechanical. The mass spectacle was not the child of October, but had been a feature of both Russian and Western theatrical life over the preceding decades. It had been used primarily to reinforce the status quo through the patriotic historical drama or a pageant celebrating the founding of a city. In America, where it was particularly popular earlier in the twentieth century, it was called the civic theater.

In fact in 1916 as Yale was celebrating its bicentenary, there were—Evreinov take note—more people gathered on the green in the shadow of its ivy-covered walls to act out a mass spectacle celebrating "for God, for country, and for Yale"—7,000 in fact—than were to gather on the Palace Square four years later in 1920 to stand for Bolshevism, Soviet power, and Lenin (incidentally, Kerzhentsev cited the Yale spectacle as a possible model for the Bolsheviks in *The Creative Theater*).[33] But Imperial Russia had been active in this area, too. For instance, in 1912 A. Ya. Alekseyev-Yakovlev had staged a mass spectacle about Yermak's conquest of Siberia which proved so successful that the following August he put on *The Fall of Azov* on a lake in a Petersburg park intended to "illuminate in the minds of the working people some moments from Russian history." This spectacle attracted an audience—at 194,000, considerably larger than the 100,000 who came to see *The Storming of the Winter Palace*.[34] Radlov must have remembered these successes because when he came to stage *The Blockade of Russia* (also on a lake in a park) he used Alekseyev-Yakovlev as a consultant.[35] Indeed, after the February Revolution the same combination as later staged *The Storming of the Winter Palace*—Evreinov as director and Yu. Annenkov as artistic director—worked on a mass spectacle in celebration of the French Revolution.[36]

In revolutionary Russia, the aim of the mass spectacle as centerpiece of the theater of mass participation was to relive the Revolution, but the Revolution meant two contradictory things. It meant, on the one hand, *the moment* in a status quo–affirming myth of origins, and thus the Revolution was comparable to, for instance, the founding of the city, a favorite subject in American civic theater. On the other hand, it meant an iconoclastic act. Thus the directors of a mass spectacle of 1920 sought both to relive the very moment of historical revolution (hence, for instance, a reenactment of the actual storming of the Winter Palace) and to revive the pathos of revolution, its élan, and its collectivist, iconoclastic spirit. But the Revolution was already three years old in 1920.

Theoreticians like Kerzhentsev might have inspired intellectuals to seek to realize a "festival of pure joy and boundless merriment" by staging spectacles in which thousands of nonprofessional actors from workers' clubs would improvise together, but this ideal eluded implementation. Doubtless, *The Storming of the Winter Palace* was more perfectly executed in 1920 than it had been in 1917, and yet it was less "revolutionary" and some of the spontaneity and pathos were lost. The actual directors of the mass spectacle subscribed to a vision of its function in the future society that was no less utopian than Kerzhentsev's, but they believed at the same time that a mass spectacle demands above all control and planning. As Piotrovsky concluded, "You cannot have a ritual without regimentation."[37]

The mass spectacles were regimented—highly organized and virtually militarized. They were organized by special troikas and committees set up for this purpose, some by the military, some by the local Soviets, some by the Provincial Department of Political Enlightenment (Gubpolitprosvet).[38] Indeed, presentations of mass spectacles in the West reached their height during World War I largely because it was only in wartime conditions that it was possible to mobilize the huge numbers of people, transportation, and so forth required.[39] Similarly, the peak period for mass spectacles in revolutionary Russia was that moment when the Civil War in European Russia was winding down, when the troops were less engaged at the front, but before they were demobilized.

Piotrovsky himself developed a system for organizing all the participants in spectacles into groups of ten arranged in an elaborate pyramid structure at the apex of which stood the directors, who were situated physically apart from the actors. Radlov, his usual co-director, ecstatically recalled in a later article how he directed operations by telephone so that a mere press of the button or brief command over the wires would unleash an attack by thousands or a barrage of canon fire; he called this, in an obvious allusion to Lenin's panacea for the backwardness of Russia, "the electrification of the theater."[40] But this also meant the directorization of theatricality.

Thus the mass spectacle may have been a theater without footlights, but it was certainly not a theater without telephone lines. It may have represented the democratization of the theater in that the masses and the professional actor alike participated in it, but this democratization was illusory, for the god-director, invisible to the spectator and set apart from the actors, directed every movement on the stage, almost as the puppeteer pulls the strings for his puppets. Piotrovsky had demanded in an article of that year "dictatorship" in the theater, and in a sense his ideal had been realized.

It was, however, not just the need for organization that threatened the revolutionary nature of the mass spectacle. One also has to question how iconoclastic its function really was. Essentially, the intellectuals who staged these spectacles wanted less to "destroy the past" than to replace one set of cultural myths from it with a new set, which happened to come largely from the past, too. The mass spectacle was an exercise in creating a new identity for the nation by reference to past models.

The New Historical Paradigms

In 1913 there had been rival accounts of the past, but in Petersburg liberal intellectuals saw Russia's identity primarily in terms of a tradition established by Peter the Great for secularizing, modernizing, and Europeanizing Russia. Proponents of these values frequently singled out the Neoclassical or Empire style in architecture as emblematic of them. Thus Russia's cultural identity implicitly stretched back to ancient Greece.

For the Bolsheviks, however, the primary historical referents, or great ages in the past to be resurrected in greater glory through their revolutionary work, were more recent and French—the French Revolution and the Paris Commune of 1871. Of the two French revolutions, the first had been the greater source of models for those who staged the mass spectacles. Indeed, the very fact that the storming of the Winter Palace was singled out as the iconic moment for the mass spectacle is symptomatic of this. This storming had not in fact been either the most climactic or the most heroic moment in the 1917 Revolution, but it lent itself to becoming *the* moment because it could be seen as Russia's analogue to the storming of the Bastille (it is of course also true that practical considerations led to the choice of the vast Palace Square as a site for mass spectacles). However, Marx, Engels, and Lenin had singled out the Paris Commune as the great harbinger of future revolution because, in their view, the Commune was the embodiment of the principle of the dictatorship of the proletariat; the French Revolution, dramatic and laudable as it was, was still only a bourgeois revolution.[41] At this time, however, Bolshevik accounts of the Paris Commune did not always stress the aspects of class struggle and dictatorship. In more leftist formulations of Marxism-Leninism, including even Lenin's own *State and Revolution* of 1917, the commune as the city controlled by the Soviet became a symbol for participatory democracy by the masses and as such was clearly a precedent for the movement for a theater of mass participation.

For most Russian intellectuals, however, the true genealogy of the mass spectacle extended back in time beyond the Paris Commune, the French Revolution, and even the writings of Jean Jacques Rousseau, which had inspired much of the cultural work of the first French Revolution (Rousseau as refracted through the recent works of Romain Rolland and Julien Thiersot that had influenced the Russians' work on their own spectacles).[42] It began in ancient Greece. The open-air theater of Greece had been an ideal for Rousseau, and a point of reference for those who organized the festivals of the French Revolution as well as for Nietzsche and for many of the theater activists. As these disparate sources suggest, there were many "Greeces."

Since well before the Revolution, Russian intellectuals had been in the grip of a Greek revival that had swept Europe in the late nineteenth and early twentieth centuries. One need only recall the figure of Isadora Duncan, who in bare feet and Greek tunic captivated audiences in the salons of Europe—and Russia. Nowhere was the Greek ideal more often a referent than in writings about the mass spectacle, which was interpreted as a veritable reincarnation of the Greek theater in that performances were in the open air and used masks and a chorus. In revolutionary Russia, Nietzsche's followers seized on the open-air Greek theater as a place where all classes might commune in harmony and have the ecstatic or mystical experience of the Dionysian rite. It might seem incongruous or foolhardy to impose this open-air Greek ideal in Petrograd, where the summers are so short and the winters so severe, but if Petersburg had long been declared the Venice of the North, why should it not become the Athens, too?

It was not so much the superficial trappings of the Greek theater, such as the tunics, that theatrical directors sought to revive—that was in fact done more in the spectacles of the French Revolution. Rather, they wanted to revive a distinctive ethos that they saw as vital, but now lost. This ethos included a true sense of community, and the subordination of the individual to the common good, as well as the emphasis on mass participation. These values more or less coincided with those of the Bolsheviks. Indeed, Bolshevik intellectuals sometimes invoked ancient Athens and the Hellenic as models for the Communist ethos, although, as was also true of the French revolutionaries, their model from the classical era was more often Sparta.

Actually, those who ran the various mass spectacles of 1920 were quite variegated in their backgrounds. For example, Dmitry Tyomkin, or "Comrade Tyomkin," of the Petrograd Military District's troika for organizing mass agitation among the soldiers was a graduate of the Petersburg Conservatory. A director of both *The Mystery of Liberated Labor* and *The Storming of the Winter Palace,* he is perhaps better known to us (in his postemigration phase) as the composer of music for such films as *Tales from the Vienna Woods*—with its Strauss Waltzes!—and that great spectacle of American national myth *High Noon.* In general, however, members of the teams that ran these spectacles represented one of three orientations. On the one hand, there were artists associated with the Neoclassical revival, such as M. Dobuzhinsky, I. A. Fomin, and V. A. Shchuko. In fact, Fomin created on Stone Island (renamed the Island of Marvels) a new amphitheater for mass spectacles stylized along classical Greek lines.[43] On the other, there were theater directors of the Meyerhold or Evreinov schools, including N. V. Petrov, N. V. Soloviev, Yu. Annenkov, S. Radlov, A. Piotrovsky, and Evreinov himself.

The most consistently represented group, however, was those who saw their own work as recapturing some version of Hellas. In fact even Evreinov—not himself a disciple of anyone, to be sure—was at about the time he was preparing *The Storming of the Winter Palace* at work on his own scholarly writings, in which he investigated the origins of Greek tragedy in the satyr play, an issue that had become important in the wake of Nietzsche's writings.[44] Sergei Radlov and Adrian Piotrovsky, though former disciples of Meyerhold who now ran an extremely popular experimental theater in Petrograd, were at the same time disciples of the principal local guru of the Nietzschean revival, Faddey Zelinsky, an extremely popular and influential professor of Classics at Petrograd University.[45] When Isadora Duncan came to Petersburg to dance in 1913, it was Zelinsky who introduced her performances. He had also been, since before the Revolution, the leader of a movement to revive the Greek theater in open-air performances for the populace and the moving force behind the journal *Hermes,* the movement's mouthpiece. Piotrovsky and Radlov themselves contributed to *Hermes,* translated Greek plays, and pursued their interests in classical scholarship. And yet these zealots of Greek revival were the most active of all in the agitational theater, writing and directing both mass dramas and mass spectacles, training Red Army and Navy recruits to act and direct, writing about the spectacles, and serving on various bodies set up to oversee mass propaganda. Piotrovsky directed the Krasnoselsk mass spectacle, which was overwhelmingly military and propagandistic.

It would be tempting to assume that this apparent split personality—serving scholarship and culture, on the one hand, and the Party's propaganda effort on the other—resulted from the necessity of earning enough to

keep starvation at bay in these extraordinary times, or responding to political pressures, while the scholarship and work in the regular theater represented Radlov and Piotrovsky's true vocation. But both these directors actually believed they were getting closer to the spirit of their beloved Hellenic
Greece with their work on the mass spectacles than they could with any
translation of actual Greek texts. Their ideal was not to revive Greece, per se,
but to found a greater "Greece" than had been achieved in antiquity.

An article by Piotrovsky of November 7, 1920 (on the eve of the reenactment of the storming of the Winter Palace), catches the pathos of their vision
of a transhistorical ethos, unbounded by time and space. Piotrovsky talks in
extravagant terms, in some respects reminiscent of the later rhetoric of High
Stalinism, about the "New Man" who is "slowly being born" in "a new generation of the October Revolution that speaks with a loud voice and has a
vision that knows no bounds and a will that cannot be broken. It is a generation of giants who breach the abysses of timelessness to join forces with their
forebears in Greece [and the Renaissance]." "The twenty-fifth of October,"
he declares, "has given the world back Aeschylus and the Renaissance. It
has given birth to a generation with Aeschylus' fiery soul."[46]

Piotrovsky and Radlov's sense of mission can be seen in one of their first
collaborative projects in the Soviet theater, a play entitled *The Battle of
Salamis*, which they wrote together for schoolchildren, drawing on sources
from Herodotus, Thucydides, and Aeschylus, and which Radlov directed in
1919.[47] The authors declared that their aim in staging this play was to work
for a theater of the future. They were eager for the young to learn from the
"talking past," but of course they wanted a particular lesson to be learned
from the story of the battle, which they saw as "the triumph of spiritual
forces over the material"—in other words, they reversed here the Bolshevik
order of priorities. The play showed its audience "the struggle of Hellenism
against the brute power of the Persians," and later "the awakening of consciousness in Hellas as a cradle of culture."[48] *The Battle of Salamis*, then,
though not a mass spectacle, was comparable with one in that it was a play
about a great historical time. And like a mass spectacle, it showed the necessity of battle in preserving a superior civilization.

We might see in the revolutionary mass spectacle incongruity between its
iconoclastic and its military-cum-ceremonial elements, but this incongruity
did not exist in the eyes of directors like Radlov and Piotrovsky, for whom
the two elements were integral, if distinct, parts of the whole. The informing
model that inspired these two, and many other theater reformers in these
years, can be sensed in Piotrovsky's remarks from an article of September
1920 entitled "The Artist and His Patron." Here he makes the claim that both

ancient Athens and the Renaissance did not know the distinction between the poet and the masses, for then the artist "knew well his social value as he fulfilled the orders of his people." "Such an artist," Piotrovsky continues, "knew his place within the walls of his city. And the city gave its artist all the inspiration of its collective heart, together with all the many and varied resources and manpower needed for decorating the city's festivals. The wise patron and the responsive artist were the enabling antithesis of all the creative epochs in the history of art." But—and this is Piotrovsky's particular version of the fall from wholeness—"the philistinism of the last century transferred the center of power from the town hall to the stock exchange and substituted commerce for art so that ordering a piece of art became a matter of buying a ready-made [shades of Benjamin]."[49]

The ideal that informed so much of the artistic activity in civil war Petrograd, then, was that of a hermetic city-state in which artists were at one with their government—a polis—Petropolis, if you will, as the city had so often been called over the past decade by intellectuals inspired by a Hellenic ideal. The city was seen as united against the philistines, the uncultured ones (as the Athenians had been united against the "crude" Persians at Salamis). These philistines would sully the city's purity and unity with the rentier-mercantilist spirit; they would degrade its fine culture with those "servile cancans." The great ages of the past such as ancient Greece and the Renaissance had featured city-states like Athens, Venice, and Florence. Petrograd, as a "commune," was in the eyes of these intellectuals a sort of modern, socialistic version of the old city-state. The next step—the move to a world commune—would entail expanding that model to embrace the entire world.

In the meantime, Petropolis was a besieged city, an island surrounded by a sea of marauding mercantilist forces who threatened it. That is, in effect, the meaning of the Civil War, the Foreign Intervention, and the Blockade. The defense of the polis takes on crucial importance, as it does in so many utopian works. Thus military maneuvers in the mass spectacle are not a concession to the powers that be but rather an ineluctable aspect of the genre.

Of course the ideal city or polis that the Petrograd intellectuals had in mind is not really a civil state in the sense that the entire rationale for its being is aesthetic rather than at all practical. In 1920 Piotrovsky called for establishing a "theatocracy."[50] One senses the dead hand of Nietzsche in these ideals except, of course, that when Nietzsche's Zarathustra wanted aesthetic or intellectual sustenance he would take himself away from the city and into the "thin air" of a mountain wilderness.

There was no lack of "thin air" in the myth of Petropolis. The grit, the smoke, and the bustle of Russia's industrial capital and major port evaporated in that vision. The image of Greece and the Renaissance on which it was based was illusory. Piotrovsky and company would fain keep commerce out of their city and yet the model cities they chose as historical paradigms' very might and power as patrons of the arts were a function of it; surely the Peloponnesian war and the battle of Salamis were less about a struggle between the civilized and the philistines—which the Persians were far from being anyway and Piotrovsky as a classical scholar must have known that—than they were about a struggle for trade advantage.

The ideal that inspired those who directed the mass spectacles of revolutionary Petrograd did not derive from the actual Greek polis, but rather from a German dream of Greek wholeness, which they had found in Nietzsche and other German thinkers popular at the time, but more directly in the works of Zelinsky and Vyacheslav Ivanov, both of whom were German-trained. More than a hundred years of German scholarship had celebrated the idea of the Greeks as the last whole society. Just as Hegel believed that we have fallen into a period of alienation and must regain wholeness (the kind of historical analysis taken up by Dostoevsky and others who saw it as Russia's unique mission to restore it), the directors of the mass spectacle were inspired by the dream of a renewed *Einheit*, a cosmic reunification, in which the people, the artists, and their patrons would be at one again and all would participate in the commmon weal. The Bolshevik slogan "All Power to the Soviets" takes on new meaning here as a dream of the people taking over the city again.

The mass spectacle was an attempt to find an analogue for the epic or tragedy in Greek society. It was to involve a mythicization of the great bonding events in the lives of the people—even of all people. The spectacle presented, in capsule version, a "living" account of the history of these events culminating in the moment when the people reclaimed the city. Thus *The Storming of the Winter Palace* represents the storming, by the people, of the citadel of an alien, bourgeois state. The myth of Petersburg, the teachings of Nietzsche and Wagner, and Lenin's *State and Revolution* all came together for a glorious finale.

Tatlin's Monument

The November 7th anniversary in Petrograd in 1920 marks the height of revolutionary utopianism in the period of War Communism. Not only was *The Storming of the Winter Palace* staged, a climax of the movement for a people's theater, but the model and designs for Tatlin's Monument to the Third International were put on display as well. This monument was never built (the feasibility of its design was questioned by engineers from the very beginning), but throughout the 1920s (and to a lesser extent since) it has functioned among Constructivists and other avant-gardists, both in Russia and at places such as the Bauhaus in Germany, as the icon of revolutionary avant-gardism.

Tatlin's Monument, familiarly known as his "tower," was a megastructure of iron and glass in which three huge glass geometric volumes, stacked one on the other, were cased in a complex system of iron vertical pivots and spirals that thrust up at an acute angle from the ground. The glass volumes were all to rotate, but each at a different speed. The lowest one, a cube, was intended for legislative use and was to complete one rotation per year; it was to house conferences of the International, and other large legislative meetings. The middle one, a pyramid, which was to complete one rotation per month, was intended for use by executive and administrative bodies of the International. The highest glass volume, a cylinder, was to complete one rotation per day and was to function as a center for information and agitation; it was to include a news bureau, a newspaper, publishing offices that would put out proclamations, brochures, and manifestoes, a telegraph, a projector for a large screen, and a radio station whose antennae would rise above the monument.[51]

Superficially, Tatlin's tower and the mass spectacles of 1920 might seem to represent different series. The spectacles were an event in theater while the tower was an event in art and architecture. The spectacles were clearly influenced by Nietzsche and Wagner, and proclaimed a lineage that stretched from ancient Greece to the present, but Tatlin's tower was intended to break with such traditions. Nikolai Punin, one of its principal champions and a head of IZO, its sponsor, proclaimed in a pamphlet published at the time to explicate the tower's significance that such a revolutionary venture could only appear then because, with the overthrow of the bourgeoisie, the classical tradition of figural statuary and the Renaissance have been reduced to "ashes" and "the charred ruins of Europe are only now being cleared."[52]

In terms of the major concerns here, however, the mass spectacle and the tower can be seen as closely related because both these products of revolutionary utopianism entail the sacerdotalization of space and highly ritualized movement through it. It could be said that Tatlin's tower derives its inspiration from the mass spectacle or even provides a way to make that spectacle permanent.

Tatlin's tower represents a new concept of the monument not just in the sense that it is nonfigural. In the first flush of iconoclasm after the Revolution, the old tsarist statues had been pulled down and replaced with avant-gardist ones, but these were still statues in the conventional sense of objects of contemplation intended to remind the contemplator of some historicopolitical or aesthetic value. Tatlin, however, like the directors of the mass spectacle (and the movement for a peoples' theater), broke down the boundary separating "viewing subject" from "work of art" so that the subject could penetrate beyond that boundary into a special space (art). Punin in his pamphlet said, in a formulation that could be taken as a virtual paraphrase of the views of Piotrovsky and others on the role of art in the polis, "The monument must live the sociopolitical life of the city and the city must live in the monument."[53] Also, both the mass spectacle and the tower use a hierarchical pattern of spaces; in the case of the mass spectacle, the highest stage is the space of the oppressors that the mob occupies, but in the case of the tower it is the space of agitation, or in other words of new-age art.

In Punin's account of the tower, one finds notions of purification of space and transcending the profane, which were so defining of intellectual ventures at this time. He insists that the fact that the inner structures of the tower are of glass "signifies the purity of their initiatives, which have been freed of any material dead weight."[54] Punin interprets the spiral, the tower's principal figure of the modules' steel casing, as "the line of movement of a liberated mankind. It is the ideal expression of emancipation; it rears from the ground, escapes from the world, and rises as if a beacon dispelling all that which is motivated by the bestial and mundane or self-serving toadyism."[55] As such, it transcends the spirit of "petty-bourgeois life," providing a "liberated life [that] rises above the earth, above the humdrum, materialistic world" (with its shops and so forth).[56] In this respect, of course, the tower project also participates in the dreams of the perceptual millenarians and other Russian visionaries of "leaving all" and going out into space.[57]

Tatlin's tower can be seen as a belated expression of the "campaign against Paris" that the members of the Petersburg group Union of Youth (to which Tatlin then belonged) undertook circa 1913. It is patently conceived against the Eiffel Tower, which had, until that point, functioned as an icon of avant-gardism and architectural *épatage*. Tatlin's tower was to be much larger than the Eiffel Tower, but it also had the potential of a perverse antimonument that resisted being symmetrical or vertical (as the Eiffel Tower is); it was to be placed at some arbitrary angle to the ground, though some have interpreted its placing as suggesting a telescope strained on the heavens or a rocket launcher.

Thus Tatlin's tower presents the paradox of monumental antimonumentalism. Of course, had the principles of its creation been adopted as canonical (as Tatlin, Punin, and others hoped at the time), the paradox would have been resolved. The utopianism of the project consists not just in its possible lack of feasibility, but also in the way it was originally conceived without a specific location. Tatlin was not sure whether it would be erected in Moscow, or Petrograd, or elsewhere, and it was only after he received a commission that it became a monument specifically for the Third International with a probable site in Petrograd. He also toyed with the idea that in Petrograd it might span the Neva River; as it were, he would be outdoing Peter in taming wild nature with culture.

The tower was a monument to and for revolution in culture and stands from our present perspective as both a *summa* and an end of revolutionary utopianism. It is important to note that the basic pattern of movement anticipated in the project is not the centrifugal dash *out*, the smashing of bounds, but rather the movement *in* to an enclosed space (no matter how transparent), and its rhythms (revolutions in the original sense) are to be absolutely regular. In this respect, the tower points the way forward to Constructivism—whose icon it became—and to the patterns of spatial movement that were defining of the next phase in the development of Soviet culture.

6

NEP AND THE
"ART OF CAPITULATION"

In the Spring of 1922, a new magazine of the avant-garde, *Veshch'/Gegenstand/Objet* (the Object), edited by El Lissitzky and I. Ehrenburg, began publishing out of Berlin. The journal was intended to realize the quixotic dream nurtured by the left artists under the Blockade that they could found an international avant-garde in the arts: although on its pages articles in Russian predominated, some were in French or German, and there were contributions from some leading Western intellectuals as well, including Le Corbusier. The lead article in its initial issue, under the banner title "The Blockade of Russia Is Ending," proclaimed the principles of the Constructivist movement and anticipated a new phase in the avant-garde's history.[1] Yet there were signs in its articles that the journal arose less out of new beginnings than out of the threat of endings.

In the next issue, under the title "The Rear Guard Triumphant," the main editorial noted with some bitterness the recent rise in Russia of an "art of capitulation." During the last year, it claimed, there had been a sudden and major shift *(perelom)* in Soviet culture: state art had been killed, so-called academic art (such as the World of Art set and the Moscow Arts Theater) now flourished under "bourgeois" patronage. The proletariat had not been able to develop their own style, and the main emphasis was now on the reactionary peasant, on an art that was "narrowly nationalistic," "superficially religious," and "traditional." The new art of capitulation was said to reflect the aesthetic tastes and lazy preference for accessibility of that favorite bugbear of intellectuals, the petty entrepreneur. The deplorable decline was epitomized in a formulation quoted from an article of that year by Piotrovsky: "We had Shakespeare in January, but got the *café chantant* in December."[2]

Of course what had happened between January and December of 1921 was that a New Economic Policy (NEP) had been introduced in March that permitted the return of limited private enterprise. In cultural life, NEP policies translated into the return of private publishing houses, theaters—and *cafés chantants*. Because market forces were given play once more, the NEP period, which stretched from 1921 until around 1927 when the shift to a planned, state-monopoly economy was announced, has often been seen in the West as ushering in a period of relative cultural pluralism, something closer to "normal" Western intellectual life, and hence a good time.[3] It should not be forgotten, however, that Glavlit, the principal Soviet censorship agency through the late 1980s, was founded in June 1922. Indeed, recent findings suggest that the state was more interventionist in the area of culture—through censorship and other means such as interfering in paper allocation—than was previously believed.[4] Some historians have even seen 1921 not as a turn to pluralism but as the death date for the great prerevolutionary cultural flowering that did not survive the witches' cauldron into which all the contradictory forces of prerevolutionary Russia were plunged in the Revolution and its aftermath.[5] Ironically, the sense that all was lost in 1921 was also felt at the time by some revolutionary zealots who saw the market as a devil incarnate and simply could not accept the betrayal of NEP; some writers left the Party in protest.

By no means should all changes that occurred in these years be attributed to NEP. It was not even really the case that in culture NEP represents a single period; a significant shift occurred around 1924-1925 (see Chapter 8). Although it is true that, for instance, several of the relatively modest private publishing houses in Petrograd that were established as a result of NEP policies made significant contributions to intellectual life, the majority of them existed in little more than name.[6]

Private publishing houses came into existence at a time when most intellectuals could not afford to buy books; the price of books in Petrograd had just gone up 300 percent,[7] and during NEP publishing costs, paper shortages, unemployment among intellectuals, and heavy taxation ensured that they progressively dwindled and were effectively eliminated well before the Plan began.[8] Moreover, "freedom" had its flip side, which is implicitly mentioned in the *Veshch'* lament—massive withdrawal of state subsidies. NEP saw tremendous unemployment among intellectuals; by July of 1923 the local branch of Sorabis (the Union of Cultural Workers) was reporting that sixteen hundred of its members were out of work.[9]

Elsewhere, I have characterized the NEP period as the era of "quiet revolution" in the sense that, by contrast with the superficially more revolutionary period of War Communism, it saw a fundamental shift in the patterns and personnel of intellectual life, a shift that extended even to the characteristic genres.[10] New faces came to dominate the cultural scene, along with new literary groupings and new institutions; most of those groups that had been prominent under War Communism, while generally not disbanded as yet, were no longer the groups of the hour.[11] Not all these changes proved enduring,[12] but what emerged during the 1930s as Stalinist culture was largely prefigured at this time (although its contours are more evident ex post facto than they were in the 1920s).

NEP played no small part in precipitating this shift. With so many state subsidies cut, the house of cards that such powerful patrons as Gorky had set up for the intellectual community began to fall. When citizens had to pay more to see plays, buy books and newspapers, and so on, many theaters and periodicals closed down virtually overnight. In addition, as Narkompros's budget was cut drastically, and as most of the soldiers were demobilized and the need for a mass cultural effort among them diminished, many of the committees on which the intellectual mandarins sat were closed or superseded by new committees. Such events effected a reshuffling of the cultural power structure.

The Party and Komsomol now began to play a more direct role as funders and overseers—patrons—within culture (except in scholarship, where state institutions still played the decisive role). The Party leadership did not direct Soviet cultural life, although some members (Trotsky, Nikolai Bukharin) began to pronounce on it more often. But during NEP the Party functioned increasingly as the body that intellectuals petitioned (see Chapter 8), while the Komsomol emerged as the principal patron of proletarian cultural endeavors.

The *Veshch'* editorial's analysis of who was to be the winner in this shift around 1921 and who was to be the loser was a little premature. The movement the journal favored, Constructivism, was not to lose out as it feared but would dominate Soviet architecture and the applied arts for the rest of the decade, while the triumph of peasant culture was short-lived.[13] But its author was not wrong in concluding that 1921 had seen a major shift in Soviet cultural life; that shift could be characterized very loosely in terms of another of the victors it nominated, academic art.

The Return to Normalcy

If one were to seek a formula to account for the many changes that took place in Soviet culture from around 1921, a good starting point would be the capsule characterization of the movement during War Communism for a people's theater made many years later by one of its most zealous activists, A. A. Mgebrov, the leader of a Proletcult theater studio in Petrograd for most of that period: "We fervently sought to break out of the kitchens of the past into the vast expanses and vistas of the coming future. Oh, how we yearned to smash and destroy the narrow, stuffy boxes of the old theater stage and in their place erect huge, free squares to which we might summon not tens but thousands of new, strong, and mighty people."[14] In this quotation, we see values iconic of the cultural ethos of War Communism: iconoclasm (smash, destroy), gigantomania (not tens, but thousands), and the hunger for conquering time. But what is most defining is the move out of the "kitchen"/"box" into the "huge, free squares."

The box had been the favorite metaphor of theater activists since well before the Revolution for representing the bourgeois theater as a confining space and a limiting, nondemocratic aesthetic. But why the kitchens? Arguably, this is a reference to Lenin's famous dictum "Every [female] cook will rule the state" ("Kazhdaya kukharka upravlyaet gosudarstvom"), his analogue to those lines from the "Internationale" much quoted here: "He who was naught shall be all." The female, as distinct from male, cook, virtually a scullery maid, stood close to the bottom of the social, economic, and educational hierarchies of prerevolutionary urban Russia, but she would be elevated to a hegemonic position. Mgebrov, in drawing a homology between the kitchens and the boxes (theaters), is identifying the movement for theater reform with that for socioeconomic bouleversement; he sees the two purposes as accomplished in the one act. The two points of origin, the kitchens and the boxes, placed as they are in apposition, are represented as functionally identical. In this respect, Mgebrov typified the expectations and policies of that firebrand time to which he looked back with nostalgia.

Starting around 1921, one finds a retreat from the "huge, free squares" into the "boxes" and "kitchens," both literally and metaphorically. This movement defines a retreat from the utopian ideals of War Communism or, as the *Veshch'* article labeled it, a shift to an art of capitulation.

One can see this retreat most literally in the case of the mass spectacle. In 1921 a new official policy was promulgated whereby the mass spectacle was to be scaled down, to be taken from those huge, free squares in a city's center to more modest suburban or factory venues and probably indoors.[15] But it was not just the venue that was changed; the whole conception of the spectacle was rethought. Now the core of all mass theater activities was to be the Unified Artistic Circle (Yedinyy Khudozhestvennyy Kruzhok, or YeKhK). Piotrovsky was one of the theoreticians of the Unified Artistic

Circle, and in its conception there is an echo of Wagner's *Gesamtkunstwerk* (the word *yedinyy* is often the one used for the German *Gesamt* in discussions of Wagner's ideas—yet another instance where translation is effectively recoding).[16] The Unified Artistic Circles, to be set up for workers in factories and city districts, were to comprise a number of subgroups in each of which participants would develop a particular specialization such as acting, choral work, or physical culture; these subgroups would be brought together or "unified" to stage skits *(instsenirovki)*, especially for local celebrations of the great revolutionary anniversaries. In other words, they would perform shorter and less ambitious works than were typical of mass theatrical work under War Communism.

This scaling down of the mass festival represents an accommodation to the realities of NEP, when the state and municipal budgets for cultural activities were reduced and, the conscripts for the Civil War having been demobilized, it was harder to organize the casts of thousands that had been a feature of the mass spectacle during 1920. However, it is also symptomatic of the general shift to greater cultural differentiation. That earlier tension between the need to use professionals and the demands of Kerzhentsev and others for a purely amateur mass theater was, during NEP, resolved by increasing apartheid. The professionals returned to the theaters from whence they had come, taking with them some of the conventions of the mass spectacle such as the placard and poster (ROSTA was closed and the heyday of the revolutionary poster was over).[17]

Once the mass spectacle retreated from the squares, one division of its personnel went to the "kitchens" (factory or local workers' cultural clubs), the other to its "box" (highbrow cultural institutions). Spokesmen for the proletarian theater advocated such a division.[18] Figures such as Piotrovsky, who had played a major role in the people's theater and the mass spectacles of War Communism, believing that the "boxes" and the "kitchens" (or shackles of class and education) could be smashed with that one blow of cultural revolution, began to run parallel but separate operations in this period. As it were, these theater activists recreated a version of the Meyerhold / Dr. Dapertutto split that their mentor had been obliged to maintain in civil service Petersburg. Piotrovsky as chief spokesman and proselytizer for the theory of the Unified Artistic Circle, and a godfather to several workers' theaters, was now, if anything, a more powerful figure than before in the movement to create a theater for the masses (for some of this period he was head of the Artistic Section of the Regional Council of Politprosvet[19]) yet he was effectively operating with a double standard: he played an active part in the highbrow theater's appropriation of German Expressionism, while for his workers' circles he advocated the skit and drawing on native Russian folk traditions.[20]

This greater social differentiation within culture is not to be associated with theater activists alone. Even Lunacharsky's statements of this period draw a distinction between great art and agitational art and thus seem to legitimize a sort of two-tiered culture.[21] Moreover, in terms of funding for theater, state subsidies went to the academic (former Imperial) theaters while studios for the workers or mass theaters subsisted unfunded in basements or wandered homeless from venue to venue.[22]

The avant-garde artists of War Communism had also been committed to taking art out of the "boxes" ("Let the streets be our palettes!" was a characteristic slogan). But during NEP—in Petrograd especially—they were no longer in commanding positions and retreated from the "streets" to a museum and a scholarly institute, that is, to the Museum of Artistic Culture (founded in 1921) and the Institute for Artistic Culture, or GINKhUK (founded in 1923), two related bodies housed together. The Petrograd GINKhUK, often called the Myatlev House after the mansion in which the two were located, was run by such giants of the Petrograd art world under War Communism as Tatlin and Punin. It was also Malevich's base during NEP and the place where he, Matyushin, and their disciples continued their experimental work on color and perception. Thus, those iconoclasts who had sought to "dynamite" the academy had retreated to academic institutions.

As all parties previously united in the cause of a mass culture of the "squares" retreated to their own boxes, this meant in effect greater specialization. Thus, for instance, the Petrograd GINKhUK no longer claimed to be "the ecumenical council of all the arts," with technology and science thrown in for good measure, as had Malevich's more utopian Suprematist organization UNOVIS, but pursued relatively specialized projects.[23]

The theater and the avant-garde artists' retreat back from the streets and into closed premises was part of a general trend toward the cameraization of culture. Whereas under War Communism culture had been to a greater extent than ever before part of the public domain, now much of the creative effort was centered away from the streets and also away from the major public institutions.

An example of this decline in the public sphere is the reduced significance of the university in most fields compared with the specialized research institute (this remained generally true of Soviet intellectual life until the late 1980s, when it was re-evaluated). To some extent, the decline was due to upheavals and political vicissitudes. During NEP, Petrograd University saw an almost unending series of reorganizations: one day a particular faculty was added to the university, the next it was rehoused elsewhere, then it was amalgamated with other faculties, and finally it was abolished.[24] The traditional humanist disciplines were combined with others in a Faculty of Material Culture with a strong sociological / political emphasis and a roster of compulsory courses. In addition, official policy required the university to admit more students of proletarian background or with Party or Komsomol allegiance, and a separate Workers' Faculty was founded in 1919 as a sort of preparatory division that gave the uneducated masses a chance to enter higher education.[25] Many of these policies were laudable (given society's past inequalities), and some leading academics gave generously of their time to serve the new age, but these policies also made it more difficult to maintain standards within many disciplines. In consequence, the major intellectual debates and theoretical work were in these years largely focused in semi-independent institutes with a small and more elitist student body, or none at all, and in which the leading scholars of the decade tended to hold positions (though many simultaneously held positions at the university). In some instances, these debates were held in unofficial fora, such as the Bakhtin Circle.[26]

A prime example of the semi-independent institute is the State Institute for the History of the Arts, henceforth to be known by its initials GIII, which saw its heyday during NEP, when it was the most lively center of non-Marxist endeavor in the arts and humanities and thus the most important scholarly institution for the purposes of this book. Originally founded in 1912 by Count Zubov, who essentially gave over his own mansion and considerable library as a private center of study where lectures were arranged, the Institute had been somewhat aristocratic.[27] Before the Revolution both Zubov and the Institute were closely associated with Retrospectivism and the movement for founding a ministry of culture. However, after the Institute was accredited by Lunacharsky in 1920, and began to accept students for tertiary courses in 1922, it took on a life of its own. The Department of Fine Arts remained largely a bastion of the Retrospectivists, but other departments became centers for forging new cultural theory and practice. Its Division of the Verbal Arts (founded in 1920) became an enclave of the Formalists where Yury Tynyanov, Boris Eikhenbaum, Shklovsky, and V. V. Vinogradov lectured.[28] The Division for the History and Theory of the Theater (also founded in 1920), where V. N. Soloviev, A. Piotrovsky, and several other theater activists taught, was no mere dry academic center but a major player in the movement for theater reform; plays were frequently produced there, and whenever Meyerhold's troupe visited Leningrad it was the place to which he gravitated to discuss his latest work. Additionally, the Division for the Theory and History of Music under B. Asafiev played a crucial role in introducing contemporary music to Leningrad and, together with the Theater Division, working out a theory of the kind of new opera pioneered by Shostakovich (see Chapter 9).[29]

The Institute's lecture series gave a public forum to some of the most serious minds of the decade; many of the major Formalist writings were aired in this way.[30] In addition, GIII maintained a close relationship with the artists working in the Myatlev House (GINKhUK), its neighbor. GIII had a Moscow counterpart, the State Academy of Artistic Culture, or GAKhN, which, similarly, maintained close relations with that city's INKhUK.[31]

When cultural life retreated toward its "boxes," one saw a return to something like normalcy, to something closer to the past intellectual life of the city. Around 1922 many of the old academic and professional associations and journals emerged as it were from the rubble of revolution and civil war, and new journals of a distinctly academic nature were founded.[32]

This trend did not entirely represent a return to prerevolutionary normalcy, however. At precisely this time Marxists and Bolsheviks also began to organize themselves into militant scholarly organizations and institutions; they launched a concerted attack against idealist and religious thought. Thus no sooner was the Petersburg Philosophical Society revived in March 1921, enabling its organ *Thought* (Mysl') to begin appearing again at the beginning of 1922, than the journal was subjected to a barrage of attacks from prominent Bolshevik intellectuals.[33]

Even as the old professional associations and journals reappeared, many intellectuals were so disaffected that they decided to emigrate (particularly in 1921, when Gorky himself left), and one hundred prominent intellectual families were expelled from the country in an infamous episode of 1922. These events, together with the death of Blok and the execution of the poet Nikolai Gumilëv in August of 1921 (for alleged White Guard activities), are landmarks in most of those accounts that see the period 1921–1922 as "the end of Petersburg," or the end of the cultural flowering, or the end of any kind of normalcy for intellectuals.

As the old professional associations went back into business, much of culture became more academic. This was especially true in the theater. The trend might seem to run contrary to the Piotrovsky complaint, intoned in the *Veshch'* editorial, that "we had Shakespeare in January [1921] but got the *café chantant* in December," but of course by Shakespeare he meant not so much the Shakespeare of high culture as a practitioner of the people's theater—the interpretation of Shakespeare shared by Meyerhold, Piotrovsky, and many others during War Communism.

As intellectuals began to use more conventional models of culture, the scornful attitude toward dramaturgy that had been particularly marked in the 1910s was reversed. The early years of NEP saw a new emphasis on the drama as a literary text rather than as a performance. Symptomatically, in 1924 the Petrograd Theatrical Department announced a reorganization in all its theaters, which were now to be directed by a troika comprising the theater director, its chief director of productions, and the head of the literary section.[34]

A defining feature of the cultural landscape of NEP was the return of literature as queen of the arts, supplanting the theater. Most of the major Party pronouncements on culture made up to 1927 were on literature (see Chapter 8). This was another sign of the way cultural bureaucrats had, de facto, abandoned the ideal of a unified culture, an ideal that at that time had to mean a nonprint culture.

The return of the word in drama was part of a general shift away from cultural models that accorded preeminence to performance, spectacle, and music. In the professional theater, the word became a dominant value, overshadowing those recent ideals pageant and improvisation. This change can be sensed in the statements of the avant-garde centered in the Myatlev House. When leading figures there presented a production of their idol Khlebnikov's trans-sense work *Zangezi* in 1923, one of the sponsors, N. Punin, insisted that it was "not a play but a long poem," while Tatlin in outlining his approach as director explained that "the word is the unit of [*Zangezi*'s] construction [actually *zdaniye*]," and hence he did not allow any "acting stunts" because they might detract from the word.[35]

With the foregrounding of the word came a sharper delineation of semantics and a devaluation of the symbolic (a reversal of the Nietzschean order of priorities). In the word, you have the possibility for more quickly distinguishing the limits of transgression, a return to what Nietzsche called the *principium individuationis,* to the particular, the defined, and the bounded.

The retreat from the "huge, free squares" to the "boxes" and "kitchens" was in effect a retreat from a more open-ended situation to one where norms prevailed, that is, the particular standards and conventions of individual fields, groups, or organizations. Cultural life was retreating from the "vast expanses and vistas of the approaching future," from that ever more centrifugally articulated periphery back toward a center (as distinct from the center from which it had retreated). Because expertise and standards were valued, cultural life was, paradoxically, both more pluralistic and more centripetal than in the immediately preceding years. Even the phenomenon of *razmezhevaniye*, the increasingly intense divisions between factions and positions in the cultural sphere, can be seen as a result of this search for boundaries *(mezhi)*—boundaries between movements, between classes, between professions, and so forth.

With the new stress on specialization and professionalism in the early years of NEP, many different factions emphasized the creative intellectual's right to relative autonomy, even to ideological autonomy, in the name of the standards of his or her field.[36] It was not just independent literary groups who spoke out against the state's mandating the kind of art to be produced. Cultural intermediaries such as Radlov called in print for the curbing of the power of the "bosses" *(nachal'niki*, a label then commonly used in this context) in order to give the professionals more control over their own work in the theater.[37] Even prominent Party officials expressed similar views: Lunacharsky, for instance, said in 1924 that art is not a state matter, and that the state could not and should not possibly attempt to encompass in its sphere of influence all of art's complexity.[38]

The general drift of cultural life was, however, centripetal. The years of War Communism had seen what was, for Russia, a marked degree of decentralization in the intellectual life of the country at large. This was partly a consequence of the chaos and confusion of revolution and civil war, partly the expression of a reaction against tsarist centripetal tendencies, and partly the result of a desire to redress cultural deprivation in the provinces. Signs of this decentralization include the mini-renaissances in such cities as Vitebsk, Baku, Kharkov, and Tiflis, and the profusion of new universities founded in provincial towns between 1918 and 1920.[39] Under NEP this trend was reversed. Lack of funding meant closure for many of the new provincial universities, and those intellectuals who had participated in the cultural flowerings in the provinces tended to drift back to the capitals or emigrate.

Another factor that contributed to centralizing cultural life was the founding of larger creative organizations combining a variety of lesser special interest groups. In literature, this process can be seen in the setting up in July 1920 of the Union of Writers (VSP), an organization that banded together primarily the nonproletarian writers. In Petrograd, VSP was initially dominated by the old literary establishment.[40]

The trend toward centralization was even more marked in publishing, where Moscow and Leningrad emerged as virtually the only active centers.[41] The founding of major literary journals in Moscow and Petrograd at the beginning of NEP particularly contributed to this trend.[42] Lesser journals whose existence was precarious financially could not compete with them in the royalties or circulation they offered.[43] Intellectuals who aspired to a place in the mainstream flocked to the new journals, while those who were disaffected, scornful, or who represented ideological or aesthetic positions that were not favored tended to publish in short-lived almanacs or factional periodicals.

As was intended, the new journals effectively created a new, mainstream Soviet culture (not, of course, singlehandedly). Those writers who achieved prominence on their pages, such as Isaac Babel, Vsevolod Ivanov, and even the returned émigré nobleman Aleksey Tolstoy, became the leading, mainstream Soviet writers. But this new culture also became progressively more Moscow-centric (as is suggested in the fact that Aleksey Tolstoy lived in Petrograd but frequently published in the thick journals of Moscow, while Babel and Ivanov had commenced their postrevolutionary literary careers in Petrograd but then moved to Moscow).[44] Unlike Moscow, Petrograd was given only one "thick" journal, the *Star* (Zvezda), which was less important and had a smaller circulation than its Moscow counterparts, which were thus able to lure away the more successful or acceptable Petrograd writers.[45]

During NEP, Moscow and Leningrad assumed in cultural life the roles they were to have for most of the Soviet period, with Moscow as the center, the home of mainstream culture, and Petrograd as the home for peripheral or out-of-favor culture. Its journal the *Star* functioned as a medium through which fringe figures on the left (proletarian extremists) and the right (such as Pilnyak, Pasternak, and Mandelshtam) could publish. While this situation afforded Petrograd the role of the more honorable, less compromised city, to some it seemed the town of the has-beens.

During War Communism, Petrograd had been more or less Moscow's equal as a cultural center and the leader in scholarly and academic life; in theater and opera, for instance, between 1917 and 1922 markedly more new productions had been launched in Petrograd than in Moscow.[46] Under NEP, however, Petrograd declined significantly in cultural importance. In part this was due to Moscow's receiving more state funds. For example, students at the Petrograd Institute for Screen Art were unfunded while at Moscow's counterpart GIK (the State Institute of Cinematography) they received stipends.[47] It is a small wonder that almost all the big names in Soviet film worked in Moscow.

For Petrograd this was a time of losses. The city even lost some of its fine treasures in the Hermitage, which were ceded to Moscow after a commission sent from the capital so ruled.[48] But for those committed to forging a new, revolutionary culture, the loss of living writers, artists, and theater people was more serious than losing treasures of the past. It was particularly galling to see that the most exciting developments in music and the theater were initiated by Petrograders, but in Moscow.[49] Already in 1921 Eikhenbaum was closing one of his articles with the desperate plea to the city's best poets: "For God's sake, don't leave for Moscow!"[50]

No longer were the most daring, new cultural events occurring in Petrograd, city of the Revolution, of the mass spectacles and Tatlin's tower. Now they tended to come out of Moscow, and to appear in Petrograd after about a year's time, if at all, and usually as imports (that is, as visiting productions), or as pale echoes of some Moscow phenomenon.

Petrograd was more conservative culturally, but for many this was a virtue. In the article by Eikhenbaum in which he begged the good poets not to leave Petrograd, he ruefully remarked that in "strict" (strogiy) Petersburg there were not, and could not be, the noisy, blustering cultural movements of contemporary Moscow such as Imagism (Eikhenbaum's claim reflects a common and enduring attitude among Petersburg writers).

Thus the lead article in Veshch' in 1922 was not wrong when it lamented a resurgence of academic art. In particular, one finds in early 1921, even before NEP was promulgated, signs that the Preservationist movement with its agenda of strict norms and uncluttered panoramas was regaining much of the ground it lost in the initial iconoclastic phase of War Communism.

When in 1918 the Academy of the Arts was replaced by avant-gardist free studios, or SVOMAS, the old art establishment had been removed from power and replaced by figures such as Natan Altman (who decorated the Palace Square in 1918), Tatlin, and the Formalist theoretician Osip Brik. On February 2, 1921, however, the SVOMAS took back their old title Academy of the Arts, a move that was far from superficial; the new leadership was swept out and replaced by more conservative department heads, such as the Neoclassicist V. A. Shchuko for architecture. Petitions were filed later that year to let such avant-garde artists as Tatlin and Matyushin retain their studios there, but in vain (hence the retreat to the Myatlev House).[51]

"He who was naught" could always become "all," but for how long? As Victor Turner, one of the principal theorists of so-called liminal times or movements has pointed out, liminal periods are generally of short duration, and structure (norms, bounds), their opposite in his scheme, soon returns.[52] But then what did Altman and other avant-garde artists have in mind when for the first anniversary of the Revolution they decked the Palace Square with such slogans?—surely that their art and their artists (which they always insisted uniquely represented the Revolution and the proletariat) should be "all." That the political establishment was never convinced of this is well known; Radlov later revealed that as early as the summer of 1920 officialdom prevented him from using Altman's designs for the mass spectacle he staged at the Stock Exchange.[53] But nor were the hard core intelligentsia convinced.

It was but a month between the high point of revolutionary utopianism, November 1920, when the model of the Tatlin tower was exhibited and the masses re-enacted the storming of the Winter Palace, and January 1921. Yet already that January, before NEP had been announced, there were distinct signs that the cultural ethos was changing. These changes were not all orchestrated from above.

In late January and early February 1921, "Pushkin Days" were organized to commemorate the anniversary of the poet's death on February 10 (January 29, old style), 1837. The Pushkin Days involved a series of evenings held at the House of Literati (duplicated at the university), at which speeches were given and commemorative poems read, the most famous being those of Blok, Khodasevich, and M. Kuzmin.[54]

In most of the speeches and poems, a somewhat bitter, elegiac mood was struck. Speakers lamented what they saw as the end of Petersburg culture; they also complained of state interference in the arts, which made it, in Blok's words, "impossible to breathe." Such sentiments had been expressed before in works such as Mandelshtam's "The Twilight of Freedom" (1918) or the apocalyptic laments about the fate of Russia by writers including A. Remizov, N. Klyuev, and A. Blok.[55] However, the year 1921 saw an unusual concentration of literary works and intelligentsia rallies where the regime of the "bosses," of the "tutor" (guvener), was denounced. Akhmatova herself contributed a poem fittingly titled "All is Plundered, Betrayed, Sold Out."

It was in that year that there appeared one of the most outspoken signs of intelligentsia alienation from the state-directed culture of the day, the newspaper Literary Gazette (Literaturnaya gazeta), mouthpiece of the Petrograd Branch of VSP (the All-Russian Union of Writers). More accurately, it did not appear since the censors confiscated the first issue after it was printed.[56] The paper proclaimed in its very title a direct link to Pushkin and other writers who had founded a periodical of the same name in 1830. V. Khodasevich, one of the contributors, associated this event with a remark Pushkin wrote to a friend in that fateful year 1825, the year of the Decembrist Uprising, about how "silence" is a "public calamity." This observation was implicitly taken up in an article by E. Zamyatin ("It Is Time") in which he calls for the silent majority—comprising, allegedly, 90 percent of the population—to be given some voice to counteract the hegemonic, Bolshevik 10 percent. Despite this militancy, which provoked the journal's closure, deeply pessimistic notes were also sounded as contributors pointed out a "significant decline" in literature, criticism, and literary scholarship.[57]

In 1921 Eikhenbaum published his essay "A Moment of Truth," in which he declares the year "marked in the history of our generation as a moment of truth" when we realize that we have no more readers and "we are needed only by History but history is cruel." Our time of " 'dreams and aspirations' [mechtatel'stvo] is over," he concludes. "A moment of terror has come. Our generation hears the steps of the commendatore."[58] The reference here is of course to the Don Juan myth, although in recent Russian reworkings of the myth, drawing on Pushkin's version in his short tragedy *The Stone Guest* and conflating it with *The Bronze Horseman* in a synthetic account of the advancing statue, the commendatore sometimes symbolized the autocratic state.

But who was the commendatore now, who was it that threatened the identity of the intelligentsia? Was it the state? or the return to a semimarket situation? or was it the fact that history had bypassed them and transposed the center to Moscow? The answer is all of the above, although at this time Spengler's *Decline of the West* was all the rage and the sense that the intellectuals were the "derniers fils d'une [culture] épuisée" was not just a response to Soviet reality but also refracted through his models of historical evolution. Whatever the referents or influences, this was a time of existential crisis. The intellectual's self-identity as a Hermes figure had received a severe battering. The return to Pushkin was a kind of *reculer* to the old values and standards, and also to a sense of tradition that took their city's poet as the originary figure.

The Pushkin Days were not all lament. As with Mandelshtam's poem "We Shall Gather Again in Petersburg" of about the same time, the message is ambiguous; the dirges are at the same time drum rolls rallying the troops. The readings essentially represented a show of strength on the part of the intelligentsia rather than an announcement of defeat. The occasion brought together on the same platform the leading groups of the non-Party and non-avant-garde cultural intelligentsia, including the Proletcult, Preservationists, the publishing house World Literature, and leaders of that segment of the prerevolutionary intelligentsia that had been particularly concerned about social causes. One finds in the occasion a general sense of cultural mission to the nation at large.

Nineteen twenty-one did not mark a jubilee year for Pushkin. He died in 1837, and thus this was the eighty-fourth anniversary of his death. Clearly the concern to mark his death in a major way outweighed the somewhat flimsy motivation. One reason for this is the fact that Pushkin's death in a duel and his fraught relations with Nicholas I had helped make him a martyr for the intellectuals' cause. Hence the celebration of his death was an obvious venue for them to express anxieties about preserving their values in the face of what they saw as an oppressive and unheeding state.[59] This was not the first time his death had served that function; the major Pushkin anniversaries of the late nineteenth century had served as massive rallying points for intelligentsia solidarity. Throughout NEP, Pushkin and his age became favorite topics for literary and scholarly texts by intellectuals of Petrograd in which they explored their own existential dilemmas. The Pushkin anniversary, then, was not merely an excuse for lamenting, but also an occasion for examining or reaffirming the consensual norms (ethical and aesthetic) of the intelligentsia and for looking anew at that perennial issue of Russia's historical destiny.

Pushkin is no neutral figure who can stand for all the intelligentsia. In the twentieth century, he has generally served as an emblem for cultural conservatism and Retrospectivism. Consequently Mayakovsky, Kruchënykh, and Khlebnikov had encouraged the intelligentsia in their Futurist manifesto of 1912 to "cast Pushkin off the steamship of modernity . . . Off! Off! Off!" During War Communism, interpretations of Pushkin's role in the new Soviet culture had been mixed, particularly among supporters of proletarian culture, some of whom denounced him, as the erstwhile Futurists continued to do, while others (a category that included Lunacharsky and the Proletcult), using a goodly measure of casuistry, found a central role for this nobleman in revolutionary culture.[60] Now, it seemed, Pushkin had not merely clambered back on board the steamer of modernity, but was in danger of being put at the helm. If the cultural tastes of the Old Bolsheviks had prevailed in revolutionary Russia, this might well have happened: consider, for instance, Lenin's famous statement: "Pushkin I understand and enjoy, Nekrasov I acknowledge, but Mayakovsky, forgive me, I can't understand him."[61] But in this instance it was an alliance of the intelligentsia, rather than the Party, that was promoting Pushkin for the new age.[62]

The Pushkin celebrations coincided with a return to prominence of the lobby for Old Petersburg. An important moment was the (re-)founding in November 1921 of the Society for Old Petersburg, whose office-holders were the Preservationist old guard and included Alexandr Benois, Count Zubov from GIII, and the grand duke K. K. Romanov. With missionary zeal the Society spawned a whole series of organizations and functions designed to propagate the Petersburg tradition within a number of spheres, not just art and architecture, but music and cultural excursions for the masses as well.[63]

In literature, it focused efforts to foster a Petersburg school in a new "Circle of the Bronze Horseman."[64]

The myth of Petersburg in general, and the Bronze Horseman in particular, resurfaced as dominant themes and concerns. Nineteen twenty-two was a vintage year for these themes in terms of the number of publications concerning them, although most must have been prepared earlier.[65] The second major redaction of Bely's novel *Petersburg* appeared that year, as did a book that has become a classic statement on the way the Bronze Horseman functions as the *genius loci* of the city, *The Soul of Petersburg* (Dusha Peterburga) by N. F. Antsiferov, a leading member of the Society for Old Petersburg. Pushkin's *Bronze Horseman* itself was published that year in a handsome first unexpurgated edition with Benois's illustrations. In fact the Preservationists became obsessed with the fate of the statue itself—decrying in the press the way vandals were allowed to desecrate it—and were ultimately appointed its guardians.[66] By 1923, the popular Petrograd magazine *Red Panorama* (Krasnaya panorama, *sic*) had a regular by-line "Old Petersburg" dominated by G. Lukomsky, who in the 1910s had been one of the chief proselytizers for Empire style.

The Preservationists were gaining institutional power as well. In 1923 the Academic Center of Narkompros incorporated the Society for Old Petersburg in its administrative net.[67] Neoclassical architects were also on the march, not only taking over in the academies and exhibitions of Petrograd, but winning commissions to design the shrines of the Revolution as well, soon to include the first version of Lenin's mausoleum, designed by A. V. Schusev. "Hands off the sacred graves!" expostulated Punin (in vain) when he realized that the jury for the competition to design the memorials at Mars Field was stacked with Neoclassicists; they also designed new approaches to the Revolution's 1917 headquarters at the Smolny.[68] But the character of the Preservationist movement was also shifting. They had not only formed a strong patron-client relationship with Bolshevik power, but had also turned to the masses rather than the elite as the target audience for their endeavors (publications, public lectures, and so on).

The Pushkin anniversary was far from the only one marked by the Petrograd intelligentsia in 1921. In fact 1921 saw the observance of an extraordinary number of anniversaries of literary figures: Hoffman, Dostoevsky, Nekrasov, and even Gleb Uspensky (the 150th anniversary of the architect Rastrelli who designed the Winter Palace was also celebrated). Among the intelligentsia, the two anniversary celebrations of that year that received the greatest attention were those for Pushkin and Dostoevsky. There was a difference in the way each was commemorated; whereas the Dostoevsky anniversary gave rise to some memorable interpretive scholarship and

debates among the intelligentsia, the Pushkin anniversary worked to insti-
tutionalize the writer it honored. A resolution was passed to make the commemoration of Pushkin's death an annual national event and to have a
decree passed to this effect. The national commemorations, its organizers
suggested, should involve not only memorial evenings and the publishing
of scholarly collections, as this one had, but also literary competitions and
dramatic renditions. The publishing house World Literature undertook to
mark the occasion every year with a series of lectures on the influence of
Pushkin in foreign literature.[69]

By 1924, a major jubilee year for Pushkin (the 125th anniversary of his
birth), the celebrations had been taken up by the state and the principal
venue shifted from Petrograd to Moscow. Yet the forms this celebration took
and many of the sentiments expressed from the platform (minus the
laments) essentially replicated the model established in Petrograd in 1921.[70]

Even the Petrograd avant-garde were not to be outdone in the business
of creating a cult of dead—and therefore martyred—intellectuals. The celebration in 1923 of the anniversary of their poet Khlebnikov's death the
previous year (from starvation and the psychophysical batterings of War
Communism) had the atmosphere of a religious ritual as Punin, one of those
who organized an exhibition in the Myatlev House to mark it, appealed
to everyone to bring forward any relics they may have, such as memora-
bilia and documents.[71] Tatlin took upon himself the mission of staging
Khlebnikov's drama in verse, *Zangezi*. This event could be seen as an answer
to the Pushkin Days inasmuch as some of the avant-garde's leading figures
used the occasion to deliver programmatic lectures about Khlebnikov's
work (it was originally intended that Radlov would co-direct *Zangezi*, which
raises yet again the question of how to place him within the cultural spectrum of the day).[72] Obviously, this occasion gave the Petrograd avant-garde
a moral lift. The *Life of Art* presented major programmatic statements about
the nature of art and of perception written by Malevich, Filonov, and other
leaders from the Myatlev establishment, and including Matyushin's statement on Zorved.[73]

The sponsors' accounts of *Zangezi* called it an "autobiography" and a
"heroic long poem."[74] Thus the intelligentsia were personalizing historical
events and trends that were broader in scope than could realistically be
contained in an individual biography. The Formalists decried this trend
to foreground the extraliterary in a literary study, a trend that was especially marked in the writings generated by the Pushkin anniversary, but
before long they too were having recourse to biographies that were in some
instances no less hagiographic.[75] Indeed, Eikhenbaum's very invocation of
"the steps of the commendatore" presages the extent to which the Formal-

ists would go to articulate their values in terms of historical precedents from the Pushkin period (see Chapter 8).

The martyrology, heroic epics, and exemplary biographies were all trojan horses that the various factions in the intelligentsia used to legitimize their positions. But the return to biography and autobiography also marked a shift from the "huge and free" schema of War Communism to more bounded (specified and conventionalized) narratives of cultural identity. Linear narrative was returning, casting aside the fragmentary and epiphanic structures typical of War Communism. Despite the avant-garde's claim that *Zangezi* defied conventional linearity, even that work provides an instance of this trend in that they adopted Khlebnikov's biography as its frame.

To smash those "boxes" and rush headlong into vast spaces is to experience the vertigo of an epiphany. Yet, no matter how vast those "squares," sooner of later one will encounter their borders. This moment is in effect a kind of falling back into time after a bout of epilepsy. But once one falls out of *kairos,* one is in a new kind of time that demands explanation and sequence. The major cultural expressions of these years no longer involved collapsing time in a series of high points (as one saw in the mass spectacle of War Communism); many wrote of the need for consistent, motivated sequence.[76] The mass spectacle in its classic versions of 1920 had really been less an etiological myth than a mass experience for galvanizing groupness, but an age of explanation always features historicism.

A cliché about literature in this period is that it saw a shift from an age of poetry to an age of prose, from an age of "short forms" *(malaya forma)*—such as lyric poems—to an age of "long forms" *(bol'shaya forma).*[77] While almost all the major poets went through a period of low creativity,[78] the novel—war horse of the Russian literary tradition—regained its prominence.

The move to longer forms can be found not only in literature but in cultural journalism, art, and other fields as well. It can, for instance, be seen in the shift among left artists from making posters and individual pictures to designing entire, integrated Constructivist stage sets and even buildings. One could account for the shift in terms of the greater possibility for producing longer works at a time of fewer upheavals and fewer problems in obtaining materials, such as paper. Arguably, the sheer length or scale of a "long form" is, however, less defining than the attitude toward composition.

Biography is in a sense the lowest common denominator of historicism, and many of the novels written during NEP were structured around biographical myths. By the 1930s the trend had devolved to a biographical master myth of the Bolshevik state through which almost all cultural production had to be in some way refracted.[79] The large number of literary anniversaries that mark the year 1921 represents a stage in the progression to its institutionalization.

In the initial years after War Communism, then, the intelligentsia of Petrograd retreated from the "streets" and "squares" to their own "boxes," and as they did so they reaffirmed the norms of their own caste in a ritual celebration of Pushkin. Most defined their culture's identity in narrower terms than before, no longer believing they could transcend in a single smashing of those airless "boxes" (kitchens / integument / sardine tins / constraining conceptual frames) class, education, and national boundaries; *pace* the *Veshch'* editorial, it was Pushkin who reigned in January 1921 rather than Shakespeare, and attention was to be focused on how he influenced the West, rather than vice versa. But as they regained their "boxes," they also confronted once again the question of norms.

The ecology of revolution is such that while a revolution occurs in a pre-existing ecosystem limiting the capacity for absolute change, still it is a revolution and is bound to disturb and even transmute the local flora. The moment of truth is in a sense the moment when differences are recognized, borders, and limits. In the ensuing phase of general *razmezhevanie,* new principles of classification and new genres have to be identified or generated. The topography had altered. In the initial postrevolutionary period, one of the borders that had been fudged by those intellectuals captivated by the euphoria of the Revolution was that with Europe, but in these years they sensed that dividing line quite palpably. Thus when the Preservationists celebrated the Rastrelli anniversary, they insisted that he, originally an Italian, thought not "in an Italian way" but "together with all of Russia."[80] The avant-garde similarly rewrote the provenance of their idols. Under War Communism, they had declared that art is a country unto itself that knows no boundaries and should even establish its own embassies in other countries, but now spokesmen had started proclaiming Khlebnikov the founder of a "national school" and claiming that *Zangezi* exposed the "collapse" (*krusheniye*) of *Western* European science.[81]

Even as intellectuals seemed to be drawing back and defining their work within a more limited purview, however, they began to look to Europe as to their "significant other" in an effort to create a culture for the new age. In Petrograd, capital of the intelligentsia, they might rein in at a moment of truth and espouse what detractors called an art of capitulation, but they had begun to look outward with a renewed sense of urgency.

7

REVOLUTIONARY CULTURE
MEETS THE JAZZ AGE

On June 15, 1924, Meyerhold's Moscow troupe staged the national premiere of *The Trust D. E.* at the Petrograd Conservatory.[1] As is suggested in the subtitle of I. Ehrenburg's novel of the same name on which the play is based—*The Story of Europe's Downfall*—the play concerns an imperilled Europe.[2] The threat comes from America, where a sinister band of monopolists has formed the organization Hand over Europe (shortened in Russian to its initials, D. E.), which is bent on conquering all of Europe, depopulating it, and colonizing it with Africans. In a variant on the old motif of Russia as a bulwark to save Europe from the yellow peril, however, the Soviet proletariat is able to rescue Europe from the enemy while the Red Army assures the success of revolution in America.

Despite this melodramatic plot, Meyerhold's production of *The Trust D. E.* is best remembered not for its themes but for its extensive use of jazz.[3] His principal device for contrasting vital and revolutionary Russia with the decadent West was to set up an opposition between the West's jazz dances and the Soviet Union's healthier physical activities. For this, he placed a jazz band on stage led by Valentin Parnakh, who in October 1922 first introduced jazz to Soviet Russia; he treated the audience to eight pop-jazz hits in the course of a cabaret-type review where lurid capitalists cavorted in shimmies, apaches, and fox trots.[4] The fox trot had by now largely replaced the *café chantant* as a cipher for Western decadence ("a new form of pornography" that has "no place in the Soviet Republic"),[5] and as a counterpoint muscular Soviets performed "sporting exercises" at the Red Sailor Stadium to the accompaniment of march music played on the harmonica. As one reviewer remarked, "The freshness, vibrancy, and healthy strength of all those movements at the Red Sailor Stadium stand out to their advantage against the background of the Americanized dances."[6]

Western commentators have tended to view a little differently the question of who stood out to greatest advantage in this confrontation. S. Frederick Starr, for instance, in *Red and Hot,* his book on Soviet Jazz, cites such factors as the extraordinary popularity of the production to support his argument that "Meierhold . . . missed no opportunity to promote the sinful allure of the jazz band. . . . Meierhold's sympathies clearly lay with the culture of jazz and the 'fox-trotting West.'"[7]

Such conclusions should not be drawn too hastily. The Soviet sportsmen in the Red Sailor Stadium did not just play soccer and do physical exercises, but also gave "a demonstration of Vsevolod Meyerhold's system of biomechanical exercises."[8] Moreover, in a speech Meyerhold made during this same visit to Petrograd, he defined his work in terms of this system.[9]

The Soviet avant-garde in general viewed jazz, and all that it stood for, with great ambivalence. Many of them interpreted jazz, and the "hot" dances then all the rage in Europe, as standing in the tradition of the cabaret and music hall, which they saw, as had the Italian Futurists, as an important aspect of their agendas for revitalization. And yet they also subscribed to the common view that jazz represented the sort of Western decadence that had to be counteracted. Symptomatic of this ambivalence, Parnakh, in the issue of *Veshch'* following the one in which the avant-garde ranted against the threat of the advancing *café chantant,* published two articles advocating jazz and the "new dances."[10]

The West and Soviet Cultural Identity

The appearance of jazz in *The Trust D. E.,* billed at the time as "the most agitational of all spectacles in the Soviet Union,"[11] focuses some of the major issues facing those concerned with the fate of Soviet culture in these interstitial years. Among the crucial issues to be resolved were the attitude toward Western bourgeois urban culture and where to strike the balance between high and low culture given the country's commitment to a "dictatorship of the proletariat." With the utopian nature of the Communist experiment and the conviction among intellectuals that market forces only "pollute" culture, these issues remained urgent throughout Soviet cultural history; all its major players were ambivalent about the West, and hence the zigzagging policies on Western culture and recurrent bouts of extreme anti-Westernism.

War Communism had provided one set of answers to these questions: between the Blockade and the government monopoly on the cultural purse strings, popular lowbrow Western culture was essentially denied access to the country and the masses were given large doses of high culture by intellectual puritans. But in 1920 when the Blockade was lifted and the Soviet Union was no longer engaging the West in an undeclared war (the Intervention), the borders became more open. Then, with limited private enterprise permitted during NEP, cultural institutions became more sensitive to popular taste. In consequence, these issues were raised again with greater urgency. Several rival solutions emerged but, initially, those that predominated in Petrograd were largely antithetical to the solutions of War Communism, and also to those that came to the fore during its immediate sequel, the "moment of truth," that is, somewhat parochial versions of the highbrow.

Between 1922 and 1924 Soviet culture was riding high on a tide of Westernism. The new cultural trends incorporated Western bourgeois or lowbrow culture, including jazz, into their purview.

The tide peaked in Petrograd, the original "window on Europe," which led the country in its obsession with the West. This fixation began quite early and was anticipated in such events as the founding there in October 1920 of the Society for the Study of Western Culture, which was explicitly set up to counteract the influence of the Free Philosophical Academy, or Volfila, an intellectual forum dominated by concerns with Russian particularity and spirituality.[12] In the city's cultural journals, the sections where the latest books and cultural events in the West were reviewed became ever longer and a new journal devoted principally to Western culture, the *Contemporary West* (Sovremennyy zapad), began publishing in 1922. Similar patterns were to be found in Moscow at this time, but there they competed with the solutions of a Russo-centric, proletarian culture to a greater extent than was true as yet in Petrograd.

A high percentage of the cultural fare to be found in Petrograd between 1922 and 1924 represents translations or adaptations (many of the adaptations were unacknowledged and were presented by authors as if they were their original works).[13] The sheer volume and popularity of Western texts so dwarfed local production that, Eikhenbaum joked, in order to be published in the Soviet Union you now had to call your work a translation and to sign it with a foreign name or at least a foreign pseudonym (admitting that in this respect he had an advantage).[14] In the country at large, 50 percent of the presses gave first priority to foreign books,[15] while in cinema, the country's dearth of new foreign films was relieved when in late 1922 Petrograd's Sevzapkino received three hundred titles from the West.[16] From then until 1927, Western movies were the main fare on Soviet screens.[17]

The traffic across the borders was not only in books, films, and plays; cultural luminaries were on the march, too. One after the other, the big names in Western film, theater, music, literature, and science came to visit (or at any rate visits were planned), while local lights sometimes got a chance to tour as well, a much sought after status symbol.[18] In contrast to 1921–1922, when many intellectuals emigrated or were expelled, some returned in these years (such as the Petrograder Aleksey Tolstoy), and even more were rumored to be returning (such as Chaliapin and Stravinsky).[19] Shklovsky published in *Veshch'* a plea to Jakobson, his fellow leader of the Formalist movement, to return from Prague because "the flood is abating and the animals are coming out of their arks."[20] This very movement back and forth also facilitated closer contact with the West.

As the West opened up after the Blockade, many Soviet Russians realized to their dismay that, despite their heroic efforts under crippling circumstances, the country had managed to slip behind the West in many areas. In physics, for instance, renewed contact with Western scholars[21] revealed that D. S. Rozhdestvensky's discoveries in the field of spectral analysis of the structure of the atom made at Petrograd's new Optical Institute in the crippling conditions of the Blockade, when electricity and fuel were hard to come by, and of which all were duly proud, could not, inasmuch as they had already been surpassed in the West, be categorized as a new discovery, but only as an incredible achievement considering the circumstances.[22]

All the old anxieties about Russia's provincialism came back into play. The situation was not helped when it was realized that "Red Russia" was being excluded from a variety of new networks linking the leading countries of Europe; new air routes between the major cities were established as well as radio broadcasts (principally of highbrow music) from one country to another.[23] This sent many to devour all that was the latest in the West with a zeal bordering on frenzy.

It might be said that the country was finally able to realize its internationalist aims, which were preached during War Communism but could then be realized only marginally owing to the limits on contact imposed by the Blockade. Just as during War Communism left artists and the Proletcult attempted to set up international organizations with branches in Europe, at this time, too, every self-respecting Petrograd cultural organization aspired to have an outlet in Europe.[24]

There was, however, an important difference. Whereas the internationalism of War Communism had stressed liberation of the underdog throughout the world, the focus of this wave was less on revolutionary struggle than on contemporary Western urban culture. The recent period when accounts of the Revolution stressed its roots in Russian native, antiurbanist traditions had virtually evaporated.[25] The literary scene was dominated by groups who were largely Western and urbanist in their orientation and who put out almanacs with titles like *The City* (Gorod).

This shift occasioned a reaccentuation of the catch phrases and values of the new society. Many of those typical of the years 1922–1924 were the same as those found during War Communism, but their referents had changed. Thus "movement" and related words such as "pace" and "tempo" remained axiomatic values.[26] However, the "movement" intended was no longer the whirlwind of revolution that sweeps away all, the upward thrust of the spiral in Tatlin or some other *perpetuum mobile,* but now more the pace of city life, of a film, or of jazz music.

Pace was all. There was a sense that Russians needed to catch up and introduce a fast-paced lifestyle, the life of the new age from which the Blockade and other disruptions had excluded them. There was even a premium on writing literary and scholarly works or getting translations of Western works out as quickly as possible,[27] and on adding pace to literary works or plays by having them imitate the tempos of the movies, a stipulation usually housed under the new slogans "cinefication" and "Americanization."[28] But such injunctions were really the surface markers of a new ethos.

The Roaring Twenties

Around 1922 postblockade Russia met the Jazz Age; in that year the first jazz concert in the Soviet Union (Parnakh's) was held in Moscow. By the Jazz Age here, however, I mean not so much the time of jazz music as the time of the "roaring twenties," captured in F. Scott Fitzgerald's classic essay "Echoes of the Jazz Age" (1931).[29] This may seem a forced comparison. One could hardly claim of Soviet Russia in these years, as did Fitzgerald of his "Jazz Age" America, that it was an age dominated by a breed of affluent pleasure-seekers who "had no interest in politics at all," for "we were tired of Great Causes."[30] Fitzgerald was of course being typically hyperbolic here, but what he characterizes as a lack of interest in politics and Great Causes could equally well be identified as a reorientation in the sense of time, and this was defining of the Soviet Union's "Jazz Age."

Fitzgerald identifies the Jazz Age in its classic phase (which for him began around 1919) with the moment when "the generation which had been adolescent during the confusion of the War, brusquely shouldered my contemporaries out of the way and danced into the limelight." This generation ignored the values and objections of their elders, for "it seemed only a question of years before the older people would step aside and the world would be run by those who saw things as they were." To them, then, "Great Causes" were essentially the causes of the older generations. Freud, the experience of the Great War, and other factors had helped them see the world anew, and thus the old grounds of authority were no longer valid for them. This also meant that not just the older generation but the past in general receded from their purview. The "flappers," the "hedonistic" and "wild" dancers, gave the moment their all; pace, the pace of the dance, the pace with which they crossed the Atlantic back and forth in search of the perfect party, was a movement through space *now*. The revolt against provincialism thus defines the Jazz Age, which entailed a movement in space (dancing, travel) to overcome the dead hand of small-town values.

In Soviet Russia, the new generation's counterparts were in most instances committed to the Revolution, and hence superficially the opposite of Fitzgerald's affluent hedonists. Yet around 1922 there emerged in Russia a new generation that had, likewise, "been adolescent during the confusion of the war" and "brusquely shouldered [its elders] out of the way and danced into the limelight," blithely ignoring them, for they were confident that time and reality were on their side.

The greatest problem in drawing such an analogy is not the question of how much the work of the new generation in Soviet Russia was influenced by jazz so much as to what extent it exemplified a libidinous, carefree, "erotic" culture. Actually, many in that younger generation—such as Shklovsky and Eisenstein—were influenced by Freud.[31] However, it was less sexual libido that obsessed them than the libido of revolutionary pathos (though some conflated the two in their imagery). In thinking through ways to avert the decline of European culture that Spengler charts in *The Decline of the West*, many fastened on revolution as a force with the necessary energy and virility to counteract the drift into effete impotence.[32] Freud and eroticism—generally combined in the Russian case with Marxism—provided a rationale for rejecting the values of the elders as a sort of false consciousness. The feisty young generation that emerged during these years claimed priority because they were young—and therefore not prisoners of their elders' illusions.

One way of accounting for the prominence of this new generation in Soviet culture is in terms of the rise of the Komsomol as a player in that field. But then, why did the Komsomol become more powerful in culture, rivaling the Party? Why, as the Soviet Union moved to an ever more committed culture, was prominence not given to that old guard of proletarian writers who had been spear-carriers of revolutionary culture for years, suffering arrest and exile, servicing *Pravda* and other Bolshevik organs with uplifting prose and verse, and undergoing apprenticeships in Paris, Bologna, or Capri at the feet of Party intellectuals? In other words, the generational changeover in Soviet culture, generally explained in terms of postrevolutionary local (Soviet) politics, might also be seen as a local version of a post-traumatic (post–Great War) shift that Fitzgerald identifies for his local context as the Jazz Age. To use a dominant trope of this book—ecology—it might be said that both in Russia and in America the young emerged to prominence as new, postcataclysm shoots.

Several groups of the young and rapacious entered the "limelight" in Petrograd at the beginning of the 1920s. The most prominent in literature were the Serapion Brothers, a group that was formed in 1921 out of a literary studio founded at the House of Arts in 1919 and included such now-famous Soviet literary figures as M. Zoshchenko, K. Fedin, Vs. Ivanov—and Kaverin.[33]

It was the youngest Serapion Brother, Lev Lunts, a mere lad of thirteen when the war began in 1914, who spoke for the Jazz Age when on December 2, 1922, he delivered his famous speech "Go West!" (*Na zapad!*) to an intimate gathering of the group. Lunts's point of departure was the crisis in literature, but he disregarded the various solutions proposed for it that involved a reaffirmation of the old values (for example, reviving the Great Tradition of "Pushkin"), declaring unequivocally that the only way to overcome the provincialism and lack of literacy in Russian literature was to learn from the West.

By learning from "the West," Lunts meant not from the great eras of the past but from the urbanized and cosmopolitan West of his day. Russian literature, he maintained, will make a great leap forward only if it passes through a period of "slavish imitation of the West."[34] Specifically, it should learn the mastery of plot to be found in the West's "adventure literature."[35] To him, a healthy injection of plot could provide an instant panacea for Russian literature's moribund condition (especially for the novel). The mistake of the Russians, he insisted in a statement that proved controversial even among Serapions,[36] was that they have given absolute priority to social commitment and contended that such formal considerations as plot construction should be waived in favor of this overriding interest. But, he countered, attention to plot does not preclude social commitment, while failure to give it its due is fatal for literature.[37]

Lunts and some fellow Serapions were far from the only groups advocating this approach.[38] By the beginning of 1924, a critic reviewing the situation in literature remarked that literary works "now could not afford not to be European," and pronounced the "hegemony" in fiction of the new generation such as the Serapion Brothers who now commanded more critical attention than Pilnyak, who had dominated as recently as 1922.[39] Lunts's main mentors, the Petrograd Formalists (themselves only a year or two older than the Serapions), held somewhat similar views. One of their number, B. Eikhenbaum, proposed in a milder formulation of Lunts's position that the road to a new Russian literature lies through "alien hills."[40]

Starting around 1921 (coincidentally, more or less on the eve of NEP) the Formalists shifted their principal concerns and began to show more interest in contemporary Western culture.[41] In that year, it was announced that Tynyanov was editing a collection entitled *The Cultural Life of the West* (which never materialized).[42] They also began to analyze Western literary genres and writers whose forte was fast-paced plot construction; names such as Conan Doyle frequently appear among the examples they adduce in their theoretical writings.[43]

The Formalists did more than discuss the formal properties of this kind of Western writing. They attempted to form an alliance of writers and theoreticians as a sort of vanguard of the new movement, setting up in January 1924 under the auspices of the Division for the Verbal Arts (their niche in GIII) a Committee for Contemporary Literature. This committee, whose aim was to "establish a link between scholarly work in literary theory and history and actual contemporary problems of literary composition and criticism,"[44] was intended to be an independent center that might influence the evolution of Soviet culture; its membership included the Formalists, the Serapions, and even Ehrenburg, a Moscow writer who for most of the 1920s lived in Western Europe (where, *inter alia*, he co-edited *Veshch'*).[45] Some of the most interesting theoretical and literary work of the time was read and discussed at the committee's sessions; at one, Zamyatin read excerpts from his banned dystopian novel *We*. The committee was closely linked with the critical journal the *Russian Contemporary* (Russkiy sovremennik), which attracted contributions from serious literary theoreticians, including Bakhtin. Also, most of its members took its agenda seriously by taking up their pens to experiment with racy Western prose genres.[46] The Formalists and their GIII colleagues resisted the notion that they were just scholars, preferring to see themselves as activists for radical cultural change. Like most such activists of this time, they took the symbolism of space very seriously and made a principled stand in resisting moving to Vasilevsky Island, the bastion of the scholarly community.[47]

The shift to an interest in adventure genres was typical of this time. Not surprisingly, the list of publications from World Literature in 1922 was dominated by works such as Pierre Benoit's *Atlantide*.[48] Such works, which were not many steps away from the boulevard romance, stand in contrast with its typical list during War Communism, which comprised largely utopian fiction and European highbrow novels.

World Literature was still high-minded as compared with many private presses that made a living by meeting the popular demand for detective and adventure literature. The state presses were less blatantly commercial in their output, but their publishing lists were also influenced by current vogues and the new requirement that they make do without subsidies. By 1924, Jack London was overwhelmingly the most published writer in the Soviet Union, coming out in sixty-seven separate editions in that year alone, followed by Upton Sinclair with thirty-four, and O. Henry with seventeen; writers such as Edgar Rice Burroughs, G. K. Chesterton, and A. Conan Doyle were also near the top of the list.[49]

The new vogues came up against that perennial bugbear of the Russian intelligentsia, the taint of the lowbrow or "boulevard." Even such relative liberals as Eikhenbaum complained about the recent craze for adventure literature, claiming that the "fare of the railway station has been brought into the town."[50] He, Lunts, and others in his coterie drew a distinction between certain of the more accomplished Western writers of adventure fiction, such as Rider Haggard and Conan Doyle, and hacks—such as Benoit.[51]

Such discrimination reflects only a mild disdain for popular literature as compared with the extreme self-righteousness of the self-appointed guardians of cultural purity who, in their comments on the vogue for Western lowbrow literature or film, did the printed word-equivalent of frothing at the mouth, insisting that this was the "muck" of an "Augean stable" that must be "cleaned out" immediately[52]—though, in actuality, the only Western popular "muck" to be cleaned out in these years was dancing on the stage; the fox trot, shimmy, one-steps, apaches, and the like were banned by a decree of the Petrograd Provincial Repertoire Committee of August 1924.[53]

Many intellectuals were less rigid and fanatical. Still, they faced the dilemma of how to counteract bourgeois culture without losing sight of the Jazz Age completely. One way to resolve the problem was to differentiate among countries in the West. Most intellectuals drew a distinction between Europe, which was misguided and imperiled, and America, where the true beast resided. Even within Europe, they differentiated between the good countries, especially antifascist, Weimar Germany, which had recently overthrown its kaiser and had undergone several attempted revolutions, and the bad—decadent and venal countries such as France and England, principal sources of the boulevard literature then flooding the market.

Soviet intellectuals had richer cultural and scientific contacts with their German counterparts than with any other country (partly because the two were the great pariahs of the postwar period). Most Soviet scientific work reached the West via a German scientific periodical in which leading Soviet scientists published their findings,[54] while in local (Petrograd) scholarly journals, the abstracts and reviews of recent German scholarship, philosophy, and literary theory crowded out most other material, leaving the impression that Petrograd was a sort of colonial outpost of German intellectual life.

Berlin functioned as Russia's new "window on Europe," even replacing Paris as the mecca for avant-garde artists. The Russian émigré community then centered there numbered more than four hundred thousand; many of them were intellectuals and they established Russian publishing houses that provided alternative outlets for Petrograd intellectuals, alternative to the state publishing houses. In film, the ties between Petrograd and Berlin were particularly close; the latest Expressionist films dominated discussion among Petrograd's intellectuals, while the latest productions of Sevzapkino were given screenings in Berlin. In literature and theater, German Expressionism was also in vogue, and in Petrograd an allied movement (the Emotionalists) was set up in 1923 with Radlov and Piotrovsky among its leaders.[55] Berlin also functioned as a "window" in the sense of a place to display Russian wares. Hence the avant-garde established *Veshch'* there, hoping through it to make its mark in the West.

Most actors in cultural life, from Party leaders to the professoriate, looked to the West but were also repelled by it. After all, the translations were for the most part *from* the West *to* Russia. Thus the country that was meant to dazzle the world with a new, revolutionary culture was in fact subsisting on an imported or at best derivative one. Even the staunchest of Westernizers, such as Eikhenbaum's fellow Formalist Shklovsky, became concerned; in an article entitled "[Put] a Tax on Tarzan," he suggested taxing foreign literature and using the proceeds to foster local writers.[56]

It might seem that no sooner had the government subsidies in publishing been eliminated and something closer to a market situation introduced, than the mirage of "culture for the starved workers" evaporated and their true tastes began to be reflected in publications (tastes, incidentally, that were not so far from those of the bourgeoisie, who also showed a preference for adventure and detective fiction). It is also possible to view this trend as symptomatic of a general reorientation in Soviet culture, however, part of the reaction against the revolutionary millenialism of the initial years. It is worth noting here that the last time Russia experienced such a vogue for adventure and detective fiction was 1908, usually regarded as a time when the reaction against the revolutionary élan of 1905 had set in.[57]

In a sense, the entire shift we have been charting is neither a devolution in culture nor a revolution, but an attempt at translation. The various shifts that took place early in NEP enumerated in this and the preceding chapter involve not just differences in magnitude—more cinematic effects, a reduced scale for the mass spectacle, younger writers and filmmakers, and so on. Intellectuals were trying to make a translation across virtually all levels of existence. It was a translation in time, as was the Jazz Age. This sub-period, more than its predecessor, saw an attempt to strike through time to a new account of reality, thus providing an example of *translation* in its most fundamental meaning. Few were content any longer with the standard fare of War Communism, the mass spectacles, posters, and agitational dramas; a broad spectrum aimed to generate a new culture that might compete successfully with that coming from Europe and America. But how might this be effected?

Some had tried to adapt Western works for revolutionary purposes in a mechanical way and the results had been ludicrous. For instance, N. G. Vinogradov, known earlier as a pioneering director of the theater of mass participation, had pirated the score for Puccini's *Tosca* wholesale for a new "revolutionary" opera, *In the Struggle for the Commune*, performed as part of the October Revolution celebrations in 1924. He maintained that he did not have to alter the original opera unduly and was able to keep *Tosca*'s "basic plot," and yet, he claimed, the opera was so revolutionary that it would have the effect of "a bomb exploding in the theater."[58] Rather than prove a "bomb," needless to say, it bombed. Clearly, more radical translations were needed.

Many literary theorists in Petrograd were engrossed in thinking through the phenomenon of translation and also models of literary evolution. They were becoming aware of the limits of mechanical translation from one language to another or from one medium to another and of how translation inevitably entails some recoding or reinflection.[59] The Formalists were particularly concerned with these questions, and they developed a theory of literary evolution that involves "translations," not just across languages, but also across literary levels; as literature evolves, what was considered high literature may be incorporated into the low, and vice versa.[60] Their model implicitly offers, if not a solution, then at least some perspective on the "muck" of the "Augean stable," that is, Western lowbrow culture, which so troubled Petrograd intellectuals and cultural authorities at this time; it raises the question of whether one should expend the labor of Hercules to clean out this "muck" when the very future evolution of literature may depend on it.

The Red Pinkerton

Some Party leaders had come to a vaguely similar position. Predictably, few in the Party were particularly enthusiastic about the idea of Western trash literature and film dominating the Soviet market, but some advocated co-opting this culture, a position not unlike that of the Formalists and Lunts. Among the Party spokesmen, the best-known advocate of this policy is Nikolai Bukharin, who proposed in a *Pravda* article of 1923 that Soviet literature produce a "red Pinkerton," or in other words, that it apply the kind of plot structures one sees in detective and adventure literature to produce fiction celebrating the triumph of Soviet Communism.[61] What Bukharin had in mind was a countermodel to the Pinkertons flooding the market, one that would use their fast-paced, entertaining plots in the service of the ideals of the new society (note that the Party [Bukharin] did not originate this idea).

This injunction did not fall on deaf ears. Many wanted to experience the Jazz Age, but they wanted to recode it as the age of revolution. Pace was one of the markers of the Jazz Age, but surely pace should be the marker of revolution *a fortiori.* Hence Jazz Age trends should be intensified in a Soviet redaction.

Whether in response to injunctions from on high, or because authors were intrigued by the challenge of recoding the Jazz Age, "red Pinkertons" appeared like mushrooms in these years. Most used some variant on a fairly standard plot (not unlike that of *The Trust D. E.*): Europe is threatened by a conspiracy of capitalists / fascists who have gained access to some device of incredible destructive power, but a valiant proletariat (usually Russian) wrests this device from the plotters in the nick of time and saves Europe; America is soon converted as well, and proletarian hegemony and international solidarity are assured.

These "red Pinkertons" represent a new phase in the evolution of Soviet culture, a departure from the conventions of War Communism. In them, for example, the cult of technology and progress was often challenged in an apocalyptic plot; science, rather than appearing as an emblem of revolution as was generally the case with the literature published during War Communism, was now often the agent of some holocaust (a trope often influenced by German Expressionism or Spengler).[62] The attitude toward technology varied among the Pinkertons, but in most other respects they followed a similar pattern, and one can adduce from them a conventionalized plot structure that focuses values defining of revolutionary culture in the initial years of NEP. The Pinkertons can be seen as emblematic of the culture of that period, as was the mass spectacle during the immediately preceding period of War Communism.

The Pinkertons' master plot points to the key shift in NEP culture, one more important than the generational and other such shifts chronicled here—a shift in the master model of history. When the Pinkerton was recoded as red, this led to a new orientation in time-space, a new chronotope—new as compared with that of the original Pinkertons, and also as compared with the dominant chronotope of the previously regnant genres.

We seek in vain in these works for any mention of Greece or revolutionary France, which were the emblems of so much of the culture of Petrograd under War Communism. We now see not a progression over time as in the mass spectacle of War Communism (then prototypically, from ancient Greece through the two French revolutions to 1917), but a valorized contrast of places (America / Europe / Russia) with historical change effected by movement between them. This emphasis on place led to a corresponding de-emphasis on time, so radical that it was not even the case that different places represent different times. This downplaying of the temporal dimension is analogous to what Fitzgerald called the "Jazz Age" with its rejection of generational prerogatives.

The new Pinkertons retain the same essential binary of oppressors and oppressed that structured the mass spectacle. In this instance, the oppressors are international capitalists-cum-fascists, and the oppressed (those threatened with extinction) are "Europe" and the socialist culture of Russia. As in the mass spectacle, most often the plot involves an opposition between two places (in this instance, Russia and America) with a third (in this instance, Europe) functioning as the equivalent of that linking "corridor" (or staircase) where, according to the conventions of the mass spectacle, the tussle between oppressors and oppressed is fought out.

In the new historical model (as defined by the "red Pinkerton") the status of that linking space is, however, much higher than in the mass spectacle (as befits a time of "interregnum"). Russian culture from 1922 to 1924 shows a marked Eurocentrism (in some instances, such as *The Trust D. E.*, there are even racist elements). It is perhaps significant that most prominent authors of "red Pinkertons" were either themselves returnees from European emigration or had spent some time in Europe in the past (for example, A. Tolstoy, M. Shaginyan, V. Shklovsky, A. Tolstoy, and I. Ehrenburg). In novels, plays, and films of this time Europe is threatened and must be saved. But when the Russian workers "save" Europe, they in a sense also consummate a marriage; Europe becomes one again when Russia joins it.

The most famous and influential of the many Pinkertons that appeared in these years was *Mess-Mend, or a Yankee in Petrograd* (Mess-Mend, ili yanki v Petrograde, 1924–1925), by the Petrograd writer Marietta Shaginyan (published under the pseudonym Jim Dollar). *Mess-Mend* tells the story of a group of American factory workers who form a secret society called Mess-Mend (that is, deconstruct-construct) that is dedicated to thwarting the sinister plans of an international conspiracy of millionaires and aristocrats bent on defeating socialism. Their evil leader, Kressling, has invented a dread device that will ensure their control over the world. However, one of the millionaires, the engineer Jeremiah Rockerfeller (named Morlender in the revised edition), falls under the spell of the Soviet Union when he visits there. He is kidnapped by the conspirators, who fake his death to incite his son Arthur to visit the Soviet Union in disguise and avenge his father by blowing up strategic factories, including the Putilov with its great revolutionary pedigree. Arthur is to kill the Soviet leadership at the Revolution Day ceremonies by handing them a bomb in the guise of a tribute. Thus Petrograd, prime locus of the Revolution, is brought to the very brink of destruction, but members of Mess-Mend follow Arthur to Petrograd, outwit the conspirators, and save the city. In the end Arthur, like his father, is captivated by the workers' paradise.

We note in this novel a reversal of the large-scale / small-scale pattern that characterized the culture of War Communism. The contrast is particularly evident if we compare this work with another that marked the climactic utopian moment of cultural life during War Communism, the fall of 1920, Mayakovsky's new epic poem *150,000,000*, which he read to gatherings in Petrograd that December. This poem has a plot similar to that of *Mess-Mend* (the workers save the world from a capitalist hyena), except that in it the heroes are 150,000,000-strong (the population of the Soviet Union at the time), but in *Mess-Mend* they compose a small band. Admittedly, the small band is but the tip of a vast network behind the secret society MM (Mess-Mend), but the network is never more than a shadowy presence in the novel. Moreover, the small band, a veritable David that takes on the Goliath of international capital, is masterminded by a single individual known as Mick Thingmaster. The shift to adventure literature has meant an unacknowledged shift from collective to individual heroes.

Mick Thingmaster shows incredible ingenuity in inventing and making devices that enable Mess-Mend's members to triumph over overwhelming odds, aiding the cause of their cloak-and-dagger counterconspiracy; they can penetrate walls, travel on power lines with the speed of electricity, and secretly record in sight and sound meetings of the conspirators. Shaginyan believed that her account of the workers' ability to produce such devices would demonstrate that those who work with their hands are superior to the effete capitalists.[63] In practice, however, it is Mick's head, his knowledge of science, rather than his actual hands, that help him outwit the capitalist conspirators. Mick appears as a combination of scientist-inventor and Sherlock Holmes, and not particularly as the fraternalist worker.

Nevertheless, Meshcheryakov, the editor of the State Publishing House, recommended *Mess-Mend* as a "novel of our time," a novel of "movement," and as such a model for the "revolutionary-adventure genre."[64] Some new novels commissioned by the State Publishing House were, explicitly, to be modeled on *Mess-Mend*,[65] and it was adopted as a model in leftist Germany as well.[66] *Mess-Mend*, and other fiction written to a similar recipe, was published in those years in printings of tens and hundreds of thousands, while printings of nonadventure fiction rarely exceeded a few thousand copies.[67]

Shaginyan originally published *Mess-Mend* in serial form in ten inexpensive booklets, thus imitating the way most popular lowbrow Western fiction had appeared in mass editions before the Revolution.[68] The booklets, however, had covers by the Constructivist artist A. Rodchenko. As this fact suggests, the attempt at adapting the formal features of Western lowbrow genres to serve the Soviet cause represents a convergence of interests between certain segments of the Party leadership and the highbrow avant-garde. Shaginyan was herself until this point best known for her essays and diaries on cultural topics and had recently become a close associate of the Formalists.

Her novel is a revolutionary utopia and to that extent similar to the standard Western fare published by World Literature during War Communism, though in this instance the classic utopia has been refracted through Constructivism and then married to the Pinkerton. The actual utopia, a futuristic Petersburg that Shaginyan calls Radio City, emerges as a sort of new and more comprehensive version of Tatlin's tower. Radio City is actually an industrial complex but, as with Tatlin's tower, it is three-tiered and topped by a radio tower. On the city's lower tier, natural resources are extracted and farming takes place. Here one sees many examples of tinkering with the ecology; for instance, in its farms everything is grown, from tropical products (coconuts, rice) to those of the Arctic (Icelandic moss), a provision that anticipates the Stalinist vogue for Michurin with his schemes for growing potatoes in the Arctic Circle and other agricultural "feats." On the second tier, the natural resources are processed, while on the third these processed materials are turned into manufactured goods. This third tier also has thousands of transport bays so that the end product can be whisked by airplanes to supply the farthest reaches.[69]

This tower-like colossus is more ambitious than Tatlin's in that it not merely celebrates revolution, but actually conquers nature once and for all. As if to symbolize this, Shaginyan tells us that it has eviscerated the infamous Petersburg swamps.[70] The magical device ensuring this achievement is electricity. In fact Volkhovstroy, an electric station in the Petrograd Region then under construction as the pathbreaker for the Leninist scheme for the electrification of the country, is cited as the source of an "incredible energy." Incredible it must be, for it enables the industrial complex to control climate and ecological conditions completely with an "electro-climate," while simultaneously fueling the city's defense system, a high-voltage electrical field placed well above the city that in the event of an enemy attack can be turned on to serve as an impenetrable shield.

In Radio City, not just defense and supply problems have been solved for all time, but also those long-standing contradictions and differences in society that concerned Marx. These include class contradictions, of course, but also the division between the country and the city and between mental and physical labor; the last has been overcome in a system whereby workers on the site intermittently leave their particular tasks to tour one of the other sections and learn about the work processes there. Radio City has also found solutions to some of the problems that utopias conventionally resolve; for instance, its planners have unlocked the secrets of retarding the aging process.

The principal agenda realized in Radio City is, however, that of the Constructivists (for whom Tatlin's tower was an icon). Besides the Constructivist fetishization of technology and electricity one finds in this novel an emphasis on utilizing science to revolutionize the pace of human movement. Arthur is amazed by the incredible pace he sees on the Petrograd streets, not just of their vehicles, but also of the pedestrians who move at an inhuman speed. He meets a Professor of Striding who explains the alterations made to human physiology to achieve this (thanks to the work of Russian scientists such as M. Bekhterev). Thus the Russians have outdone even the Americans and produced the ultimate pace. The Jazz Age has met revolutionary utopia.

"Here there is everything," the narrator exults, but in fact this "everything" is in just the one place—Petrograd.[71] It was of course no longer the capital, and yet in Shaginyan's utopia it is all, the center of a unified socio-economic-political system. This denouement is presented as the triumph of proletarian internationalism; all the nations are represented among those who work in the giant complex.

In this utopia, ethnic and social problems have been eradicated, but at the price of homogenization. Shaginyan proudly proclaims that all production processes are standardized in a "single [yedinyy] method of economic activity."[72] She likens the way everything is centrally coordinated in Radio City to a symphony in which "each performs his own partitura but hears only the symphony"—hardly jazz![73]

Generically, by contrast, the novel is a hybrid made up of elements from different genres.[74] With such a melange, it exemplifies what Shaginyan's friend Tynyanov called the literature of the "interregnum." In his account in "The Literature of Fact" (1923) of the evolutionary dynamic that gives rise to that kind of literature, Tynyanov posits an ongoing dance between genres at the "center" and those at the "periphery" (note how, as was typical for the culture of this time, he uses a spatial model for a temporal progression). According to Tynyanov's model, it is genres on the periphery that save (or regenerate / supersede) the dominant genres at the center. His model, then, is analogous to that of this new kind of fiction (drama and film) in which peripheral Russia saves Europe. Such works, as it were, mediate the technology gap no less than the menace of fascism. Their basic plot also saves Russia from that recurrent phobia, provincialism: in *Mess-Mend*, the international conspiracy is sending assassins to Russia in order to become the rulers of Europe.[75] Petrograd, so recently supplanted as Russia's capital, suddenly becomes the center of the world. It is probably no accident that while most Moscow writers of this new kind of literature set their works in some place only vaguely identified, almost all the Petrograd writers set their works in Petrograd itself.[76]

Tynyanov's general model in this essay, though intended to describe a dynamic in literature, was analogous to an account of cultural evolution in general that was more broadly found among the Petrograd coterie associated with the Committee on the Study of Contemporary Literature and the Serapion Brothers, and in effect represents a version of the one found in Kuhn's *The Structure of Scientific Revolutions*. Like Kuhn, they posit an alternation between a period of the canonical, or "normal" science / literature, and a period of the noncanonical, as the old norms are what Shklovsky might call "defamiliarized."[77] Zamyatin, another of the Serapions' mentors, in his essay "On Literature, Revolution, and Other Matters" (which he read to the Committee), figures his account of revolution in culture primarily using the alternation to be found in the theory of thermodynamics between energy and entropy, the slide into entropy being analogous to Kuhn's slide into "normal science." Thus the main distinction between the models of Tynyanov, Shklovsky, and Zamyatin, and those of Kuhn is their respective valorization of "normal" and "abnormal." Zamyatin and the Formalists idealized heretics and those who "explode" or confound canons.[78]

Kuhn's model of alternating periods of "normal" and "abnormal" science was essentially descriptive, but the corresponding theories of Zamyatin and the Formalists were also *prescriptive*—hence the Committee. In seeking to influence the direction of Soviet literature with their prescription of "adventure literature," they as lovers of "heretics" warned against the pitfalls of slavish imitation or adaptation of existing models, recommending instead parody.

The Formalists gave parody a crucial role in their account of literary evolution, where they described it as a kind of translation that more often than not involves deflation or lowering of the models of high culture. Shaginyan claimed that *Mess-Mend* was written as a parody of the adventure story, hence somewhat in the spirit suggested by the Formalists.[79] However, the critics missed the point—as did the workers who snatched up copies and read them avidly.[80]

In Petrograd, the contemporary masters of parody were the young members of FEKS (an acronym for the Factory of the Eccentric Actor), a group founded in 1922 by two young enthusiasts from the provinces, Grigory Kozintsev (from Kiev) and Leonid Trauberg (from Odessa). The FEKS members, or FEKSy, were most representative of the nexus of things we have been discussing in this chapter—Westernism, co-option of Western lowbrow culture, Americanization, jazz, and a racy pace. They were young—they saw the Great War as teenagers—and they took these trends to an extreme. In that sense, they can be seen as emblematic of the age.

The FEKSy picked up the baton from the avant-garde theater of War Communism, and particularly from Radlov's Peoples Comedy Theater, which also sometimes called itself "eccentric." As if to indicate this, they engaged as an instructor and performer in their "factory" the famous circus acrobat Serzh, who had been used by Radlov's theater (in Russian one of the meanings of "eccentric" refers to a clown).[81] They were nevertheless careful to define themselves as younger and more truly avant-garde than such predecessors. In this endeavor they were joined by their Moscow friend and ally, Sergei Eisenstein (unfortunately, the friends' dream of combining forces in Moscow or Petrograd was never realized, but some claim that Eisenstein's theory of montage was really first conceived by FEKS). In these years the FEKSy and Eisenstein did remarkably parallel work in Petrograd and Moscow, respectively, as can be seen in their first films, FEKS's *The Adventures of Oktyabrina* (December 1924) and Eisenstein's *Strike* (April 1925).[82]

The FEKSy were more radical than Eisenstein and went well beyond him in the area of *épatage*. But they were bent on shocking not just the bourgeoisie per se but more the tribal intellectual, the one who would react at the very mention of "the boulevard," the *"café chantant,"* or "America," which the FEKSy proclaimed cardinal values.[83] FEKS reveled in all those aspects of modern-day America that most of their contemporaries found repellant: not only the technology (focused in their cult of Edison as emblem of electricity and inventor of the cinema), but the strident, loud sounds, the ubiquitous advertisements, and even its lowbrow culture—Pinkertons, movies, jazz, and the music of the *café chantant*—was not merely to be tolerated, but proclaimed "the art of today" and put at the center of its cultural program.[84] Yet they were also fervent revolutionaries, insisting that art be "truly agitational, entertaining, and eccentric."[85] The juxtaposition of these three qualities would seem to be a conundrum and in some senses FEKS represents a sort of zany version of Constructivism—Dadaist Constructivism, if you will.[86]

The first major production of FEKS was an adaptation of Gogol's play *The Wedding* (Zhenit'ba), which affronted its audience of 1922 with a cacophony of competing sounds, flickering lights, and a confusion and profusion of action on the stage. Figures dressed in garish clothing exchanged shouts and reprises about topical issues; they sang couplets and acted out strange pantomimes with dances and acrobatic feats. The affianced pair from Gogol (in conventional theatrical guise) were mixed in with constructions moving about on wheels. Then, in a flash, the backdrop was changed into a screen on which was projected a clip of Charlie Chaplin fleeing from the cops. Actors dressed and made up in the same way as those on the screen burst onto the front of the stage to act in parallel play with the movie. A circus clown shrieking ecstatically turned on a *salto mortale* right through the canvas of the backdrop, while "Gogol" bounced around on a platform with springs from which he was propelled to the ceiling.[87]

Thus Gogol was "translated" into postrevolutionary Russia. Clearly, however, this was less a translation than some sort of parody. In the earlier playful examples of revolutionary culture such as those found at the People's Comedy Theater or in the mass spectacle where the farcical essentially alternated with the tragic or elevated, the lines between genres and modes were preserved, but in this instance one finds an almost Postmodernist flouting of such borders—almost, but not really.

The term "eccentric," which this group used to nominate its art, is a bit misleading because in the West it has connotations of something aberrant, unique, or even anarchic. The FEKSy did not, like many Dadaists, for example, look to the "gratuitous gesture" as a paradigm for the sort of system-confounding art they represented. On the contrary, though they took the ideal of playful experimentation to an extreme, they were also absolutely serious about their pro-Soviet message. They were also not "eccentric" in the sense that for them cardinal values were control and discipline (even in executing the "hot" dances).[88] To them "montage" meant "strict timing," a position shared by Meyerhold and Eisenstein at this time.[89]

In these years, the Formalists, together with representatives of left art such as the Constructivists, emphasized in their writings the necessity of organizing a given artifact or situation (be it a building, a musical piece, a painting, or a poem) and studying how it was put together. Yet at the same time the Formalists focused on the arbitrariness of a work's length or plot structure. They saw particular merit in playing with the devices in a given work, in stringing along episodes or devices, retarding plot development, and various techniques for playing with the direct chronological sequence of events (an interest in adventure and detective fiction was a natural for them).[90] Thus they and other members of their coterie wanted to usher in an age of "plot" (organization) in literature. Yet at the same time what they advocated was a kind of antisystematic system.

So, then, was this systematic, or not? And what, too, is jazz? Is it improvisation, or is it timing? Is it cacophony, or is it the new-age symphony? Is it a "carnival" form, or is it, as Gorky was later to contend, pornography? Is it the vice of the upper classes, or is it the voice of the oppressed (of the barely freed slaves)?[91] Is it a new form, or is it a corruption or degradation of the old? Is it "mess" or is it "mend"? Thus we are up against the paradox of revolution again—revolution as iconoclasm and demystification but also as affirmation on a monumental scale. This time the paradox emerges in a different articulation.

One problem with the Formalists' analysis is that a parodic literature tends to be a posterior literature. The question is, how do you get from abnormal to normal science? In order for the antisystematic to become system it has to be perceived as such; much depends on institutional history and what it is modish to call "situatedness"; today's parody may become tomorrow's canon—especially if it proves to be popular, as was *Mess-Mend*. Moreover, a "permanent revolution" of systems, such as Zamyatin advocated, essentially militates against meaning. Even Shklovsky began to sense this. In a 1925 foreword to *Mustard Gas* (Iprit), his contribution to the "red

Pinkerton" (a novel he co-authored with the Serapion Brother Vs. Ivanov), he confessed that in this book he had overdone "playing with the clichés" of the translated novel of adventure, that there was excessive "stylization" and "ironic parody" that he hoped to correct in his future efforts.[92]

By then, many had begun to think that the "red Pinkerton," the hasty reconfiguration of Western adventure novels and films as "revolutionary culture," was only a bandaid solution.[93] To say "Go West" through "alien hills" is essentially to say ditch the cult of Pushkin, ditch the norms and sacred cows of the intelligentsia. The Petrograd Formalists were not prepared to do that. Hence they oscillated. They were suspended between the Jazz Age of the immediately younger generation and the authority figures among their elders.[94] There were also extraliterary factors fostering a reappraisal of Western genres, as the next chapter will show. Thus the "red Pinkerton" formula for the new culture was not productive for long. Consequently, this period proved to be more of an "interregnum" than even Tynyanov anticipated.

And yet, this interregnum did not prove entirely sterile. All was not "plundered, betrayed, and sold out" as even Akhmatova recognized, but rather it had to be rethought, reconfigured, regenred. The next three chapters outline successive attempts at creating new models for a truly Soviet culture, and, as we shall see, each in its own way has distinct links with *Mess-Mend* and the "red Pinkerton"—and even with the work of FEKS.

8

THE ESTABLISHMENT OF
SOVIET CULTURE

In September 1924 Leningrad was engulfed by a disastrous flood. The Neva broke its banks, covering such landmarks as Nevsky Prospect and Vasilevsky Island. Since so many cultural institutions were situated in the center of town, they were particularly hard hit. In many theaters, for instance, the costumes or the heating and lighting were destroyed; in the case of the Bolshoi Drama Theater, the roof was torn off.[1]

The fact that this flood occurred exactly one hundred years after its famous predecessor, the great flood of 1824, did not go unremarked. The high-water mark of that flood was the focus of newspaper reports trying to gauge the severity of the more recent one; the flood of 1824 rose to thirteen feet seven inches, whereas the flood of 1924 rose to thirteen feet, thus coming closer than any other flood to reaching the level of 1824.[2]

Needless to say, comparisons with 1824 need not only be in terms of high-water marks. Since the 1824 flood was the subject of Pushkin's *The Bronze Horseman*, the principal text of the myth of Petersburg, this flood brought into sharper focus once again the city's existential dilemmas, and also the issues of modernization and the authoritarian state that many have assumed to be aired in Pushkin's poem.

On October 7, 1924, the same day that the *Life of Art* printed an appeal for flood relief, it also published extracts from a new play by Evreinov called *The Commune of the Righteous* (Kommuna pravednykh), which draws on the biblical story of Noah and his ark. The play, written in a "heroic grotesque," is about how the idealist hopes of an intelligentsia tragically remote from real life "run aground" as they are dashed against the reality of a more worldly working class who do not share their quixotic idealism and are easily able to gain the upper hand. Most of the action of the play takes place on the deck of a "hermit ship" that houses an anarchic "commune of the righteous" inspired by a poet who has been nicknamed "the crazed one." One can't help speculating whether the play is not in part a dig at Mayakovsky as the author of *Mystery-Bouffe*, another free interpretation of the biblical legend of Noah's ark.[3] Thus, effectively, Evreinov is announcing not just the end, but also the failure, of the ethos that inspired the cultural Renaissance of Petrograd during War Communism.

Evreinov himself emigrated in 1925 when his troupe went on a European tour. Other fellow directors of the mass spectacle, such as Yury Annenkov and Dimitry Tiomkin, left the previous year (Alexandr Benois emigrated a year later). Most of the would-be theatrical renovators remained, however, to experience a more fundamental shift in the dominant patterns of cultural life than the Revolution had as yet effected. In the mid-1920s, approximately 1924–1926, we can already find the contours of those patterns—institutional, ideological, and aesthetic—that in the 1930s were to re-emerge as defining a culture we call "Stalinism."[4]

The shifts around 1924 were so major that one may talk of the emergence of a post-NEP culture.[5] Of course it was not entirely the case that NEP had disappeared as a force in cultural life, but in literature at any rate stiff taxes and other factors conspired to reduce the number of private publishing houses, and especially the number of their titles.[6] Moreover, some literary groups had begun to disavow the principles of pluralism and creative autonomy that they had insisted on just a few years before.[7]

An obvious starting point for this shift would be Lenin's death on January 21, which raised the possibility that the new leadership might effect a change in cultural policy. The direction this change was to take was not immediately apparent and was to emerge in increasingly heated debates conducted over the ensuing ten years. There were some disquieting signs from the very beginning, however. For instance, in Leningrad the censors became more active.[8]

A palpable sign of change after Lenin's death was the decree of the Petrograd Soviet on January 24th that the city should be renamed Leningrad.[9] Zinoviev, the ambitious head of the Party in the city, had pushed the new name through immediately, hoping, presumably, to emphasize Leningrad's status as cradle of the Revolution—the "city of Lenin."

The renaming of the city and the ensuing flood were superficial markers of change. Yet with their ominous resonances both events lend themselves to interpretation as signaling that perennially proclaimed "end of Petersburg," the end of a time when a distinctive ethos informed the city's cultural life, and the beginning of the dark days when a sort of "bronze horseman," or highly authoritarian central power (now located in Moscow), sought to impose its will on creative activity.

Leningrad intellectuals, already taunted by the thought that they were passé, were being invaded by new cultural trends from Moscow that many found alien and threatening. These trends were not only Constructivism (which was often welcomed) but the self-styled "proletarian" or "revolutionary" cultural organizations that were militantly opposed to most of the trends that had dominated in the city over the past ten years.

Around 1922 there had formed in Moscow a plethora of proletarian or revolutionary cultural organizations, each representing a different branch of the arts. In literature, the dominant organization was VAPP (the All-Russian Association of Proletarian Writers, founded in 1921); in music, it was RAPM (the Russian Association of Proletarian Musicians, founded in 1923); and in art, it was AKhRR (the Association of Artists of Revolutionary Russia, founded in 1922). There had of course been other proletarian and revolutionary cultural bodies before (notably the Proletcult), but these new organizations were markedly more militant vis-à-vis others in their field; a Soviet literary historian aptly titled his book on the VAPP leadership *Implacable Zealots*.[10] Each was actively committed to eliminating particular groups or trends from Soviet culture, especially the avant-garde and the modernists. VAPP's particular *bête noire* was the so-called fellow-traveler (*poputchik*), or, in others words, the uncommitted writer who was generally sympathetic to the Revolution but not yet won over completely to its cause. To VAPP's dismay, Trotsky had argued in *Literature and Revolution* (1923), influential in these years, that the proletariat were not sufficiently cultured to produce a world-class literature and hence the *poputchiki* would be the mainstay of Soviet literature during the current interim period before a classless society was achieved. Members of VAPP were outraged at the notion that bourgeois writers could be so much as tolerated in these revolutionary times and demanded hegemony for the "proletarians," by which they largely meant those associated with the Party or Komsomol.

For those fearing an art of capitulation, the invasion of proletarian culture from Moscow was ominous because these groups generally equated revolutionary aesthetics with the traditional realism of the nineteenth century, against which had been directed the energies of the pre- and postrevolutionary avant-garde.[11] AKhRR also amalgamated in its ranks or included in its many exhibitions members of several prerevolutionary highbrow artistic groups, including some from the World of Art who had originally risen in reaction against realism but were now offended by the avant-garde's nonrepresentationalism.

In Leningrad, the threat of a general changeover in culture grew stronger as one by one branches of the militantly proletarian Moscow organizations were established there. LAPP, the Leningrad branch of the writers' organization VAPP, was formed in late 1922.[12] AKhRR formed local branches in 1923, and by 1925 it had secured control of the Academy of Arts in Leningrad with the installation of Ye. Ye. Essen, its new director.[13] By 1924, Malevich was to remark bitterly, "[Leningrad's] art world is full of 'the spirits of the time of Pericles' who nurture hopes of 'Parthenonizing' [oparfenochit'] or 'Renaissancizing' [orenessansit'] this dynamic modern age, of 'Turgenevizing' [oturgenit'] literature."[14]

With this changeover, youth became an even greater value than in the preceding two years, but now what was meant by "youth" was not young people in general but politically committed youth. "Worker youth" became a veritable slogan, but it contained the implication "Komsomol." That a given kind of art did not serve the young became in these years almost as valid a grounds for attack as the charge that it did not serve the workers; it was, for instance, under these terms that the high-minded, socially conscious Mobile Traveling Theater of Gaydeburov, one of the cradles of the movement for a people's theater, was vilified and forced to close in 1924.[15]

It was not just the Komsomol that was emerging as a major force in culture, but also the Party. Leading figures within it, such as Trotsky and Bukharin, had become more active on the cultural front than before, arguing that the Revolution's ultimate goals could not be reached without a massive cultural transformation.[16]

A defining feature of these years was a new militancy for a truly Soviet rather than just some wishy-washy "revolutionary" culture. By 1925 a new troika of slogans had come to dominate the articles in Leningrad's cultural journals: "Marxism," "sociology," and "workers" (or "workerization" [orabocheniye]). Hardly new, they were now de rigueur and every player in the game of establishing a new culture had to invoke them and justify his or her position in terms of them. As a corollary, in cultural journals the two most frequently found negative labels were "apoliticism" and "aestheticism"; bald content was in (the correct content, of course). To ensure this in the theater, a temporary commission was formed to oversee the repertoire of the State theaters in Moscow and Leningrad whose members included the Party historian V. I. Nevsky, Lunacharsky, and Voronsky;[17] also, senior representatives of the Party, trade unions, and proletarian writers' organizations were put on their repertoire commissions.

A sign of the new times, in September 1924 a new journal appeared in Leningrad, the *Worker and the Theater* (Rabochiy i teatr), which, continuing through the 1920s, was to rival the *Life of Art* as the principal weekly cultural organ. Even in the *Life of Art* the weighting of traditional sections shifted, giving more space to the activities of the various proletarian cultural organizations. Similar shifts can be found in most fields; for instance, during the publishing year 1925–1926 there was a marked increase in the number of works by proletarian writers;[18] scholars and cultural bureaucrats began to make studies of worker responses to plays, films, art, and literature, and architects and artists turned their attention to designing workers' homes, clubs, and even clothing.

Such trends were particularly fateful for that cluster of Leningrad intellectuals loosely composing the Formalists and their disciples both among the Serapion Brothers and among the students and organizations attached to the Division of the Verbal Arts at GIII. They began 1924 feeling confident. Many of their articles appeared in the *Life of Art* and the *Russian Contemporary,* and they formed the Committee for Contemporary Literature. Their particular changeover in literary theory and practice never got very far off the ground, however; their names disappeared from the *Life of Art,* and the *Russian Contemporary* made only four issues before being forced to close down. Later that year the Formalists were subjected to sustained attacks by Marxists (hitherto, the main attacks had come largely from the right, including religious thinkers).[19]

GIII was also called to task for its inattention to that new troika "Marxism," "sociology," and "workers."[20] In response, it hastily formed in 1924 a Circle for the Marxist Study of Art (at which Piotrovsky was invited to give lectures).[21] Soon thereafter, it set up a Committee on the Sociology of Art, whose particular mandate was to "study contemporary Soviet art" and to try to involve in its work that valuable commodity "young students."[22] The director even claimed that this committee was the "heart" of the Institute.[23] GIII also set up a Section for the Study of the Arts of October (that is, of the mass spectacles, placards, and so on), which in turn set up a "permanent museum of Red October" at the Academy of the Arts, proclaiming that the displays would be mounted in accordance with something it called the "complex Marxist method."[24]

The "art of the circus tent" had been taken inside to the museums. The era of flamboyant revolutionary culture was waning; symptomatically, one of its colorful figures, the poet Sergei Esenin, committed suicide at the end of 1925 (he actually did so in Leningrad, having just "moved" there from Moscow to escape what he experienced as its stifling atmosphere).

Yet one need not see Lenin's death as the cause of a major shift in cultural politics that took place at approximately that time. It could be argued that an event of late 1923 was more consequential. This event—or nonevent—was the failure of the German revolutionary uprising of October–November.

There had been too many failed revolutions, and this one delivered a coup de grâce to the long-nurtured expectations that an international proletarian revolution was imminent. Although Trotsky continued to insist that revolutions in Europe and the East were both essential and inevitable and would be followed by a confrontation with the capitalist hyena in America,[25] few were able to sustain his faith. The sort of internationalism that had defined early revolutionary cultural endeavor was fast receding; there was even a backlash of anti-Westernism.

In the new anti-Western climate, hopes for a cosmopolitan or sophisticated urbanist culture were particularly threatened. Symptomatically, the publishing house World Literature was closed in 1924, and in that same year Lunacharsky introduced a new slogan for the theater: "Back to [the Russian nineteenth-century dramatist] Ostrovsky!" Critics took this as their cue to argue that the "left" theater was manifestly illegitimate in revolutionary Russia because it did not develop out of national traditions but came from Europe, or worse still, from the infamous United States.[26] Even the Fine Arts Section of GIII, its most conservative in aesthetic terms, and its Moscow counterpart in GAKhN were attacked in 1924–1925 as "hotbeds of West European art" and subjected to purges on that basis, while AKhRR in its programmatic statements rejected "taking forms of art from the West . . . such as Cézanne, Derain, and Picasso—and transplanting them into a soil that is alien to them both psychologically and economically."[27]

To some extent, militant anti-Westernism among Party and proletarian circles went along generational lines, with the younger generation usually the more conservative. The older leaders were more cosmopolitan in their outlook than a new, Komsomol generation that entered cultural politics through Party work during the Civil War and was at this point a rising force. One can sense this division in a moment during the Central Committee meeting of 1924 called to clear the air on the issue of "proletarian literature" when Trotsky discussed theoretical issues in terms of Dante and an Italian Marxist, but his opponents from VAPP replied with references to Vissarion Belinsky and the debates in which that pre-Marxist champion of a national school of socially committed "realist" literature was embroiled in the nineteenth century.[28] The two generations were talking past each other.

As revolutionary internationalism declined, the previously dominant historical models informing literature, film, and drama that figured progress over time in a distinctly Euro-centric purview lost currency. The new focus on Russia alone in official ritual, film, literature, and so on meant a loss of geographic scale. The temporal (historical) dimension gained correspondingly in importance. As compared with that of the earlier mass spectacles, however, this scale was also reduced; the grand sweep from ancient Greece through the present and beyond had been cut to a span of a mere century or so.

Around this time the official genealogy of the Revolution was revised (a revision that stood for the next sixty years). The version that informed most cultural production charted the road to October not from ancient Greece or the French Revolution but from the Russian peasant revolts of the seventeenth and eighteenth centuries (Stenka Razin and Pugachev) as a sort of prelude, through the Decembrist uprising of 1825, to the 1905 Russian revolution. Sometimes other moments were added, such as the reigns of Peter the Great or Ivan the Terrible, but there were no non-Russian milestones.

It might seem that cultural workers were hastily adjusting their models in response to a shift of policy made by Stalin (the doctrine of "Socialism in One Country" first aired publicly in an article he wrote in December 1924). In fact, it was Bukharin who first formulated this shift in policy; Stalin popularized it.[29] Moreover, as was remarked in Chapter 6, a shift had already occurred among some intellectual circles to a more Russo-centric sense of identity, seen in events such as the Pushkin celebrations of 1921. Indeed, since around 1922, that is, at the same time as the "red Pinkerton" with its atemporal, Euro-centric narrative had been a model for a wide range of cultural production, there had been a growing vogue for works on Russian historical topics. This was particularly the case in workers' theaters, where the 1825 / 1905 / 1917 genealogy for the Revolution had structured many of the skits prepared for them, characteristically by Piotrovsky or one of his associates, but typically based on a conflation of earlier texts from writers such as Blok and Dmitry Merezhkovsky (the latter had emigrated!).[30]

By the mid 1920s, when this genealogy had assumed official status and the Party was even putting its historian (Nevsky) on theater boards, any Euro-centric model of revolutionary progress was precluded. Clearly, the movement for creating an Athens on the Nevsky, Piotrovsky's passion of slightly earlier times, was doomed. He and Radlov still sporadically staged reworked versions of the classical Greek theater, but their efforts were labeled "alien to a worker audience."[31] Instead, a whole series of plays for factories was developed covering topics from the Russian past, not only revolutionary subjects, but also the history of Petersburg.[32]

The emphasis in cultural policy was no longer on iconoclasm but on creating new and enduring icons. Editorials insisted that mass spectacles for the revolutionary holidays were to be considered not ephemeral events, but rituals to be passed on to "future generations" to help give them a vivid and uplifting sense of revolutionary history.[33] The audience was to be given "real history, not a tarted up version of the Old Regime fare of the fairground tent. . . ."[34] Lenin also gained a more central role in mass celebrations of revolutionary days, and by 1925 huge portraits of him became *de rigueur*.

This shift to a more enduring iconography was a crucial development in the evolution of the genus "Stalinist culture." Parallel with the shift to historical subjects had come a shift in the dominant cultural field from theater to literature. Two Central Committee resolutions on literature, one of 1924 and especially that of 1925, functioned for some years as the *ex cathedra* pronouncements on culture in general.[35] Moreover, around the mid-1920s emerged some of the key works to be singled out in the 1930s as models for socialist realism.[36]

Nineteen twenty-five was a particularly crucial year in the evolution of the new, official culture. That year F. Gladkov's novel *Cement* and S. Eisenstein's film *The Battleship Potemkin* appeared. Both were hailed by the powers that be as the long-awaited models for a Soviet culture, while works such as Marietta Shaginyan's "red Pinkerton" *Mess-Mend*, promoted so recently, faded from view. *Potemkin* had a gratifyingly proletarian and revolutionary subject—the mutiny of sailors on the *Potemkin* as a symbolic encapsulation of the 1905 revolution—and officialdom buried their prejudices against avant-garde endeavors for the moment to endorse it. *Cement* was even more promising in that it was a popular novel by a writer from the proletarian literary organization "Smithy" (Kuznitsa, actually a rival of VAPP). Its hero combines in his biography all the desirable givens: he is a factory worker, Party member, and a highly decorated hero of the Civil War. Hence the novel's appearance in a year when everyone was clamoring for "workerization" was particularly timely.

The novel was greeted in official quarters with the most inflated praise. Lunacharsky outdid his peers by pronouncing, "On this cement foundation we can build further."[37] Actually, Soviet culture did not get to build much "further" for some decades in the sense that *Cement* became the single most influential novel in providing the basic patterns for the conventional plot of Soviet literature of the Stalinist 1930s and 1940s—a cement "overcoat."[38] In the Stalin years it was the novel rather than the theater or film that emerged as the leading genre of official Soviet culture—its analogue to the Peking Opera for PRC culture—but we do see a shift in other genres in these years. Indeed, in 1925 Piotrovsky was already talking about the "novelization" of the theater.[39] The crucial development in the direction of socialist realism was not "novelization" per se, however, but the emergence about this time of a formulaic biography informing both cultural products and political rhetoric that enacted the principal political myths of the Bolsheviks. *Cement* played a distinct role in this development, and hence its appearance in 1925 has to be regarded as an even greater milestone than the leadership's hyperbole claimed it to be.

Cement and *Potemkin* had an analogue in art, in this case contributions from the Leningrad figure Isaak Brodsky, who emerged in these years as the nearest thing to an official artist. Brodsky, with a prerevolutionary record of leftist sympathizing and consistent opposition to abstract and "decadent" art, largely devoted himself after the Revolution to creating an official iconography (primarily portraits of Bolshevik leaders).

Two works of 1924–1926 established his position as artist laureate and the Russian Revolution's David, the Neoclassical official artist of the French Revolution. Both these works were singled out at the time as models for the new Soviet culture. The first was his epic canvas *The Official Opening of the Second Congress of the Comintern* (1920–1924), a huge commissioned work that depicted the Congress's six hundred Soviet and foreign delegates. Functionally, it was a sort of *Tennis Court Oath*, David's most famous revolutionary canvas (although in execution it was more reminiscent of the "architectural landscapes" of Neoclassical Petersburg done early in the twentieth century). The second, *The Execution of the Twenty-six Baku Martyrs* (1925), commissioned by Kirov, who was then head of the Party in Azerbaidzhan, was like the *Oath of the Horatii* (David's most famous Neoclassical work) in that it also illustrated the theme of civic duty as the higher calling.[40]

Brodsky joined AKhRR in 1923, and his popularity with prominent Bolsheviks is a major reason AKhRR flourished, especially in his native Leningrad. His works became centerpieces for the organization, which, together with various government agencies, arranged exhibitions of the paintings and their sketches in Moscow, Leningrad, and other major cities patronized by the Party leadership.[41]

Brodsky was particularly valued because he could be construed as standing in a direct line of succession going back to Repin, with whom he once worked and whom members of AKhRR identified as their model. The Soviet authorities were courting Repin to return from emigration in Finland with the hope that he might produce just such occasional paintings as did Brodsky (the closest they came to that was getting his son to do a commissioned work).[42] They were courting Gorky as well, with whom Brodsky also had associations.

Thus the young were no longer "muscling" the older generation aside. In many quarters, including the official, there was a tremendous premium on establishing a senior authority figure—ideally, one with a prerevolutionary pedigree—to function as emblem for each field in culture. This trend re-emerged in the 1930s when Gorky assumed that function in literature, as did Nikolai Marr in linguistics.

Thus it might be said that the flood of 1924 was a harbinger of the new hege-monic culture. Many Leningrad intellectuals—supporters of high art and supporters of left art alike—fought valiantly against its tide,[43] but ended up as devastated as were the theaters in the flood. But clearly this account is too simplistic. In 1924–1926, for all the saber rattling of the proletarian groups and other militants, for all the political pressures to "workerize," and so forth, the country's culture was still essentially in transition and open-ended. After all, each of the three official models for the new culture—Cement, Potemkin, and the art of Brodsky—represents a different school. Moreover, not all three models were to enjoy this status into the 1930s (Potemkin was by then out of favor and Brodsky had been eclipsed by Sergei Gerasimov). With the benefit of hindsight one can pick out the contours of socialist realism in the variegated landscape, but they were not so clear at the time.

An important aspect of this open-endedness was the extent to which cul-tural groups in the two capital cities were in dialogue. The new Moscow cul-tural empire did not simply colonize Petersburg. When Leningrad branches were formed of the new Moscow proletarian organizations, often they stood for very different things from those of the parent organization in Moscow. A striking case of this would be LAPP (the Leningrad Branch of VAPP), which housed several factions, each espousing a position quite different from that of the "implacable zealots" of the VAPP leadership in Moscow: initi-ally, LAPP was dominated by the "Cosmists," a group of utopian fanta-sizers, some of whom (the "Biocosmist" faction) saw in the Bolshevik Revolution a hope for achieving biological immortality;[44] later, the associa-tion included the Komsomol literary group Changeover (Smena), which looked to a sort of international "urbanist" tradition that included among its models Baudelaire, Proust, and Gumilëv (a "white guardist")—a far cry from VAPP's models Belinsky and Tolstoy;[45] and after 1926 LAPP was joined by the Moscow group thrown out of power in a recent leadership tussle in VAPP, that is, by ultra-leftist, even more implacable, zealots.

Another, widespread form of dialogue with the emerging official culture to be found in Leningrad was the way intellectuals appropriated the new official genealogy for 1917 (1825 to 1905 to 1917) as a vehicle for exploring their own existential dilemmas and presenting their own programs. Around 1925 this practice was most evident because that year marked special anniversaries of the first two dates in the triad, the one-hundredth anniversary of 1825 and the twentieth anniversary of 1905. In official commemorations, 1825 was eclipsed by 1905, receiving very little coverage in the press or public rituals.[46] On the whole, avant-gardists foregrounded 1905 in their work, too; for instance, the 1905 revolution is the subject of Eisenstein's *Potemkin*. But among Leningrad intellectuals, including Eisenstein's erstwhile allies in FEKS, the topic of choice was events associated with 1825.[47]

For intellectuals to take a period one hundred years earlier as their paradigmatic time, one that is not temporally contiguous with the present but rather parallel at a century's remove, is to opt for allegorical rather than etiological potential. They focused on the movement from 1825 (and its buildup) to the succeeding decades under Nicholas I because they could engage in this mediated way the movement from a time of revolution to one of reaction. Eighteen twenty-five emerges in their works not just as a revolutionary high point, but more as a nodal point leading to the 1830s and 1840s, that is, to Nicolaevan Russia, which became a particular obsession of intellectuals around this time as an exemplum, generally presented in the grotesque mode, of stagnation, bureaucratism, obtuseness, and provincialism. The focus on 1825 could also be seen as intellectuals' immersing themselves in a time when they enjoyed more aristocratic status, a retreat in the face of rising anti-intellectualism to be found even in public ritual and culture (it is quite marked in *Cement*).[48]

The intellectuals' obsession with 1825 was most marked in literature. A good example is the Formalist Tynyanov's fictional account of the Decembrists in his novel *Kyukhlya* (1925). *Kyukhlya* concerns the life of Wilhelm Kyukhel'beker, a minor literary figure and peripheral and inept participant in the uprising who later died in Siberian exile after years in solitary confinement in tsarist prisons. With Kyukhel'beker as his ostensible focus, Tynyanov contrived to include in the novel an almost encyclopedic sweep of the literary intelligentsia of that time. Against this broad canvas he explored the theme of the intellectual who is out of step with, or a casualty of, his times ("vybyl iz vremeni"), a theme of obvious contemporary resonance that was taken up in other studies of Nicolaevan Russia from this time.[49]

Thus Tynyanov could be accused of biographism, along with the rest of the Formalist crowd working in literary theory at this time. They had earlier attacked the emerging Pushkin cult in Russia for its biographism. In the mid-1920s, however, whether in response to pressures to do scholarship with a more "sociological" methodology, or whether in the course of their own evolution, they became immersed in Russian literary history. The Leningrad Formalists Tynyanov and Eikhenbaum—and Shklovsky, who was now in Moscow but maintained close contact with his associates in Leningrad—produced several critical biographies of nineteenth-century writers, and also became interested in the literary and publishing politics and economics of that time. Thus they in a sense reverted to their roots in the Vengerov Circle (a famous study group Tynyanov and Eikhenbaum attended while students at Petersburg University and which pursued rigorous if somewhat conventional scholarship on Pushkin and his contemporaries), even though they had always defined themselves as Formalists against its approach to the study of literature. Indeed, the novel *Kyukhlya* itself can be regarded as a return on Tynyanov's part to the subject of his long paper "Pushkin and Kyukhel'beker" which he wrote for this circle but which was destroyed by fire in 1918.[50]

Ironically, in *Kyukhlya* Tynyanov was partly using biography as a vehicle to attack the creeping biographism of the times. One of his missions was to demystify the plaster saint Pushkin and also to provide a healthy antidote to the recent vogue in plays and films about historical figures (tsars and writers) for titillating detail and sensationalism. More important, Tynyanov's barbs in this book seem to be aimed principally—more than at extracultural, political targets—at defending the principles of perceptual millenarianism against AKhRR and other spokesmen for a tame or romanticized culture.[51] Some key passages are effectively polemics for the crucial role to be played by "contingency" in any revolutionary culture and attacks on the cult of "precision" and "standardization."[52] Moreover, although the bumbling Kyukhel'beker is in the foreground of his novel, the writers Pushkin and Griboedov emerge unmistakably as its unofficial heroes whose work exemplifies preferred approaches. Thus Tynyanov is not only demythologizing but also simultaneously countermythologizing, much as he has taken the official genealogy of revolution—1825/1905/1917—but reinflected it.

From the mid- to the late 1920s the debate about the nature of revolutionary culture was at its most intense. Hence not just "political interference" but also intra-intelligentsia theoretical rivalries were a major factor in the evolution of that culture. As the various parties debated what a "revolutionary" culture might be around 1925, there were some who were in the thrall of facts and the culture of "everyday life" (something analogous to *Neue Sachlichkeit* among the avant-garde of Weimar Germany)[53] while others sought a "monumental" culture of heroic pathos. The dominant positions in this debate can be found right across the proletarian/nonproletarian or Marxist/non-Marxist spectra. In other words, there was no correlation between participants' political positions and their aesthetic agendas. Within particular movements, and among adherents to particular isms, notably that elusive "realism," individuals took opposite positions in the debate.

Thus the mid-1920s saw a shift to a more proletarian and tendentious art, but debates on the nature of Soviet culture were still fierce and its direction not yet set. The firebrands from organizations like RAPP, RAPM, and AKhRR posed the greatest threat to nonproletarian and experimental groups were they ever to be given much power, but at this point it was still an open question whether they would be or not. Significantly, the principal VAPP organ, *On Guard* (Na postu), which was intended to appear monthly, had trouble with funding and paper and was able to secure publication for only five issues for the entire period the journal ran between 1923 and 1925; by contrast, the principal fellow-traveler organ, *Red Virgin Soil* (Krasnaya nov'), appeared monthly and enjoyed the largest circulation of any literary journal. Moreover, in 1924 and 1925 Party leaders acted as defenders of the fellow-travelers against proletarian attacks, calling a meeting of the Central Committee Press Section in response to their petitions.[54] The meeting's resolutions, which generally reasserted the principle that the proletarian associations could not exercise hegemony, were those documents that functioned for some years as the *ex cathedra* pronouncements on cultural policy in general.

Bolshevik leaders were probably reluctant to endorse proletarian movements because they did not see them as sufficiently cultivated. Trotsky consistently withstood VAPP pressures to promote its writer Yury Libedinsky and label Pilnyak a pernicious bourgeois, calling Libedinsky's writings "the work of a schoolboy" who needs to do more work if he is to be taken seriously as a writer.[55] Similarly, although Lunacharsky clearly felt obliged to praise *Cement* fulsomely, he was reluctant to suggest that it represented any final answer (writers must "build further"). Moreover, far from praising proletarian ventures only, Lunacharsky in his review articles on the cultural scene frequently singled out for commendation such works as N. Erdman's *Mandat* (first produced by Meyerhold) and the modernist composers Stravinsky and Prokofiev.[56]

The Party was far from a monolith at this time and in it cultural issues were hotly debated (as were economic and political issues). It was virtually a mirror of the cultural intelligentsia inasmuch as most factions in the intelligentsia's debates could find sympathizers somewhere in the Party hierarchy. AKhRR's battle with left art in Leningrad was largely a struggle to see who could find the most powerful patrons in the Party. The left artists had their patrons who resolved in their favor, but AKhRR was able to appeal to officials at a higher level.[57]

The problem of who and what (which groups, which approaches) the state, Komsomol, and Party would favor in culture had its own very practical aspects. The later years of NEP were a time of galloping unemployment for intellectuals. Yet the issue of which approach was to be favored was resolved not by the Party per se but, to a greater extent than has been recognized, by popular taste (which many Party functionaries also represented). The masses were not going to the very cultural institutions which, in theory, the Revolution had freed them to enjoy. The highbrow theater was perilously underattended and, as surveys at the time established, people weren't even going to the workers' theaters or reading proletarian literature[58] (Cement's popularity, anomalous in those days, was undoubtedly a factor in its official endorsement). The bogeyman of intellectuals, proletarian culture, really represented a small fraction of cultural production at this point, and an even smaller percentage of cultural consumption. Everyone was watching American films.

Nineteen twenty-five was not only the year of Cement and Potemkin, but also the year when such films by Douglas Fairbanks as Robin Hood, The Thief of Baghdad, and other Hollywood versions of the exotic adventure movie absolutely dominated the Soviet screen.[59] The overwhelming majority of the new films shown at this time were from the United States, outnumbering even Soviet productions four to one.[60] Fairbanks and his actress wife Mary Pickford—the king and queen of the Western public—were the heartthrobs of the Russian populace, and when they visited Moscow in 1926 they were virtually mauled by frenzied mobs of fans.

Such Western films represented to many of those in authority the filthiest of that muck in the "Augean stable" which an enlightened Soviet government had to clean out. Reviewers of Fairbanks' films were generally quick to point out the misguided representation of class relations in his historical romances.[61] Yet Soviet movie houses continued to show Western films. Moreover, those shown were far from foreign imports smuggled in as part of the laxness and state-sanctioned private enterprise of NEP. Most of them were part of a huge purchase made by the Old Bolshevik L. Krasin in 1924.[62]

Similarly, under state patronage prerevolutionary vogues and even institutions for exotic adventure literature were revived. In 1925 two popular mass journals were launched that were explicitly dedicated to providing Soviet versions of such fare "in the American style"—Thirty Days (Tridtsat' dney), which specialized in short stories and essays, and the Universal Investigator (Vsemirnyy sledopyt), which called itself a "monthly journal devoted to travel, adventure, and science fiction."[63] Thirty Days had a profile very similar to that of *Argus,* a popular Petersburg journal of the 1910s, right down to having the same editor, V. A. Renigin. The *Universal Investigator* was edited by Popov, the former editor of the prerevolutionary popular journal *Around the World* (Vokrug Sveta),[64] itself to be revived by the Komsomol in 1927.

Such ambiguous actions on the part of the state in regard to the "Augean stable" are patent in perusing any issue of the journal the *Life of Art* from 1925. Frequently, on the front cover of a given issue would be a photo of Fairbanks, Buster Keaton, or some other Hollywood star, usually from his or her latest movie. Then, immediately inside the cover, the editorial would rail against this kind of art, and call for cleaning up the cinemas and producing healthy, proletarian art. The ensuing pages would more or less continue the theme, but the supplement at the end frequently carried movie chit-chat about the latest exploits of the exotic Hollywood stars, and possibly of émigré figures such as Anna Pavlova and Chaliapin as well. Clearly, the journal had to sell, and material about the Hollywood stars would ensure that they did just that. As if to confirm this, an article in the journal that year pointed out that while programs with Soviet movies accounted for 27–30 percent of all showings in movie theaters, the returns on them were only 14–19 percent of the total.[65] The *Life of Art* did, however, have to establish its credentials as a fighter for the cause of revolutionary proletarian culture (a cause that was probably genuinely espoused by the editor, at least). But the leadership was also aware that it was faced with a dilemma. While Lunacharsky dismissed *The Thief of Baghdad* as "rubbish," he went on to point out that purely didactic and agitational films are no antidote. Effective agitational movies will have to be "gripping" and "fictional"—like these Hollywood products.[66]

The Fairbanks films are dominated by the figure of Fairbanks himself, the larger-than-life swashbuckler who defies physical limitations to leap, swing, or even fly as he overcomes daunting obstacles and attains impossible goals—a Tarzan of the historical romance and a Superman before his time. As even some Soviet reviewers noted, Fairbanks is exuberant, fearless, always smiling and optimistic, and the epitome of robust youth and physicality (despite his forty years when he made *The Thief of Baghdad).*[67] Frequently naked from the waist up or with his shirt half open to reveal a rippling torso, Fairbanks was dubbed "Mr. Electricity," a term that, in this instance, meant sheer pulsating energy rather than icon of the new technology. He performs breathtaking feats with great exuberance, but always for good causes, whether the cause be love (as in *The Thief of Baghdad*) or defending the oppressed (as in *Robin Hood*).

Some historians of the cinema have analyzed Fairbanks's films in terms of their function of mediating the passage the masses must make to a corporate America.[68] But his kind of action hero proved no less functional in the Soviet Union as a model for marrying the "boulevard" romance to the Soviet ideological parable. A version of this model can be found in Gladkov's *Cement*.

Many contemporary critics and theoreticians thought that novelists should present realistic accounts of work on the factory floor, but in the adventure romance Gladkov had effectively found a better formula for "the production novel." *Cement* tells of how a cement factory that fell into disrepair during the Civil War is restored and brought back into production by a group of local enthusiasts led by the larger-than-life Gleb Chumalov. This hero achieves economic successes in that prosaic world of the provincial cement factory but is depicted in the style of the swashbuckler operating in exotic climes. Gladkov consistently identifies each step in the restoration with Chumalov performing some heroic, seemingly impossible physical feat in the natural world—a Fairbanks-like feat. Such feats—saltos—had greater potential than the Pinkerton for allegorical representation of spectacular political-cum economic-progress. This strategy was to become fairly standard in classical Stalinist culture where "men of action" perform tasks more quickly than seems at all feasible according to the dictates of science. In other words, though it is assumed that socialist realism and the dominant political tropes were established by the Party, popular taste for the adventure romance was undoubtedly a significant factor.[69]

The "red Pinkerton" had jettisoned its detective and been "reconfigured." The movement from Mick Thingmaster of Mess-Mend to Gleb Chumalov is the movement from the mastermind to the quintessential worker who scorns ratiocination and operates from his essential class nature. Gleb's world has no need for a Professor of Striding, for he has been drawn against the iconography of the Russian epic hero, or *bogatyr'*, which gives him seven-league boots.

If this, then, was the kind of fare (American, adventure, and exotic) that the majority of the populace preferred to digest in both film and literature, Gladkov's novel *Cement* came closer to resembling it than did *Potemkin* (and was much more popular at the time). *Potemkin* barely survived the 1920s as a model, whereas *Cement* enjoyed that status for decades, well beyond Stalin's death in 1953. In the mid-1920s, the singling out of larger-than-life heroes was anathema to large sections of the avant-garde intelligentsia. Thus Eisenstein in making *Potemkin* had tried to show the feats of the masses rather than individuals. His colleagues lionized *Potemkin* and loathed *Cement*.[70] But by the 1930s *Cement* with its titanic hero remained unchallenged as the "cement foundation" of socialist realism while *Potemkin* was eclipsed by new films about Russian and Soviet heroes.

Another defining aspect of Stalinist culture that can be associated with *Cement* and this Fairbanks interlude is the fantastic transformation of space. If, in the "red Pinkertons" of recent years, the heroes had to go to Europe to save it (or, conversely, the yankees had to go to Petrograd), now in literature heroes made such progressions from the diseased to the whole, the drab to the magnificent, within their local space. There was no need for the journey in time or place as a frame for extraordinary transformation. The fantastic was in place, now.

When, in *Cement*, Gleb first enters the factory after a long absence fighting in the Civil War, he passes through a surface area with piles of rubble, stale smells, and desultory workers—a prosaic and rundown world. But when he descends into the "austere temple of the engines" he sees the factory not as an everyday reality but as a kind of King Solomon's mine: "The diesel engines stood like black marble idols, bedecked with gold and silver . . . like altars demanding their sacrifice."[71] This is no underground Metropolis, no Expressionist nightmare, and it anticipates a basic topos of Stalinist culture.

On whose shores, then, had that "Noah's ark" bearing the intelligentsia's utopian hopes and schemes been dashed? And what was the nature of the "flood" that had swept so many of them away?—the demands for "marxism," "sociology," and "workerization"? or mass popular culture? The standard Western account of what happened in Soviet culture during the late 1920s, the time this narrative is now entering, generally chronicles a descent into ever blacker times. The problem with such accounts is that they reflect the adoption of the bad habits of Stalinist historiography, rendering it as a chiaoscuro with its logical telos, Stalinist culture. But cultural history is no socialist realist novel and has no swashbuckling, all-powerful heroes. All actors in it were negotiating a very complex landscape. Undoubtedly, if many of the leading figures in cultural life of the 1920s were to look back on that time from the vantage point of the late 1930s or 1940s they would, with the advantage of hindsight, see it somewhat differently from the way they saw it at the time.

Any particular moment in ecohistory is constituted by different states and different velocities of change, all of which are hard to read at its present moment. Also, what makes an evolutionary change in a given species successful at one point may be the very feature that will cause that species' downfall in another. But in any case different species may evolve in quite various ways in response to a single new set of ecological conditions (such as a flood). With so many and such various "false starts," no single evolutionary line can be charted.

The way a "flood" is interpreted depends on one's point of view. When during War Communism a flood was a favorite metaphor for revolution, it was often described in terms of removing the hardened scab of the stagnant and outdated—thus purification.[72] If one were to look at the 1924 flood in Leningrad from the perspective of those who dreamed of a cultural "breakthrough," it could be seen not as an apocalyptic sign, but as the promise of a new beginning. The "scab" that had formed under the Old Regime was being removed, but what would emerge from under it? As the next chapters will show, many were not cast down by the flood qua pressures for "workerization," "youth," and a more "Marxist" and "sociological" approach, but were instead challenged by the task of providing a coherent account of a postbourgeois culture.

9

PROMETHEAN LINGUISTICS

On December 19, 1926, Rykov, then head of Sovnarkom (the Council of Peoples Commissars), opened the Volkhovstroy hydroelectric station. Located near Leningrad and intended to remedy the city's chronic power shortages, Volkhovstroy also had tremendous symbolic importance as the first major realization of Lenin's dream of electrification, encapsulated in his famous formula presented to the Ninth Party Congress of 1920: "Communism Equals Socialism Plus the Electrification of the Entire Countryside." Thus the event was a guarantee of that Promethean dream which presented scientific progress as the emblem of revolution.

A poem written for the occasion, Gennady Fish's "Current from the Volkhov," celebrates how the vapors from the murky swamps (a clichéd image from the myth of Petersburg) were "eviscerated" by a mighty current.[1] Thus what *Mess-Mend* had foretold was realized: in the realm of the Bronze Horseman a mightier current—electricity—had triumphed over the untamed waters. Nature had bowed before culture.

Lenin was far from the only Soviet figure who was captivated at this time by the magical possibilities of electricity and the promise of Volkhovstroy. Avant-gardist groups such as FEKS and the Constructivists took Edison and Volkhovstroy as their icons. Such enthusiasts did not wait until the project was finished, but began to photograph and film it obsessively even as it was being constructed;[2] photographs were manipulated to give it a semimagical aura, establishing it as, in the words of the title of a film about the project for which Piotrovsky wrote the scenario, one of the "victors over the night" (pobediteli nochi). In making speeches officials fell over themselves in their efforts to find grandiose comparisons for Volkhovstroy (such as the pyramids of Egypt), and at every opportunity they took foreigners to view the site.[3] Volkhovstroy had become an icon of Soviet technological, aesthetic, and political superiority.

It also became a symbol for liberation from the past. In *Edison's Woman,* an agitational film scenario written by FEKS in 1923, Edison creates a robot that comes to Petrograd to save the city from the "cult of the past," of "Petersburg." Once the light of Volkhovstroy is turned on, the old Petersburg disappears.[4] In official rhetoric and culture, the bringing of electricity (light, energy) became virtually synonymous with revolution. Thus in Gladkov's *Cement* the hero's principal task could not be fulfilled—the cement factory could not be restored—until a power station had been built. This sequence established a paradigm for representing the Promethean ideal in Soviet novels of the ensuing decades whereby a backward region is propelled into the modern age by the building of a power station.

In the Stalin era, *rapid* industrial progress became the marker of ideological advance. In 1927, with the Stalinist faction who had pushed for rapid industrialization in the debates now dominant, Party policy made a decisive shift to giving industrialization absolute priority. Since Volkhovstroy was opened more or less on the eve of this shift, that event represented more for Leningrad than the ritual fulfillment of Lenin's directives now already erected into political myths. To build a power station on the nearby Volkhov river had long been considered crucial for that lapsed capital, the only way of saving it from its likely fate of becoming a rust-belt city—not just a political but an economic and industrial has-been.[5] Inasmuch as Leningrad had traditionally been Russia's major industrial city and also the seat of the scientific-technological intelligentsia, the timely "electrification" of the city afforded it a second chance.

The national goal of industrializing Russia gave the scientific-technological intelligentsia a renewed sense of the crucial role they might play in the country. In 1927 the heads of the various scientific bodies and the government's Industrial Bureau (Prombyuro) organized a series of conferences in Leningrad to discuss how to proceed with industrialization. They invited scientists and industrial managers to attend. They also arranged, under the auspices of KEPS, for research institutes to link up directly with the appropriate local factories so that these enterprises might benefit from the scientists' expertise.[6] The Leningrad Institute Gipromez was assigned responsibility for planning the four most ambitious projects of the First Five-Year Plan.

A perusal of the Leningrad press in 1927 yields a plethora of extravagant statements about the crucial contributions its city's scientists would make to industrialization and about the privileges and rewards they should receive as a result. One commentator, writing of Gipromez, waxed lyrical with the words: "It is with a feeling of joy that I leave this laboratory of our future. The cream of our technological expertise is located in it."[7] Yet another crucible of a transformed world had been claimed.

The tragic fact is, however, that the scientific intelligentsia of Leningrad could no longer be counted on to lead the country into that long-sought "leap out of backwardness." On the eve of the Revolution, Russian science and technology were world-class in many areas, but war, revolution, lack of foreign capital, and isolation had taken their toll. All of the major projects of the First Five-Year Plan were designed by foreign experts and used imported equipment (a partial exception being Dneprostroi, which used some generators designed and built in Leningrad). Even Gipromez, which masterminded the great construction projects, though it had a Russian director to be sure, comprised predominantly foreign experts. For the Volkhovstroy electric station, built before the plan years, some Soviet-made generators were used as a compromise (made in Leningrad).[8] In 1927, however, the very year the Leningrad scientific intelligentsia were making extravagant claims for what they could do to transform the country, the dynamos of Volkhovstroy kept breaking down, seriously reducing the city's electrical power.[9]

Those sections of the avant-garde who sought in their work to marry science and the new art also experienced a blow with the power station itself. Its exterior (designed in 1923–1925) was eclectic Gothic, anticipating some of the styles typical of the Stalinist 1930s.[10] Obviously, or so many thought then, there was a contradiction between the power station, a beacon of the technological future, and its *passéiste* Gothic casing. Many saw this as a travesty of revolutionary cultural ideals, but in the 1930s and 1940s, when Promethean ideals were married to conservative cultural models, this would be seen as a marriage of culture and science.

Just two days before the lights of Volkhovstroy went on, another light of the avant-garde went off. On December 17, the Leningrad GINKhUK, the stronghold of such avant-garde artists as Malevich, Filonov, and Matyushin (and, until 1925, Tatlin), was closed down and merged by decree with its friendly neighbor institution, GIII.[11]

This closure and allied events might suggest that 1926 saw an acceleration of the process whereby a centrist, hegemonic, Muscovite culture assumed dominance over local Leningrad culture. Moreover, Leningrad was increasingly identified by those pressing for cultural revolution as not just an economic but also a cultural has-been, the symbolic home of an intelligentsia that was deemed bourgeois and passé; the city was considered the last bastion of non-Marxist, nonproletarian, and "nonsociological" intellectual movements. Thus, although L. Leonov was a Moscow writer of the 1920s who set his novels in Moscow or the provinces, when in 1924 he chose to write about a retrograde intellectual in "The End of a Paltry Person," he set the work in Leningrad.[12]

Far from alienated, however, many intellectuals saw this as a time of great opportunity; to them, it promised to be the creative period of Soviet culture. Moreover, although the two capitals remained cultural rivals with distinct profiles, to an increasing extent the changes were being called not by "Moscow," per se, but by institutions and figures that formed a Moscow / Leningrad axis. Symptomatically, in 1925 Leningrad's principal cultural journal, the *Life of Art*, became an organ of both capitals, though it was still published in Leningrad.

The Search for a New Cultural Theory

Even before the Promethean fire at Volkhovstroy began to sputter, another was making promising beginnings, a fire conceived as Promethean although it was outside the fields of science and technology. Many intellectuals were focusing their attention on the possibility of a radical transformation (or revolution) centered not in the natural sciences but in the social sciences and the humanities. They sought a sort of metaphysical Volkhovstroy of cultural theory, one they believed would prove in its own way more effective than Volkhovstroy itself.

Starting around 1925–1926, one finds among Soviet intellectuals of leftist persuasion a sense that the Revolution had to finally come into its own. They looked for ways to forge an entirely new and comprehensive postrevolutionary culture. The Soviet Union was the first state to declare itself Marxist but there was little precedent in either history or Marxist writings for establishing what a Marxist, materialist, postrevolutionary culture might be. Those accounts that did exist were held by many to be primitive, eclectic, or otherwise inadequate. There was some pressure from on high to work out an academically respectable Marxist aesthetic; this was, for example, the burden of the leading address given by Arvid Pelshe, the head of the Department of Political Enlightenment, to its All-Union Conference in December 1925.[13]

The leftist intellectuals did not need officialdom to nudge them into producing an intellectually respectable account of the new culture. They felt confident that if only they provided such an account, the "progressive" forces of the world would follow their lead. There was some reason to believe this, given that prominent leftist theoreticians in the West had begun making pilgrimages to the Soviet Union with ever greater frequency (such as Benjamin, whose friend Asja Lacis had begun publishing in the *Life of Art*). To this end, in 1926 there was an attempt on the part of Glavnauka (The Central Scientific Administration) in Moscow to convene an international conference on the sociology of art, to be attended by prominent intellectuals from abroad. The announcement proclaimed: "We live at the very beginning of a new epoch defined by a renaissance in socialist thought." Much of the existing Marxist theoretical writing on culture is too amateur, eclectic, and simpleminded, it suggested, and thus the field needs professionalization.[14]

This conference was not to have the desired impact, but that did not deter the enthusiasts. During this time, the issue of what might be a Marxist, materialist theory of culture was debated with great intensity. A new central focus emerged in these debates—linguistics—a scholarly and hence seemingly unlikely discipline for revolutionary ideologues, but one that was seen as located at that crucial intersection of ideology, everyday life, and scholarship and therefore an essential component of any would-be comprehensive Marxist theory of culture. Within linguistics itself one finds reflected in the mid-1920s the general shift to a more Marxist or minimally "sociological" orientation in theory and practice and a correspondingly greater emphasis on "applied linguistics" and "psycholinguistics."[15] Science was to be married to language, leading to the triumph of a Marxist, materialist linguistics over that cottage industry known as philology.

In the scholarly sphere, the mid- to late 1920s saw a tremendous rise in interest in linguistics. At the national congress of the Academy of Sciences held in 1927, the opening address was given by the linguist Nikolai Marr, while senior members of the Academy whose work related more directly to the proposed scientific-technological revolution spoke only later.[16] New institutes or departments devoted to linguistic questions sprang up in the capitals and the older ones experienced a rejuvenation. In the mid-1920s members of the Bakhtin Circle redirected their interests from literature and philosophy to the study of language.

The new emphasis on the crucial role of language was not confined to scholarship. Around 1925, debates on cultural policy suddenly became obsessed with the question of what kind of language should be used in a particular genre, and what kind should be used by citizens (and especially proletarians) themselves. "Language" also supplanted "music" or "performance" as the shibboleth of revolutionary culture. The question was which "language," or which policy on language, could truly transform man.

The Leningrad Formalists had for some years laid claim to the notion that their approach was putting the study of literature and language on a scientific footing for the first time, hence they might seem logical candidates for providing the definitive account of this. But by 1927 the sporadic Marxist campaign against that school was in high gear and Formalism was no longer politically viable. Indeed, the theories of language rising to prominence at this time were billed as more truly scientific—more materialist—and therefore better able than their ill-defined predecessors to combat the Formalist, idealist hyena.

The various participants in this new movement to found a Marxist or sociological linguistics all took as their point of departure an attack on the Formalists. This common point of departure had strong institutional backing. In 1926, several institutes concerned with the humanities and arts formed into a powerful Moscow-Leningrad axis under the umbrella of a new body called RANION (the Russian Association of Research Institutes in the Social Sciences), which for the next few years continued to gobble up institutes in the two capitals to house in its empire, so that by the end of NEP these institutes numbered fifteen. RANION was originally conceived as an alternative to the Communist Academy, thus it represented fellow-traveling, leftist (including Marxist and Bolshevik) scholarship and was in a sense analogous to the Writers' Federation (FOSP).[17] But when the Communist Academy and RANION adopted a militantly anti-Formalist position, the cluster of institutes they incorporated, forming a Moscow-Leningrad axis, made them a particularly effective actor in the campaign.

In linguistics, the leading Leningrad institution in this movement was the Institute for the Comparative Study of Literatures and Languages of the West and East (ILYaZV), a RANION body. Founded in 1921 as a center for research and graduate training in linguistics and literature within Leningrad University, this institute housed most of the members of the Formalist circle and their associates and also many other reputed scholars, including Piotrovsky[18] (in the late 1920s V. V. Voloshinov became a graduate student there). In 1925, however, the Institute was restructured and several additional linguistics sections were opened. Despite the continued presence of Formalists within its ranks, it then adopted a more militantly anti-Formalist stance, becoming at the same time more sharply focused on the task of working out a new sociological and Marxist theory of language and literature.[19] The anti-Formalist profile is particularly palpable in ILYaZV's list of compulsory readings for all students in 1927, which comprises almost exclusively anti-Formalist tracts (the only exception being volume 10 of Plekhanov's works). The reading list of the sister institute in Moscow, the Institute for the History of Literature and Language, was very similar.[20]

The militantly anti-Formalist approaches to linguistics that in the mid-1920s were worked out at such institutes were many and various. I will isolate here only those that were to prove the most formative in the evolution of Stalinist culture. Thus I will not discuss one of the dominant trends, what I call "vulgar materialism," whose adherents took a physiological approach to the analysis of language, which was discussed in terms of "conditioned reflexes" and other Pavlovian categories; some of them formed at ILYaZV a Circle of Linguist-Biomechanists.[21] This trend is of obvious interest in charting the evolution of Meyerhold's theories of Biomechanics, but its impact on cultural history pales before that of another which was less confined to the research institute but espoused by a wide range of political and cultural figures.

Among the many theories of language advanced at this time, I am singling out a trend for which I have coined the label "Promethean linguistics." Promethean linguistics is to linguistics as scientism is to science; it is an attempt to generate a significance for a discipline that exceeds its professional bounds. That extraprofessional element is what made this unlikely field so important in the formation of Stalinist culture.

Promethean linguistics cannot be described as a coherent movement, but rather as an identifiable position espoused by a range of powerful figures and their epigones, principally by Party ideologues, by representatives of the avant-garde, and by professional linguists. Among them, I am foregrounding Leo Trotsky; a subset of the Constructivist movement known as the Productionists,[22] who emerged with particular strength around 1925 and whose chief spokesman on questions of language was Boris Arvatov (this was essentially a Moscow group, although most of Arvatov's articles on language were published in Leningrad's the *Life of Art*); and finally N. Ya. Marr, the infamous linguist whose school was to hold sway for most of the Stalin period.

Trotsky was an early advocate of linguistic Prometheanism. His book *Problems of Life* (Voprosy byta: Epokha kul'turnichestva i yeyë zadachi), which appeared in late 1923, is a largely forgotten moment in Soviet cultural history; indeed, Trotsky's contribution is remembered more in terms of his *Literature and Revolution*. But the latter was largely an appraisal of the current literary scene whereas *Problems of Life* was virtually a *domostroy*, or manual, of revolutionary culture and became in the mid-1920s—especially in the Leningrad of Zinoviev—the authoritative text for cultural revolution.

Trotsky's book addresses a variety of questions, including creeping bureaucratism, family morality, alcoholism, religion, and secular rituals. But it is more than a miscellany of essays; from the very outset it tackles the problem of providing a more comprehensive account of culture than is available in existing Marxist texts. The most crucial material on this is to be found in Chapters 6 and 7 (added for the second edition), called—by the activist who would mourn *The Revolution Betrayed!*—"Civility and Politeness as a Necessary Lubricant in Daily Relationships" and "The Struggle for Cultured Speech," respectively.

Trotsky's concern for language went far beyond the need to express manners and civility. He contended, in a move defining for a Promethean linguist, that language is not just a means or a style to be used in expressing ideas but the heart of the ideas themselves. It is the key to culture because it is the very shape of consciousness (Arvatov took a similar position).[23] Consequently, if you changed the language people use, you could change the way they think. Moreover, he concluded, language reform is pivotal for any program of modernization and political progress, the twin aims of Soviet society. In *Problems of Life* he identifies the contrast between what he saw as retrograde, and correct language with that between "swamps and impassable roads," and the modern industrial utopia, effectively conflating in his negative term the myth of Petersburg ("swamps") and those impassable roads that both Marx and Lenin identified as impediments to forging the new society;[24] just as the current of Volkhovstroy "eviscerated" the swamps, so the correct language would "eviscerate" all manner of obscurantism.[25] In effect, Trotsky identifies the use of standard, educated Russian with political progress and the Promethean ideal; what Gellner in *Nations and Nationalism* identifies as an effect of modernization whereby linguistic and cultural localisms and particularisms are eliminated as "high culture" becomes standard was to be its means.[26]

This, then, is the meaning of the term "linguistic Prometheanism," the idea that language can serve as the ultimate vehicle for the kind of transformation sought by revolution. Just as Prometheus transgressed epistemological boundaries and stole fire, one could, in order to give "fire" to the people, intervene in the natural course of language evolution and regulate it. The Productionists, a militantly utilitarian group, labeled this "linguistic engineering,"[27]and hence the Party ideologue A. A. Zhdanov at the First Writers Congress in 1934 partly cribbed from them when he defined Soviet writers as "engineers of human souls."

Trotsky and the Productionists both identified folkisms, grammatical infelicities, and most other forms of substandard speech as tendencies in language that impeded rational and efficient patterns of speech and thought and should therefore be banned. This position can be seen as part of a broad reaction at this time against the cult of the peasantry and peasant speech.[28] But they also railed against the other end of the linguistic spectrum, against using artificially bookish and long-winded expressions. Trotsky called the resulting spare and pared-down language "cultured speech," which he saw as marked by its "inner discipline."[29] Thus the Bolshevik state was by his account to mandate the language of the classes it had ostensibly overthrown! Trotsky obviates this problem by maintaining that "the foremost elements of the workers regard such false simplicity [peasant language and other such substandard speech] with instinctive hostility, for they justly see in coarseness of speech and conduct a mark of the old slavery, and aspire to acquire a cultured speech. . . ."[30]

Trotsky and the Productionists insisted on "casting out of our speech all useless words and expressions" leading to "precision and correctness of speech"—a position that was clearly at cross purposes with the perceptual millenarian wing of the Russian avant-garde who favored the whimsical, chance, or eccentric.[31] They wanted social and linguistic mores to be put on a more scientific basis, to be regulated and standardized. Their linguistic reforms were conceived as part of a general program for overhauling patterns of daily life that included rationalized communal living.[32] Thus they can be seen as a staging point on the route to Stalinist cultural homogenization. But what in the theories of the Productionists and Trotsky most anticipates that distinctive culture we call Stalinist (Trotsky!) is not its "totalitarian" impulse toward standardization in language. They did not want to mandate some invented new language for all, like Esperanto and other versions popular in Russia and the West in the 1910s and 1920s. Rather, they wanted society to adopt a standard language, a language crafted from the existing one by a process of rationalization. It is the values informing this process of standardization that can be most clearly associated with Stalinism.

A crucial value for Trotsky and the Productionists was that their single, standardized language would be not only rational but also, no less than the housing, hygienic. Trotsky, for instance, drew an analogy between the eradication of substandard language and physical hygiene: "The struggle against 'bad language' is a condition of intellectual culture, just as the fight against filth and vermin is a condition of physical culture."[33]

The implicit theoretical armature of all their claims for a revolutionary culture is a highly restrictive image of the body. The deep structure of their argument envisions society as a body that must be guarded to preserve purity. Their accounts betray a fear of pollution, of invasion, infection, or defilement by unclean or substandard elements. By the end of the decade when the first Stalinist purges began, apologists were equating "filth" and "vermin" with political deviance.

In the mid-1920s, a new concern for sexual purity and hygiene became marked in the writings of a broad spectrum of actors in the sphere of culture and morality. Symptomatically, at the very time these various versions of linguistic Prometheanism were rising to prominence in cultural debate, a new movie studio was founded with a mandate to educate the masses with films that were to popularize scientific work and also serve social causes.[34] The two main movies made under this rubric were *Abortion* (Abort, 1924) and *Syphilis* (Sifilis, or Pravda zhizni, 1925).[35] To be sure, syphilis, abortion, and some of the other projected topics such as gonorrhoea and tuberculosis have to do with very real social and public health problems of the time, but the choice of such topics is also indicative of the obsession with bodily purity. Inasmuch as this purity was linked to rationality and overcoming superstitious folk culture, it seems fitting that, at the same time these films were being made, Vsevolod Pudovkin, then an emerging director, was working at Pavlov's institute in Leningrad on what was to have been his first film, *The Mechanics of the Brain* (Mekhanika golovnogo mozga, 1925–1926).[36]

Official social and cultural policy was becoming markedly more puritanical, as was reflected in the new marriage code (1926) and the growing attacks on Freud. At this time, a series of fictional works appeared that treated the theme of sexual libertinism among Soviet youth and overcoming bourgeois prejudices on that score.[37] These sensational works gave rise to a heated press debate about the place of love and sex in the new society, with the works' detractors declaring the offending writers counterrevolutionaries who should be banned if not worse, and their defenders maintaining that the authors in question were depicting genuine social problems, if in exaggerated terms. Several members of the Party leadership took part in the debate, including Lunacharsky, who participated in the main debate, conducted in the Leningrad press. This question happened to coincide with the bitter ideological struggle over Trotskyism and related issues. Trotsky had enjoyed particular popularity among the student youth, and although his cultural policies were puritanical, sexual license among the young was implicitly identified with his ideological deviance.[38]

Bodily, sexual, and linguistic purity was being identified increasingly with ideological conformism. Conversely, many contended that an individual who showed sexual license or used bad language could not be trusted politically (in *Cement,* which had come out as recently as 1925, an ostensibly positive Party boss was also a rapist, an aspect of the novel that was toned down in its later redactions). This reached such extremes that when authority figures invoked the slogan "workerization" as often as not it was used to mean incorporating squeaky-clean heroes in literature, plays, or films and having them talk in only the most *comme il faut* language. This fear of pollution by unclean or substandard elements is of course a variant of the fear of invasion by commercialized popular culture, which threatened the purity of the true culture, that we have seen as a fundamental trait of the Russian intelligentsia since before the Revolution.

The pure and continent body had, then, become a controlling model for both political and discursive practices.[39] The trend is of course far from unique to Russia. Stallybrass and White in *The Politics and Poetics of Transgression* analyze the phenomenon in terms of the normative model of the "classical body," which they see as "far more than an aesthetic standard or model. . . . In the classical discursive body were encoded those regulated systems which were closed, homogenous, monumental, centered and symmetrical. It began to make 'parsimony' of explanation and 'economy' of utterance the measure of rationality, thus institutionalizing Lenten rule as a normative epistemological standard." Everything excluded from these norms, they contend, everything marginal or low was figured as a kind of "grotesque body" that has "*its* discursive norms, too: impurity (both in the sense of dirt and mixed categories), heterogeneity, masking, protuberant distensions, disproportion, exorbitancy, clamor, decentered or eccentric arrangements, a focus upon gaps, orifices and symbolic filth. . . ."[40]

Trotsky and the Productionists can be counted among those who advocated making "parsimony of explanation and economy of utterance the measure of rationality." Thus it is tempting to see the introduction of a "totalitarian" culture in the 1930s as a case study in the dynamic that Stallybrass and White discuss. In that sense, Boris Groys is right when in *The Total Art Work of Stalin* he argues that militant avant-gardists, such as Arvatov, were the secret legislators of Stalinist culture. But it is not actually Arvatov's particular version of Promethean linguistics that prevailed in the 1930s—let alone that of the "Judas Trotsky." Writers were to be "engineers," to be sure, but engineers of human *souls,* a very un-Productionist term.

There was more than one version of Promethean linguistics, and another one was more defining for the culture of the 1930s.

As powerful as the classical body theory may appear to be in its capacity to describe Stalinist culture, it leaves out a very important vehicle for the metaphor, and that is time—growth. Trotsky and Arvatov tend to focus on an eternal present, but in Stalinist culture lines of descent were crucial.

Nikolai Marr

Lines of descent play a dominant role in the theories of a third "Promethean" linguist, Nikolai Yakovlevich Marr (1864–1934),[41] which may cast light on why such eccentric theories as his became canonical in the 1930s. They were eccentric in some senses of the word used by Stallybrass and White in the quotation above, that is, the theories were noncanonical, hybrid, and ex-center, although not in the precise way Stallybrass and White mean ex-center, namely, as grotesque or parodic.

Marr is best known for his Japhetic Theory. This theory was launched around 1908, when he published a treatise claiming links between the Georgian and Semitic languages. The theory's title comes from his having labeled Georgian and certain other languages from the Caucasus "Japhetic" after the third son of Noah, Japheth, while he identified Semitic with another son, Shem.[42] Over time, he expanded his Japhetic theory, accommodating within its general contours more and more Caucasian languages. When, with first war and then revolution, his travel to the Caucasus for fieldwork became more difficult, Marr began casting his Japhetic net more broadly and ambitiously, adding first some languages that Indo-Europeanists found hard to accommodate in their schemes, such as Basque, Etruscan, and Pelasgian, and later Dravidian, Hittite, and others. As he extended his Japhetic Theory to an ever greater number of languages he saw as linked, Marr worked out progressively a comprehensive historical model for the evolution of all language. Its purview stretched from sea to shining sea, or more specifically from the Pacific Ocean in the Far East to the Atlantic, extending southward to incorporate some of Africa, and even potentially embracing some Native American languages.[43] But his two main groups were the Indo-European family and the Japhetic, one which hitherto had been largely unknown or ignored, but which in his scheme had a central role.

Many of the basic contours of Marr's Japhetic Theory had, then, been worked out well before the Revolution, but his theories did change fundamentally under Bolshevik rule. In 1925, he renamed his theory "The New Theory of Language" (novoye ucheniye ob yazyke), although he sometimes still used the term Japhetic Theory. In 1926 and 1927 he published two collections of his essays as the canonical sources for the New Theory: *Some Stages in the Development of the Japhetic Theory* (Po etapam razvitiya Yafeticheskoy teorii, 1926) and *The Japhetic Theory: The Program of a General Course on Linguistics* (Yafeticheskaya teoriya: Programma obshchego kursa ob yazyke, 1927).[44] The first of these was an anthology of Marr's recent essays, and the second comprises a series of lectures he gave to students. Thus the latter, both in its genre and in its subtitle, bears similarity to Ferdinand Saussure's path-breaking *Cours de linguistique générale,* which had been published in Russian translation in 1922.

The similarity is intentional. Marr identified himself as a linguist who followed Saussure's stance against basing linguistics exclusively on written sources.[45] The implication of his subtitle, however, is that he is presenting a further stage in the evolution of linguistic thought, in the tradition of, but superseding, the great Saussure. His was to be a truly materialist linguistics. Marr insists in his writings of the 1920s that the evolution of languages is in sync with, indeed determined by, the process of evolution in economics. He identifies three major stages in language evolution that correspond to Marx's three major stages of socioeconomic evolution. Moreover, he assigns language a place in the superstructure rather than the base;[46] thus any major changes in language have to be a function of major socioeconomic changes.

Such "vulgar materialism" might seem questionable, but more significant for the inquiry in this book is Marr's insistence that all languages are impending toward unification (just as are all classes and nations) and that ultimately, in the classless society, there will be a "single and unified language," what he calls a *yedinyy yazyk,* a language that will be more "precise"[47] and will be spoken by all peoples.

In this ideal of a single, spare, unified, and more precise language Marr's linguistic theories seem comparable with those of Trotsky and the Productionists. Moreover, like them, he insisted that language should be regulated and the process of unification speeded up.[48] However, and this is a crucial distinction, while Trotsky and the Productionists articulated their concern with bodily purity synchronically, in terms of keeping the body "pure" in an eternal present, Marr gave overwhelming emphasis to the diachronic or vertical aspect; he consistently outlined his theories in the terms of evolution.

A key term in Marr's account of the dynamic of linguistic evolution toward *yedinyy yazyk* is "crossing" or "hybridization" *(skreshcheniye).* In canonical Marr, languages are said to have evolved not so much when tribes migrated or when one language group borrowed from another, but rather in a process akin to hybridization; when two tribes or other language groups were thrown together by common economic need or practice, their two languages were crossed, resulting in a single language. The more crossing that had occurred in the evolution of a given language, the higher a linguistic form it would represent.[49] Over time, this process would lead to total linguistic unification.

Marr, then, foregrounded evolution as a place where a theory of change might be found. In this sense, he anticipated Stalinist culture, in which genetics played a key role in figuring revolution. It is no accident that many of the authority figures of Stalinist culture worked on genetic issues (Michurin, Lysenko). Marr was himself the son of a botanist working in agriculture, hence he used in a more figurative sense the vocabulary of his father. But at the same time, like the good Oedipal son, he rejected genetics.

Marr maintained that the history of linguistic evolution is not about bloodline or race, not even figuratively.[50] He insisted that the term "hybridization" has nothing to do with biology.[51] As he conceived it, hybridization involves a kind of fusion of two languages that occurs when there is a marked change in the economic-cum-social life of the two language groups causing a concomitant change in the sort of language they speak.[52] There are, he insisted, no ethnic groups established by bloodline and no national languages.[53] He substituted class for biology, maintaining that the language of one class will in its typological features be closer to the language of the same class in a different ethnic group than it will be to that of another class in the same ethnic group.[54]

Here Marr dovetailed with the legitimizing myths of Stalinist culture. The key myths had to do with replacing the bloodline as a value or system of reckoning with a line determined by political allegiance; Stalinist rhetoric gave priority to the "Great Family" (the state) as contrasted with the "little," or nuclear, family.[55]

Another defining feature of Stalinist culture anticipated in Marr is evolutionary impatience (to be seen in Lysenko, Michurin, and others). Marr urged a "creative" approach to linguistic evolution, guiding it and helping it to accelerate.[56] Thus the "creator" in Marr is, as in the culture of High Stalinism, the man who defies natural evolution.

In a speech of 1924 he proclaimed: "Down with the *Venus de Milo!*"[57] This may sound like the opening salvo in a Futurist manifesto, but that is deceptive. Marr was not calling for the *Venus de Milo* to be dynamited as the typical Futurist would have in his time, but rather he was insisting that she yield her place on the throne of culture; radiant as she was, she had been eclipsed. The salvo is aimed at the regnant European school of linguistics, the Indo-European School, which had, since well before the Revolution, been his chief bugbear.

But the target is broader than the Indo-Europeanists. In Marr's works of the 1920s, he rewrote the consensus account of Western civilization because his theory of language evolution established priority for the Japhetic peoples as providing the earliest cradle of language and civilization.[58] He included in his account of the genealogy of Western civilization all the usual elements—Egypt, ancient Greece, and so on—and offered as its "creative center" the Mediterranean area (hardly original) but reconceived the account so that its original culture is Japhetic. Thus he adduced a new theory of origins whereby a previously unknown or marginalized group (the Japhetic peoples) became the center, the originals for all of Europe and, in an ever expanding purview, the world; center and periphery were transposed.

The *Venus de Milo*, housed in the Louvre, is an icon of European cultural dominance, but Marr was questioning that assumption. She must yield her place as the "center" because she is not an achievement of the group with priority. Marr, phrasing this in terms of his own field, asserted that though the Europeans may have a superior technology, in linguistic thinking they are still in the nineteenth century.[59] Such assertions fit well the needs of a regime that sought legitimation and put forth Promethean claims that local conditions made difficult to realize. Indeed, Marr associates the rise of Indo-European theory with the rise of European imperialism.[60] Here his theories are like those of the Formalists in that both enact revolution as an inversion of center and periphery. The scale of his inversion is more fantastic, but a more crucial difference derives from the fact that Marr's move against "the center" (hegemonic, West European culture) entails a countermyth of origins.

Marr also renegotiates center and periphery within the great Russian empire. In his writings, he constantly urges that the ethnic minorities be given a voice and that their dialects not be discriminated against as "primitive" but be accorded respect equal to that of written languages. Thus he was an early voice for giving greater status to non-Russian elements in the empire, a process that saw its tentative beginnings in the 1920s (especially in the late 1920s, when the minority peoples of the Soviet Union finally gained a position of prominence in Soviet public rhetoric and many of them were given the alphabet for the first time).

In Marr, we find what is in some ways a cult of the bastard, the mongrel, of racial indiscriminateness. Here there may have been personal motives since he was himself a mixture of an ethnic minority (the Georgians) and a foreigner (a Scot) in a Russian-dominated empire. He seems to have felt this situation most keenly in terms of language; in his autobiography Marr recounts how his mother, who spoke the Gurian dialect of Georgian, and his father, who spoke English, essentially did not understand each other. Hence an amusing aspect of his theories is that both the Gurian dialect and the Celtic have a place in the Japhetic family;[61] as it were the entire theory is one great fantasy that enables mummy and daddy to speak to each other, if in some primordial past.

Marr's theory of the "single language" purports to provide the route to true internationalism—so that all mummies and all daddies can speak to each other, and in the present. His recommendations would also seem to militate against Russian dominance; Marr consistently promoted the manifest virtues of linguistic internationalism *(yedinyy yazyk)* as the antidote to linguistic parochialism. But of course as long as the path to a "single language" is "regulated" in only the one country, the Soviet Union, the meaning of rejection of blood or tribal ties is creating a more cohesive state. Moreover, even as Marr seems to be rejecting the hegemonic status of Russian language and culture, certain of his statements shade over into some of the myths of Russian particularism popular at that time. He repeatedly urged linguists to look not at Greek and Sanskrit in their quest to understand literary evolution, but rather at such early Japhetic languages as Scythian (other favorites frequently listed in this connection include Sarmatian, Khazar, and Bulgarian).[62] Of course, these assertions are part of his attack on the Indo-Europeanists for whom Greek and Sanskrit were paradigmatic sources of examples, and also of his "Saussurian" campaign to have the "living language" be the focus of linguistics rather than dry and highly formalized studies of written languages.[63] But this foregrounding of the languages of the wild tribes of the Russian area such as the Scythians also suggests the curious inversion of the nature / culture hierarchy that is implicit in the slogan "Down with the *Venus de Milo.*"

Marr did not merely proclaim in that 1924 lecture "Down with the *Venus de Milo,*" but added immediately, "Long live the hoe and hoe culture." Thus just as the genealogy of Prometheanism was being shifted, so were its ideals. He explained this strange predilection for the hoe by going on to say that only something that is truly grounded in material culture is of any value. The hoe is scarcely the "engineering" of Arvatov, nor are dialects such as Gurian particularly close to the "cultured speech" Trotsky sought; Arvatov and indeed most avant-garde leftist cultural groups at this time were absolutely opposed to using any folkisms. Marr seems to take an antimodernist position. In one of his articles he even entertains the lost civilization of Atlantis as a candidate for his Japhetic empire.[64] It would seem that to Marr that which is primitive and from an earlier time—the hoe—is more signifi-cant than that which represents a later stage of human development and greater sophistication, the *Venus de Milo*. But the inversion is not wholesale because Marr will not admit any hierarchy of primitive and cultured in his theory.[65]

All this seems strangely out of sync with the culture that erected Volkhovstroy as one of its icons. Marr's predilection for the oral and folk highlights some of the major ambivalences in Stalinist culture, which advanced as models both, so to speak, hoes and Volkhovstroys.

Marr's theories come perilously close to representing yet another glorifi-cation of the Folk. Updating it for the October Revolution, he has the prole-tarians perform the messianic role which, in the past, most assigned to the peasantry, yet there is little sign of anything intrinsically proletarian in his account of them. Indeed, his frequent foregrounding of the Scythians, coin-ciding as it does with a time when Scythianism was a dominant literary movement in the Soviet Union, suggests that he may share that movement's antiurbanist bias.[66]

In Marr's writings the "single language" is always represented as a futur-istic one. In his essay "On the Origin of Languages," for instance, he allows that by the time the single language emerged, sound language might be sup-planted by "another technical means which enables humans to express their thought more precisely [*tochno*]."[67] Yet he gives the lion's share of attention in his account of linguistic evolution to the languages of traditional peoples. Before the Revolution, he did some work in archeology, but in the mid- to late 1920s he developed a particular line of inquiry, shifting the center of his attention from the vast range of languages to be accommodated in his theory—its "spatial sweep"—to accounting for language in its "prehistoric" phase, looking at the "paleontology" of languages, at the possibility of "pre-logical" languages.

Marr contended that before there was sound language there was kinetic or linear speech, a kind of speech defined in terms of gestures and mimicry.[68] In this speech, the chief organ was not the mouth but the hand (sound was used chiefly for expressing emotion but not involved in a system of commu-nication). True to his sociological-materialist method, he insisted that the emergence of this kind of speech presupposes acquisition of some labor processes, but as yet only with "natural implements" (for example, stones). The transition to sound speech he associates with the acquisition of man-made implements.[69]

Marr pronounced the hand the center of production and the center of presound language (gesture). At the same time, he identified it as the great "creative agent." By elevating the hand to the status of hero of prelogical speech, he was able to make an identification between speech, labor (that all-important value to the Marxists), and creativity. Indeed, even the development of reason he attributes to "ingenuity" *(nakhodchivost')* and "inventiveness" in doing manual labor processes, a finding that reinforces the then current biases in favor of practical reason over theoretical, of applied linguistics over "Formalist schemes," and so on. But these postulates are also strongly weighted in the direction of a romanticism of the uneducated classes as "creators." Moreover, even after that "revolution" that was the shift to sound speech, Marr claims, the imprint of linear speech was still felt in language. Indeed, "The ideological remains of linear speech are still with us."[70]

Some of these moves read today as singularly clumsy. Many, such as Lawrence Thomas, the author of the main monograph on Marr in English, have wondered if his transition in the 1920s to a more Marxist articulation of his theories was not a little forced or opportunistic, particularly given his meteoric rise to power then. Thomas also interprets Marr's move into the prelogical period as trying to get himself out of the dead end he had created in overextending the purview of the Japhetic Theory.[71]

Certainly, Marr's rise to power was extraordinary and not commensurate with his scholarly standing (there was no dearth of detractors before the Revolution). He had been a prominent member of the Academy of Sciences since before the Revolution and his seat of operations had always been Petersburg. In the mid-1920s, however, he began to head institutes and other organizations in both capitals and is therefore an example of the emerging bicapital, Soviet culture. In this way, Marr progressively gained a dominant position in the scholarly world, heading ever more institutes, and establishing his own Moscow-Leningrad power axis with bases in the Communist Academy, in a range of scholarly institutes under RANION, the university, and the Academy of Sciences. Nineteen twenty-eight, marked as the fortieth anniversary of Marr's scholarly career, appears to have been a watershed year in his official elevation. The leading Bolshevik historian and cultural bureaucrat M. Pokrovsky in a May article in *Izvestiya* proclaimed: "If Engels still lived among us, every student at an institution of higher education would be studying Marr's theories because they would enter the mandatory list of sources for a Marxist understanding of human culture."[72] In the 1930s his power was to grow even more and "The New Theory of Language" was to become mandatory for all of linguistics, and allied fields as well.

This extraordinary rise to power was not without its ugly incidents. The most famous of these was the losing battle against Marr waged by a founding member of OPOYaAZ, Ye. D. Polivanov, who was by the late 1920s the only linguist of stature to make a concerted public stand against him. Despite the many common points in the positions of the two linguists (such as an emphasis on nonwritten language and advocacy of the languages of the ethnic minorities),[73] Polivanov took absolute exception to Marr's theories, particularly to his anti-Westernism and the way he rode roughshod over the facts in his zeal for establishing his theories. The bitter struggle between the two was essentially resolved in a series of debates and lectures held between December 1928 and February 1929 at the Communist Academy, but they were weighted against Polivanov, who was blackballed from all scholarly enterprises in the two capitals. From then until his arrest (1937) and execution (1938), he was essentially in exile in Central Asia, where he was able to accomplish fruitful work on the local languages.[74]

One might be tempted to seize upon Polivanov's struggle as either another example where proletarian and Party hacks or their stooges terrorize unwitting non-Party or bourgeois intellectuals, leading sooner or later to their repression, or, more specifically, as a prime example of the persecution of the Formalists. At the time, Polivanov was obliquely made a hero in Kaverin's novel about his intelligentsia set, *The Troublemaker* (Skandalist) of 1929.[75] But the problem is that Polivanov, although a founding member of OPOYaZ, was really only active in the group between 1915 and 1919 (in part because he was away from Leningrad for much of the 1920s). From 1926 to 1929 he served as head of the linguistics section of a Moscow institute within RANION (the consortium of institutes pitted against the Formalists), and in 1927 he was made head of its Linguistics Section. More important, Polivanov, a leftist even before the Revolution, joined the Party in 1919, worked some time for the Comintern, and joined the Bolshevik forces in putting down the insurgents at Kronstadt. He left Petrograd in 1921, a move that is often attributed to the hostility among his colleagues at the university to his support for the Bolsheviks.[76] Polivanov always insisted that his linguistic theories were Marxist.

Marr's Marxism, by contrast, is problematical. He joined the Party only in 1930, essentially after his triumph in Soviet linguistics was complete and Polivanov had been sent to rout. Until the late 1920s he had always insisted that although his theories coincided with the Marxist position, they were not specifically Marxist. Thereafter, he allowed that they might be Marxist, but did so very hesitantly and sometimes disclaimed this identification.

Marr was born in the mid-1860s, and hence the formative years of his intellectual career essentially occurred before Marxism became an issue in Russia; by the mid-1920s, he was sixty. Thus his career provides a good example of what I am calling the "ecology of revolution," of how Stalinist revolutionary culture was neither sui generis nor "created" by the Party or Komsomol, and of how many prerevolutionary trends were modified, but far from obliterated, in the postrevolutionary period. When Marr's "New Theory of Language" was married to Marxism this illustrates a general phenomenon in the ecology of revolution as particular intellectual orientations find themselves in a new force field. Such an explanation does not necessarily imply repression, opportunism, or calculated moves.

Actually, we need a slightly broader purview to look at the Marr phenomenon. In such a context, his socioeconomic theory of language development does not have to be written off as a crude attempt at accommodating the Marxists, but can be seen as an elaboration of some of the theories of A. N. Veselovsky (1838–1906), that grand old man of Russian literary and linguistic theory who died in Petersburg in 1906, precisely the time Marr was working out his first major move from purely philological scholarship to the Japhetic Theory. Indeed, one of Marr's many institutional bases of the 1920s, ILYaZV, was originally called the Veselovsky Institute. In other words, it was named for Veselovsky, who, although discredited in the 1940s as too "cosmopolitan," at this time provided a favorite frame of reference for critiquing the Formalists. Veselovsky was himself a leftist but no Marxist, and many of the scholarly agendas and positions he pursued were analogous to those taken up by Marr, including his championing of historical poetics, as distinct from a poetics that sought to adduce invariants. Also, Veselovsky developed a stadial theory of the history of language that is in its general contours quite similar to Marr's, while Marr's interest in prelogical language also has ample precedent in Veselovsky, who also worked on the paleontology of languages.

We can look at Marr's theories in an even broader purview. Promethean linguistics in general and Marr's theories in particular can be seen as part of a European theory dating from at least the German Romantics, who believed that language is thinking (as they put it, "Die Sprache als Energie"). One of its grandsires was the German Wilhelm von Humboldt, who influenced such leading Russian theorists of language as Veselovsky, Aleksandr Potebnya, G. Shpet—and Vygotsky. Indeed, even the "hack" S. Danilov from the Communist Academy cited von Humboldt's statement "Language is the agent of human interaction" as the banner quotation for his pro-Marrist speech of 1928 made to the Department of Political Enlightenment (Politprosvet). At the same time, in this speech he pronounced Marr's theories the only possible version of a Marxist linguistics that showed how to "regulate the collective," but in this context he cited Trotsky (in 1928!) on the necessity of ensuring "hygiene" in language. The doctrine of "hybridicity" was itself an intellectual hybrid.

There is another important extra-Bolshevik aspect to Marr's theories, in this instance having to do with his interest in prelogical language. This can be viewed as yet another version of that general tendency of the 1910s and 1920s which I have labeled "the Wagnerian project." Marr in his study of prelogical language and culture was particularly concerned with the relationship between physical gesture, sound, and music and with the whole question of rhythm. In other words, he was also attracted by the possibility of a truly syncretic culture in primordial times.

Marr did not pursue these interests in isolation but in the late 1920s became a member of a study group that included L. Vygotsky, Luria, and Eisenstein.[77] All of these men were committed to establishing a materialist account of such questions as language acquisition and the survival of primitive expressive forms in our languages of today. But their investigations did not focus on Marxist thought; they were largely conducted at the intersection of linguistics, new psychological theory (particularly that coming out of Berlin and including Freudianism),[78] and aesthetic theories, in particular those of Nietzsche and Wagner and later theorists who were influenced by them. Eisenstein tried to uncover the gestural bases at the depths of the meanings of words and was particularly interested in Nietzsche's observations on this in *The Birth of Tragedy*.[79] One can also see some of his theoretical and practical explorations into syncretism in some essays he wrote in the late 1930s and early 1940s in connection with his productions *Alexander Nevsky* and *Ivan the Terrible*.[80]

Marr died in 1934 but his school only grew in power, making it difficult to ascertain to what extent he was responsible for its canonization. Its sway came to an end in 1950, however, when Stalin joined a debate on linguistics in *Pravda* with three essays attacking Marr.[81] The essays are of considerable interest for the question of cultural evolution because they contain a hybrid message. One of their chief functions was to debunk Marr's contention that language is part of the superstructure and changes as a function of changes in the base; this move freed much Soviet scholarship from an excessive economic determinism. But there are two other important moments in the essays. First, Stalin called the strangle hold that the Marr school enjoyed in linguistics an "Arakcheev-like" regime, thus likening it to the repressive military colonies set up by Arakcheev during the reign of Alexander I. This remark gave license to writers and intellectuals to attack all manner of "Arakcheev-like," overly authoritarian trends in intellectual life. Thus the critique of Stalinism that we associate with the thaws under Khrushchev actually began before Stalin died. In *Not by Bread Alone* (Ne khlebom yedinym), the most explosive book of the 1956 thaw, Vl. Dudintsev was in a sense taking his cue from Stalin when he attacked Stalinism for what he explicitly called the "Arakcheev-like" regimes in intellectual life.

The second moment undercuts this impression of the essays as a milestone in liberalization. In Stalin's critique of Marr's theories, he used for "hybridization" the word *skreshchivaniye* rather than *skreshcheniye*. As is so often the case, the difference of a mere few letters spoke volumes: *skreshchivaniye* has negative connotations of interbreeding that are absent from *skreshcheniye*. In these articles, Stalin railed against Marr's notion that there can be no such thing as national languages and also attacked the Bund (a Jewish socialist group persecuted by the Bolsheviks). Thus the essays were in effect a call to greater "purity" of the line, and must be seen in the context of the anticosmopolitan campaign, the doctors' plot, and an increasingly rabid Russian chauvinism.

Finally, we must ask why, if Marr so successfully served Stalinism, was he in the end denounced publicly by Stalin himself? One answer to this question may be found in a kernel of truth in Marr's own theories. History is always everywhere at work, even in a totalitarian state, and the Soviet Union found itself in a different historical moment when there was a need to realign once again the symbolic borders.

In 1926, the very point when Marr, by his own account, had finalized his "New Theory of Language," the political power structure in Leningrad changed radically. Zinoviev, who had been Party head of the city ever since the capital was moved to Moscow in 1918, fell from power. As "socialism in one country" emerged as the de facto and then the *de jure* policy, he, in his other capacity as head of the Comintern, had become less important. But he ultimately fell from power because he had started to ally himself with Trotsky. In February 1926 the Central Committee sent a huge contingent from Moscow to Leningrad, and at the Thirteenth Extraordinary Session of the Leningrad Regional Party Conference the "new opposition" was routed. A new Regional Party Committee was elected, headed by Sergei Kirov, the former Party head from Azerbaidzhan who was considered a relative unknown who would be easier to manipulate. Leningrad is generally reckoned to have become, thanks to this comprehensive purge, the first Stalinist city.

The "unknown" Kirov was in actuality already known to some Leningrad cultural circles as the person responsible for commissioning the memorial to the Baku massacre and the Brodsky painting commemorating it, commissions won by architects and artists who were anathema to the avant-garde. Nevertheless, Kirov, for all his Stalinist identity, was probably more enabling for the avant-garde than Zinoviev had been. Certainly in the initial years of his tenure in Leningrad the city regained some of its lost status as a cultural trendsetter.

Even as Marr's linguistics and allied movements directed at "a single, unified language" (*yedinyy yazyk*) were gathering political strength, there came another avant-garde response to the task of creating a truly revolutionary culture. This new wave, which essentially set itself up in opposition to that "single language," was centered in Leningrad. The dynamos of Volkhovstroy might break down, but the city's engines of cultural revolution were still churning.

10

STRAIGHT TALK AND
THE CAMPAIGN
AGAINST WAGNER

In an article of 1928 Polivanov claimed that "the language of the Pioneer-Komsomol generation of today is quite different from that of the prerevolutionary intellectual or the average Russian of 1913." He contended, moreover, that the differences amount to not merely two dialects but two separate *languages* as that word is defined by linguists, that is, "in terms of mutual incomprehensibility." He went on to invoke a common trope of utopian writing in claiming that if someone had gone to sleep in 1913 and woken up in 1928, he or she would not be able to understand what was being said.[1]

One might contest Polivanov's view that the radical differences between the Russian spoken in 1913 and that of 1928 amount to two distinct languages. Nevertheless, he is accurate insofar as he is describing two generations that were separated by events so revolutionary that they often seemed unable to communicate with each other. In order to assess this shift in language we should turn to Bakhtin's contribution to the understanding of the sociology of language practices—the belief that we need to study not only languages but what he refers to as "images" of languages.

Bakhtin notes that within the mass of data that linguists study as language, there are highly marked "social languages" that give a distinctive profile to particular generations, classes, professions, and so on, "a profile that by defining itself through semantic shifts and lexical choices can be established even within the boundaries of a linguistically unitary language . . . [It is] a concrete sociolinguistic belief system that defines a distinct identity for itself within the boundaries of a language that is unitary only in the abstract." Such a set of practices gives a recognizable face to a world view; it is, then, less a language than an image of language, "an image assumed by a set of social beliefs, the image of a social ideologeme that has fused with its own discourse, with its own language."[2]

The difference in language between 1913 and 1928 described by Polivanov is really a difference between images of language. It is a discursive break. But it might also be described more broadly as a radical reorientation in the dominant image of culture itself to be found among certain mainstream and avant-garde intellectual groups in the second half of the 1920s. Although this shift could be seen as following the official agenda of "workerization," a more sociologically oriented scholarship and so forth, it actually had no necessary connection to the Party, the Komsomol, or the Revolution; analogous shifts can be found elsewhere in Europe at this time. This reorientation was toward foregrounding cultural forms that, in crucial respects, represent the opposite of those that obtained in the 1910s and the first half of the 1920s.

Arguably, culture in the first half of the decade labored, consciously or unconsciously, under the shadow of Wagner, but in this period it began to emerge from under that shadow. That is not to say that in the early 1920s Wagner's music was imitated or revered—although it was to a certain extent—but more that what might be called the materiality of the word was downplayed in favor of such values as music (or the sound qualities of language), theatricality, spectacle, and monumentalism. The theater veered off decidedly in the direction of pantomime and bouffe, or alternatively of pageant-like "mystery," and some productions dispensed with words altogether.

A good example of Wagnerism is the mass spectacles of the 1920s, which incorporated much pantomime. Because words used in the spectacles were often lost in the melee of thousands of actors on a vast open-air stage, the verbal text was of necessity kept to a minimum and largely involved choral recitation or singing. But the downplaying of the word was due to more than sheer necessity. In its place, music assumed a major role; the duel between the two classes locked in a revolutionary struggle was frequently represented in terms of a duel between two pieces or kinds of music. In *The Storming of the Winter Palace*, for instance, the triumph of the revolutionary forces was represented by having the Communist hymn the "Internationale" progressively drown out the music of the "Marseillaise," which was deemed bourgeois because it was associated with the French Revolution. During the early years of NEP, the verbal text had experienced a comeback. However, the official model of those years for organizing performance groups in workers' clubs, the so-called Unified (*yedinyy*) Artistic Circle, or YeKhK, was patently influenced by Wagnerian principles. In 1927, a sign of new times, YeKhK was debunked in an Agitprop (Department of Agitation and Propaganda) conference on the theater; in other words, the shift described in this chapter was felt very broadly, though not universally.[3]

At the center of this shift were a movement for opera reform and an allied movement in linguistics. That it should be focused in opera is not surprising. Even before the Revolution, theatrical activists had been particularly concerned with the Wagnerian agenda of conceiving a new interrelation among three key elements in opera—sound (or music), text (words), and bodily movement. Now they returned to the same problematic, focusing particularly on the interrelation between sound and word (or, in opera, between score and libretto). A parallel shift can be found in linguistic theory, one that set itself up in opposition to those who advocated a "single and universal language" *(yedinyy yazyk)*. Whereas Promethean linguists had emphasized linguistic standardization, the emphasis in this new movement was on variegation and interrelation—between sound and word, between text and context, and so on.

Thus the implications of this shift were not confined to opera or language use / linguistics. The shift can be seen as a marker of a broad cultural change that is best generalized in the following terms: in each of several discourses (literary and linguistic theory, the performing arts, and even music), there was a tendency to move away from formal categories that drew attention to their own abstractness in an attempt to capture more closely the actuality of spoken language. In each case this move was seen as a gesture toward a new image of language in the broader sense.

This trend cannot be called a movement, just as Promethean linguistics cannot be called a movement. It is reflected in the work of very disparate groups and individuals, many of whom would scarcely have been prepared to see any common cause in their theories. Although some were active proselytizers, they did not go in for writing manifestoes or any of the other activities that had become standard for the many new movements that proliferated over the previous ten years or so.

The anti-Wagnerian trend stood against a tendency, found in all areas of the arts at this time, especially art and architecture, to monumentalism, or exaggerated heroic pathos. In fact, it represents virtually the opposite of heroic monumentalism, that is, a paradoxical attempt at monumentalizing the trivial. I mean trivial here not in the sense of kitsch, but rather in the sense of privileging a discourse that had previously been marked as minor and mundane, the discourse of everyday speech, and particularly of nonstandard speech.

The cult of everyday language can be seen as an effect of interest in two particular movements in contemporary Europe. These were, on the one hand, new developments in the Austro-German modernist theater and music then centered around Berlin, and, on the other, contemporary Francophone linguistic thought, and particularly the work of Saussure and Antoine Meillet. These disparate trends came together in Soviet Russia in a union facilitated by the peculiar historical and political conditions of that time. This interaction was fostered by such factors as the increasing cooperation of the German and Soviet military industrial complexes, but particularly by the founding in 1925 of VOKS (the All-Union Society for Overseas Cultural Links), an organization that sponsored not only the visits of Benjamin and other leading leftist intellectuals, but also concert tours, art exhibitions, and film showings both in the Soviet Union and in the West; the majority of all VOKS activities at this time involved movement back and forth between Berlin and the two Soviet capitals. Two particular VOKS-sponsored events in Leningrad proved seminal for the new trend.

The New Operas

At the very end of the 1926–27 season the Leningrad Maly Opera House fitted in somewhat surreptitiously the premieres of two highly controversial new operas, Ernst Krenek's *Leap over the Shadow* (Der Sprung über den Schatten, or Pryzhok cherez ten') and Alban Berg's *Wozzeck* (Votsek). Both had premiered in Germany as recently as 1925. Krenek's later opera *Johnny spielt auf* (Johnny Strikes Up [the Band], of 1925–26), which premiered in Germany in February 1927, was staged in Leningrad in 1928. These operas, which opened later in Moscow as well, were to have a major impact on the development of Soviet music and theater over the next few years. Their librettos feature characters from the lower classes of the city and its demi-monde, a significant shift when compared with the aristocrats and rustics who had been the basic fare of opera, though their plots largely rehearse the recognizable themes of love, jealousy, imputed infidelity, and revenge. The impact of the new operas derives less from the new subject matter, however, than from their formal strategies.

Writing about the premieres of 1927, Boris Asafiev, the leading Soviet champion of modernist music, listed among these operas' qualities their ability to convey the insistently everyday and nonheroic, what he referred to as "humdrum life in a humdrum town" ("seryy byt serogo goroda"). More significant in terms of innovation, however, was in his view the unusual structure of the operas, which were built on "chance conversations, unexpected meetings, words dropped casually in street language . . . and drunken ramblings."[4] The conductor Nikolai Malko developed these observations further in a succeeding article on Krenek's *Leap over the Shadow*, claiming that the operas represented a step forward beyond Prokofiev's *Love of Three Oranges* (which also premiered in Russia that year). *The Love of Three Oranges*, he said, mocked false operatic romanticism, and in so doing prepared the ground for these new operas, which are actually "preparing the . . . inevitable revolution." These works point to a way out of the "essentially antediluvian" condition of the current Soviet opera, he contended, because they actively confound the dominant opera traditions of Wagner and Strauss by eschewing "sentimental, sweet lyrics," "cheap love pathos," and beautiful arias. The new operas are deliberately antimelodic; nearly all their music is polyphonic, atonal, or polytonal; their sounds seem cacophonous, but this is because they are built on the principle of dissonance; the apparent confusion of voices is not as unsystematic as it might seem because it is controlled by a "strict rhythmic pattern."[5]

Before long, these operas were having their impact on Soviet music. The most celebrated instance of the influence of the new German operas on a Soviet is D. Shostakovich's *The Nose* (Nos), which is loosely based on the Gogol story and premiered in 1930. This opera, like so many other interpretations of Gogol made in this period, satirizes Nicolaevan Russia as an emblem of all that the avant-garde of the day abhorred: oppressive regimes, a bureaucratic cast of mind, and above all cultural philistinism.

The musicologist I. I. Sollertinsky wrote in his review of the opera: "[Shostakovich] is perhaps the first among opera composers to make his heroes speak not in conventional arias and cantilenas but in living language, setting everyday speech to music. . . . The opera theater is at a crossroads. The birth of Soviet opera is not far off."[6] Sollertinsky was of course wrong in claiming that Shostakovich was the first to use the "living language" in his opera. His dramatic claims for the significance of *The Nose* seem particularly inappropriate given that Sollertinsky became a close friend of Shostakovich's while the latter was working on the opera, and was one of those who collaborated in the writing of the libretto.[7] His claim for the opera is also in a sense understated, however: *The Nose* was a sign that not just the opera but Soviet culture itself was at a critical crossroads; indeed, it seemed to many that the birth of an entirely new culture might not be "far off."

Asafiev concluded his article on the new operas with the claim that their unusual compositional strategy was essentially "directed against high culture." This was certainly so in terms of the music, which was deliberately democratized; in the new opera, nonreceived, lowbrow forms and even instruments were used. Jazz, which when first introduced in the Soviet Union in 1922 was scorned as decadent and bourgeois, stormed the citadel of the opera. Subcanonical instruments were also incorporated in the operas' orchestra; for instance, Shostakovich included a balalaika in his score for *The Nose.*

The most radical step of these new operas, however, was toward a new kind of libretto and a new relationship between libretto and music. Previously, a Wagnerian sense of this relationship dominated; in his *Gesamtkunstwerk,* or "total art work," all the elements—text, sets, acting, and so on— were ultimately subordinated to the music, which was itself controlled to a large extent by the principle of the leitmotif or recurrent musical signature, which was to play a large role in conveying meaning. Now it was the libretto that was to control the opera rather than vice versa. As Shostakovich himself stated in his introductory remarks to the first edition (1930) of the libretto (echoing what was by now a commonplace about the new opera), "The music in this work [*spektakl'*] is not an end in itself. Here the emphasis is on the presentation of the text."[8]

At the same time, there was a shift in the writing of librettos from the use of the literary language to the spoken vernacular. Here I mean literally the spoken vernacular, not some idealized version of the folk that essentially becomes part of the literary language. This shift necessitated the writing of an entirely different kind of music. When the libretto reproduced the actual patterns of vernacular speech, this militated against conventional musical form, which was geared to more idealized and regular verbal patterns more readily amenable to translation into melodic form. The privileging of conversational language led to music's imitating the patterns of that speech rather than vice versa. Shostakovich, in several of his scores for musical dramas and films from this time, had individual instruments parody the intonational patterns of everyday speech.[9]

In the new opera, the libretto was not synchronized with the music. Much of the effort in composition was directed at undercutting melodic expectations or at using a form of recitative that was nonsynchronous with the musical line. The new music was so difficult for a singer with conventional training, however, that many complained of "a campaign against the voice."[10] Indeed, composers in their zeal took the attack on melodic music to an extreme. Thus in *The Nose* the main part was sung in a nasal voice effected by putting the hand over the nose.

The downgrading of the musical component in opera took such extreme forms that when Radlov was appointed as an opera director in 1928, the lack of musical experience in his background was considered of no importance. Certainly he was not troubled by it for, in an article of 1930, he declared war on the kind of opera that is defined as "singing in costumes and wigs against a background of sets," and in which music is seen "as the only self-valuable element in the opera that presides over it magisterially as its essence and meaning." "Instead of the singer, equipped with the appropriate makeup and gestures," he continued, "we will have a performer who . . . [makes] use of the entire intonational range [*vsem intonatsionnym bogatsvom*] from the spoken to the sung word. . . ."[11]

A sort of apotheosis of the Wagnerian trend is Meyerhold's production of Gogol's *Inspector General,* which premièred in December 1926 and was, by Meyerhold's own account, subordinated to the principle of "musical realism," by which he meant that musical forms such as the fugue and the leitmotif governed the rhythm of the production; the text, acting, and even the sets were all geared to the demands of these controlling forms. Also, some of the scenes in the play were wordless.[12] Shostakovich was close to Meyerhold and even lived in his Moscow apartment for a time (where he wrote some music for *The Nose*), but arguably, although both works use Gogol as a weapon to debunk petty bourgeois philistinism and the bureaucratic cast of mind, Shostakovich's approach is in many ways opposed to that of Meyerhold; whereas Meyerhold nominated "tragedy" as the genre of his production and explicitly rejected for it his old ideals of bouffe and the *commedia dell'arte,* Shostakovich looked to parodic grotesqueness, buffoonery, and laughter.[13] A central means for such effects was the slippage between the music and the action, between the verbal text and the music, or between pompous, bookish, or clichéd verbalizing and "straight talk."

The significance of this shift extends beyond the opera, and analogous shifts can be seen in many other branches of cultural activity. The ballet, one of the most unlikely mediums, was also being revamped to incorporate the word. Even that old chestnut *The Nutcracker* was totally reworked for a production of 1930 to "demonstrate a whole series of new forms [*priyёmy*], such as dances without music and word dances [*tanets-slovo*]."[14]

The Resurrection of the Word

The new trends of 1926 and beyond sought a "resurrection of the word," but in a different way from the one Shklovsky and his Formalist and Futurist allies had sought. In Formalist analyses, words were frequently regarded only for their sound potential, or as "technique-fodder." At this later time, those who privileged the spoken language wanted to "make the stone stony" once again, but they believed they were doing so more literally than the Formalists. In this sense, their project can be seen as analogous to the new wave found in Germany from around 1925 which called for *Neue*

Sachlichkeit, for basing art more in the actuality of the world, to give it, as *Sachlichkeit* is generally translated, "objectivity."

The prerevolutionary Futurists in their quest to go "beyond sense" *(za-um)* wanted essentially to break through the constraints of "sense" *(um)* qua the stale conventions of language and even epistemology to reach an extrasystemic—revolutionary—meaning. Proponents of the newer trend, however, sought the opposite. They glorified discourse that was prior to such semantic conventions. They rejected an academic and dictionary attitude toward language and language that was clichéd and *comme il faut*, in favor of one that was richer and more variegated because it had not submitted to these constraints. Obviously, and as many theorists of this time such as Bakhtin stressed, some sort of conventionality or system in language is neither good nor bad but rather unavoidable if there is to be meaning. There is no way to get beyond what Frederic Jameson calls "the prison house of language," and the Futurist quest for extrasystemic meaning was essentially utopian semantics.

The avant-garde of the late 1920s were no longer interested in the sort of total iconoclasm one finds in the theory of trans-sense *(zaum)*, which, in seeking meanings that cannot be communicated through the conventional system of semantics, is in danger of becoming a solipsism. The figures discussed here turned their attention to actual, nonbookish language, and particularly to oral and proletarian forms, because these forms did not have to be made up, as did *zaum*. Unlike *zaum*, they could communicate meaning readily, and yet they were, it was felt, a source that might truly "resurrect" language. Clearly, even before the Revolution members of the less transcendental wing of Russian Futurism, as represented in Mayakovsky, were also interested in incorporating in their writing nonreceived language, including street talk. However, with their emphasis on *sdvig* (displacement) and on breaking through to a new order of meaning by means of incongruous and unexpected juxtapositions—their mania for manipulation—they gave priority to the orchestration of such language forms over their materiality.

The main group in Leningrad's literary avant-garde of the late 1920s, OBERYu (an acronym for the Society for Real Art, sometimes known in the West as the Russian Absurdists), marked an absolute distance from their Futurist predecessors in rejecting *zaum* and advancing actual, spoken speech as a remedy for a dead "literariness."[15] "We are the poets of a new sense of the world and a new art," they declared in their manifesto of 1928. "We are the creators not only of a new poetic language but also of a new sense of life and of objects. . . . We broaden and deepen the meanings of objects and words but never destroy them. A concrete object cleansed of its overlay of the literary and conventional is made into something from the sphere of art." [16] It is not surprising to discover, then, that in the late 1920s Shostakovich and other composers in the movement for opera reform worked on new operas to librettos by Daniil Kharms and N. Oleynikov from the OBERYu set (the projects, unfortunately, came to nothing).[17]

A similar concern with authenticity in language can be seen in the new orientation in linguistics. Whereas earlier the members of the Formalist circles looked to linguistic methodology as providing a key for a more scientific way of studying literature, now many regarded linguistics as providing a key for renewal in culture generally, but rejected the Formalist emphasis on the literary language and written forms. Instead, in almost all schools of linguistics the emphasis was now on "applied linguistics," "speech culture" *(rechevaya kul'tura),* and "nonwritten forms" *(bespis'mennost').*[18] In state-sponsored scholarship the importance of "actuality" *(sovremennost')* was constantly stressed as a priority so that even the study of traditional philological subjects was modified; those who worked on the language of the ancient Greeks, for instance, endeavored to reconstruct "living antiquity" *(zhivaya starina)* and its "sociological bases."[19]

The emphasis on the living word, or *zhivoye slovo,* was seen as not merely distinctive from the Formalist approach, but actively in opposition to it. This was clear even in the canonical attacks on the Formalists. For instance, an article by Bukharin of 1925 described Formalism as a phenomenon that was broader than the group of literary and linguistic scholars who have generally been given that name. He defined it as the impulse, whether found in linguistics, economics, jurisprudence, political theory, science, or elsewhere, to analyze the subject by reference to phenomena solely from within that field, without taking into account any other phenomena. What was called for, he contended, was a "new philology," a "renewed approach to examining the data," which would entail, in the case of literary and linguistic scholarship, a reorientation toward "practical life" and "living language," and toward studying the language of the proletariat.[20]

As was discussed in the last chapter, several different schools of linguistics were ranged up to combat the Formalist / idealist hyena, including a sort of vulgar materialism that took a physiological approach to the analysis of language, which was discussed in terms of "conditioned reflexes" and other Pavlovian terms and "biomechanics";[21] and also versions of "vulgar sociologism" such as can be found in appropriations of Marr.

Another approach, one characteristic of the broad trend described here, sought to be less "vulgarly" sociological in defining language in terms of its dependence on the social.[22] This definition covers a range of positions, but in each account language proceeds not from system, or from individual expression, or even from the body per se, but from interaction. Meaning resides neither in the object, nor in the expressive subject, but between persons in the give and take of their dialogue. Its adherents stressed the immediacy of spoken language.

In 1926 two works were published that were to define this new trend, R. Shor's *Language and Society,* which was to become an obligatory primer in all those institutes forming the anti-Formalist axis, and Bakhtin (Voloshinov)'s[23] "Discourse in Life and Discourse in Art."[24]

Shor's work gives a highly schematized account of how different social classes produce different languages. The division of labor is the base on which the superstructure of linguistic differences is erected. Although oversimplified, the account draws on the latest linguistic thought in the West, citing primarily sources published between 1921 and 1923, with Saussure playing a leading role. Indeed, Saussure might have been bemused to discover that at that time the most militantly Marxist theoreticians of language claimed him as a materialist.

Saussure was also an important figure for members of the Bakhtin Circle, who, after 1924—and under the impact of the new urgency that discourse formation assumed in these years—were seeking to rethink the Neo-Kantianism that had dominated their earlier discussions. In his 1926 essay Bakhtin (Voloshinov) essentially conflates the basic insights of his early texts, including "Author and Hero in Aesthetic Activity," with some of the more powerful work being done in linguistics. As a result, Saussure's privileging of abstract, systemic *langue* over the messiness of real spoken language, *parole,* is utterly overturned by Bakhtin (Voloshinov), who brings into the picture such previously marginalized factors as the intonation with which a particular utterance is pronounced.

It is in this aspect that the new linguistics intersects with the movement for opera reform. Bakhtin (Voloshinov) in his work of this time on the way meaning is grounded in social interaction singled out the very phenomenon Radlov had stressed in his account of the new opera, that is, "the entire range of intonational possibilities." Radlov had said "from the spoken to the sung word"; the equivalent in Bakhtin's writings would be "from the spoken to the written word." Indeed, there was actually a link between the new opera and the Bakhtin school in that I. I. Sollertinsky, who, starting from the time when Shostakovich was working on *The Nose* became his intellectual mentor,[25] was also at the time a member of the Bakhtin Circle.

Intonation assumed importance in some Formalist writings as well, but there it was more a matter of sound patterns. In Bakhtin's studies, intonation stands in for the contextual basis or situatedness of meaning.

The emphasis on contextuality and situatedness that challenges Formalist assumptions was at the heart of a serious attempt to define a new, sociologically based poetics. As theoretical inquiry turned in this direction, there was a revival of interest in the theories of Veselovsky from the last century; the insistence on the situatedness of meaning that informed his "historical poetics," based on "concrete material," was all too frequently used to beat the Formalists over the head[26] (given that Veselovsky was also important for Marr, it should be clear that the "three" anti-Formalist approaches identified here are only constructs and the distinctions between them are not absolute).

This was a time of millennial expectation, which was, paradoxical as it might seem, focused on everyday language, and particularly that of the masses. Enthusiasm for the language of the proletariat reached an all-time high in these years (fostered of course in part by the new emphasis on "workerization"). Scholars rushed around collecting and categorizing different examples of urban speech, looking particularly at such things as the patois characteristic of workers from different trades, for example, print workers, metal workers, and so on.[27] Even the study of folklore was now insistently on the folklore of the proletariat.[28] Thus when Propp's pathbreaking study of the morphology of the folktale came out in 1929, it was by then anachronistic compared with the new trends. (It was a product of the Formalist stronghold, GIII, where most of the chapters were originally presented as lectures.) The new generation of writers who entered Soviet literature at this time experimented with writing in the language of the factory worker.[29] Even OBERYu invoked the proletariat in its manifesto of 1928.

This faith in the power of the language of the proletariat is a sort of analogue to the Romantic cult of the "folk" of the German 1820s. A few years earlier, Soviet literature had seen late-blooming echoes of this cult in Scythianism and allied movements of "peasant writers," but they were largely discredited and even actively persecuted at the end of the decade. The vogue for proletarian discourse, however, amounts to more than merely idealizing the culture of one group from the masses rather than another. Proletarian culture is more urbanist and cosmopolitan, or is at least conceived as being so. In it, one does not generally find the "kvass nationalism," as Belinsky called it, or the saccharine religiosity that in Russia have so often informed peasant-inspired writing. Street talk is meant to cut through such cant, to be direct and realistic. It should be added that at about this time in America the hard-boiled detective novel of Dashiell Hammett and others was being developed, a genre in which a sure mark of the heroic status of the detective protagonist was his ability for laconic and pithy street talk, frequently contrasted favorably with the bookishness or longwindedness of lesser or negative characters.

How can a romanticism of proletarian straight talk be related to Shostakovich's opera based on Gogol's "The Nose," that is, on the language of an essentially preproletarian petty bourgeois? Actually, *The Nose* was untypical of Shostakovich's compositions from the late 1920s; most of them were on contemporary themes. For instance, a later work, *The Bolt* (1931), billed as "the first industrialized ballet," tells a somewhat hackneyed tale of worker sabotage in a factory, incited by a bourgeois. The ballet culminates in the necessary arrests, which lead in to a "dance-play" by the Red Army.[30] Another Soviet opera that premiered in the same year as *The Nose*, V. Deshevov's *Ice and Steel*, which features highly colloquial conversational recitatives and other techniques typical of the new opera, draws on a simplistic revolutionary plot concerning the Kronstadt Uprising whereby the young Komsomol firebrands Musya and Sanya prevail over conventionalized versions of the bourgeois, who are undermining proletarian solidarity among the sailors and hence contribute to the tragic mutiny.[31] The weapons the figures in these new operas fire at the bourgeois blackguards are not just the guns of Kronstadt, but also what intellectuals such as Shostakovich believed to be even deadlier: the words of nonauthoritarian discourse. But such discourse is also available in nonproletarian, and even noncontemporary, sources.

"The Nose" was far from the only text by Gogol to play a major role in the culture of the late 1920s. As one contemporary observed later, "Our age was in love with Gogol."[32] However, this eyewitness was in the late 1920s a member of "the Changeover," a Komsomol group of self-proclaimed proletarians who looked, as the name of their group implies, to the "Great Breakthrough." Thus Gogol was the hero of the hour in an age of industrialization, and furthermore he was a hero among certain proletarian cultural groups no less than among the Formalists and other so-called bourgeois intellectuals.

Here we must make a distinction between the cult of street "straight talk" and the more "Gogolian" project whereby a technique known as *skaz* is used to parody Soviet newspeak. An interest in *skaz*, or substandard oral narration, was marked already in the early 1920s. Clearly the phenomenon described here did not emerge out of the blue in 1926. There was, rather, a distinct evolution in the theory and application of *skaz* over the course of the decade.

The Formalists of GIII took an interest in *skaz* early in their careers. However, in their initial studies of it, such as Eikhenbaum's "The Illusion of *skaz*" or "How Gogol's 'The Overcoat' Was Made" (both of 1918), this technique for incorporating substandard, oral speech in literature is defined in terms of its theatrical and musical potential ("improvisation," "intonation" defined as sound patterns, references to the *komediant*, that is, to the actor in *commedia dell'arte*, and "pantomime gestures").[33] Indeed, the very term "illusion" in Eikhenbaum's title implies that *skaz* is a form of *uslovnost'*. By the second half of the 1920s, however, Eikhenbaum had shifted his account of *skaz*, and as other linguists and literary theoreticians such as R. Shor, V. V. Vinogradov, and Lev Jakubinsky delved deeper into the implications of *skaz* they developed a dialogic theory of language.[34]

Zoshchenko, the most famous master of *skaz* as parody of Soviet newspeak, began publishing in 1921, but his day was really the second half of the 1920s, when he became a household word and could not even move in the streets without being mobbed.[35] Nineteen twenty-eight was the year of his greatest fame and greatest number of publications. In that year the institutions that published his work or books on him ranged from the proletarian mass series Deshëvaya biblioteka to GIII itself. Zoshchenko, like Gogol, was so popular partly because of the way he debunks officialese (in his case Soviet) and the bureaucratic cast of mind in petty officialdom. In this respect, there are parallels between what Shostakovich and Zoshchenko sought to do. Indeed, although Zoshchenko is not known to have been involved in the movement for opera reform, another major practitioner of *skaz* from the 1920s, E. Zamyatin, collaborated on the libretto for *The Nose* (allegedly he wrote the third scene of act one).[36]

What Zoshchenko was doing in his stories was essentially reactive. His kind of appropriation of the speech of the semieducated of his day exposes the gaps in the officialese they parrot, the ignorance, cant, and ludicrousness of it; it also catches moments when overly formalized language systems constrain the "living language." Shostakovich used Gogol to similar ends, but at the same time his project was proactive. Like other figures working in different domains, such as Bakhtin, he was seeking to establish a different image of language (in the broader sense) that many of those involved in the project, in the nakedness of their naïveté, associated with throwing off the shackles of "bourgeois" or "petty bourgeois" discourse and aesthetics. They were also conducting a concerted campaign against *yedinyy yazyk* (the single and unified language that Marr, the Constructivists, and all too many others wanted to see mandated to all).

In works such as Shostakovich's *The Nose*, the aim was not so much to debunk Nicolaevan Russia, or authoritarian and highly bureaucratic regimes, or even to expose "petty bourgeois philistinism" *(meshchanstvo)* per se. All this had been done a thousand times before. And as for Shostakovich's use of such techniques as parody, dissonance, and cacophony—all these had been perennials in the inventory of the avant-garde over the course of the 1920s. At this point, the old war horses were mustered under a slightly different flag. Among Shostakovich's stated purposes in choosing "The Nose" as his principal text for a new opera was to find the Gogolian text with the most "colorful" language, and this he believed was "The Nose."[37] What he meant by "colorful language" was of course not just quaint folkisms or pithy expressions from a bygone age. Rather, Shostakovich had in mind the way the Gogolian text debunks the language of authority, just as his own music was intended to debunk the musical language of authority. This represents an expansion of the sort of project Zoshchenko undertook. But as Shostakovich's opera drew on the "wealth of intonational possibilities" as part of the inventory of techniques for debunking, it simultaneously pointed to the possibility of richer cultural expression in a liberated, "living" language.[38]

Thus, were one to seek to define this new trend, the use or nonuse of substandard language—street talk—would not be its most crucial feature. Street language in the romanticized conception of writers and librettists is essentially a trope for the forces that conspire to challenge and undermine "music." The issue is whether the materiality of the word will be given its due, or whether conventionalized, but now hackneyed and allegedly "petty bourgeois" *(meshchanskiye)*, systems for achieving "beauty," such as the standard literary language, the principles of harmony, and overriding, music-like constructions, will prevail and thus keep back the "great breakthrough" to a new culture. As Kozintsev said at the time about Shostakovich's *The Nose*, in it "urban lore . . . stormed the citadel of the Aidas and Trovatores."[39]

Thus there was a strong iconoclastic element in the culture of this time, but the iconoclasm was not an end in itself; it was a necessary feature of the route to a new, postbourgeois culture. This can be seen in the case of a contemporary film, Eisenstein's *October*, made in 1927 to celebrate the tenth anniversary of the Revolution. The film opens with an iconoclastic act, the dismantling of an Imperial statue, and culminates in the storming of the Winter Palace. But the charge on the Winter Palace in this film was aesthetic no less than it was political. As Sergei Tretyakov wrote in the *New Left Front*

(Novyy lef) after *October* was released: "The Winter Palace had to be taken twice. In 1917 it was demolished as a political citadel. Now it is time to demolish it as an aesthetic citadel. The ironic and destructively mocking manner in which Eisenstein shows all those tsarist-aristocratic monumental accoutrements—the Hermitage, the carpets, the porcelain, the pictures, and the statues—points the way for storming the aesthetic. But the storming of the aesthetic to be found in Eisenstein's work covers only one of the areas to be attacked, because the 'aesthetic Winter Palace' with its artistic philistinism [*meshchanstvo*] has spread over the whole country, penetrated into every apartment and become an ingrained habit."[40] Thus in the film the objects in the Winter Palace that Eisenstein singled out are in heavy, bad taste, and smack of the very Biedermeier against which the entire film is directed.

In *October,* after the insurgent masses have penetrated the Winter Palace, a small group of them finally breaks through into the tsar's apartments. Here they experience a moment of truth as they uncover boxes of military medals represented as sheer baubles, exposing the "masquerade" of giving one's life for the tsar in the Great War. And then they find the tsarina's bidet juxtaposed with an icon-like picture of the royal family receiving divine blessing: the tsar is not just a figure who sits on horseback in full regalia at a review of troops, but also one who engages in sex.[41]

The aim of such work was of course not just to debunk authority figures by using scatology. There is a difference between tearing down a statue of the tsar and penetrating into the tsarina's water closet, and it has to do with different levels of dehierarchization. The second is the more complex of the two and difficult to define, but we are helped in developing a theoretical account of what occurs by such works as Bakhtin's book on Rabelais, in which the body plays a central role.[42] In that work, Bakhtin describes how the sense of the body can be limited and formalized to exclude its ungainly protuberances, leaving a smooth and orderly surface (more or less what Stallybrass and White call the "classical body"). But in what he calls "carnival," the bodies intermingle and such protuberances take on a crucial role in enabling communication. While Bakhtin's account stands on its own as an analysis of carnival, it can also function as a metaphor for a pervasive concern of his writings in the early 1930s, the distinction between sanitized, authoritative speech and the myriad possibilities available in natural language.

Those who looked to a new discourse were concerned not so much with annihilating the regnant aesthetic and linguistic conventions as with enlarging, demystifying, and democratizing them. Similarly, as writers, dramatists, and filmmakers branched out to include the bodily functions in their accounts of sacrosanct authority figures, they were essentially using the body as a metaphor for the general field of discourse. While most Constructivists were advancing a version of the "classical body" (stressing "hygiene," trying to ensure that the surfaces of their buildings be as clean as possible, trying to restrict movement to a rationalized minimum, and so on), the account of the body that informs the work of the many disparate groups that can be associated with this trend admits of its protuberances and orifices. It is thus not surprising that "The Nose" became the basis of a path-breaking opera. As we know, the nose is the most visible of human protuberances—that is, when we are dressed—and is often interpreted as standing in for the male member.[43]

A postbourgeois culture is not necessarily Communist, let alone Bolshevik. This is amply demonstrated in the fact that members of the Leningrad avant-gardist group OBERYu were for a time co-opted, if peripherally, into the movement for opera reform, and, as many have remarked, their works were often informed by a religious consciousness.[44] Also, an important aspect of this movement for opera reform in Leningrad was a sense of common cause with leading leftist figures in the musical and theatrical world of Berlin. For example, Brecht and Weill—who actually began their collaboration in 1927, around this same time—were well known to the Leningrad lobby for opera reform. Several of Brecht and Weill's compositions were put on at places such as the Academic Capella in Leningrad.[45] Activists in the movement for opera reform in Leningrad visited Brecht, a great enthusiast of Soviet culture, in Berlin and reported back on Brecht and Weill's *Mahagonny* and *The Threepenny Opera*. Leningrad productions of these two operas were mooted, but the worsening cultural climate of 1930 (see Chapter 12) meant that they were nipped in the bud and it was only in Moscow that it was possible to stage a production of *The Threepenny Opera*.[46]

If one looks at the work of most avant-gardists, and here those who sought to create the new opera are no exception, one will be struck by the extent to which they were making what might seem to be conflicting gestures, to be participating both in heroic, propagandistic ritual and in "carnival," modes most see as antithetical. Moreover, these composers and the operas' directors frequently went from one mode to the other in works produced at the same time or even within the one work. Consider, for instance, Shostakovich, who at more or less the same time as he wrote his grotesque and playful opera *The Nose* composed a great deal of occasional music in the heroic mode (cantatas, symphonies) and also his ballet *The Bolt*, which celebrates the new age in a major key and has a somewhat primitive, agitational plot about wreckers in the First Five-Year Plan.[47] His colleague V. Deshevov's attempt at the "first Soviet opera," *Ice and Steel*, has (as already outlined) an equally primitive, agitational plot, and its first production under Radlov combined exaggerated revolutionary poses such as one finds in Chinese revolutionary operas with highly colloquial recitatives in the manner of Berg and Krenek, together with Constructivist musical simulations of factory sounds in the tradition of Arthur Honegger's *Pacifica 231* and Darius Milhaud's *Agricultural Machines* (both then very popular in such circles).

What does this mean? That the government was reluctant to sponsor "carnival" and that therefore the avant-garde were obliged to serve the propaganda cause in order to survive, or in order to make it possible for their more carnivalesque works to get a public airing? This was surely partly the case. But this confusion is also a marker of their romanticism. Essentially, both modes represent an attempt at getting out of ordinary time via a romanticized version of the other (the proletarian). Thus we find the two extremes of the iconoclasm / icon-creation spectrum, or to put it in terms of Mayakovsky's play, both "mystery" and "bouffe."

It was also the case that many intellectuals at this time were extremely ambivalent about the Revolution, its culture, and their own role. While many supported "revolution" and, in those terms, the Bolshevik experiment as well—even Mandelshtam to some extent—they were tormented by its actuality.[48] They were also tormented by a fear that they had become marginal, were as passé and pathetic as so much rhetoric of the time represented them as being. Such fears were perennials among Soviet intellectuals. Indeed, in some senses the entire society was haunted by a fear of being marginal—hence so many compensatory narratives (such as those we have seen by Marr, Shaginyan, and Tynyanov) whereby that which is marginalized or "peripheral" regenerates "the center." At the same time as the movement for a new opera was at its height in Leningrad a spate of novels appeared about the intellectual misfit of which the Moscow writer Yu. Olesha's *Envy* (Zavist', 1927) is the best known. Such fiction generally tells the tale of how some quixotic intellectual flounders in his encounter with Soviet reality. In this genre, as in so many others, Moscow and Leningrad represent quite different patterns. Not only were these novels about intellectuals overwhelmingly a Leningrad phenomenon, but the Leningrad variant, unlike its Moscow counterpart, was typically a Petersburg-centric *roman à clef* about the respective author's own set.[49]

These novels are ostensibly self-flagellating lampoons written by literary intellectuals about their own kind. But, for all the grotesque caricature to be found in them, their authors are generally maneuvering in the Aesopian tradition to air the problems of the intellectual in such complex times (as emerges only after decoding). Some present a countermythology and countermartyrology (of the intellectual) as an answer to the myth of the proletarian hero which was fast becoming even more entrenched, but most remain obdurately ambiguous.[50]

Although ambiguity was very characteristic of intellectuals' stances at this time, it was not the case that they all felt alienated and retreated into an obsession with their own set. Avant-gardist groups in Leningrad had begun to consolidate forces and create a more cohesive lobby with a coherent agenda for revolutionary culture. Not only had some association formed between the lobby for a new opera and members of OBERYu, but around 1926 members of OBERYu started negotiations with Malevich about merging with his Suprematist group UNOVIS.[51] Another Leningrad school of perceptual millenarianism, that of the artist Pavel Filonov, was also gathering strength. In 1925, he and his students had formed into a Collective of the Masters of Analytical Art, and in 1927 this Collective was given public prominence when it received a commission to design the sets for a production of Gogol's *Inspector General* (by I. Terentiev) at Leningrad's Press House; they seized the opportunity and organized an exhibition of their own Analytical Art there as well. Though this work was attacked for its "pornographic" aspects and bald "physiologism,"[52] the collective continued undaunted and Filonov was able to organize a further exhibition of his work in 1929.

But the movement for a new opera, the allied reconception of linguistics, and such attempts at amalgamation emerged at a time when Soviet society was on the cusp of another "cataclysm," the cultural revolution of 1928–1931.

11

THE SACRALIZATION
OF EVERYDAY LIFE

In 1927 the Revolution was ten years old. But even as the country was celebrating the anniversary of the old revolution, it was looking to the next great one. The second revolution was to involve a more fundamental restructuring of the country than had been achieved after 1917. The principal means were to be rapid industrialization and collectivization, but what concerns us here is its concomitant cultural revolution. This "revolution," or set of policies, attempted to turn the old order in culture on its head. In a speech to mark the revolutionary anniversary in 1929 Stalin proclaimed a *bol'shoy perelom,* or "Great Breakthrough," that would finally bring about an absolute rift between the old and the new.[1]

Nineteen twenty-seven to nineteen thirty-one were the peak years of a militant campaign to institute a collective, proletarian culture and also of the movement for a socialist architecture. Such features do not represent isolated events but are interrelated as aspects of a totalizing drive for a radically new way of life replacing the old, bourgeois one. I use the term "totalizing" rather than totalitarian because the latter implies that the culture is mandated from above and indeed imposed by force and terror. Although there was certainly no shortage of government direction in these years, and there were already large scale purges, to a remarkable degree Soviet culture was translating the visions of intellectuals into actuality.

"Militarization" became a twin slogan with "industrialization" as shorthand for the priorities of the age (military preparedness became an obsessive concern in the wake of a war scare of 1927). Yet—and here we sense the utopian element in the age—neither could ultimately be seen as self-valuable; the ultimate aim of the industrialization drive was not so much to turn out dynamos as to turn out the "new man." But what defines this age as utopian must be found above all in the radical privileging of place over time, that is to say, as in all radical utopias, there was an attempt to efface change, to create conditions so perfect that time would cease to exist.

As the emphasis reverted once again to the transformation of man and mass culture, the theater eclipsed literature in prominence and resumed its position as queen of the arts and principal focus of official policy. The signal of this shift was a meeting of Agitprop in May 1927 devoted to the Soviet theater. During NEP, the two major Party pronouncements on culture—those of 1924 and 1925—had been on literature but their guidelines became binding for all the arts. Now, analogously, all cultural workers, Party and non-Party, including those in literature, were expected to follow the steno-graphic report of the 1927 Agitprop meeting as a sort of little red book of the new age.[2] It is no accident that this conference was conducted in Agitprop whereas the pronouncements on literature issued from Central Committee meetings. The conference heralded a shift to a more instrumental conception of the function of culture and to a greater emphasis on agitation.[3] It was also symptomatic of a return to greater theatricality and ritualization in culture generally.

The New Mass Spectacle

In these new times, the mass spectacle was rescued from the peripheral role it had been consigned to and pronounced the backbone of the new revolu-tionary culture. We associate the mass spectacle with the heady times after the 1917 Revolution, but what is not generally recognized is that by weight of sheer numbers it has to be considered the genre of the second cultural rev-olution even more than the first. During 1929, the year of the "Great Break-through," in the major cities and even in their suburbs mass spectacle fol-lowed hot upon mass spectacle, with often as few as three days between them. By comparison, during 1920, their peak year during the first cultural revolution, there were only five in Leningrad and even fewer in Moscow.

The difference here is not just one of statistics. The first revolutionary mass spectacles were meant to function as crucibles for transforming con-sciousness among the illiterate masses, to help break down the gulf between actors and audience, between cultural professionals and the masses. It was believed that if the masses participated in a ritual reenactment of revolution, they might experience a revolution of their very psyches. The utopian aim of breaking down the gulf between art and life that eluded realization then was in this later period taken to an almost farcical extreme as the country attempted to take the mass spectacle out beyond its already vast stage to encompass all of life.

The new mass spectacles, as examples of one of the cruder agitational genres, capture the defining features of Soviet culture in these years. One can sense the dominant structures of the new political culture in one of the first of the spectacles, which marked the revolutionary jubilee in 1927. This spectacle, with the somewhat unimaginative title *Ten Years,* was staged in Leningrad, which was still considered the originary site of the Revolution, but it was attended by Party heads who came from Moscow to officiate at the spectacles.

Members of this spectacle's production team—Sergei Radlov, Adrian Piotrovsky, and N. V. Petrov as directors and scenarists, with Valentina Khodasevich as set designer—were all veterans of the mass spectacles of 1920. However, they chose to avoid duplicating the setting for that year's revolutionary jubilee spectacle, *The Storming of the Winter Palace.* Instead, they set their spectacle on the other side of the Winter Palace, that is, primarily on an expanse of the Neva River around the bridge from the Palace across to the Stock Exchange, but they also used such buildings on the river's opposite banks as the Peter and Paul Fortress and the Mint.

As this list suggests, a striking feature of *Ten Years,* and one that typifies the mass spectacle of the late 1920s, is its monumental scale. A vast scale had been a desideratum of the earlier mass spectacles, too, but in them the scale had been measured primarily in terms of the number of participants and the size of the audience. Now, it was the spatial scale rather than human numbers that was to astound; the audience, at one hundred thousand, was comparable to the largest in 1920, while the cast was smaller—there were two thousand at most—and the majority of members were in a mass choir. The area taken up by the mass spectacle was truly astounding, however. The audience alone stretched over one and a half kilometers. Similarly remarkable was the sense of stage. *The Storming of the Winter Palace* had been largely set on two specially constructed stages on the Palace Square, with a bridge structure joining them. *Ten Years* was given its "stages," too, but they were not specially constructed ones. The set designer, Valentina Khodasevich, identified as the "proscenium" a large stretch of the Neva River between two bridges, while she called the "main stage" the Peter and Paul Fortress, with the Mint nominated as the "rear stage" and the Kronkversky Canal functioning as "wings." The auditorium, she claimed, was "the entire population of Leningrad."[4]

These Leviathan dimensions were a marker of the utopian character of the spectacle itself. They also rendered impractical the earlier conventions for the mass spectacle with its huge cast of amateur actors (who could of course be neither heard nor seen across such vast distances). Instead, the spectacle was transformed into a sort of *son et lumière* piece that made extensive use of searchlights, sirens, fireworks, cannonfire, and above all huge banners and figures representing the main actors in the Revolution which were transported on boats (the Revolution's enemies were said to be "two stories high").[5] The mass element in the spectacle was largely realized in a huge choir and orchestra, both made up by combining worker musical groups.[6]

Commentators pointed to these features in claiming that the spectacle met the central demand of the times: industrialization. This mass spectacle was said to show the way for the "industrialization" of the theater, in which "the main principle of the staging is to shift the center of gravity from living forces [*zhivaya sila*] to mechanical devices."[7] As the director Radlov put it, "The [acting] troupe comprises torpedo boats, launches, factory smokestacks, tugboats, pulling boats, emblems in light, and letters picked out in fire," and he went on to boast of how much larger his cardboard representations of the actors in the Revolution were by comparison with actual human figures.[8]

As luck would have it, the weather that November night was inclement, with the characteristic "Petersburg" rain and fog, which proved a poor ally of the industrialized theater. Some of the searchlights could not be seen in the fog, and the fireworks were too damp to ignite so that some of the most striking effects did not work. Also, the telephone connections between the directors' bridge and their far-flung network of participating groups kept breaking down, throwing coordination off.[9] Nevertheless, the directors proclaimed *Ten Years* the model for future spectacles.[10] Members of this team went on to produce the principal mass spectacles of both Leningrad and Moscow in 1929–1930.[11]

Industrialization in the mass spectacles became an important element both formally (in terms of techniques and apparatus used) and thematically. Most mass spectacles had as their centerpiece a mighty machine or construction. These figures were not there merely to affirm success in industrialization; the machine or giant industrial complex had become for many intellectuals the master metaphor for the new organization of Soviet society, a model for the way all the parts might be integrated into a whole.[12] Thus the sense of human nature and of the function of people and culture in society was a very mechanistic one.

When the machine became the master metaphor, as a corollary people generally receded in significance against the vast panorama of industrialization. In literature, the image of the individual emerges as one of a swarm of industrious ants dwarfed by the giant construction project.[13] Similarly, industrializing the mass spectacle did not just mean enhancing the "scale" of the dramatis personae but also an extra degree of abstraction. Actors in history were increasingly represented not by individual human actors but by mummers (chuchelo-maska) and especially by huge cardboard figures and massed choirs.[14] This reduced significantly people's represented role in history, and especially their role in the Revolution, which still functioned as *the* paradigm of history. The conventions for depicting the Revolution itself changed radically (compared with the paradigms of 1920), as is clear in *Ten Years.*[15]

In this spectacle, the need for the masses to mobilize for revolution is conveyed in a sequence that presents in symbolic, capsule form the twin slogans of industrialization and militarization; searchlights pick out factory smokestacks (as in Eisenstein's *October*), and then a siren signaling danger sounds from a torpedo boat. The searchlight illuminating center stage sweeps upward, and all becomes dark. But "suddenly" the searchlight sweeps down again and out of that darkness it focuses on a steam launch on which a "dazzlingly bright red shield" depicts the "radiant" *(svetlyy)* silhouette of Lenin, who then proceeds slowly, *against the current,* from one end of the Neva stage to the other. Torpedo boats fire 360 rounds of ammunition, and a conflagration of "blazing bonfires" is simulated on the Neva. The Revolution has been won.[16]

This revolutionary apotheosis utilizes fire and light, two of the oldest and hence most multivalent symbols of political and religious ritual. It is interesting to note, for instance, their centrality in German Nazi ritual of this time. But in this case, as in many of the mass spectacles of this time, the fire of revolution represents primarily a scorching fire that destroys the old, making way for the new.

The cutoff between old and new had of course been a paradigm of revolution in Soviet culture all along. In the earlier mass spectacles, the passage to Communism was less abrupt and proceeded through a long series of revolutionary uprisings of ever greater magnitude and ever greater degrees of success; hence, the dominant temporal model was linear (although time was divided into a series of Great Times, or peaks, with lulls or troughs in between).

In the new mass spectacles, changes occur suddenly, without linear historical development. Most typically, events shift back and forth thematically from war to industrialization to revolution.[17] But there were also frequent travesties of chronology. For instance, in the May Day antireligious spectacle staged by Radlov in 1929 the central event, the trial by medieval monks of Giordano Bruno, was, as newspaper reports described it, interrupted in a bizarre way: "Suddenly, something unexpected [occurred]" as masses of Young Pioneers invaded the trial and drove out the clerics.[18]

This example was but one of many from that time where changes are not only without historical motivation, but actually entail a temporal reversal such that recent times act upon the past. This reversal is in its own way represented in *Ten Years* when the Revolution occurs as Lenin proceeds against the current, which could be taken as a symbolic reversal of the flow of time.

One reason for such temporal reversals in political rituals was the extraordinary emphasis laid in official rhetoric on the present moment and the considerable pressures placed on writers and all others to treat only "current issues." So great was the emphasis on the present that it provided the template for the past. Indeed, at a meeting in Narkompros of 1927 to set policy in the theater a delegate defined the demand to treat "contemporary themes" as "illuminating the past from our present point of view."[19]

To a marked degree, the past was expunged from the purview. Films about industrialization made at this time typically used a version of the phoenix myth whereby, to quote from a review of a Leningrad film of 1930, A. Room's *Plan for Great Works* (Plan velikikh rabot, actually the first Soviet sound film), "the outlines of the new world appear out of the ashes of the Civil War."[20] A striking example of this phoenix myth is *Happy Street* (Shchastlivaya ulitsa), a feature film of 1930 about the iconic Soviet revolutionary factory, Red Putilov (located in Leningrad), that was directed by the former FEKS member Sergey Yutkevich. In representing the Revolution, it focuses on Yudenich's White Guard attack on Petrograd in October 1919 and the role of the Putilov workers in defending the city. When the workers prepare to meet the foe, as part of a sort of scorched-earth policy they burn down some of the buildings on Happy Street where the factory stands (a historical fact), and "with them all that is rotten." And so, *now,* where Happy Street once was there rises up Tractor Street "with its totally new way of life."[21] The notion that a fire will destroy the old and bring about a total break between past and present was so pervasive in the political culture of the late 1920s that in the press the workers were sometimes referred to as the "fire victims" *(pogorel'tsy)* who are building on the ashes of the revolutionary fire the great cities of a new world.[22]

Of course, the historical models informing these mass spectacles do not allow for society to pass from the old to the new merely by incendiarism, as Futurism sometimes seemed in danger of suggesting. Historical change had its agents, even though the masses were represented as playing a very reduced role in it. In the new mass spectacle, it is Lenin who makes the

Revolution—or the Revolution *is* Lenin, as we saw in *Ten Years*. Similarly, in Room's film *Plan for Great Works* the principal motivation for the way the industrial utopia arises out of the ashes is a "monumental figure of Il'ich with his arm stretched out."[23]

Lenin is not a mere historical actor, but of a totally different order of humanity from that of ordinary citizens. Consequently, it is really only Lenin who can go back into history (or forward). He is both extrahistorical and a maker of history, and so he represents something like the Aristotelian category of the God. Consequently, the Young Pioneers who invade the trial of Giordano Bruno are not individual actors in history but symbolic representatives of Lenin, as are all other collective agents of his will. In this way, the mass spectacles of 1927–1931 personalized a very complex and impersonal historical process in one figure, Lenin. This is a general human tendency, but it has been hyperbolized in this case.

It is a cliché in talking about Stalinist ritual that it was religious in nature. Essentially, what we find in these rituals of the late 1920s is the structure of a conversion experience. The past evaporates as the "born again" subject experiences a totally new reality. If it is a conversion experience, however, it is one of a singular kind. This is most strikingly apparent in "Industrialization Day," a festival staged in August 1929. For this festival, untypically, there was no mass spectacle to mark the day's climax. Its "celebration" was a workday made out of the ordinary because every single worker worked— or so it was said—including even chronic laggards and absentees; furthermore, the workers performed prodigious feats in the workplace, giving the press ample material for ecstatic reports.

The aim of "Industrialization Day" was to replace a particular religious festival, the Transfiguration of the Lord. Part of the rationale for sending everyone out to work was to help keep them out of church and out of the taverns, a practice adopted in this year for undermining most of the major religious holy days.[24] At the end of the day everyone was to go out into the streets for a festive promenade. The festival was primarily intended to show how "the ordinary work day" *(trudovye budni)* can become what was called "a great festival of industrial transformation" (the word used for "transformation," *preobrazheniye*, is also the one for "transfiguration," as in the name of the religious feast day they were replacing), a great "prototype for communist labor forged by the proletariat."[25]

As this example shows, much public ritual in these days was directed toward conferring on the ordinary the status of the extraordinary. Industrial labor could function as the ritual observance of a kind of new religion and was seen as the route to salvation. For social deviants and the unreconstructed bourgeois, it was believed, the experience of laboring on production could bring about a complete transformation in their identities, enabling them even to overcome class allegiances. That doctrine justified the labor camps in these relatively early and modest years of the Gulag system.

"Industrial Day" is a particularly grateful example of the mass festival of the late 1920s because it entails radical displacement of the site of action. Instead of having actors performing for an audience, the audience has been turned into the actors. Thus, the space of ideology has been expanded beyond the limits of a stage, even a stage as enormous as the Neva River, and has invaded the workplaces of the city. The space of high ritual is not a temple or even a theater but a place of the most prosaic reality. Moreover, the space of the ritual has been extended into leisure time. This points to the totalization. This new mass festival provides the missing link between the aesthetics of festival and the aestheticization of everyday life that can be perceived in the movement from ideology organizing the masses in theatrical events to ideology organizing the masses in every aspect of their lives. The "cameraization" represented by the cornerstone of NEP policy for the mass theater, the (now discredited) Unified Artistic Circle, or YeKhK, has been overcome.

Time was flattened out, but in compensation space gained both in importance and in extension. The culture of the late 1920s provides manifold examples where society tried to get out of ordinary time by foregrounding an *extra-ordinary* space. It seems to have been seeking a new space that might be adequate to the new time, and thereby trying to extend the scope of effect. The underemphasis on time contrasts with revolutionary culture during War Communism, which charted an ascending progression through the ages culminating in the Revolution (mirrored in new architectural projects, such as Tatlin's tower, many of which are articulated in a vertical spiral[26]).

The shift in spatial imagery was not just a matter of inverting perspective. The dominant metaphors were generally articulated horizontally rather than vertically, a shift that enacts a reorientation in societal values. In the culture of the late 1920s one finds an extreme horizontality in orientation, reflected in trends such as the tendency toward designing new model towns that stretch out in long and impractical ribbons or curves of settlement, and in the emphasis on the far-flung construction site or outer, workers' suburb as the locus of regeneration for workers and intellectuals alike. It is also found in an extreme democratism that flattened the traditional hierarchies to the point where they were virtually inverted, and a militant empiricism.[27]

Socialist Architecture and Collectivist Zeal

Reforming domestic architecture was a major aspect of the ritualization of space at this time. Architects and town planners were given a key role in transforming the country. Their stock agents of transformation were the "socialist town" (sotsgorod), which meant an entirely new town or workers' suburb designed to create a "healthy environment," not just in the literal sense of clean air and so forth, but principally in the sense that it maximally conduced to collective, socialist mores and work habits, and the "communal house" (dom-kommuna), which represented a sort of socialist town in miniature, realized within the confines of a gigantic apartment house for workers or a complex of residential and service buildings. Neither of these concepts was new. Indeed, there had been sporadic attempts to establish residential communes since 1918, and over the course of the 1920s several new worker neighborhoods had been built in various towns. Even more had been planned. The difference was that in approximately 1929–1930 the idea of totally transforming the Soviet city into a socialist town became a key concept of cultural policy. According to the values of the time, the new industrial project, no matter how gigantic, could be nothing without the accompanying socialist town or suburb as symbol and enabler of the new life that the industrial complex had been built to achieve. Thus, for instance, Magnitostroi, the icon of socialist construction, was inconceivable without its town, Magnitogorsk.

This movement for erecting socialist towns and communal houses is generally associated with Constructivism. Indeed, much of the theory of the "commune house" was articulated during NEP by Constructivists such as Alexei Gan and especially Mosei Ginzburg; also, the Constructivists gave prominence to the idea of the communal house when in 1926 they organized a competition to design one conducted by their journal Contemporary Architecture (Sovremennaya arkhtitektura).

As the communal house was conceived by Constructivist theoreticians, it was to be a "social condenser," a term that received its most classical formulation in an article by Mosei Ginzburg of 1927.[28] The theory of the social condenser rests on the assumption that architecture can influence the psychological development of the masses by functioning as an active force for social change. The Constructivists believed that by placing workers and their families in an environment in which the majority of social and domestic functions (human interaction, political activity, self-improvement, study, entertainment, cooking, housework, child-care, and so on) had been communalized, in an environment where the layout of the building itself was designed to encourage collective human interaction, those very same families would shortly be transformed into model Soviet citizens steeped in the new socialist way of life. The corollary of this view, argued as early as the first major Constructivist tract, Aleksei Gan's *Constructivism* of 1922, was that if one left Soviet towns and domestic architecture as they were, that is, left intact the "staunch allies of counterrevolution," this would only conduce to a bourgeois consciousness in Soviet citizenry and frustrate efforts at transforming the country into a socialist society.[29] By the time of the First Five-Year Plan with its militant proletarianism, such views were given even more extreme formulations; for instance, in 1929 the Constructivist group OSA in its "Theses on Housing" rejected altogether the idea of including apartments in socialist residential architecture on the grounds that they are "a material manifestation of petty bourgeois ideology."[30]

In Ginzburg's 1927 formulation of the theory of the social condenser, he developed the "flow diagram" for analyzing and minimizing a worker's movements around his apartment and compared it with the conveyor belt that connects the various subassembly sites within a factory. Once such "scientific" analyses had been made, he contended, the "basic spatial structure" of a dwelling could be devised. And with this model in place, architecture would become an active force for social change; "in the habits and attitudes of the mass population, low-voltage activity and a weak consciousness would be focused through the circuits of these 'social condensers' into high-voltage catalysts of change."[31]

Ginzburg is using "condenser," a term that denotes the apparatus where change occurs in a *variety* of physical processes, such as condensation of steam, in the *specific* context of electricity (where it means an apparatus for accumulating or increasing the intensity of an electrical charge). Thus he is implicitly identifying his theory with Lenin's famous maxim of 1920: "Communism equals socialism plus the electrification of the entire country." But the particular electrical apparatus Ginzburg chose as his central trope, the condenser, provides the added implication that the effect of the social condenser will be not merely to convey "electricity" but to intensify it, thus the end sought was not merely a more proletarian society, but also a society that had stepped up to a higher intensity of living. Through its *byt*, that is, through the ordinary and everyday, society would, paradoxically, attain the extraordinary.

Thus the dominant approach to architecture at this time involves applying to domestic architecture something like the principles for NOT (Nauchnaya organizatsiya truda, or the Scientific Organization of Labor, a Soviet movement favored by Lenin during War Communism which applied Taylorist ideas in the workplace).[32] Indeed, the plan years represent a high point in the history of NOT in Soviet culture. Taylorist theory was being applied not just in the workplace but to every area of life, even the most banal. In the place of NOT, a new term was coined, NOZh, the Scientific Organization of Life.[33] It is probably no accident that this acronym is also the Russian word for a knife. At this time the idea of the scientific organization of life was inseparable from the notion that in order to achieve it one had to destroy the old, whether by taking a metaphoric "knife" to it, or by destroying all in a cleansing pyre.

Figuratively, these years were to be a time of slash and burn. But in the landscape thus purified a totally new culture was to be erected. This was an uncompromising age of totalism. Every aspect of the traditional city was to be transformed (communalized, proletarianized) so that, in theory, in leisure, in work, and even in their daily ablutions, individuals would be living the collective, postbourgeois existence.

Between 1929 and 1930 the movement to transform the landscape of the Soviet city assumed such fantastic proportions that it had clearly gone beyond the bounds of "proletarianization," "industrialization," or even the "scientific" organization of the dwelling space; it had taken off from its beginnings in Constructivism and town planning. One can sense the element of the fantastic even in the area of scale. In the early 1920s, competitions for designing collective dwellings usually stipulated that they should be for around thirty families, but by 1929 projects were being approved for new communal houses for twenty-five hundred.[34]

The communal house was to be a "cell" of a future utopia. In 1930 that long-standing admirer of Campanella, Lunacharsky (ousted as Minister of Enlightenment in the fall of 1929 but nevertheless intoxicated with the spirit of the times), gave a public address on the theme "Restructuring Life and Art" in which he announced that "the time has come when the utopias of Fourier and Moore can get their practical application." Now that Lenin's campaign for electrification has given us this potential, he continued, we must "build towns in such a way that it will be impossible to live in them in the old ways."[35] Many of the new architectural projects of 1929–1930 seem to have less to do with Marxism than with Fourier (who was one of several utopians published during War Communism by the Petrograd publishing house World Literature).

Most of the communal houses designed in the Soviet Union at this time took the collectivist zeal of the age to an extreme, reducing to the barest minimum not only privacy but even the possibility of performing some action at a different time from the other inhabitants. The designers seem to have taken a leaf from Zamyatin's dystopian novel *We* (My, 1920), with its strictly regimented day, inasmuch as something like his "Table of Hours" determines all activity in the communal house, right down to the "private hours" (times for sex). It was fairly standard to build these communal houses without kitchens—"Let's be rid of the kitchen stench" was the common cry, the stench being seen not only literally, but in terms of the distasteful obscurantism of the old individualistic lifestyle.[36] In the socialist town built around a new hydroelectric station at Dubrovsk in the environs of Leningrad, not merely were there no individual kitchens, but there was no way to eat except in the cafeteria in a different building located on the way to work; bachelors did not have individual rooms, but slept in sleeping rooms housing ten; individuals were not allowed to keep their outer clothing in their rooms, but had to keep it in a locker room near the entrance; and all leisure activity was to take place in two large rooms, one for "noisy" activities, the other for quiet.[37]

Someone like Zamyatin might conclude that such plans were intended to reduce workers to being mere production machines who lead totally regimented lives. The champions of the socialist town and communal house, however, saw them as leading not to the workers' greater enslavement, but to their emancipation. The well-designed town would enable workers to become less the mere slaves of the machine, as Marx had dreamed. In Trotsky's *Problems of Life* (1923), he recommends that in order to achieve a rationally organized lifestyle, the Soviet citizen's day be divided up into three equal portions of eight hours: eight for sleep, eight for work, and eight for eating, leisure, and so on. In the press of these years, however, one frequently finds a new ratio for the average day with a shortened workday so that workers can indulge in "creative" cultural activity.[38] A typical account of future life in the projected dwelling complexes spelled out this ratio as seven hours for sleep and seven for work, because "for at least ten hours" the worker, having been liberated from domestic cares, will want to be "above all in the library, the museum, studying, in the gymnasium or sports field, at mass festival promenades, at the popular musical theater, art gallery, or movies." The author concluded, "[We must have] TEN HOURS A DAY OF IMPROVING LEISURE!"[39]

This outline seems all too reminiscent of the sewing artel in N. Chernyshevsky's *What Is To Be Done?* (1863) whose workers live communally but also take part in improving activities in their leisure time. But the proposals of the late 1920s did not prove to be merely dreamy schemes. The vogue for collective living was particularly marked among radical intellectuals, who throughout the 1920s banded together to build communal houses or student hostels, or organized themselves into spontaneous communes. In other words, many of these communal arrangements were not, as Zamyatin anticipated, imposed on intellectuals by the state, but were examples of their zeal and idealism. It might have been more accurate to say that the communes were imposed by the intellectuals on the workers, who were conceived as would-be intellectuals.[40]

By the late 1920s the conception of the worker as would-be intellectual involved a limited sense of what being an intellectual means. The word "culture" was generally applied in a very reduced sense as compared with what the *Kulturträger* of War Communism had in mind. Often, for instance, it was virtually synonymous with sport; a huge sports stadium was generally the centerpiece of the new Houses of Culture. In this period, an entire spectrum of cultural activists conceived the culture of the future in terms of synchronized bodily movement or eurythmics; Meyerhold advocated in an address to a Leningrad audience of 1929 that the "theater of the future" would have "theatricalized sporting games" to be staged in huge stadiums like other sports,[41] while the state organized mass sporting "Spartakiades." As in Nazi culture, there was an emphasis on bodily strength and health, sport and coordination to rhythm; an individual's body became an organic analogue to the powerful machine as an expression of might and indomitable will. This is apparent, for instance, in a sequence from the film *Fragment of an Empire* (Oblomok imperii), made by the Leningrad director F. Ermler in 1929, in which monumental men, naked from the waist up, perform tasks as super machines.

As bodily movement in mass formations returned to prominence, so did the question of theater design. Most theater activists, particularly Meyerhold, became involved in this question and urged an end to the small theater serving a local audience. They recommended instead that huge mass theaters which essentially conflate the functions of the sports stadium and the theater be erected in their place. In Leningrad's GIII, researchers at the theatrical laboratory, under the rubric "industrialization of the mass theater," were working on a model for a "theater of the future" with seating for ten thousand; it was to "utilize all the contemporary architectural and technological achievements," and in so doing might even incorporate "real towns."[42] Thus when Valentina Khodasevich, the set designer for *Ten Years*, declared one and a half kilometers of the Neva and the adjoining buildings her "stage," and all of Leningrad her "audience," her claim was, by the standard of those times, relatively modest.

Those who worked on the "theater of the future" insisted that it would not provide "art in the old sense," for in it "the theater bursts out into the streets like a raging river during a flood and art dissolves in the mighty surge of creativity. . . ."[43] In other words, the dreams of the theater activists since before the Revolution that they might break down the borders between theater and life seemed on the verge of realization. In the new culture, with its mass spectacle using the city as its "stage," and its ordinary working day billed as a "festival day," the theater had truly burst beyond the footlights at last.

The utopian architecture and town planning that distinguish this era in Soviet culture are in their own way symptomatic of the dominance over cultural forms of highly ritualized mass theater. The communal house or socialist town can be seen as a ritualized space, a sort of stage set for a cast of two thousand to act out everyday life, complementing the mass spectacle itself, where *extra-ordinary* life is enacted on an equally massive scale. In both cases, there is no temporal movement involved in this ritualized action. The communal house and the socialist towns are like a machine in that in them a limited number of processes are repeated in a synchronized way; thus one gets a perpetuum mobile, but no development. This is the true meaning of what Ginzburg called the "social condenser." Even self-development, the apparent aim of such institutions, does not represent development so much as process: the machine of the architectural structure processes its inhabitants, who are actors in a limited sense, as they are also actors in a limited sense in the mass spectacle or mass choir.

Thus the boundary between literature and life was shifting. Life was now nonhistorical insofar as it had been textualized. No one was going anywhere because all were locked in a fixed unity like a text. The Constructivists had attempted initially to turn the factory into a piece of art, but this transformation was to have been more comprehensive. It might be said, as Boris Groys has argued, that reality was to become a sort of ballet or *Gesamtkunstwerk*. Here we also are reminded of Siegfried Kracauer's concept of the "mass ornament"[44] or of the applicability to the Soviet case of Walter Benjamin's remark that fascism "logically amounts to . . . an aestheticization of political life."[45]

In the culture of 1927–1931 one finds an impulse toward homogenizing all elements in society in a *Gesamtkunstwerk* in which, as in the Wagnerian scheme, "music" predominated; in other words, the campaign against

Wagner had a very tenuous hold. In the late 1920s, music emerged as one of the dominant art forms for mass culture. Where before it had largely remained the preserve of the highbrow with its institutions left virtually intact in their prerevolutionary forms, now it assumed a central role in many of the accounts of the cultural revolution and became one of the principal battlegrounds as rival factions within the intelligentsia, Party, and state each sought to implement its own program; RAPP's counterpart in the sphere of music, RAPM, though founded in 1923, essentially assumed prominence only in these years. While bourgeois institutions such as the opera and symphony did not disappear during 1929–1931, the entire orientation of Soviet music began to change, guided by the slogan "music for the masses" *(muzyka-massam)*, which became the name of a new national organization founded in 1929.[46] In 1929, also, there were highly publicized purges in the Moscow and Leningrad conservatoria that sought to rid them of recalcitrants still wedded to the bourgeois model who resisted the ideal of a mass music. As music was forcibly democratized, the mass choir became a mainstay of Soviet musical life, playing a major role in all mass spectacles and also in the newly organized musical olympiades and numerous singing festivals in sports stadiums.[47]

In official rhetoric music became, together with architecture, one of the principal sources of metaphors for describing the new society to be ushered in after the cultural revolution. As, for many in the late 1920s, *stroy* (structure) and *perestroika* (restructuring) became axiomatic ideals, much of the culture was informed by a homology among the machine, the collective producer of music (for example, an orchestra or massed choir), the military unit, and the architectonically perfect factory or dwelling *(dom-kommuna)*. One can see this, for instance, in M. Tsekhanovsky's film *Pasifik,* made in Leningrad in 1931, which is an attempt to translate into the medium of the screen a musical composition by Arthur Honegger, *Pacific 231* (1923), celebrating the locomotive. Tsekhanovsky used dissolves, superimpositions, and other montage techniques to identify the movements of a locomotive's wheel and driving axle with the movements of the musicians in the orchestra as they played the Honegger piece.[48]

Music and architecture were not just sources of metaphors for *perestroika,* but seen by many as crucial agents of it. A key element in the alleged efficacy of both for *perestroika* was rhythm. It was the pattern of articulation, the rhythm that citizens were said to acquire as they were subjected to a particular architectural structure or musical composition, which would help restructure their psyches. Lunacharsky in his address to the First Musical Conference in 1929 (held in Leningrad to celebrate the shift to "mass

music") presented as a model for social organization a "symphony of movement and labor" and went on to define the role of music in the new society
as "capturing the spirit of our time" and giving it "order."[49] His statement
seems virtually modeled on the principles of organization for Radio City in
Shaginyan's *Mess-Mend* (this particular emphasis on the "symphony" probably has something to do with the somewhat maverick emphasis that figures such as Bakhtin and Sollertinsky placed on "polyphony" in their writings of this time).

The "order" offered by music, or more generally rhythm, bespeaks a centripetal pattern of organization with some "conductor" or other figure(s) at a
central point establishing the rhythm for the entire orchestra.[50] It is perhaps
no accident that in the imagery of films made at this time there is a marked
tendency to foreground the morphological patterns of some machine organized on a horizontal axis but with a central part controlling the revolutions
or movements of all others. Thus, in Dziga Vertov's *The Man with a Movie
Camera* (1929), the central motif (replicated in other imagery) is the textile
machine with a revolving spindle and assorted bobbins and spools rotating
around it, their movement controlled by the rotation of the central spindle;
this image is in turn related isomorphically to the action of a machine for
editing film (hence art and technology are as one). But it was not just Constructivists who used such imagery. Most films from this time foreground
electric poles, train lines, telephones, or some other products of the technological age that radiate out from the urban centers to their peripheries. Often
the heroes follow them in their journey from the village or provincial town
to the capital or industrial center and then return with a tractor, a Party
directive, a technical manual, or some other magical agent to transform the
local world so that it may pulse with the same rhythm as "the center."

Such imagery celebrates the introduction of a planned economy, which
entailed a shift to a more centripetal pattern in economic life. Other recent
developments in the country, such as the spread of radio overcoming its celebrated tyranny of distance, were likewise center-reinforcing phenomena.
Even the purges (a feature of the Plan years) seemed to feel honor-bound to
follow a centripetal pattern. Within Leningrad they progressed over the
course of 1929 from the main Party Committees to the borough committees,
to government bodies, and so on, until by late December they had worked
their way all the way down to the bakeries: "The Class Enemy is in the
Bakeries" became a rubric.[51]

Bread and baking played a central role in 1917. Not only were the bread
lines the immediate cause of its first revolution, but the bakery is more or
less the locus of the "female cook" whom Lenin at that time envisaged as

"ruling the state." This second cultural revolution was to be her coming-out party.

In general, however, the "female cook" was not the main loser at this time. In the purges (in Leningrad especially), besides Party officials intellectuals and engineers were major targets. These two categories might seem to be crucial players in the industrialization effort. They also potentially represent that category in Plato's *Republic* the philosopher-kings, or in other words enlightened legislators—the kind of figures to whom Vernadsky and other liberal intellectuals in the years immediately preceding the Revolution wanted to give a greater role in running the country. Lenin's own conception was not so far removed when in his famous speech about electrification he talked of a future time when the legislators would be not professional politicians but "engineers and agronomists," that is, practical experts.[52]

The contradictions between the intellectual/engineer's enhanced role and his being a prime target for repression evaporate if one assumes that the "female cook" will become the "engineer"/philosopher-king while the superseded, bourgeois usurpers to such a title whose hearts pulsate with a different rhythm will, in turn, be shown the gates of the city. This was more or less the scenario that underwrote many of the purges. Actually, the Soviet state was a little more charitable and these so-called has-beens—or more literally "former people" *(byvshie lyudi)* (note how both the past and the present are represented in the present)—were given a chance to reform in places of exile or incarceration on the periphery.

Many Leningraders who were deemed socially alien were taken to a camp on the Solovetsky Islands in the far north or to the Baltic-White Sea Canal project. Their (forced) labors on the canal and the miracle of the regeneration were attested to by individual convicts, and also by several of the town's most distinguished writers, in a glossy book later presented to Party delegates at the Seventeenth Party Congress in 1934.[53] In this book we read of one "former person," the engineer Magnitov, who finds that at the White Sea Canal he begins to develop a quicker pulse and faster thought processes and reflexes. "He begins to take on the new tempo, to adjust his reason to it, his will, and his breathing." The authors of the sketch report: "Engineer Magnitov thinks of the old engineer Magnitov, and for him that person is already alien. Magnitov calls that person 'him.'"[54]

The "female cooks" were ruling the state to a farcical degree, a single, unified language and a single rhythm were mandated to all, and the "transmission belts" carried this rhythm out from the center to the farthest-flung corners, all this the dastardly deed of the Party and other co-conspirators such as the NKVD. Actually, I would argue that is was not entirely so. For a start, the *Gesamtkunstwerk* was never very fully achieved, not even during the cultural revolution (or the Great Terror of the mid-1930s); those transmission belts were never as dominant in actuality as Constructivist works implied.

It was not really the case that the Party or the state imposed models of collective living on the populace. The Party and the government saw the mass spectacle and the *dom kommuna* as the route to achieving such eminently practical ends as increased productivity, political socialization, and solving the housing shortage. Intellectuals were the more utopian by inclination and many of them saw such collective ventures as the route to the aestheticization of life. We see here a kind of synchronization of art and politics, though of a more complex kind than the clichéd version whereby the Party controls the intellectuals as, virtually, puppets on strings.

The Party eventually proved to be opposed to the extreme collectivism of the *dom kommuna*, which they began to label, by analogy with politics, a "left deviation" or "leftist excess" (*levyy zagib* or *levye peregiby*).[55] Yet it was not the case that "the state" or "the Party" killed the movement for the communal house and socialist town. Predictably, most of those built proved a failure, a failure that was in some measure due to good old flux as residents grew up, got married, gave birth, died, and above all divorced.[56] It was just such banal things that undermined the perfect choreography necessary for such large-scale collective living and caused many a communal house to fall apart.

One always has to ask oneself how ineluctably tied to Marxism or even socialism the socialist towns and communal houses were. After all, the "bourgeois" architect le Corbusier was in the 1920s the main mentor for Constructivist architects and also designed several major Soviet projects (including an attempt at radically redesigning Moscow).[57] The socialist towns might also be seen as implementations of the dreams of the early 1910s of those who advocated the garden city or some other kind of planned workers' settlements. Indeed, one of the ways proposed for marking the three-hundredth anniversary of the Romanov dynasty in 1913 was to build a model town for workers in the environs of Petersburg.

In some senses, the mass spectacles and communal houses of the years 1929–1930 represent a version of some of the agendas and ideals of disparate groups of intellectuals from the period immediately preceding the Revolution. In them, we can see the ideals of the Preservationists who sought government support to create a perfectly designed environment with massive complexes constructed to ensure an "overall harmonious interconnectedness of all . . . component parts." Such principles are not so remote from those that guided Constructivist architects and designers in the

1920s.[58] If one considers that in the culture of the late 1920s the concept of these "component parts" was extended to include people, one might say that at this time such aims seem to come together with the programs of the theater activists who pinned hopes for humanity's salvation on a renovated theater in which the masses were to participate rather than be passive spectators. Additionally, the centrality of rhythm in the rhetoric of both Soviet officialdom and the Constructivists is reminiscent of the emphasis on rhythm during the prerevolutionary years by so many of these theater activists, ranging from Meyerhold to the Russian followers of Dalcroze (Dalcroze, it will be recalled, had been invited to Hellerau by idealists who were setting up a model workers' town and believed his work on rhythmic movement to music might be a crucial ingredient in enabling the workers to realize their true identities as proletarians). There are many such specific similarities, but the main point is that the culture of this time seems to have realized—or perhaps taken to an extreme—these groups' common aims of transcending the mundane and banal (or the commercial and petty bourgeois) and attaining a greater intensity of experience in religious-like and generally communal rituals (Ginzburg's "social condenser" was in a sense a metaphor from the technological sphere for this scenario).

What was truly daring about the cultural experiment of the late 1920s, however, was its paradoxical assumption that through the common such a remarkable self can be achieved. Accounts of cultural transformation lay stress on regularity, rhythm, the masses—the ordinary. As we see in the case of the engineer Magnitov who intensified the pace of his rhythms and was transformed, regularity was represented as miracle.

Thus in the culture of the late 1920s the Revolution was respatialized, an event that points forward to the 1930s, when space was even more highly ritualized. Although in this chapter the basic pattern of spatial articulation in the late 1920s has been identified as centripetal, in fact centrifugal patterns were no less characteristic. The economic and political life of the country was directed at ever greater centralization (central planning, and so on), suggesting a centripetal pattern, but at the same time the fundamental principle of the cultural revolution was radical hierarchy inversion (a centrifugal pattern). The implications of that agenda, if taken to the extremes some sought, are a transvaluation of values. It was the vertigo of that possibility that drove many intellectuals between 1927 and 1931 to attempt the ultimate in cultural revolutions.

12

THE ULTIMATE
CULTURAL REVOLUTION

Recall that in 1918, as part of the decorations for the first anniversary of the Revolution, the artist N. Altman had made a huge banner for the Winter Palace with the lines from the "Internationale": "He who was naught shall be all." But thus far, though many others had blazoned forth this slogan, its implications had not become reality. During War Communism, the first revolutionary phase when Altman had erected this banner, the state had looked to the regeneration of the masses through high culture, and intellectuals were expected to devote themselves to this cause. During NEP, Soviet society had retreated even further from the ideal of a single, "proletarian" or "peoples' " culture and in large measure established de facto separate cultural institutions for highbrow and mass culture.

The cultural revolution of the First Five-Year Plan was essentially the only time in Soviet history when such slogans were taken literally, a time when utopian zeal drove true believers to attempt an entire series of such paradoxical inversions. But these inversions also rendered more problematical any centripetal model for the organization of society.

During the Plan years, the hierarchy reversal was so radical that not merely were the lowly ("naught") to be elevated, but canonical culture (the heritage of the past) was deprecated. Those who enjoyed a privileged position in society by dint of their alleged access to Knowledge and Culture—intellectuals—were to be thrust down the ladder. As recently as February 1927 a national meeting of scientific workers in Leningrad had made grandiose claims about their indispensability as scientific experts, but by 1930 a meeting of intellectuals concluded that the common worker who is closer to socialist construction knows more than the engineer.[1]

The role of intellectuals was radically reconceived. In some of the cruder formulations, it was now defined as one of effecting a rise in the level of production.[2] All professional cultural workers' "expertise" or "creative genius" was devalued as an obdurate "individualism" that must be "broken,"[3] for it was considered that they had acquired more of the tools and skills for their particular branch of cultural production than the workers only as a result of social injustice; workers had been systematically denied access to them but were manifestly superior to any professional cultural workers because they were closer to the mysteries of the production process itself.

The intellectuals' job was to hand over those tools. In a *volte-face*, they were transformed from gods to servants. They were to organize libraries in factories and kolkhozes, run their theaters, art circles, clubs, and newspapers, train beginning writers, artists, and actors from the ranks of the workers, lecture to them, organize exhibitions for them, help collect archives and oral history from them, compose slogans and appeals to them, and if after all this they had time for their own "creative" efforts, these were to consist of production sketches that essentially functioned either as a conduit of information from worker to worker, or as purely agitational pieces.[4]

As intellectuals were reduced increasingly to a service role, he who had been peripheral in the running of cultural life became a legislator. Rather than intellectuals' taking the masses under their wing, as during War Communism, individual workers and also factories were asked to undertake *shefstvo* (a supervisory role) over cultural institutions. This was a progressive process, but it culminated in 1930, when, for instance, Leningrad's Red Putilov factory was among those asked to supervise the National Federation of Soviet Writers,[5] while the artistic councils of major cultural institutions in Leningrad (for theater, music, and film) were reformed as two hundred and fifty workers and fifty worker correspondents (*rabkory*) were assigned to them.[6] In the theater, the arbiter of value was no longer the professional critic but the factory audience.[7]

As the factory became the locus of the legislators, there was, in effect, an inversion in the hierarchy of place. The factory became the new cathedral, library, university, public monument, and opera house all rolled into one. The old factories were most likely to be located not in the center of any town—where the cathedrals, libraries, and statues were—but at its periphery, while the new industrial complexes were to be built in far-flung places. Thus at the same time so much of cultural production was structured by a centripetal spatial model, it was challenged by a radically centrifugal model that represented "the center" (of the town) as a condemned / polluted / retrograde space, full of intellectuals and bureaucrats, unlike the periphery, the locus of the laboring workers. "The outskirts" (*okraina*) emerged from obscurity as the favorite term for designating by place that which was preferred as the new culture; thus, for instance, subcanonical music, now favored over the canonical, earned that status as "the music of the *okraina*."[8] *Okraina* refers not only to the outskirts of a town, but also to the periphery of the country; in this period the national minorities first emerged on the Russian cultural map on any scale.

In these years, it was felt that representatives of the tainted-but-redeemable sociological categories (bourgeois intellectuals and trained professionals) should be sent to a place of labor on the periphery as the necessary route for their regeneration. Some were sent to exile or labor camps as social aliens; in the more common and more benign version they were assigned to a factory, collective farm, or construction site where they might serve the new class and imbibe some of its ethos. The movement was both voluntary and coerced. Some likened it to the Populist movement of the early 1870s and called it a "movement to the people,"[9] although it should not be romanticized since the last years of NEP saw rampant unemployment among intellectuals and the "brigades" of cultural workers provided a welcome opportunity for income.

Editorials spearheaded this centrifugal trend, calling for decentralization of culture. There was even a move to make Kuzbass (one of the raw industrial cities of the Urals) into the cultural center of the entire country.[10] This pattern stands in contrast to that of the immediately preceding years when one finds, particularly in the writings of the Moscow-based avant-garde, a cult of Moscow as the purported center of Soviet, and even world, culture. Writers such as Mayakovsky then urged that all turn their "gaze [*vzglyad*] to Moscow" (and specially to them).[11] As a virtual corollary, Leningrad became in their accounts the apotheosis of all that is doomed, retrograde, or repressive—a "swamp."[12]

In order for the cult of Moscow to emerge, Petersburg / Leningrad as the rival claimant to the status of symbolic national center had to be eliminated. But the slaughter of Leningrad in avant-garde culture was largely a ritual one;[13] the concrete historical reality of the city had become increasingly irrelevant in articulations of the myth. Thus Eisenstein's *October* (1927–1928), which treats the Bolshevik Revolution in Petrograd, opens with the dismantling of the statue of a tsar, but the particular statue shown was actually located not in that city as its presence in the film implies, but in Moscow. Indeed, for this movie Eisenstein did much of his filming of "Petersburg" in Moscow.

The tendency to build up Moscow as some sort of mecca and to deprecate Petersburg / Leningrad as its antithesis waned as the country moved into the Plan years themselves. While many in the avant-garde still urged that the entire world turn its gaze to Moscow, and to use imagery that was essentially centripetal in its organization, the analogues of a centralized polity, the more marked trend during the Plan was to reverse this.

Leningrad grew in stature again. It could lay considerably greater claim than could Moscow to the title of industrial city and many considered it a preferable headquarters for the new, proletarian culture. The city's factories with their revolutionary pedigrees and emphasis on heavy metal industries became major symbols of the age. It even had its factories located on the mandatory "outskirts"; most of them stretched in a ribbon at the north end of the Vyborg side (across the river from the city's center), while the famous Red Putilov factory was in the Moscow-Narva district far to the southwest.[14] Hence there was a series of moves to make Leningrad a national center for mass festivals or home of a new institute of proletarian art.[15]

The traffic pattern between the two rival cultural centers, Moscow and Leningrad, which during NEP had become overwhelmingly one-way (from Moscow to Leningrad), was substantially reversed. The new and revolutionary no longer came to Leningrad from Moscow with a time delay. However, in most instances the new cultural paradigms from Leningrad were for a proletarian, mass culture. For instance, the First All-Union Musical Conference (1929), which launched the movement for "music for the masses," and most of the first musical olympiades, were held in Leningrad. Leningrad could also boast taking the lead in developing new mass spectacles, the first Soviet sound movies (both documentary and feature),[16] some of the critical national meetings called to decide the direction of revolutionary culture, and even a new journal for training proletarian recruits for literature, *Literary Study* (Literaturnaya uchëba).

As Leningrad regained stature on the cultural map of the country, there was also a de facto shift in its symbolic status and a reaccentuation of the myth of Petersburg. The tenacity of that myth in the Russian imagination was such that even in this ostensibly most Soviet of cultural revolutions one senses its lingering power in providing tropes for the sweeping changes taking place. This trend received some impetus because Stalin in his address to the Central Committee of November 19, 1928, used the example of Peter the Great to describe the mighty transformations the Plan promised,[17] although the parallels with the building of Petersburg have their own logic apart from (or perhaps informing) Stalin's invocation of Peter.

Most of the gigantic construction projects of the First Five-Year Plan lent themselves to an identification with the myth of Petersburg because they entailed the massive transformation of semiwilderness (a "naught"), the taming of waters with canals and hydroelectric schemes, and the triumph over adverse natural conditions—the triumph of culture (or technology) over nature. One could even speculate whether the myth itself did not have some effect on the outcome of debates over which sites should be developed as giant industrial complexes since the far-flung and completely undeveloped ones generally won out over those that were to have been located in more settled places (it should be noted that these choices were also influenced by the theories of the American economist Alfred Weber, who contended that industrial complexes should be located near sources of raw materials, rather than of labor).[18]

This new appropriation of the Petersburg myth did not mean that the city itself was suddenly re-evaluated from a "swamp" to a positive place. But in order to represent Leningrad in a positive way there had to be a major shift away from seeing the city as full of statues and grand canals to seeing it as dotted with smokestacks, the new statues of an industrial romanticism. Thus Soviet rhetoric began to insist that there were two Petersburgs, the old Petersburg, which must be destroyed completely, that is, monumental Petersburg as oppressive Imperial capital, and the new Petersburg as an industrial city and hothouse of the new culture. But the two were also said to have separate locations. As Shklovsky remarked at the time: "Peter[sburg] is creeping to its periphery and has become like a bagel-city [actually *bublik*] with a beautiful but dead center."[19]

Thus in a range of ways the cultural revolution entailed taking very literally that old slogan from the "Internationale." This "revolution," in its extreme expressions, entailed a movement away from all kinds of canonical thinking: geographical, institutional, in the way professions were constituted, anthropological, and so on. Culture in this period reached one of the outer limits in playing down the aesthetic. Moreover, all of these shifts were essentially in sync because they were masterminded by the great centrifugal spatial model whereby the locus of value was shifted from the center to the periphery.

In almost every area of cultural life one sees a shift from the "central" (normative, authoritative, canonical, of a lofty position on some hierarchy) to the "peripheral" or noncanonical: instead of the famous writer, it was to be the worker or the peasant correspondent; instead of highbrow instruments and music it was folk music or jazz and noncanonical instruments such as the accordion and the balalaika;[20] instead of the cultural institution undertaking *shefstvo* over the factory's cultural life, the factory was to undertake *shefstvo* over the cultural institution, and so on. Even textual space was mapped in these years by analogy with social space; the so-called *bol'shaya forma* or (literary) "long form" such as the novel was to be supplanted by the much shorter *malaya forma*, that is, by such marginally literary genres as, in literature, the highly journalistic *ocherk*, or sketch, or, in drama, the *agitka*, or agitational dramatic sketch; analogously, in all cultural productions instead of individual heroes (the *bol'shoy chelovek*) as characters, there were to be myriad "little men"—the collective of common workers. From the avant-garde Constructivists to the movement for worker writers there was an emphasis on factual writing and showing how "little men" performed simple tasks that tended to result in shapeless and fragmented works as practical details crowded out plot development or heroization.[21] This general de-emphasis on plot also accompanied a reaction against adventure genres in literature; such terms as "detective" or "adventure" became standard negative terms in criticism.

But "he who was naught shall be all," while dramatic and appealing, is in the last analysis vague. At best, only a tiny minority in society could qualify for the categories "naught" or "all." Above all, how might the lowly become "all"? In culture, such a dramatic turn involves obvious problems of sheer professional expertise (even in 1917 Lenin's opponents liked to ridicule his model of the "female cook"). Not surprisingly, no sooner did Glaviskusstvo, the main body supervising cultural matters, assign two hundred and fifty workers and fifty worker correspondents in Leningrad to sit on the boards of most of the city's major cultural bodies than they had to turn around and set up courses to train these workers in cultural competence.[22] And then the question arises: Who should train the Great Unwashed, and in what will they be trained? And in what sense can a worker who has completed training be said to be able to legislate, unmediated, from the factory floor?

Needless to say, there were also vicious battles about who could be considered the "he" who could inherit the "all," and also about what this "all" might be. These arguments split the radical intelligentsia, and Leningrad became the major battleground where the issue was fought out. The story of TRAM, an acronym for the Leningrad Theater of Worker Youth (Teatr Rabochey Molodëzhi), of its meteoric rise to power and national prominence in the years 1928–1931 as an extremist agent and emblem of the cultural revolution, provides an excellent case study that focuses the dynamic and the vicissitudes of the period as a whole.

TRAM Rides the Roller Coaster of Cultural Revolution

TRAM, a Komsomol theater for workers, had existed for most of NEP as a minor cultural institution.[23] After the Agitprop conference of late 1927 on the theater, however, and especially during the initial years of the Five-Year

Plan when industrialization and cultural revolution were cornerstones of official policy, TRAM attracted the attention of the state as a theater totally devoted to the work lives and mores of the proletariat. Indeed, it was in many respects the theater of the historical moment. During the late 1920s, as never before or since, the Komsomol played a leading role in guiding Soviet culture, and TRAM was riding on the crest of its wave. A Komsomol theater of worker youth could not miss.[24]

Actually, in the late 1920s there was no shortage of Komsomol and worker theaters to claim this historical moment as theirs, but TRAM proved one of the few truly viable ones in the sense that it was able to turn agitational dramas about factory life into pithy, rollicking, and enormously popular productions (no mean feat).[25] It also appealed to the cultural bureaucrats. In June 1928 the theater went on a highly successful tour to Moscow, where its performances impressed the heads of both Glavpolitprosvet and its parent body, Narkompros (that is, Pelshe and Lunacharsky), and its standing in the theatrical world began to increase even more dramatically.[26]

By 1929, TRAM had emerged from its modest beginnings to become a major force in the Soviet theater. It had already begun to sprout branches in cities like Moscow and Baku, but after the Moscow tour of 1928 the movement took off, expanding to seventy branches by 1929,[27] and three hundred by 1932.[28] "Cells" of TRAM, or *tramyadra*, were established in all the major Leningrad factories and then throughout the country.[29] It also expanded its empire into the other arts, sponsoring IZORAM in the fine arts in 1928, followed shortly by KINORAM (or KRAM) in film, MUZORAM in music, and BALETRAM in ballet.[30]

In late 1929, as the November 7th anniversary approached, TRAM formed an alliance with three other leftist and agitational theaters known as the Revolutionary Front, or Revfront.[31] The four theaters met on November 3rd at TRAM headquarters (together with invited guests from the press, the Party, and the government) and drew up and signed a "revolutionary contract" according to which Revfront took upon itself the task of eradicating from Soviet culture all vestiges of the traditional theater, leaving the stage free for a truly revolutionary, proletarian, mass agitational theater such as those they represented. In practice, this meant eradicating primarily the academic theaters, that is, places such as the Bolshoi, the Mariinsky, the Bolshoi Drama Theater, and the State Theater (the former Alexandrinsky). Among them, Revfront wanted to abolish above all its absolute *bête noire*, MKhAT (the Moscow Arts Theater), as, allegedly, quintessentially bourgeois. After signing their "contract" in an atmosphere of elation, those present at the meeting streamed out of the hall to form columns and march to Ostrovsky

Square in front of their closest local target, the Academic Theater, where with loudspeakers mounted upon trucks they staged a confrontational protest against "academic art," shouting the slogan "The Liquidation of MKhAT as a Class."[32]

TRAM was in a position to take this revolutionary stance because of its proletarian revolutionary purism. Its director, Misha Sokolovsky (1901–1941), one of those Komsomol activist firebrands who refused to ever wear a tie and insisted on being called "Misha," the most informal version of his name,[33] had from the theater's very inception zealously guarded TRAM's profile as strictly worker and Komsomol.[34] On *his* stage, he would claim, "the working lad plays himself," and thus in a sense both acts out and even realizes his own transformation in the very act of helping transform his peers.[35] Originally, the theater was conceived as being strictly amateur and used only full-time workers. Here we see lingering from War Communism a romanticism of the eternally amateur theater as the formula for social transformation found in the theories of Platon Kerzhentsev and others. Now, however, the notion of the "people's theater" has been rigidly confined to the proletarian and Bolshevik.

The plays were by the workers and Komsomols, of the workers and Komsomols, and for the workers and Komsomols (at every performance there would be a huge block of cheap seats reserved for Komsomol organizations). The young authors who wrote TRAM's plays (together with the "collective"), such as Arkady Gorbenko, Nikolay Lvov, and Pavel Marinchik—names not to be found in any literary encyclopedia—all allegedly came from a worker milieu and were completely inexperienced as writers.

As TRAM gained power and prestige, it began to advance ever more inflated claims about the role it would play in forging the new man and the new society, insisting that it be seen not as just a theater but rather as "the Agitprop of the Komsomol,"[36] or even as an entire social movement of youth, called "tramism" *(tramizm)*.[37] When Revfront was formed, it published a declaration contending that theatrical circles had to be replaced by "agitational-propagandistic brigades."[38]

Thus when, on November 3, 1929, the members of the four theaters making up Revfront, led by TRAM, lined up on Ostrovsky Square facing the Academic Theater and insistently chanted their demand "The Liquidation of MKhAT as a Class," this incident had all the makings of a black day in that black year. From TRAM's very inception in 1925, it had taken as its slogan the famous lines from the "Internationale" "We shall build a new world, our world / He who was naught shall be all."[39] Now, with their new slogan "The Liquidation of MKhAT as a Class," they were essentially implying that the institutions such as MKhAT that had previously enjoyed the status in the cultural sphere analogous to that of the kulak in the village, those who had been "all" by virtue of their purported monopoly over that currency called culture, should now be "naught." Potentially, this incident has all the signs of being yet another onslaught by the underprivileged on the position of the educated and professional classes, yet another purge of an intellectual institution as part of a twin campaign for "proletarianization" and Party / Komsomol hegemony, and hence comparable with the purges at this time in the Academy of Sciences, the conservatoria, publishing houses, and countless other institutions. At the same time, TRAM's claim for hegemony might seem to have been informed by a crudely mechanistic sense of the function of culture, its only utility being what it might achieve as a form of agitation or as a means of raising economic yields. Thus we seem to have a scenario where Culture's very existence is threatened by primitive propaganda.

All these conclusions are valid, but they do not tell the whole story. In many senses, the campaign by Revfront with TRAM at its head was not a moment when the Great Unwashed confronted the cultural elite, nor when Soviet power attempted to destroy culture, but more a matter of internecine warfare within the intelligentsia, a category which at that time included a lot of Party and Komsomol officials. For a start, although TRAM was originally founded as an amateur theater, in the 1927–28 season a decision had been taken to go professional and its members had been given extensive theatrical training. As TRAM became more professional, however, it seems to have become more militant vis-à-vis the established theaters and, in consequence, more directly those theaters' rival.[40]

One of the major motives in the Revfront demonstration seems to have been its four theaters' frustration at seeing little improvement in the chronic paucity of material and administrative support they received from the cultural bureaucracy in a year when official rhetoric would seem to suggest that they were the theaters of the hour; in the months immediately preceding the demonstration their subsidies had been cut,[41] while Stanislavsky and Nemirovich-Danchenko, the ideologues of what they called the "bourgeois" theater, were reinstalled as unchallenged directors of MKhAT.

When Revfront stood on Ostrovsky Square, it was in a sense an exercise in that ultimate utopianism of intellectuals who took too literally the words "he who was naught shall be all." "The Liquidation of MKhAT as a Class" can be seen as a direct translation of this—their—slogan into the sphere of the theater. The demand that the new theater be by, for, and of the proletariat is a purist interpretation of the inversion of cultured and uncultured. The emphasis on propaganda and the immediate concerns of the workers reverses the conventional hierarchy whereby art with its claim to aesthetic value was seen as the highest form of communication and the purely propagandistic or journalistic was seen as lower. Also, the turn to local and current topics represents a shrinking of horizons as compared with those of "high art."

Yet the reality of TRAM did not quite conform to its claims to be exclusively a workers' theater. While histories of TRAM allege that its authors were untutored workers who came to the theater straight from the factory floor, further examination reveals that many of them had already established themselves as career Komsomol cultural workers or had previous experience in a theater or theater school (both are true of their director, Sokolovsky[42]). Others in the theater did not even fit the mold of the Komsomol activist. The acknowledged "godfather" of TRAM, technically head of the Literary Artistic Section but in practice its chief theoretician and mastermind—and its chief spokesman on Ostrovsky Square—was no raw worker youth but Adrian Piotrovsky.

Piotrovsky was not the only exception to this rule that TRAM was to be the pure working-class theater. The Theater Department of GIII was essentially a Svengali of TRAM, and TRAM's Musical Section, MUZORAM, was headed by Shostakovich, who composed the music for several of its plays, as did V. Deshevov; both came, like Piotrovsky, from a background in the professional classes and with higher education—in this case from the Conservatory—and both were heavily influenced by contemporary Western music.[43] Other avant-gardists were associated with other theaters in Revfront; for instance, Filonov and Malevich did work at different times for the Red Theater.[44]

"The Liquidation of MKhAT . . ." was in a sense the agenda of the prerevolutionary theater activists, champions of *uslovnost'* against the bourgeois "realist" theater. To some extent, TRAM can be seen as part of the diaspora from Meyerhold's studio on Borodinskaya. Many of its leaders, such as Piotrovsky, Sokolovsky, and Shostakovich, had in the past had some association with Meyerhold and the movement for a peoples' theater, while two other leaders of that movement, Radlov and V. Soloviev, had been among those who began giving the TRAM actors theatrical training in 1928.[45] As masterminds of TRAM, however, they emerged as direct rivals of Meyerhold with their own extremely ambitious agenda for theatrical reform.

TRAM, Piotrovsky, Deshevov, and Shostakovich were also central players in the movement for opera reform. Indeed, as Revfront was formed (on November 3, 1929) rehearsals were well under way for Shostakovich's *The Nose*, which was to premiere in January.[46] Yet while, even in this period,

Meyerhold was making public statements (including in Leningrad) praising the Wagnerian opera for the way it resolved the relationship between word and music,[47] TRAM was being praised by the theoreticians of the new opera for the anti-Wagnerian way its productions orchestrated that relationship.[48] There were no actual operas in the TRAM repertoire, but music played a central role in all its productions, which were typically satirical comedies or melodramas interlarded with musical numbers, or outright operettas. The leaders of TRAM frequently called their plays "musical dramas," using the term most often adduced by the proponents of opera reform to categorize the genre of the revamped opera.[49]

In some respects, TRAM's aims can also be seen as a development of the basic program of the Russian avant-garde from even before the Revolution. Like them, TRAM wanted to transform not just the external behavioral patterns of the audience members but their mindsets as well. The first step toward this was, as with the Russian Futurists and Eisenstein, to shock the audience into paying attention by presenting all manner of contradictions, incongruities, radical "displacements" (sdvigi), and "montage."[50]

TRAM, however, starting from its production of Molten Days (Plavyatsya dni) in May 1928, attempted more radical kinds of incongruity. In this play, incongruity was to be found not just in imagery or language but in plot, characterization, and temporal sequence.[51] Members "rejected" the "single and integrated psychic image" as a "fiction" together with the notion that characters should be individualized. The directors sought to break down the identification between actor and character by having their actors critique their roles even as they were acting them (here we see how their theories come close to Brecht's concept of alienation).[52] They aimed to present a conflicted and multilayered account of reality such that no single and coherent account of anything should be presented; its opposite should always be there simultaneously.[53]

A TRAM script was to present no conclusions to its audience as a guarantee of true collectivity (no overriding voice). There should, the group maintained, be no finality, a characteristic they identified with a Marxist account of the dialectic whereby all would be in a state of contradiction, of becoming. There was even to be no final version of the script. The cast and director were to keep working on it collectively not only as they rehearsed but after the play premiered (until at least the third or fourth performance, and even then the version was to be considered only provisional).[54]

Thus in a TRAM play each identity projected was to be relentlessly undermined in manifold ways, and there was to be no explicit message. But how could such complex and confusing plays meet Agitprop's central stipulation in its decrees on drama of 1927 that plays be readily accessible to the masses and effective as propaganda? The answer given by the theoreticians of TRAM was that their theater was truly radical because the synthesis of the manifold contradictions inherent in a TRAM play's text and staging should be made not on stage, but in the consciousness of the audience. The audience was to be the author.[55]

TRAM, then, tried to overthrow the most fundamental conventions of theater, and with them, the way in which its audiences perceived reality. Its primitive and pedestrian melodramas and comedies of the factory floor had, willy-nilly, to become the agents of epistemological revolution—very weighty baggage for such a medium to bear.

The theorists of TRAM liked to insist that their spectacles did not feel bound by any genre,[56] and even that the parent TRAM was not a canonical exemplar. Yet if one reads the texts of their productions, one is struck by the extent to which the majority represent variations on stock favorites of the lowbrow theater such as the family melodrama or the comedy of errors, in which, to be sure, the setting is generally the workers' hostel or holiday camp, but the characters' workday lives are minimized to make such a graft possible; the factory or blast furnace simply looms up larger than life for the triumphant finale.[57] Are, then, the claims of TRAM theoreticians to be a-systematic and a-generic deluded?

In any event, TRAM's noisy campaign came to naught and it was unable to storm the citadel of High Culture. Within a year of its dramatic challenge, it was under serious attack, and by 1931 it had been reduced to a minor player on the cultural scene.[58] This "denouement" hardly seems surprising given that, during the Plan years, one after the other contenders for the title principal theoretician or exemplum of the new culture experienced a rapid fall from grace. In 1925 the Party, in its pronouncement on literature, had advocated relative pluralism in cultural trends, as long as all were sympathetic to Bolshevism. But the prevailing mood in culture at this time demanded that among all the trends claiming to represent the new culture, one must be named.

Explanations of TRAM's demise are often made in terms of cultural politics. Such explanations foreground its losing battle against its main rival and arch opponent as chief legislator of the new revolutionary culture, RAPP. Both groups were riding high on the wave of Komsomol culture, which both represented. A struggle between these two mastodons within the Komsomol was probably inevitable. Their rivalry came to a head during 1929–1930. As the confrontation intensified, each group attempted to expand its empire, incorporating a broader sweep of cultural organizations. RAPP poached into TRAM's territory, the theater, adopting MKhAT, the flagship of "realism" in art, as its chosen vessel for proletarian theater. TRAM, for its part, began in 1929 to organize its commune as a center for discussions on what should be the new socialist culture.[59] Then in 1930 it encroached directly on RAPP's domain, literature, adding to the members of Revfront a dissident faction within RAPP itself, Litfront.[60] Litfront was based in Leningrad and in 1931 the RAPP leadership decamped there for an infamous national convention that was in effect the final showdown (for them, victorious) with this opposition within its ranks. By late 1931 TRAM was a very reduced force politically.

Thus the rise and fall of TRAM and Revfront could be explained in terms of political intrigues, factional politics, lobbies, and power plays. It should be noted, for instance, that Revfront was formed soon after Lunacharsky, the long-standing supporter of the conventional "academic" theater, was ousted as Commissar of Enlightenment (in the fall of 1929) and replaced by A. S. Bubnov, who was determined to "proletarianize" more radically.[61] Also, TRAM and, ironically, RAPP as well, ultimately lost out because of their megalomaniacal claims, which stood in the way of the Party's own ambitions for hegemony.[62] But literary politics cannot provide a complete explanation of their demise because they in themselves represent surface manifestations of more fundamental developments. TRAM was essentially the theater of the hour for the years of the First Five-Year Plan and the cultural revolution, but it did not wear well as the country entered the 1930s.

Anti-Westernism

In the closing phases of the cultural revolution, there was a shift in the dominant Soviet attitudes toward two things TRAM particularly valued—current Western trends and the proletarian. TRAM's "westernizer" stance became increasingly problematic as the country became more obsessed with defining the borders between "us" and "them." The attitude toward the West had always been fraught, but it was in some senses even more so during the Plan years because of the West's increasing importance at a time of industrialization and modernization.

For all the decade much of Soviet intellectual life had been heavily influenced by new directions or theories from Germany: Expressionism, Neo-Kantianism, the new physics, and aesthetic theory (Heinrich Wölfflin), to name just a few. Indeed, though Mayakovsky in 1927 might summon his colleagues in the international avant-garde to turn their "gaze to Moscow," in reality Soviet leftist intellectuals and avant-gardists had their eyes trained on Berlin: in the theater, there were some for Max Reinhardt and others for Erwin Piscator, but what was happening on the Berlin stage was always a landmark around which the Soviet avant-garde oriented themselves; the movement for opera reform came from there, not to mention trends in art (the Bauhaus), film, and music. The only major exception seems to have been in literature, where in the late 1920s the Soviets had stronger links with contemporary French and Anglophone trends.[63]

In some ways the Plan years saw an intensification of this Western trend. The country was visited, as never before or since (until recently), by a major influx of foreign workers, technological experts and equipment—and avant-garde architects;[64] many came as starry-eyed volunteers, fleeing a doomed and collapsing West after the Great Crash of 1929 and bent on building the socialist tomorrow. Soviet experts also went to Detroit, Deerfield, and such places to study Western technological achievements and organization.

Yet at the same time, in this militantly proletarian age the recurrent anxieties about ensuring cultural purity in the face of a bourgeois West needed to be alleviated. Though for many the terrain encompassing "us" definitely stretched at least to Berlin, now it was necessary to re-examine such assumptions. Should one differentiate between two "Berlins," just as there were now two Leningrads, one the Berlin of bourgeois culture and theory, and the other the Berlin of leftist proletarian culture, or even, since the latter movement split at about this time as the result of bitter fighting, of Communist proletarian culture? Thus many intellectuals, including the theoreticians of GIII, had to recant because their orientation had been to non-Communist German theoreticians.

There was also a movement to fuse the cultural effort in Soviet Russia with Communist and proletarian groups in Germany. This was particularly so in the theater[65] (TRAM, for instance, formed an alliance with a German counterpart): proletarian groups from each of the two countries toured analogous theaters in the other; there was an attempt to found a single "[proletarian] international theater"; alliances and "socialist competitions" were formed between Soviet and German leftist cultural bodies; and terminology and names from the milieu of German Communist culture (such as Rotfront and Jung-Sturm) were adopted by Soviet proletarian theaters and other cultural bodies.[66] This trend for identification became mutual; Brecht began to write a play about Lenin, and when Piscator, who had been scheduled to come to Leningrad and direct a production, was arrested in Germany he announced that if war were to break out between his country and the Soviet Union he would fight for the latter.[67]

Despite TRAM's emphasis on its links with German proletarian culture, in this later phase it proved out of sync with the times because it was heavily influenced by Western modernist trends and fell afoul of an anti-Westernist campaign that began even as Revfront was forming. In 1929 there began a series of attacks against prominent non-Party intellectuals couched in terms of their suspected Westernism,[68] including a particularly virulent one on the Leningrad Formalists that led to a purge of the Department for the Verbal Arts in GIII, their stronghold. By the end of the year this anti-"Formalist" campaign had extended its purview to include such representatives of the avant-garde as Eisenstein, Meyerhold—*and* Piotrovsky, Shostakovich, and Sokolovsky.[69] In November 1930, TRAM's Svengali, the Theater Department of GIII, which had been spared in the 1929 purge, was singled out and "reorganized" in a purge.[70]

Nineteen thirty, the height of this campaign, was the time when RAPP, in a strong position by virtue of its Russo-centric aesthetic, exacted its revenge on the masterminds of TRAM for their hubris in challenging it. Taking advantage of TRAM's weakened position, RAPP emasculated that organization and added it to its empire. TRAM, in an effort to preserve its position, disavowed its "godfather," Piotrovsky, at a national meeting of TRAM organizations in February 1930,[71] and bowed to pressures to draw closer to RAPP and the Theater section of the Communist Academy in Leningrad (which was then headed by the RAPP leader Libedinsky).[72] The Communist Academy was on the march at this time and since 1929 it had been absorbing a large number of leftist cultural bodies, including many institutes formerly allied with RANION.[73]

Unfortunately, it was not only the anti-"Formalist" forces that used this moment to make vicious attacks. Piotrovsky in turn lashed out at Meyerhold.[74] The avant-garde under pressure also began to recant. As these disavowals rolled off the assembly line in 1930–1931, one after the other the theoreticians of the avant-garde theater from GIII confessed that they had "suddenly" realized how much their thinking had been influenced by German theorists.[75]

The anti-"Formalist" campaign of 1929–1931 was not only informed by a xenophobic reaction against Western modernism but also directed at the question of "norms." In the attacks, Eisenstein, Piotrovsky, Shostakovich, Filonov, and others were not just reproached for falling prey to Western bourgeois tendencies, an accusation they were prepared to recant on (even earlier the theoreticians of the new Soviet opera had started to insist that it had outgrown Western influences).[76] In the attacks, less emphasis was given to the priority these figures give to form than to the absence of conventional structure in their work (Formalism!), and their disregard for conformist taste and the *comme il faut* (their "pathological anatomy").[77] A typical vicious journal attack on the "Formalists," one delivered in the militantly proletarian Leningrad journal the *Worker and the Theater* in February 1930, was headed "Let Us Put an End to Formalism, Bad Taste, and Lack of System," all three being equated as "prime values of bourgeois art theory."[78]

These qualities (attributed to the West) were perennial bugbears of Soviet criticism. As yet, however, such articles were not to have the status of *ex cathedra* pronouncements (as became the case in the mid-1930s), but were more salvoes in the most intensely fought battle of the day, the battle over norms. It is no accident that in the same issue of the *Worker and the Theater* as contained the above-mentioned attack on Formalism, I. I. Sollertinsky (one of the principal ideologues of the new opera) published his programmatic account of Shostakovich's *The Nose* under the rubric "'The Nose' Is a Long-Range Weapon."[79] Similarly, the campaign against Piotrovsky did not result in his expulsion from TRAM; he continued to work in the theater and to direct its productions and, despite consistent attacks on "Formalists" in film, he remained the artistic director of the Leningrad Film Studio (originally the Leningrad Factory of Sovkino), a post he held from 1928–1937. There were casualties of this campaign, however. Mayakovsky, another representative of leftist avant-gardism forced to join RAPP in 1930, committed suicide that December. At the time, he was working on a production in the Moscow circus of his play about the 1905 revolution, *Moscow Is Burning* (Moskva gorit), directed by Radlov, in which he, the erstwhile Futurist who in the manifesto of December 1912 had called for "throwing Pushkin . . . off the steamship of modernity," had his oppressed intellectuals gravitate toward that very bard's statue.

The Major Shift to the "Great Culture of Bolshevism"

Thus the anti-Formalist / anti-Westernist campaign of around 1930 was a major setback for TRAM (and particularly for its allies in GIII) but not its nemesis. Around 1931, however, a series of events occurred whose overall impact amounted to the dismantling or reversal of the distinctive culture of the Plan years—and the consequent diminution of TRAM's presence in culture. The most crucial reversal was on the official policy of "leveling" (*uravnilovka*), or treating all as equal in the workplace and in wage scales. This effectively called a halt to dreams that "he who was naught shall be all." In most aspects of Soviet life there was a reaction against the extreme emphasis on the low and "peripheral."

The move to greater hierarchization in Soviet society translated into a shift away from the common workers and their labor as the main subject for cultural production. But it also returned to the intellectuals some of their erstwhile status and promised that the standards and conventions of their caste would henceforth receive less battering. In the sphere of culture, the campaign was used as an occasion for regularizing and improving conditions in the various professions and the system of royalty payments. At the national plenum of Rabis, the Union of Cultural Workers, held in Leningrad in October 1931, five days were spent on this issue.[80] When the Writers Union was founded in 1932, its principal initial concerns had to do with improving the material position and social status of its members.

It is no accident that the same Rabis plenum discussed the inadequacies of the characteristic "short forms" of Plan culture and recommended a new emphasis on "long forms." The age of the agitational sketch was coming to an end and literature was reclaiming its traditional place as queen of the arts, a status returned her during 1931–1932. A new slogan of 1931, "The Great [bol'shaya] Literature of Bolshevism," was used as a signal to halt the battering that traditional professional standards had received in all areas of culture.

The country was finding worker mores a less compelling subject for its theater, and hence TRAM had lost much of its original purpose; its clumsy attempts at adjusting to new trends were deemed by critics pedestrian and boring. By the second half of 1931, TRAM had already disappeared from view in the cultural press by comparison with the preceding two years or so when it remained at the center of attention and controversy (in the mid-1930s, the remaining TRAM theaters were superseded by Theaters of the Leninist Komsomol).

The demise of TRAM can also be seen as an effect of the moment when the inherent paradoxes and ambiguities of the Plan years were resolved. Those years had been a very liminal time, a time when the dominant cultural patterns were both centripetal and centrifugal. Thus in some instances rather than cultural organizations undertaking shefstvo over a factory, or vice versa, one found a situation of mutual shefstvo. The city of Leningrad can be seen as both locus and icon of ambivalence in a liminal age. Was it a "center"? the periphery? the stronghold of the old intelligentsia? or of the revolutionary proletariat? Was it the home of the ancien régime or of the new? Likewise, one has problems in trying to define TRAM. Was it a workers' theater? the Agitprop of the Komsomol? or a sandbox for intellectual romantics?

TRAM (and Revfront) of 1929 as a marriage between avant-garde experimentalists bent on transforming the landscape of culture, on the one hand, and theatrically gifted workers, on the other, was bound to come unstuck, since the partners were ill-matched in so many ways. Shostakovich, for instance, had to work overtime on the worker youths of TRAM to persuade them that the new music was more truly proletarian than the more melodious and schmaltzy revamped Tchaikovsky and Mussorgsky peddled as "revolutionary music" by RAPP's counterpart in music, RAPM. In a sense, 1930 represents the year the marriage began to fail. The next year a bitter Shostakovich responded to the attacks by giving notice that he would not serve the country any more as an "applied composer." In language reminiscent of Brecht's attack on the opera as "culinary," he condemned such hackwork as aimed at "pleasant digestion" (it is to be noted that he started work on his opera *Lady Macbeth* in that year).[81]

Around 1931 the root ambiguity of the Plan years was resolved: the entire country in all its many aspects—political, social, symbolic, and cultural— became unambiguously centripetal and hierarchical in its organization. But then, who or what set this new direction? Undoubtedly two major landmarks in the fundamental shifts that year were Stalin's famous speech in June to a meeting of industrial managers that reversed the policy of "leveling,"[82] and his letter published in *Proletarian Revolution* (Proletarskaya revolyutsiya) in October which attacked one of that journal's articles of the previous year (by Slutsky) about Lenin's role early in the century vis-à-vis the German Social Democrats. The terms of this latter attack had immediate bearing on the great debate about revolutionary historiography in the 1920s, and the related debate about "revolutionary" representation, between those who contended that it should be based on actualities and those who contended that the Marxist-Leninist account of history should guide the historian's pen. Stalin took particular exception to the way Slutsky insisted that more documentation was needed for studying the issue of Lenin's relations: how could one need documents to evaluate a figure of the stature of Lenin ("The editors should raise the study of the history of Bolshevism to a more appropriate, high level")! In effect, Stalin made it clear that Party leaders are ipso facto exemplary and cannot be accorded mundane or negative traits.[83]

In this essay in *Proletarian Revolution* Stalin also took the anti-Western trend further and undermined the theory of the "two Berlins"; he drew a qualitative distinction between German Communists (Rosa Luxemburg) and Bolsheviks, favoring the latter.[84] From approximately this time, it was not enough to be leftist or even Communist to be acceptable in Soviet Russia. One should note the humiliation that year of the European avant-garde architects (such as le Corbusier) in the competition to design the Palace of Soviets, an event that is conventionally taken as the end of the international avant-garde's happy marriage with Soviet power.

As it were, Stalin put his thumb on the page of *Proletarian Revolution* and the whole country did a turnabout—from the cult of "little men" to the cult of "big men," from having close links with Western leftist avant-gardism to cultural autarchy, and so forth. This situation may seem similar to that in the nineteenth century when the tsar allegedly drew a line arbitrarily between Moscow and Petersburg and that became the route for the rail-line, even though it meant taking the line through bogs and other needlessly difficult terrain. Once Stalin's "thumb" hit the page, once the revolutionary culture had been named, all the other contending versions became non- or anti-trends.

Stalin's letter can be seen as one of a series of landmark occasions—the most notable being the Central Committee's 1925 ruling on Soviet literature, the anti-Formalist pronouncements of 1936, the Zhdanovist decrees and attacks of 1946, and Stalin's articles on linguistics of 1950—where pronouncements from "the highest levels," often from Stalin himself, appear to set a new direction for Soviet culture, thereby excluding from it other vital trends advocated by leading intellectuals. But in most such cases, including this one, the *ex cathedra* pronouncement represents not a shift but the endorsement of one position in a very heated debate. The Stalin article appeared toward the end of 1931, thus it represents the most authoritative formulation of tendencies that were already marked. Moreover, the cultural shifts to be observed in 1931 did not occur in a single moment but evolved over time.

Stalin's remarks, unlike the lines for the railway, were not arbitrary. They reflect the general responses to a particular nexus of circumstances the country found itself in at that time. For example, 1931, annus horribilis as it has been called, was a crisis year in the West. The Party was alarmed at the rise of fascism in the West and Japanese incursions into Manchuria in the East, and responded with a policy of greater economic autarchy, making cultural autarchy more probable. Additionally, the Party was affronted by the meeting of the Second International that year in Vienna; hence a shift on the pages of *Pravda* over the course of the year from articles in praise of German Communists to articles denouncing them. Finally, and most crucially, 1931 was that critical moment when the First Five-Year Plan was winding down and the Party was planning the second. It was a time of stocktaking when the quixotic nature of extreme democratism and its costs in practical terms were becoming all too apparent. Some have suggested that it was not Stalin who initiated the debunking of "leveling," but Sergo Ordzhonnikidze, who in November 1930 had been made head of Vesenkha (effectively the ministry of industry) and was anxious to deliver[85]—but perhaps it is pointless to speculate about priority: Stalin in his function as absolute authority promulgated changes, but their roots were "deeper." The economic stocktaking of that year was accompanied by ideological stocktaking as well; in *Pravda*, together with articles on production and foreign affairs came an unusual number of articles on ideological and philosophical issues. They were partly occasioned by the anti-Trotsky campaign, but were symptomatic of a need to normalize after the upheavals (cataclysms) of economic, social, and cultural revolution.

The Plan years might have been a liminal time, but liminality cannot be sustained, as Victor Turner, one of its chief theoreticians, has pointed out.[86] How viable could the new culture be if, characteristically, it placed hyper emphasis on the "periphery," the noncenter—the "naught"? So many of its programs seem a sort of reductio of the movement to take the theater out onto the streets; as it was put at the time, "The theater bursts out onto the street like a river during a flood . . .," representing it as a spontaneous act. But if the theater really empties out onto the streets, if the bounds of the theater become fuzzy, you lose theater (culture) as a distinctive institution. Also, as the bounds between spectacle and spectator are broken down, there are no subjects. A genre means restraints, borders. As the center is emptied out, where is the source of authority?—is it the worker?

In a sense, during the Plan years the zealots of cultural revolution went to the edge almost literally—they followed the path to the "periphery" to its outer limits. To some extent, state policies did so as well. In the theater, policies came closer than before or since to "Liquidat[ing] MKhAT as a Class," but each time they did so, segments of the public or the cultural bureaucracy panicked and a reverse trend set in. In 1929, for instance, the Leningrad State Theaters were taken off the budget of Narkompros (after Lunacharsky, their patron, was "retired"), but not for long.[87] And then in 1930 the Bolshoi Drama Theater, the theater Gorky and others founded shortly after the Revolution to bring high culture to the masses, was dropped from the roster of subsidized state theaters, but the decision was revoked after a public protest.[88]

In a highly centralized society such as the Soviet Union a mass exodus to the "periphery" becomes a necessary gesture if one is to reorient the culture. Certainly it is a gesture that has been made each time Soviet culture has rethought itself, although it is difficult to ascertain in each instance whether the gesture was aimed consciously at reorienting the culture. Such inversions can be found in the post-Stalin era when cultural production acquired a new symbolic geography based on the assumption that the only way of recovering from the blow delivered by the revelations of Stalinist infamy made at the Twentieth Party Congress in 1956 was to leave the corrupt "center" for a construction site or other such place on the periphery where individuals might discover an untarnished expression of the Communist ideals that would help them find a new faith and values and enable them as well as the country to return to a recuperated "center." Later, under Leonid Brezhnev, and particularly in so-called village prose, the questing hero (or author) was to push farther out from the center to some remote village where he might find intact not a Communist ethos but the truly Russian (pre-Soviet) one, a topos that underwrote the religious and nationalist revivals and even led directly into perestroika (the cultures of non-Russian ethnic groups soon followed suit, a prelude to their quest for national self-determination).[89] Under Gorbachev, however, a new "periphery" was found as an antidote to such a potentially xenophobic locus; the preferred icon became the provincial town presented as a model for a more pluralistic and federalist society with its modest local associations and market promising greater weight for civil society and an antidote to Communist big brotherism.

The actors in the cultural life of the Plan period were, analogously, "going to the edge," not to find a permanent new locus, but to find new borders (norms) as they undertook this journey. There can never be a period when the "periphery" is all. For a start, there is really no such place as "periphery" because it is not bounded and can be defined only negatively, as "noncenter." If all is periphery, there are no bounds or norms. Thus, any period when periphery is a dominant value can only be liminal at best (hence in a sense TRAM's demise was inevitable because they had staked so much on "decentering"). Moreover, any theory of decentering is itself a new center, as one saw in the 1980s and early 1990s in the new "Postmodernist" orthodoxy.

As the cultural revolution of the First Five-Year Plan progressed, one saw to an increasing extent the next phase of the dash to the "periphery," that is, attempts at defining norms and boundaries. Symptomatically, as early as 1930 several institutes of RANION identified the question of genre as the linchpin of their inquiries and together founded a special commission to oversee the reorientation of their institutes to this focus.[90] This project anticipates the major work on genre theory done in the 1930s by figures such as Lukács and Bakhtin.

The return to genre had ramifications extending beyond literary or theatrical forms. As Bakhtin has explored in his theory of the chronotope, at the heart of any literary genre is a particular understanding of the nature and interconnection of space and time (a chronotope), an understanding that defines not only the genre of a particular time but in some senses that time as well.[91] The return to an interest in genre coincided with new spatial and temporal models.

The rejection of the principle of "leveling" meant that there was a reorientation toward the vertical, which brought with it a new emphasis on the dimension of time. As literature and plays were reordered around sequences of events in time, biographism returned, including biographies of major historical figures.[92] The Senyas and Musyas, those faceless "little men" who were the mainstay of literature and theater during the Plan years, retreated from center stage. In their place came figures who represented the Party leader; Kaverin and some other intellectuals matched this trend with hagiographic biographies about "heroes" of their own caste.[93] As plot and historical subjects returned, heroic adventure experienced a revival in literature.

In 1931 the principal Leningrad cultural journal, the *Worker and the Theater* (having absorbed the *Life of Art* after 1929), began to feature an entirely new type of cover with photographs not, as before, of worker theatrical collectives or cultural leaders, but of wild and frequently Asiatic horsemen. This trend had been prepared for in cinema, which during the Plan years had been somewhat out of sync with literature and drama and had in many films presented a different version of the periphery—not the construction site with its ant-like swarm of toilers, but the exotic steppe of the Civil War or prerevolutionary underground as the setting for adventure.[94] Such exotic orientalism is, as Edward Said and others have shown, frequently the flip side of imperialism. In the 1930s (and especially the 1940s) the Soviet Union was to emerge as a more nakedly imperialistic power, and though the "orientalist" aspect of the trend had largely faded by then, engagement with the wild and untamed, a swashbuckling-like heroism, became the mainstay of culture.

Soviet society might around 1931 have, de facto, abandoned the ideal that "he who was naught shall be all," but its literature continued to present parables of this process. Writers had learned a bitter lesson from the Plan years, however—that sketches about "little men" and their practical tasks make for unreadable literature that piles up in warehouses but has little demand. As Gladkov had shown with the great success of *Cement*, this tale had to be recast in an adventure plot that transformed the factory floor or kolkhoz field into an epic canvas. In heroic struggles with elemental or elemental-like forces, "he who was naught" became that "all," which by then in the national Imaginary meant the form of the Bolshevik leader. Novels were generally set in some peripheral location, but as the hero triumphed over the overwhelming odds there he also completed a symbolic journey from that periphery back to the "center."

The best known of the films from the late 1920s about revolutionary engagement in exotic settings is V. Pudovkin's *Storm over Asia* (originally called *The Heir to Genghis Khan* [Potomok Chingiz Khana], 1928), set in the Buriat Mongol steppe. In its famous ending the hero, Bair, a Buriat Mongol youth, escapes from the British, who have tried to set him up as a puppet leader, and joins the local revolutionary uprising. As the expeditionary forces pursue him a great storm blows up, overwhelming the British, who are blown back in retreat while Bair and his people meld with the storm and drive them out. The original screenplay by the Formalist Osip Brik provides for a more elaborate version of this ending. The hero escapes on his horse and rides furiously over the steppe, through Mongol hamlets, across rivers, and over mountains. As his pace quickens he sees a mirage in the distance. He presses his pace even more and as he draws closer he sees it is a town. Moving now at breakneck speed he rides to meet it and the mirage is revealed to be the gleaming city of Moscow.[95]

This proposed ending with its cult of Moscow was arguably rejected because it was ahead of its time, but it prefigures the shape of culture to come. As the wild horseman gallops over the steppe to meet the shining mirage, the audience gets both its cowboy movie and those monumental panoramas of stately *(tsarstvenno-velichavyy)* buildings the Preservationists sought. Just as in 1913 "all of Paris" was captivated by the elemental, "Asian-daring" dancing of the Polovtsians in *Prince Igor,* so could all of the Soviet Union be captivated by the daring physical exploits of its new heroes. As they made their journey to Moscow (symbolic or actual), they mediated the gap between high culture and low, between agitation or status quo–affirming rituals and entertainment. The periphery, now even more than during the Plan years *the* locus of novels and films, became more "wild," but thereby, paradoxically, it became more tame. As heroes breached the gap between center and periphery, they also proclaimed an end to the period of "abnormal science"—and hence, in effect, of revolution.

EPILOGUE:
THE THIRTIES

Stalinist culture did not appear overnight. Nor was its evolution linear, gradual, and incremental. A more appropriate model for the pattern of intermittent periods of extremism is that of "punctuated equilibrium," a model proposed for natural evolution by theoreticians including Stephen J. Gould. They have argued that in many instances evolution is not an even process but is marked by periodic cataclysms or spasms that tend to make superfluous or weaken a spectrum of possibilities and to advance others. What remains after such spasms is changed as well thereby.[1]

This book has charted two such "punctuations"—the period of War Communism and the time of the cultural revolution. In the 1930s, another can be found in the time of the Great Purge, the "terror" of 1936–1938.[2] One might characterize the pattern in terms of an alternation of peaks and valleys, or of revolution (extremism) and normalization. The "valleys," the intervening times, are, though less dramatic, also critical in the evolution of Stalinist culture. The peaks largely determine which among those possibilities represented in the valleys will go and which will be advanced, but generally a more formative period is the time of recovery and consolidation between cataclysms (or "peaks"). One such "valley" can be found in the wake of the cultural revolution.

The day the *Literary Gazette* reported Gorky's return to the Soviet Union in May 1931, it published his article "Concerning Work with Language."[3] It might have been expected that Gorky would mark his triumphal return at such a critical time with a major political statement, but reform of the language of literature was for him a crucial priority; indeed, his crusade was to prove one of the most fateful moments for Soviet culture.

The following year, 1932, all independent writers' organizations were abolished as a single Writers Union was established with Gorky as its head.

This shift, first orchestrated in literature, was progressively replicated in every field (music, architecture, film, and so on) and the new policies for literature—socialist realism—set the model for the other arts. Theater was no longer queen.

In 1934, when the Writers Union held its First Congress and the doctrine of socialist realism was being finalized, Gorky was still crusading for language reform. In January 1934, as delegates were attending the Seventeenth Party Congress, he was conducting one of his most crucial power struggles—this time with a block of writers headed by Fëdor Panfyorov. Panfyorov was at that time an extremely important writer: he was one of two delegates to the Congress from the literary sector, and his novel *Bruski*, a saga of collectivization, was one of the two literary works presented to all the Congress delegates (the other being the infamous Belomor Canal book about the regeneration of convicts through labor on the canal).[4]

Gorky and Panfyorov were, at this critical moment, arguing about language, or more specifically about whether the extensive use of substandard folk language in literature (a characteristic of Panfyorov's *Bruski*) represents, as Gorky termed it, "language pollution," and as such should be excluded from Soviet literature. Panfyorov was supported in this argument by the Old Bolshevik author A. S. Serafimovich and several other prominent writers.[5] The issue was laid to rest when M. P. Yudin, the nonliterary, Party-appointed head of the Writers Union's Organizational Committee and the other spokesman on literature at the Seventeenth Party Congress, supported Gorky at the Committee's plenum in March 1934.[6]

A debate about language is never innocent. It is no wonder this one was put to an end by statements from on high. Starting from such earlier disputes as that between Lomonosov and Tredyakovsky in the eighteenth century, or the series involving Admiral Shishkov, Karamzin, Pushkin, and others that heralded the emergence of modern Russian literature early in the nineteenth, debates on language have tended to mark interstitial times in Russian cultural history. In the Soviet period, the impact of such debates became decidedly more political. Consider Stalin's famous essays on linguistics of 1950 that reversed the base / superstructure model in this sphere and ended the sway of Marr's school in linguistics; in so doing, they set in motion, or were a sign of, a major reorientation in Soviet culture that was intensified during the thaws under Khrushchev.

Arguments about language are often arguments about authority and system. As was said in a *Literary Gazette* editorial when the canonical theory of socialist realism was being worked out: "The struggle for cultured language [*kul'tura yazyka*] is at the same time a struggle for the language of socialist culture and even more broadly a struggle for socialist culture in general."[7] A similar position was taken by the Party spokesman at the First Writers Congress, A. A. Zhdanov, who in his speech to the Congress (a canonical source for the theory of socialist realism) stated: "In order to be an engineer of human souls one must struggle actively for cultured language [kul'tura yazyka]. . . ."[8] Thus "cultured language" was a cornerstone of socialist realism, together with "Party-mindedness" (partiynost') and the "positive hero."

Socialist realism was also defined negatively, by a list of taboos, the key constraint being the parameters of language. Gorky mandated that all dialecticisms and substandard expressions be kept out of Soviet literature. Thanks to his policies, the "living speech" of the urban proletariat so idealized in the late 1920s by writers, linguists, and reformers in the theater and opera was now expunged with particular zeal. Writers were expected to follow what were allegedly "folk" models for their positive heroes. In practice, however, their characters were to speak an incongruously bookish language.

The significance of language reform extends beyond the question of what kind of language could, and what could not, be used in literature. Gorky not only mandated this kind of language as opposed to that; he mandated an *image* of language and thus also a function. In so doing, he essentially proscribed its noncanonical, demystifying, eccentric aspects, thus eliminating one of meaning's polarities as Ricoeur has defined them (see the Introduction). The boundaries for "bouffe," as distinct from "mystery," became narrower and conventionalized. Socialist realism has thus with some justice been called a form of classicism, that is, a normative system that emphasizes purity, restraint, and decorum.

Socialist realism was, then, essentially a version of what Stallybrass and White call cultural "Lenten rule." Together with the insistence on linguistic purity went a rejection of "naturalism" (sex and other intrusions of the baldly physiological); Gorky also condemned these aspects of Panfyorov's novel.[9]

The new language policy for literature seems comparable to the one advocated in the mid-1920s by such Constructivists as Arvatov, who also used the metaphor of the "engineer," and by Trotsky, who recommended "cultured speech" too. There was a significant difference, however. Trotsky's and Arvatov's agendas for language reform had as their master norms utility, science, and technology—making language dignified and efficient, and eliminating rhetoricizing flourishes and other such "redundancies." Gorky's emphasis was on avoiding the prosaic; his model was the language of epic, rhetoricized language.

The institutionalization of socialist realism saw the return to a standard inventory of models as a pillar of Soviet culture.[10] But socialist realism did not mean a return to the same canon that had held sway before the Revolution. The claim to canonicity of works by Aleksandr Fadeyev, Gladkov, and others, which were repeatedly cited as models, had a very different basis from that which had assured such predecessors as Pushkin, Dostoevsky, and Tolstoy a place in the prerevolutionary canon. In the new canon, the grounds for inclusion, while allowing some aesthetic criteria, were predominantly political; the primary function of all cultural products was now legitimization of the status quo.

In a sense, the mad dash to the "periphery" made by TRAM and others in the period of cultural revolution had been a necessary preliminary step to such a radical recentering of the canon away from the old giants. The institutionalization of the new Soviet culture—the paradigm shift—had been preceded by what Kuhn might call a period of "abnormal science."

But what was Gorky's role in this? In the initial postrevolutionary period he had been chief advocate of the Petrograd intelligentsia, attacking the government for its excessive violence and its cavalier attitude toward the nation's cultural treasures and then negotiating on their behalf, persuading the state to fund institutions and cultural enterprises that maintained them morally and physically. But now he had become an apologist for the purges and allowed himself to head an organization that ensured direct state control of literature. One popular explanation of this apparent *volte-face* is that Stalin duped Gorky into returning and assuming such a role; another is that his career was spent in the West and he had to return in order to regain the stature and style of life to which he had become accustomed.

There are, however, elements of continuity in Gorky's later actions that make them seem less of an absolute reversal. For instance, much of the initial activity of the Writers Union had to do with ameliorating the lives of writers (increasing royalty payments dramatically and constructing privileged apartment buildings, dachas, and "houses of creativity" for writers in idyllic vacation sites[11]). In that sense, Gorky's role as head of the Writers Union is analogous to the one he assumed in civil war Petrograd as a Lorenzo the Magnificent, a patron extraordinaire of intellectuals. More important, as head of the Writers Union Gorky was able to institute the kind of culture he had advocated after returning to Russia from exile in 1913, and also during War Communism in projects such as the Bolshoi Drama Theater, which sought to provide high culture and "tragedy" for the masses, or his various encyclopedist ventures.

The debate over the kind of language that should define Soviet literature was, then, a critical moment in the evolution of Soviet culture. But it did not, in this instance, involve a conflict between avant-gardists and traditionalists, or between the Party or Party hacks and true intellectuals or dissidents.

Rather, it was a struggle conducted almost exclusively within the Party-cum-proletarian literature camp. However, a similar battle could have taken place within the avant-garde as well. But we must ask ourselves the question: do these events show that the Party did in fact set the direction for Soviet culture circa 1934? And, if so, was the Party (through Yudin) supporting "its man" (Gorky) or was it, rather, supporting a particular image of language, a particular understanding of culture? The answer to the latter question has to be both: the invitation to Gorky to head Soviet literature was based on certain assumptions about the kind of literature (and culture generally) that his stewardship might foster. But the answer to the first question is more complicated.

Gorky was able to argue for "Lenten rule" in literature because many of the values he espoused had been internalized by the Party. To argue as to whether it was Gorky or the Party who made socialist realism, or Stalin, or someone else, is to overpersonalize. The shift to Lenten rule and the positive hero, the twin pillars of socialist realism, should not be attributed to the agency of Gorky alone (although one can see ample precedent for them in his earlier writings), or of Stalin, but can be seen in the context of that major societal shift mentioned in Chapter 12 from the cult of the "little man" and minor genres to the "big" or "great" man and great literature; Gorky himself made a similar shift in his own writings of 1931 as compared with those of the period of the cultural revolution.[12] Moreover, at about the same time analogous shifts can be seen in the work of many European intellectuals.

When the new canon was formed the old canon was not jettisoned, as the erstwhile Futurists might have advocated. Rather, it was adjusted to the new age. Some of its more "naturalistic" and "obscurantist" figures and works were blackballed, such as Dostoevsky, whom Gorky had long attacked for these qualities, especially in polemical articles of 1913.[13] The expurgated old canon was given a place in a teleological account of literary evolution toward a culmination in socialist realism. A milestone in this process was the literature occasioned by the Pushkin Anniversary in 1937.[14]

In 1937, the blackest year of the Great Terror, the one-hundredth anniversary of Pushkin's death was marked throughout the country on an unprecedented scale: every small town, every kolkhoz, and even the most minor enterprise was obliged to honor Pushkin with lectures, readings, performances, and scholarly efforts from citizens of all educational and social levels. Pushkin was used in 1937, as in 1921 when the intelligentsia themselves organized the first major Soviet commemoration of the poet's death, as the official progenitor of a Russian national tradition and guarantor / emblem of its linguistic and aesthetic norms. By 1937 these norms had been nominated "socialist realism," but in both instances they were conservative in aesthetic inclination.[15] It is no accident that Benois's illustrations for *The Bronze Horseman* were republished for this event, along with several other Preservationist texts (even though the authors had often emigrated). In both commemorations of Pushkin's death there were elements of intellectual patriotism, which by 1937 had taken a nakedly imperialistic course.

Even as, in 1937, so many Russian intellectuals were setting out in the diaspora of the Gulag—most, if we are to believe Evgenia Ginzburg's memoirs, with Pushkin in their hearts—[16] the bard was making his own journey across the major linguistic barriers of the Soviet Union as he was translated into the languages of ethnic minorities. In many cases, these minorities were newly literate, in others they had recently acquired a Cyrillic alphabet to replace the roman one given them in the late 1920s by, among others, Polivanov (Marr's vanquished opponent then in Central Asian exile). Pushkin was the name of the Russian intelligentsia, but in the late 1930s he also became the name of Russian cultural hegemony and imperialism.[17]

It was an edited version of Pushkin that was advanced when the state proclaimed him "ours"[18]—Pushkin the bard of Lenten rule and a Neoclassical tradition, not the Pushkin noted by others as an irreverent, irrepressible, and even bawdy poet. Mandelshtam had yearned for a time when "we shall gather again in Petersburg" and the "buried sun" could rise. This anniversary was a cruel parody of that long-awaited moment, but it was welcomed by many. The celebration of classical Pushkin pleased the aesthetic majority and the expurgated image of the bard projected in 1937 remained tenacious indeed, although some of the cruder political claims made for Pushkin in that year—such as that in spirit he was with the kolkhoz system—were soon jettisoned. Even under Gorbachev, when a noncanonical account of Pushkin was suggested the response from many intellectuals was outrage at the sacrilege.[19]

A *Veshch'* editorial of 1922 had, under the title "The Rear Guard Triumphant," complained that an "art of capitulation," an "academic art," had triumphed in revolutionary Russia.[20] In reality, however, the true triumph of academic art occurred in the 1930s. Pushkin was far from the only author from the canon celebrated then.

Symptomatic of the triumph was the revival in 1938 of Meyerhold's production of *The Masquerade,* by Pushkin's self-proclaimed successor, Mikhail Lermontov. The term "revival" is in this instance fairly accurate given that the Golovin sets and the Glazunov score were used "as much as possible" as they had been in 1917.[21] Yuriev, the twenty-fifth anniversary of whose acting career had been honored at the 1917 premiere, played the central role of

Arbenin once again, inappropriate though it now was for such a geriatric actor. During the cultural revolution, Yuriev had been viewed by the theater activists of Leningrad as a retrograde actor; the director of the Academic Theater had eased him out and he had taken umbrage and retreated to Moscow to return only in 1932, when Revfront and other such threats to "academic art" were a thing of the past.[22]

The production of *The Masquerade* preserved the pomp of the old sets, so decried at the time for their lavish extravagance, but not the bite of the original endeavor, which had been directed at transforming humanity via the theater. No doubt, however, this revival particularly suggested itself in this period of high Stalinism because the Golovin sets celebrated Imperial Petersburg and its Empire style. In the original (prerevolutionary) production, the sets were meant to suggest a ghostly veneer masking a corrupt and degenerating Imperial power, but now they could dazzle with the promise of a great tradition already being resurrected.

The Academic Theater where *The Masquerade* was staged was the very place Piotrovsky and Revfront had picketed with the slogan "The Liquidation of MKhAT as a Class." But few of the theater activists from the 1920s seemed to be pursuing that cause now (it would have been a trifle foolhardy given that its Stanislavsky had been elevated to the status of absolute authority figure within theater, a role comparable to that of Gorky in literature and Marr in linguistics). Already by the 1931–32 season Radlov, one of the activists for the new opera, was presenting the Wagner ring cycle at his theater using the old Benois sets.[23] For most of the 1930s, he was to make his mark as a director of Shakespearean plays.[24]

The revival of *The Masquerade* had been intended to save the career of Meyerhold, who was invited to direct it because he was under attack and his own theater had already been closed. But this invitation represents a sad reversal of the situation when he first directed the play in 1917, then believing that with such productions he as director might save his audience.

Meyerhold had fallen victim to a particularly virulent anti-Formalist campaign that had been launched in a *Pravda* article of January 20, 1936, attacking Shostakovich's opera *Lady Macbeth of Mtsensk District*. This campaign, soon to be followed by the Great Purge, can be seen as one of the "cataclysms" that made the ensuing years a "peak" time in Soviet cultural evolution.

The *Pravda* article, "Muddle instead of Music," condemned the opera as "leftist art," which with its "deliberately dissonant, confused stream of sound . . . denies for the theater simplicity, realism, comprehensibility of imagery, and the natural sounds of words" and is riddled with "rotten naturalism." "Leftist distortion in opera," it continued, "stems from the same source as leftist distortion in painting, poetry, education, and science." It also concluded that *Lady Macbeth* represents a translation into opera and music of "the most negative features" of what it termed "Meyerholditis."[25] This target emerged more strongly a week later when another *Pravda* article condemned Shostakovich, this time for his ballet *The Limpid Stream* (Svetlyy ruchey), but the attack focused primarily on the libretto written by Piotrovsky in cooperation with Leningrad's leading choreographer F. Lopukhov, which was condemned for following the principle of *uslovnost'* and using puppet-like figures rather than realistic representations of its kolkhoz worker characters from the Kuban; symptomatic of this cavalier attitude toward realism, the article continued, was Shostakovich's reuse in this ballet of some music from his industrial ballet *The Bolt*.[26] Thereafter was orchestrated a general public discussion on Formalism and naturalism in art. The "discussion" of the parameters extended to most branches of the arts, and one after the other many of the most famous avant-gardists and modernists were obliged to come forward and disavow their previous work (although many dragged their feet on this, particularly in Leningrad).[27]

Meyerhold was a particular focus of the campaign. On December 17, 1937, Platon Kerzhentsev, then head of the State Committee on the Arts, which largely orchestrated this discussion, published an article about Meyerhold's theater in *Pravda* entitled "An Alien Theater" (Chuzhoy teatr), an event that heralded the theater's closing early in 1938 (Kerzhentsev signed the order).[28] Kerzhentsev was, ironically, the author of *The Creative Theater*, which, with its slogan of "the eternal studio" where the audience could say not "I am going to see something" but rather "I am going to participate in something," functioned throughout War Communism as the little red book inspiring the directors of the mass spectacles and other programs for realizing a truly people's theater (he was also considered generally sympathetic to Meyerhold's work).

Hence the need to save Meyerhold by having him direct *The Masquerade*. But all such attempts, including magnanimous gestures by his erstwhile opponent Stanislavsky, were in vain: he was arrested in June 1939 and shot as an enemy of the people in 1940; his wife and leading actress, Zinaida Raikh, was brutally murdered in their apartment shortly after his arrest.[29] Yuriev was officially credited with *The Masquerade*'s production.[30]

Among those who had fought for a revolutionary, people's theater, Meyerhold's fate was far from unique. Kerzhentsev was himself purged the same year as he signed the order to close Meyerhold's theater (1938). Piotrovsky was also arrested in that year, even earlier than Meyerhold.

Already in the Remand Center in Leningrad, an eyewitness, the poet N. Zabolotsky, reported, this visionary who had hoped to bring "Aeschylus' fiery soul" to the proletariat "had lost all human semblance in his grief, paced about the cell, scored his chest with a nail, and at night he did shameful things right in front of everyone in the cell";[31] he died in captivity that year. Radlov, regrettably one of those who had attacked Meyerhold, his erstwhile mentor, during the anti-Formalist campaign of the mid-1930s, was spared until the 1940s. During the war, in ambiguous circumstances he and his wife were taken to France by the German occupying forces, and on their return to Russia both were sent to the camps; she perished there in 1949, while he survived to die in 1958.[32]

There is an element of the arbitrary in who succumbs in a purge and who is elevated. Whereas Meyerhold was shot and Piotrovsky imprisoned, other actors in the heroic saga of theater reform in the 1920s (such as the Proletcult director A. A. Mgebrov) found an honored place in the Academic Theater, where *The Masquerade* was revived.[33] Shostakovich quickly recovered his status as a leading if embittered Soviet composer. One finds a similar pattern in literature. A prominent category of those who suffered during the purges of intellectuals in the Great Terror (1936–1939) was those who in the 1920s had been of a leftist or proletarian orientation, such as the leaders of RAPP, that is, Piotrovsky and Meyerhold's erstwhile archenemies. But while some leaders of RAPP were purged (Averbakh, Kirshon) and Libedinsky, who had gone to Leningrad in the late 1920s to set proletarian culture straight there came under suspicion and never recovered his status in literature, the RAPP leader Aleksandr Fadeyev was elevated in 1939 to First Secretary of the Writers Union, a post he held until Khrushchev came to power (he committed suicide in the wake of the anti-Stalinist revelations). At the same time Kaverin, that staunch champion of perceptual millenarianism, was in the 1930s to produce one of the classics of socialist realism, *The Two Captains* (Dva kapitana, 1938), without "capitulating" substantially (after Stalin died, he played an active role in literary destalinization, and in the 1970s and 1980s was a patron of "alternative" and dissident culture). And as for the Preservationists, while Benois, Dobuzhinsky, and some other leaders were in emigration, Benois's nephew E. Lanceray designed murals and ceiling panels for several iconic Stalinist buildings (the metro, the Hotel Moscow, the Palace of Soviets, and the Bolshoi) and went on to win a Stalin Prize for this work in 1943.

Although the patterns in purging individuals may have been inconsistent, the far-reaching effects of the anti-Formalist campaign of 1936 in restricting the parameters of Soviet culture should not be underestimated. The two

Pravda articles are unsigned—and hence all the more authoritative—but they clearly emanated from the highest levels (speculation has it that they issued either from Stalin or from Zhdanov). Allegedly, this entire series of events began when Stalin went to see *Lady Macbeth* and was outraged by the cacophonous music—it is said that his box was unfortunately over the percussion instruments. Was this major shift in the direction of Soviet culture, then, due to the arbitrary whims, tastes, or reactions of a potentate?

Here we have a situation comparable with the one Tolstoy discusses in *War and Peace* in which it is unclear whether a battle was "lost" by Napoleon because of this or that strategy, or military hardware, or degree of troop preparedness. Or was it "lost" because on that day Napoleon woke up with a cold? Obviously, when official cultural policy is made so radically restrictive more than Stalin's reactions to a specific opera are involved (though they may well have served as the immediate cause of the chain of events). The attack on naturalism and Formalism in the name of simplicity, accessibility, the natural, and the real has countless precedents in the cultural history of the Soviet Union and, mutatis mutandis, of prerevolutionary Russia and Europe. Similar attitudes inform Gorky's formulations for socialist realism and also the anti-Formalist campaign of 1929–1930.

The Party leaders did not invent these attitudes and policies, but rather had them implemented with singular rigor. The policies reflect prejudices widely found among Soviet intellectuals. The linguistic and visual puritanism of socialist realism proved persistent and generally outlived Stalin himself, as well as socialist realism. The ban on scatology, on so-called *nepristoynoe slovo,* was one of the last fortresses of Stalinist culture to fall, an event that really happened only after the Berlin Wall itself had gone.[34]

Nineteen thirty-six to nineteen thirty-eight was a time of extremism, a time when trends already apparent in 1931, such as Gorky's language strictures and their broader ramifications, were intensified and applied to the elimination of other trends and figures. It was a "peak" time. Somewhat analogously, in the preceding "peak" time of 1928–1931 such doctrines as "workerization," already established in 1924–1925, were applied more rigidly than ever before.

The struggle of Gorky between 1931 and 1934 to ensure that the language of high culture was used in Soviet literature can be seen as a struggle for normalization after a time of revolutionary extremism. That this was a period of normalization can also be seen in the fact that, starting with the formation of the Writers Union in 1932, the various branches of intellectual activity acquired their own separate guilds or unions. The goal of a single culture embracing all of the arts had been abandoned. Another sign of normalization was the partial retreat from the ideologically based extremism of the cultural revolution. Symptomatically, the Communist Academy was closed down and merged with the Academy of Sciences. With the publication of "Muddle instead of Music" and the ensuing anti-Formalist campaign, however, the policies that were intended to normalize intellectual activity were implemented with "catastrophic" force, eliminating a sizeable number of options for the culture's future evolution.

This pattern of "punctuated equilibrium" did not cease in the 1930s. The 1940s saw another bout of extremism in the anticosmopolitan campaign. Since the central thrust of state cultural policy in the 1940s was to secure the norms of socialist realism, however, "Stalinist" culture in its classical form had essentially evolved by the mid-1930s.

Stalin's interest in culture was not an arbitrary whim. He shared the intellectuals' faith in its transformative powers. But culture also functioned as a means of aggrandizement and legitimation. This was effected in part by cultural myths, but also by the myth of culture itself. Stalin had pretensions to expertise in a range of cultural fields and frequently acted as an arbiter in them while members of the Party leadership were pillars of high culture. Habitués of the Bolshoi, they could, from March 1936, watch operas such as *Quiet Flows the Don* by a composer with the felicitous name of [Ivan] Dzerzhinsky, hastily put on as a counter to Shostakovich's *Lady Macbeth.* Quiet flowed the Don, and quiet flowed Soviet culture.

Soviet culture flowed quietly in the sense that the central tension between monumentalism and iconoclasm had been resolved. Potentially iconoclastic tendencies were censored out. This was largely the meaning of the anti-Formalist campaign with the *Pravda* article on *Lady Macbeth* calling for "simplicity."

Yet, as this book has argued, for all the "totalitarian" xenophobia of the Stalin era, Western popular culture continued to be a major player throughout the 1930s. Its influence was particularly marked in film and music. Effectively, there was a division within culture into two bailiwicks: literature dominated by its titular head, Gorky, and film dominated by its titular head, Boris Shumyatsky. The reign of Shumyatsky, who sought to found a Hollywood in Soviet Russia, is best known for the Busby Berkeley–style, propagandistic musicals produced under him by Grigory Alexandrov (who in the 1920s had been Eisenstein's assistant director) in which the star was Alexandrov's wife, Lyubov Orlova, the heartthrob of the 1930s. Soviet film, which at that time attracted some of the best writers and composers, was closely implicated in the mania for the popular song that everyone recalls as the hallmark of those days.[35] Jazz and romances were thriving at the height of Lenten rule.

Thus Soviet culture of the 1930s may have been totalitarian, but it was far from homogenous or relentlessly grim. It became more "monolithic" in the 1940s when film conventions drew closer to the literary, but that was also the time when the culture lost much of its capacity to generate new paradigms as the state sought with particular zeal to safeguard the canons of socialist realism.

In the 1930s, however, many intellectuals had not given up all hope that they might pursue the Great Experiment. The framework in which it was to be conducted became ever more circumscribed, the perils of pursuing it ever more dire, but with the perspective of Nazi Germany to the West and increasing leftism among intellectuals in France and Central Europe, some hope could still be found.[36]

One of the principal focuses of new work was that old project "music," perhaps a reason why the "signal" article of the anti-Formalist campaign was addressed to a musical work (Shostakovich's *Lady Macbeth*). Music was extremely important in the culture of the 1930s. Examples range from Stalin's own fantasies of being an opera connoisseur and perhaps even a talented performer (one of the many facts of his biography that suggests the way his self-image may have been influenced by intellectual fads) to the role of military music and popular songs in consolidating allegiance. Many of the most talented intellectuals undertook serious work on producing films in which music played a crucial role. Music, opera, and musical theater were for them not just a means of livelihood; they were key vehicles of a regenerative project. Thus in many instances from the 1930s, as intellectuals worked on the music of films, lines of continuity from avant-garde experiments of the 1920s (especially from Leningrad) met "Stalinist" propagandistic projects closely supervised from above.[37] The lingering dream of a new wholeness to come from music can be seen in several of the most propagandistic films of the 1930s, such as the Vasiliev "brothers" *Chapaev* (1934), Kozintsev and Trauberg's *Youth of Maxim* (1935), and even films by those FEKS leaders' erstwhile co-conspirator from the early 1920s, Eisenstein, who in his own accounts of making *Alexander Nevsky* (1938) and *Ivan the Terrible* (Part I, 1944) foregrounds his quest for an "inner synchronicity between picture and music" along the lines of the Greeks, Nietzsche, and Wagner, a "single wholeness and higher unity."[38]

The famous Stalinist musicals of the 1930s and the popular musical theater of that time used material that derived not only from America but also from experimental work for a new musical theater done in Leningrad in the late 1920s.[39] Several of these shows, though essentially light musicals or revues, were staged in Leningrad's Academic Maly Opera Theater, one of Radlov's bases and the place where the new opera was launched in the Soviet Union. Some were produced by theater activists who had directed the mass spectacles (such as N. V. Petrov, before the Revolution a compere at the intellectuals' Stray Dog Cabaret); others by a director of Soviet highbrow theater Nikolai Akimov. Even Shostakovich tried his hand (in fact some of his compositions for one musical, *Declared Dead* [Uslovno ubityy], of 1931, were recycled for later works, including *Lady Macbeth*[40]). The key roles in these productions were played by Leonid Utësov and I. O. Dunaevsky, the two leading names in Soviet popular music of the 1930s and the two most responsible for the music in the Alexandrov films.[41]

Paradoxically, then, literature, run by an intellectual (Gorky), was more restricted than film, run by one of the proverbial "Party hacks" who were appointed to administer some area of culture even though they were not particularly educated and had no cultural experience (Shumyatsky had been a Party worker in Siberia before going to Leningrad as one of the "Stalinist" contingent of 1926 sent there to clean up that "Trotskyite" stronghold).

These few sketchy examples that bespeak the extremely complicated evolution and function of music and popular song in the films of the 1930s show that, however much the state bullied and applied censorship, it was not able to eradicate completely the agendas of intellectuals who found ways of prosecuting them, if in drastically reduced forms. These cases also illustrate how difficult it is to answer the question who made "Stalinist" culture (the regime? the intellectuals? particular groups? popular taste? or even Western trends?), or to suggest any kind of linear progression in its "evolution," or predictable trajectories through the 1920s and 1930s for individual actors in its "making." It is also worth noting that although the Party nomenklatura frequented the Bolshoi, they also loved jazz and popular music; Utësov was a personal favorite of Stalin. Analogously, was socialist realism propaganda doggerel, or was it an attempt, however jejunely realized, at translating intelligentsia ideals into actuality?

Sooner or later one has to ask the accursed question of Soviet cultural history, that old Leninist maxim "Who whom?"—in this case not who will get whom, but rather, who influenced whom? Although members of the Stalinist regime unquestionably created a new force field for culture, might it not be the case that the myths and models by which they were operating and which they were mandating to intellectuals had been influenced by ideas generated by intellectuals themselves?

The specific mix of narrative norms and practices that composed "Stalinist culture" was "made" as—a banal truism—a particular cultural ecosystem entered a particular historical moment. In the 1930s, the momentous upheavals of the purges notwithstanding, the Soviet Union had clearly passed through its revolutionary phase and was in a period of national consolidation.

Moscow: Capital of a Colonizing Power

During the 1930s, the Soviet Union established itself as a nation. In this process, it confronted a paradox. On the one hand, it was already a relatively old and long-established nation. But, on the other, the country had in some senses colonized itself; the Bolsheviks had formed a colony out of Russia.

When a new nation is formed, typically its leaders or intellectuals seek to establish a new and unique identity for the country and hence feel the need to give it a unique or new language. For example, when Indonesia became independent it sought a single national language where there existed only a host of languages and dialects, so it invented Bahasa Indonesia, a language that as such did not exist, but is made up from an amalgam based primarily on a Sumatran-cum-Malay dialect.

The development of socialist realism is in effect an aspect of nation building in the 1930s—providing new myths of cultural identity and a new "language." Like Bahasa Indonesia, socialist realism did not exist before it was instituted (in this instance before the term was coined in 1932), but it did not emerge *ex nihilo*. It was put together as an amalgam of previously existing theories and practices, many of them associated with revolutionary or proletarian culture.

The next defining act in establishing a cultural identity for the new nation, one that occurred at about the same time, was the creation of the myth of Moscow, the nation's capital. Although the city had since 1918 functioned as the seat of power in an increasingly centralized state, it was not yet inscribed on any scale into official myths. In some senses, therefore, the Petersburg era came to an end around 1931.

A great nation needs a capital adequate to its stature. Hence the "dead" center of the "bagel" cities that so many fled so resolutely in the dash to the periphery of the Plan years had to be revitalized. The center had to be repurified (social deviants were to be expelled), but it also had to be recast. This process began in 1931 at the June Plenum of the Central Committee, when members decided to replan all the major Soviet cities with the lion's share of money and resources allocated to Moscow.

The remaking of Moscow was partly an effort to redress a period of neglect, to repair and modernize the capital and its system of transportation. But the urban revitalization was conceived as the nodal moment in the new direction the country would take; the First Five-Year Plan was entering its last phase and the Party leadership was already stocktaking and planning the second. In official speeches and *Pravda* editorials of that year (1931), a particular historical model based on architectural tropes provided the framework for the various new policies proposed: allegedly, with the Revolution, the leadership had cleared away the old; during the 1920s, and particularly with the industrialization and collectivization during the Plan, they had built the "foundation" of the new society; and now it was time to erect the "socialist building" *(zdaniye)*.[42] As Party leaders expanded on this new model, however, they concluded that it was time to rebuild Moscow as the "model" for the new socialist cities of the country, and as a model for proletarians and Communists throughout the world who would be inspired to follow it. Outlines of what such a rebuilding would entail effectively reversed the model of compromised center / purer periphery *(okraina)* that had underwritten so much cultural production during the Plan years; rather than transpose the center of cultural life to the "periphery," those implementing the changes would further purify the "center" as a domain of culture; there was to be a ban on building industrial plants in Moscow, and the number of residential buildings in its central areas was to be substantially reduced.[43]

In the rhetoric surrounding these new proposals, actual building and practical considerations are conflated with ideological models. Drawing on the fact that Marx and Engels had used terms from construction for their primary model for society—base / superstructure—Party rhetoric used the building of Moscow as the central figure for, and legitimation of, the increasing "bolshevization" (colonization) and centralization (or some would say "totalitarianization") of the country.

With the ban on further industrialization of the capital, the romance of the proletarian was beginning to wear thin. Now frequently the adjective "socialist," or more particularly "bolshevik," was interpolated in places where one might have expected to see "proletarian."[44] Even *bol'shoy*, as in such new catchphrases as "the big man" or "great literature," sharing as it does a common root with "bolshevik" (originally coined to give the illusion that Lenin's faction was the majority in the Party), suggests a model citizenry and culture marked by its loyalty to the colonizing regime. At this time one also finds in rhetoric increasing reference to the principle of *par-*

tiynost', which can be somewhat crudely translated as "Party-mindedness" but essentially meant active loyalty to the new regime.

The downplaying of "proletarian" also meant de-emphasis on the class basis of historical progress—bolshevization rather than sociological bouleversement. Significantly, the Great Unwashed were now not to occupy the center of the new capital, as had occurred on a symbolic level in the mass spectacles of 1920 and in actuality in resettlement policies of the 1920s, but rather to be at least partially redirected to the suburbs. If the Party no longer had such a clear class mandate to lead, however, it had, as if in compensation, to promote itself as extraordinary, the most common meaning of *bol'shoy* (big, great). Actually, the main speech to the Plenum about urban revitalization invoked the Leninist maxim "Every female cook should rule the state," but now it was used to introduce proposals in the more domestic context of providing nurseries, children's playgrounds, and so on. The new society was to be achieved by paternalistic munificence rather than by revolutionary seizure; speakers outlining proposals for urban revitalization foregrounded the Party's concern with workers' "well-being."

The Party presided very literally over the rebuilding of the capital. Lazar Kaganovich, a member of the leadership (he was first secretary of the Moscow Party Committee from 1930–1935 but also a manager of collectivization) who made the main speech at the Plenum on the rebuilding of Moscow, functioned as institutional head of the enterprise, his remarks the locus classicus. In 1933 Stalin created an architectural review board, Arkhplan, also headed by Kaganovich, who was given the power to amend any proposal submitted for approval. In effect, Kaganovich became the great patron of architecture. In the 1910s the Preservationists had sought just such a patron, and their style of architecture (Neoclassicism) was now favored.

As the center of Moscow was remade and aggrandized, the city finally became the symbol for the nation. There was no architectural pathos left in Leningrad; indeed, although some gestures were made toward rebuilding it as a "model" city, *its* model was to be the new Moscow.

As Moscow grew in status, Leningrad's erstwhile role as center of the Russian intelligentsia was increasingly undermined. In 1934, the Academy of Sciences' headquarters and many of its institutes were moved to Moscow. This decimated the city's scholarly community. It is, however, only the most dramatic instance of the Petersburg diaspora, a diaspora that began immediately after the Revolution and continues to the present day as emigration, purges, and the lure of the money and power available in the capital have chronically leached the city's intellectual community. The problem for the city's intellectuals was not only the fact that they were losing their talent and resources, however, but also the fact that their city—"Petersburg"—functioned as a symbolic home of alternative culture (or cultures). Virtually every time there were major campaigns against creative intellectuals, figures from Leningrad were singled out as the negative paradigms. For instance, the anti-Formalist campaign of the mid-1930s hit many of the most prominent figures in Leningrad cultural life. But this was to be the pattern. In the next major campaign, in 1946, some of the city's leading writers, including Akhmatova and Zoshchenko, and literary journals (*Zvezda, Leningrad*) were scored in an attack by the Party's spokesman on ideological matters, Andrei Zhdanov (*Leningrad* was closed down and Zoshchenko and Akhmatova could publish little until the Khrushchev years).

Was Petersburg, then, to return to the "nothingness" from which it arose, as some versions of the Petersburg myth had insisted it would? Actually, even while, in the 1930s, the cultural reserves of the old capital were fast being depleted, in many senses "Petersburg" (as opposed to Leningrad) experienced a resurgence.

Petersburg had played, and would continue to play in manifold ways, a major role in the formation of Stalinist culture. As Moscow was rebuilt it was turned into a Petersburgian city; it was "clad in granite" (as Pushkin had described Petersburg in *The Bronze Horseman*), its waterways were "tamed," and it was given monumental buildings together with those other features so sought after by the Preservationists of the 1910s—clear spaces, grand vistas, and imposing facades[45] (another city redesigned in the late 1930s, Novorossiisk, was explicitly intended to be yet another "Northern Venice"). The original proposals called for "straighten[ing] out the . . . crooked streets and lanes," "to broaden them and eliminate that jumble [*pëstrota*, a negative label for the Preservationists] . . . of structures there at present."[46] Thus in that old battle between Moscow and Petersburg, two cities whose characteristic street formations stood for radically opposed world views, Petersburg had won. But it might also be said that "straightening out" crooked lanes (the iconic Moscow streets) was a standard gesture of modernization (under which the myth of Petersburg can be subsumed); that and building broad streets (better for troops to march up) were also standard moves of imperial or militaristic powers.

Hitler had a comparable plan for rebuilding the center of Berlin as a monumental city, but it was largely unrealized.[47] Central Moscow was substantially rebuilt, though most of the grandiose plans for public buildings were never executed. The funding required was simply not there and in the 1930s some of the more banal projects, such as the Hotel Moscow, were built while the more ambitious were not.

The projected colossi of the new Moscow which were never built, such as the Ministry for Heavy Industry, should not be seen as merely cases where ambition outran the pocketbook. In the Stalinist 1930s, architecture, the building of a new city grander than any thus far realized and embodying the fundamental ideals, was a key trope.

While literature reigned supreme as *the* art form—the flagship of Soviet culture—and film and popular song functioned as auxiliaries more consciously targeted at popular audiences, architecture, the architectonics of spatial arrangement, was the iconic—ideal—cultural form that underwrote all three. So many novels and films of this time include a fleeting segment involving a vision or even the construction of a fantastic city that emerges phantom-like *ex nihilo* (or from the rubble created by an orgy of dynamiting) and is often gleaming white. Such scenes had their visionary, mirage-like quality because, as with the grandiose plans for public building in Moscow, they were not representations of reality but more proleptic rhetorical devices. They were both a promise of the great and glorious future as yet not totally realized and a template, a guiding model. As proleptic devices, they are also anticipated in Zhdanov's capsule definition of socialist realism made at the First Writers Congress: "A combination of the most matter of fact, everyday reality and the most heroic prospects."

Let us return here to the horseman speeding toward Moscow, the projected ending of Pudovkin's *Storm over Asia*, discussed at the end of the last chapter as a paradigm for the new conventions emerging in Stalinist culture of the 1930s for reconciling center and periphery. In this projected ending, as in so much subsequent cultural production, the new Soviet citizen is yearning, impending, toward the "heroic prospects" Zhdanov stipulated; their symbolic embodiment is Moscow and its buildings. In Pudovkin's film, a gleaming city is a beacon that orients the horseman as he keeps quickening his frenzied pace. As he presses his pace to an absolute extreme, the beacon is revealed to be the city of Moscow. At that point he has, as it were, entered into a hyperspace that transforms the familiar terrain of the Central Asian steppe (somewhat as a plane or rocket might in theory attain such a high speed that it would first break the sound, and then, ultimately, the light barrier). Many of the more visionary Russian thinkers from before the Revolution, such as Nikolai Fyodorov, spoke of "overcoming time" *(pre-odoleniye vremeni)*. The rocket engineer Konstantin Tsiolkovsky wanted to reach, in the words of his science fiction novel first published in full after the Revolution, "beyond the earth" *(vne zemli)* to that "freedom" that is not undermined by gravity's pull. Here, of course, the model also intersects with the perceptual millenarianist scenario of a journey at breakneck speed to a radical otherness—or of the Scythians' call to "renounce time" and hurtle across the steppe, wild and free (see Chapter 1). A crucial difference between the Stalinist paradigm and these earlier models, however, is that the gesture is no longer centrifugal; it is centripetal and the route is not "wild and free," but charted, or planned. Indeed, by the 1930s it was not just intellectual visionaries who spoke of "overcoming time." Stalin in a famous speech of 1931 said that the country was behind the West by fifty to one hundred years but would make up the gap in ten (his formulation was thus less extravagant and more pragmatic than the intellectuals').[48]

In the 1930s, the city of Moscow functioned as a kind of hyperspace that had transcended time and was hence of a different order of reality from that of familiar parts (Stalin, its human counterpart, was also of a different temporal order—of being, rather than becoming—and so was depicted in film and art as static and vertical or, if moving at all, doing so at an exaggeratedly slow and deliberate, monument-like pace). But the capital also had a very real, concrete, and even banal existence.

Architecture is in some senses the most concrete and material of all art forms, but at the same time—as architectonics—one of the most abstract. It functioned in Stalinist culture much like the icon in Russian Orthodox culture in that it had simultaneous existence in two orders of reality, both sacred and profane. Like Alice's looking glass, it reflected an image and yet was also a portal.

Thus some architecture already in place functioned no less than the visionary designs as emblems and legitimators of the new order. In this respect, Alexandrov's hit musical *The Circus* (Tsirk, 1936) provides paradigmatic moments. In the film, the hero and heroine first come together as they compose a song at the grand piano in a stateroom of the Hotel Moscow; its opening line is "Broad is my native land." This song went on to enjoy a curious status as simultaneously one of the most popular songs of the decade and also, de facto, an auxiliary national anthem. In subsequent shots from the film, first the Kremlin looms into view on one side of the hotel, and then the Bolshoi on the other. As it were, the two buildings flank the site where the song is composed as guarantors of its political and cultural legitimacy (and hence of the new nation—"native land"—that the song extols). Architecture guards the sacred. But at the same time it also guards an enhanced profane. When the Kremlin appears, it is at the window of the heroine's luxurious stateroom, and the Bolshoi looms into view while some characters are eating frivolous cream cakes in the hotel's roof garden; in other words, both buildings rear up in the background as patrons of the new good life. Yet both these buildings are emblems not of the new Moscow, but of the old.

Moscow did not get a new center. On the contrary, the gigantic Palace of Soviets that was intended to recenter the capital was never built and its traditional center (the Kremlin) was reinforced as the symbol of the nation and its leaders. Similarly, the Great Tradition of Russian culture had been revived, to be seen in such examples as the restaging of *The Masquerade*, something that was unthinkable during the cultural revolution.[49] But it might be said that the revival of *Masquerade*, now without its Meyerholdian bite, was a kind of second-order masquerade, a masquerade of a masquerade, and as such a sort of synecdoche for Stalinist culture. It might seem that, with the "Petersburgization" of Moscow and the return to prominence of the Academy of Sciences, together with the emphasis on heavy industry, defense, and modernization, Peter the Great (the founder of the Academy of Sciences) and his values had triumphed over "obscurantist," retrograde Moscow. This triumph of a secular order where the arts and sciences flourished had been prepared for in the cultural revolution; one of its principal thrusts had been against religion and the church. But this triumph of the values of "Peter" was deceptive. Or, rather, only one meaning of Peter had been comparably achieved—Peter as Imperial potentate.

The new Moscow, like Petersburg, was largely designed using Neoclassical or Renaissance models as an Empire style. Nikolai Punin had, in his laudatory article on Tatlin's tower of 1920, declared that thereby the traditions of the classical and the Renaissance had been reduced to "ashes," but their resurgence should not be read merely as the victory of Stalinist entropic forces over the avant-garde. In fact both Tatlin and Malevich (especially in his portraits of 1932–1934) had themselves begun to draw inspiration from the Renaissance; already in 1929–1932 Tatlin had worked on Letatlin, an individual (as the name implies) flying machine closely linked to the famous project of Leonardo.

In Moscow's new architecture the Empire style was not maintained consistently; it also appropriated Russian national and Gothic styles, although the Neoclassical predominated.[50] The adoption of Neoclassical models suited the historical moment but its strictures were never followed with rigor (the famous wedding cakes, actually erected in the late 1940s and 1950s, in effect conflate the classical, Gothic, and national traditions, but another, unacknowledged model is the new architecture of New York and Chicago). The buildings erected in Moscow are full of needless ornamentation (Albrecht Speer's designs for Berlin realize more consistently the Neoclassical ideals). Essentially, each style was favored for its monumental potential and because it had a suitable pedigree establishing heroic precedents.

The apparent revival of Neoclassicism and the setting up of Arkhplan to oversee the more systematic rebuilding of the capital and other major cities suggest the possibility that some of the agendas and ideals of the prerevolutionary intellectuals were now being realized after that "hiatus" of revolutionary upheaval (even though, admittedly, Arkhplan resembled the old Imperial Chamber more than it resembled a branch of the Ministry for the Arts). Perhaps, to invoke this book's central trope of "ecology," many of the old "flora and fauna" had essentially survived the "cataclysms," though of course they had undergone mutations. The Soviet Union was now entering an obsessively citational period, but the constant need to establish precedent also tended toward a more conservative culture; does recycled but "reframed" material represent "continuity" or "change"? Often, in a pattern somewhat akin to the one Fernand Braudel outlines in *On History*, the changes amounted to the "resurfacing" of dormant paradigms. One can also find marked continuities. Any account of the movement from the 1920s and the 1930s made in terms of (predominant) "continuity" or (predominant) "change" is inadequate to the dynamic, however. Though many features of High Stalinist culture had been present before, under the impact of the new historical conditions there had been significant restructuring and reinflection of these features.

As we saw in the example of the most famous Neoclassical artist, David, who served in succession the aristocracy under Louis XVI, the successive leaders of the French Revolution, and then Napoleon, Neoclassicism is often the name of a marriage between political power and the intellectual elite. In a state as highly politicized as the Soviet Union was in the 1930s, style cannot be all. The shift in that decade to new styles in art, architecture, and literature can be seen as surface manifestations of a shift to a new function for culture, and hence for intellectuals as well.

As the Russian intelligentsia went into the Revolution, they hoped to function as Hermes figures who might mediate between the language of a higher truth and that of the imperfect world around them. Many were particularly attracted by the possibility that they might act as the great demystifiers. Now, however, their role was closer to that of the comprador. By comprador I mean that special institution that emerged in the era of European economic domination in Asia. The comprador was the non-European who mediated between the local people and the European commercial enclave. He spoke two languages, the vernacular (his own language) and that of the particular European community he served. Originally, he spoke the European language only haltingly. Over time, he became increasingly fluent in it.

By the 1930s, the typical Soviet intellectual had become a comprador in that his task was to mediate between the language of high culture, which he spoke "natively," and that of his masters, the language of ideology and power. At first, he might speak the latter imperfectly, but in time the successful comprador passed more and more for a member of the elite group. He could enjoy many of its privileges (cream cakes), but only as long as his linguistic skills proved useful.

Earlier, in 1921, the intellectuals' turn to Pushkin after a bout of revolutionary extremism had been a kind of *reculer* to the old values and standards and a show of intelligentsia solidarity during what Eikhenbaum had called a "moment of truth" when they feared that "history" might be passing them by. What the intelligentsia did not realize then was that though the Soviet state they so feared was to be an oppressor, it was also in some senses to be their savior (particularly for those who felt that the Great Tradition was threatened). This paradoxical message was received most loudly in the 1930s. The state's role as oppressor is all too evident in tales such as the story of the Meyerholds' fate. But as savior it would stem the tide of historical evolution, inflating artificially the numbers of intellectuals, according them a highly privileged role in society, insulating them in unions of creative workers, institutes, and publishing houses (all bankrolled by the state), and staving off the devolution of nineteenth-century literature as compared with the West, where the grand old novel and other such cumbersome baggage of earlier eras had been downgraded. Above all, the state would save them from the market, from reckoning with flux. Small wonder so many of the Romantic Anticapitalists of Central Europe were burrowing away in the institutes of Moscow during the 1930s. In this respect, the real "moment of truth" would come not with the entrenchment of the Soviet regime in the 1930s and beyond, but with its dissolution and the turn to a market economy after the system's collapse in the 1990s.

But what of the intellectuals' original projects and dreams? Clearly, the Hermes role had been pre-empted by Stalin, who was now represented as the one who, uniquely, could "see, really see." But did Stalin pre-empt this role, or was he inscribed into it by "hacks"? And again, one might trace a line through the mass spectacles of the early 1920s and the work on the new opera to some of the musicals of the 1930s, but of course a clearer line led to the parade on Red Square, which was in some senses those spectacles' apotheosis. In the 1930s, the mass ritual celebrating a revolutionary anniversary (May Day or November 7) no longer included a theatrical centerpiece but mostly comprised what Siegfried Kracauer has called the "mass ornament" (physical culture formations often organized around banners, portraits, slogans, or fetishized objects symbolizing political, military, or industrial achievement). This was not in itself the most telling difference, however. If in the spectacles of the early 1920s "the people" were to be transformed by a ritual enactment of transgression, by occupying the space of the hegemonic classes, now they were to process across Red Square, past the reviewing stand, and on beyond it as rapidly as possible. For all its "ornamentation," the parade was essentially a candidate for the world's longest receiving line; it was an act of homage. An analogous pattern is to be found in that other sacred ritual, viewing Lenin's body in the mausoleum (which, after a long wait in line, was seen for only a matter of seconds as the viewer filed past).

The parade was a ritual affirmation of the "center" (locus of power) rather than an act of iconoclasm or demystification. "The people" were never really to occupy that hegemonic space. In actuality, had they tried to climb the stairs (of the reviewing stand), as had the oppressed classes in *The Mystery of Liberated Labor*, they would have been shot. The reviewing stand-cum-mausoleum was placed outside the Kremlin walls and only a chosen few from "the people"—primarily heroes of aviation, sports, culture, or production—were taken inside for an actual meeting with the great leader, which was itself generally represented in rhetoric as an epiphanic moment.

Such rituals reaffirmed the central hierarchy of the new society vested in a symbolic hierarchy of place. The leadership's place was at the center; the place of the "people" was at the periphery (most socialist realist novels are set there), and the parades and formalized meetings represent a brief moment of contiguity—not really even meeting—between center and periphery (they have to be as brief as possible lest the aura of the center dim). Their function is, as with the mass spectacles of the 1920s, to transform the participants (generally in proportion to their getting closer to the great leader); they are to be inspired to return to their place at the periphery to work to make it as much as possible like the center, to make it less peripheral. The division between center and periphery is nevertheless absolute and untransgressable. In scenarios such as that projected for the ending of *Storm over Asia*, the exemplary citizen might make a frenzied "ride" toward the capital (perform extraordinary feats) in an effort to bridge the gap, but he will never actually reach "Moscow." Like the perceptual millenarian, he can enjoy the thrill of the dramatic quest, but he will never be oppressed by the enigma of arrival.

Thus, in essence, these rituals were neither centripetal nor centrifugal events. They neither enacted revolution as an explosion that eliminated the hegemonic center, nor enacted it as a centripetal event whereby the "periphery" takes over. The ritual was closer to enacting another agenda shared by many intellectuals in the prerevolutionary period who saw the panacea for the profane not in terms of revolution, not even in rituals of revolution, but in terms of elevating the intelligentsia to a greater status enabled by consolidating a center, a pure culture, unsullied by commerce and secured by norms.

When Moscow was redesigned in the 1930s, an important aspect of the transformations, much heralded at the time, was to clean out the stalls and petty shopkeepers *(lavochniki)*. The intellectuals had finally found a "Christ" who would drive the moneychangers out and purify the polis as a temple of that secular religion called culture. But the city's status as preserve of the sacred was a chimera (a masquerade), as was their sacerdotal role in it. They were kept by the center, but only as compradors. Just as Nietzsche was disillusioned with Bayreuth and mourned the way Wagner's original conception had been profaned by an "imperialist" mentality, the intellectuals could see their ideals for culture realized in only the most bowdlerized version as an imperial sublime. Culture served power rather than vice versa. And there was blood all around.

ABBREVIATIONS

NOTES

ACKNOWLEDGMENTS

INDEX

ABBREVIATIONS

A	*Apollon*
Ar	*Argonavty*
As	*Argus*
B	*Beseda*
BG	*Byuleten' GAKhN*
Bv	*Birzhevye vedomosti*
G	*Gryadushcheye*
Ge	*Germes*
Gf	*Gazeta futuristov*
I	*Izvestiya*
Ig	*Igra*
Ii	*Izobrazitel'noye iskusstvo*
Ik	*Iskusstvo kommuny*
Iko	*Iskusstvo kino*
IPs	*Izvestiya Petrogradskogo soveta*
Kg	*Krasnaya gazeta*
Kir	*Kniga i revolyutsiya*
Km	*Krasnyy militsioner*
Kn	*Krasnaya nov'*
K-n	*Kino-nedelya*
Kp	*Krasnaya panorama*
KP	*Komsomol'skaya Pravda*
Ku	*Knizhnyy ugol*
Kz	*Kinovedcheskiye zapiski*
L	*Lef*
Lg	*Literaturnaya gazeta*
Lgd	*Leningrad*
Lii	*Literatura i iskusstvo*
Lim	*Literatura i marksizm*
Lkta	*Lyubov' k trëm apel'sinam*
Lo	*Literaturnoye obozreniye*

LP	*Leningradskaya Pravda*
Lz	*Literaturnye zapiski*
Mg	*Molodaya gvardiya*
Mi	*Mir iskusstva*
N	*Nachala*
Niyer	*Nauka i yeyë rabotniki*
Nk	*Novaya kniga*
Nl	*Novyy lef*
Nlp	*Na literaturnom postu*
Nm	*Novyy mir*
Nr	*Nauchnyy rabotnik*
Nrk	*Novaya russkaya kniga*
Nz	*Novaya zhizn'*
O	*Ogonëk*
Os	*Ocharovannyy strannik*
P	*Pravda*
Pir	*Pechat' i revolyutsiya*
Pl	*Plamya*
PP	*Petrogradskaya Pravda*
Pzm	*Pod znamenem marksizma*
R	*Rech'*
Rit	*Rabochiy i teatr*
Rs	*Russkiy sovremennik*
Rso	*Russkoye slovo*
S	*Smena*
Sa	*Sovremennaya arkhitektura*
Sk	*Sovetskaya kul'tura*
Sm	*Sovetskaya muzyka*
Som	*Soyuz molodëzhi*
St	*Sovremennyy teatr*
Sz	*Sovremennyy zapad*
T	*Teatr*
Tii	*Teatr i iskusstvo*
V	*Veshch' / Gegenstand / Objet*
Vl	*Vestnik literatury*
Vo	*Vneshkol'noye obrazovaniye*
Vopzitil	*Vestnik obshchestvenno-politicheskoy zhizni iskusstva, teatra i literatury*
Vt	*Vestnik teatra*
Vtonkpp	*Vremennik teatral'nogo otdela narodnogo kommissariata po prosveshcheniyu*
Yeit	*Yezhegodnik imperatorskikh teatrov*
Yail	*Yazyk i literatura*
Z	*Zvezda*
Zi	*Zhizn' iskusstva*
ZptGiS	*Zapiski peredvizhnogo teatra Gaydeburova i Skarskoy*

NOTES

Introduction: The Ecology of Revolution

1. David Remnick, *Lenin's Tomb: The Last Days of the Soviet Empire* (New York: Vintage Books, 1984), p. 332.

2. Gennadiy Gor, "Zamedleniye vremeni," *Z*, no. 4 (1968), p. 179.

3. The novel saw three main redactions: the first was published in the journal *Sirin* between 1913 and 1914, the second in Berlin in 1922, and the third in Moscow in 1928.

4. Andrei Bely, *Petersburg*, trans. Robert A. Maguire and John E. Malmstad (Bloomington: Indiana University Press, 1978), p. 2.

5. The original name, Sankt-Piterburkh, was actually Dutch.

6. Among the major interpretive studies of this myth are Yuri M. Lotman, "The Symbolism of St. Petersburg," in *The Universe of the Mind: A Semiotic Theory of Culture*, trans. Ann Shukman (Bloomington: Indiana University Press, 1990), pp. 191–202, and the articles in *Semiotika goroda i gorodskoy kul'tury: Peterburg*, an issue of *Trudy po znakovym sistemam*, XVIII (Tartu, 1984), esp. its version of the Lotman article and V. N. Toporov, "Peterburg i Peterburgskiy tekst russkoy literatury (vvedeniye v temu)," pp. 4–29.

7. The noted scholar of the Petersburg myth N. Antsiferov documents the many discrepancies between the myth and historical fact in his *Byl' i mif Peterburga* (Petersburg: Brokgauz i Efron, 1924).

8. See Edward Shils, "Center and Periphery," in *Center and Periphery: Essays in Macrosociology* (Chicago: University of Chicago Press, 1975).

9. See Carl E. Schorske, "The Idea of the City in European Thought: Voltaire to Spengler," in Oscar Handlin and John Burchard, eds., *The Historian and the City* (Cambridge, Mass.: M.I.T. and Harvard University Presses, 1963), pp. 95–114.

10. Clifford Geertz, "Centers, Kings, and Charisma: Reflections on the Symbolics of Power," in Sean Wilentz, ed., *Rites of Power: Symbolism, Ritual, and Politics since the Middle Ages* (Philadelphia: University of Pennsylvania Press, 1985), p. 30.

11. The most influential text in this development was N. M. Karamzin's *Memoir of Ancient and Modern Russia* (Zapiski o drevney i novoy Rossii), circa 1811.

12. N. Antsiferov, *Dusha Peterburga* (Petersburg: Brokgauz i Efron, 1922), p. 27.

13. During the 1920s, most major works of fiction involved some reworking of the Petersburg myth. Examples range from Ye. Zamyatin's dystopian novel *We* (My, 1920), then banned from publication, to F. Gladkov's socialist realist classic and prototype of the production novel, *Cement* (Tsement, 1925).

14. Donald Fanger, *Dostoevsky and Romantic Realism: A Study of Dostoevsky in Relation to Balzac, Dickens, and Gogol* (Cambridge, Mass.: Harvard University Press, 1965).

15. Lewis Mumford, *The City in History* (New York: Harcourt, Brace and Jovanovich, 1961), p. 49.

16. This was the position taken by many in the avant-garde (see Chapter 1) and also by writers such as Boris Pilnyak in *The Naked Year* (Golyy god, 1922).

17. Brodsky's essay "A Guide to a Renamed City" (1979, reprinted in Joseph Brodsky, *Less Than One: Selected Essays* [New York: Farrar, Straus and Giroux, 1986]) provides one of the most eloquent accounts of the meaning of "Petersburg" and its fate in the Soviet period. See also Yevgeniy Rein, "Sotoye Zerkalo: Zapozdalye vospominaniya," *Z*, no. 12 (1991), esp. pp. 189–192, 193, 195.

18. Thomas Mann, "Tod in Venedig," in Thomas Mann, *Gesammelte Werke*, vol. IX (Berlin: Aufbau-Verlag, 1955), esp. pp. 489, 490, 508, 524–525, 529.

19. James H. Bater, "Between Old and New: St. Petersburg in the Late Imperial Era," in Michael F. Hamm, ed., *The City in Late Imperial Russia* (Bloomington: Indiana University Press, 1986), pp. 58–60.

20. Peter Stallybrass and Allon White, *The Politics and Poetics of Transgression* (Ithaca, N.Y.: Cornell University Press, 1986), for example, p. 145.

21. Fernand Braudel, *On History*, trans. Sarah Mathews (Chicago: University of Chicago Press, 1980), esp. pp. 3–4.

22. See Braudel's statement "But the step [for the historian] from bright surface [events] to murky depths—from noise to silence—is difficult and dangerous" (ibid., p. 39).

23. *Capital* is available in different redactions, but see Chapter 15 in the Penguin Classics edition of 1990 (trans. Ben Fowkes), p. 493.

24. Zeev Sternhell, with Mario Snajder and Maia Asheri, *The Birth of Fascist Ideology*, trans. David Maisel (Princeton: Princeton University Press, 1994), pp. 5, 6, 7, 3.

25. See Michael Löwy, "Naphta or Settembrini? Lukacs and Romantic Anticapitalism," *New German Critique*, no. 42 (Fall 1987), esp. p. 18.

26. G. Lukács, "Über den Dostojewski Nachlass," *Moskauer Rundschau* (March 1931).

27. See Robert Sayre and Michael Löwy, "Figures of Romantic Anticapitalism," *New German Critique*, no. 32 (Spring–Summer 1984), pp. 42–91.

28. See Aleksey Kruchënykh's "Heights" (Vysoty), first published in *The Croaked Moon* (Dokhlaya luna, Moscow, 1913).

29. Richard Pipes, *Struve: Liberals on the Right, 1905–1944* (Cambridge, Mass.: Harvard University Press, 1980), pp. 67, 79–80, 180–184, 190; Alfred J. Rieber, *Merchants and Entrepreneurs in Imperial Russia* (Chapel Hill: University of North Carolina Press, 1982), pp. 261, 277–278, 297, 319–322.

30. See, for example, E. J. Hobsbawm, "Intellectuals and Communism," Chapter 4 of *Revolutionaries: Contemporary Essays* (New York: Pantheon Books, 1973).

31. See Alexander Bogdanov, *Sotsializm nauki* (Moscow: Proletarskaya kul'-tura, 1918), p. 15.

32. See, for example, Siegfried Kracauer, "Der kleinen Laden Mädchen gehen ins Kino," *Frankfurter Zeitung*, March 11–19, 1927; O. Kameneva, "Plany budushchego," *Zi*, no. 6–7 (1919), p. 74; Lenin in *State and Revolution* uses the terms *meshchanskiy* and *melkoburzhuaznyy* with even greater opprobrium than *burzhuaznyy*; V. I. Lenin, "Gosudarstvo i revolyutsiya," in N. Lenin (V. Ul'yanov), *Sobraniye sochineniy*, vol. XIV (Moscow and Petrograd: Goz. izd., 1921), pp. 311, 316, 323, 324, 355.

33. See Katerina Clark, "Not For Sale: The Russian / Soviet Intelligentsia, Prostitution, and the Paradox of Internal Colonization," in Gregory Freidin, ed., *Russian Culture in Transition*, a special edition of *Stanford Slavic Studies*, vol. VII (1993).

34. This term was coined by Friedrich Meinecke in 1912. See Wolfgang J. Mommsen, *Max Weber und die deutsche Politik, 1890–1920* (Tübingen, 1959), pp. 188–206.

35. V. I. Lenin, *What Is To Be Done?* (Chto delat', Stuttgart: J. W. H Dietz, 1902).

36. Fritz K. Ringer, *The Decline of the German Mandarins: The German Academic Community, 1890–1933* (Cambridge, Mass.: Harvard University Press, 1969), esp. p. 7.

37. See also Noel Annan's remarks on the "aristocracy of the intellect" in nine-teenth-century Britain, in *Leslie Stephen: The Godless Victorian* (London: Weiden-feld and Nicolson, 1984), esp. p. 3.

38. See, for example, Walter Gropius's "Programme of the Staatliches Bauhaus in Weimar" (April 1919).

39. See the article by F. F. Zelinsky (the moving force behind *Hermes*), "Antich-nost' i klassicheskoye obrazovaniye," *Ge*, no. 1 (January-July, 1918), pp. 17–34.

40. Katerina Clark, "Political History and Literary Chronotope: Some Soviet Case Studies," in Gary Saul Morson, ed., *Literature and History: Theoretical Prob-lems and Russian Case Studies* (Stanford: Stanford University Press, 1986), esp. pp. 232–233.

41. Nadezhda Mandelshtam writes in her memoirs of how Radlov tried to recruit her husband for his group; *Hope Abandoned*, trans. Max Hayward (New York: Atheneum, 1970), p. 120.

42. Boris Groys, *The Total Art of Stalinism: Avant-Garde, Aesthetic Dictatorship, and Beyond*, trans Charles Rougle (Princeton: Princeton University Press, 1992).

43. Paul Ricoeur, *Freud and Philosophy: An Essay on Interpretation*, trans. Denis Savage (New Haven: Yale University Press, 1970), p. 27.

44. Karl Marx, *Das Kapital* (Berlin: Dietz Verlag, 1989), p. 791.

1. Revolution as Revelation: The Avant-Garde

1. See Gail Harrison Roman and Virginia Hagelstein Marquardt, eds., *Avant-Garde Frontier: Russia Meets the West, 1910–1930* (Gainesville: University of Florida Press, 1992).

2. Katerina Clark, "The Avant-Garde and the Retrospectivists as Players in the Evolution of Stalinist Culture," in John Bowlt and Olga Matich, eds., *Laboratory of Dreams* (Stanford: Stanford University Press, 1995).

3. Walter Benjamin, "Surrealism: The Last Snapshot of the European Intelligentsia," *Reflections*, trans. Edmund Jephcott (New York: Schocken Books, 1986), pp. 179–180.

4. See the memoirs of L. Zheverzheyev in *Mayakovskomu: Sbornik statey* (Leningrad, 1940).

5. See Aleksey Kruchënykh, "Novye puti slova" (a possible source of the term *zaum*), in V. Khlebnikov, E. Guro, and A. Kruchënykh, *Troye* (Petersburg, 1913), pp. 23–33.

6. V. Shklovsky, "Iskusstvo kak priyëm," in *Sbornik po teorii poeticheskogo yazyka* (Petrograd, 1917), p. 7.

7. Ibid., pp. 7, 8. In a footnote to the latter quotation Shklovsky refers to a similar point he made in *Voskresheniye slova*.

8. Ibid.

9. V. Shklovsky, *Voskresheniye slova* (Petrograd, 1914); A. Parnis and R. Timenchik, "Programmy 'Brodyachey sobaki,' " in *Pamyatniki kul'tury: Novye otkrytiya 1983* (Leningrad, 1985), p. 221.

10. See, for example, his essays of 1929: "The Cinematographic Principle and the Ideogram" and "A Dialectical Approach to Film Form," in Sergei Eisenstein, *Film Form: Essays in Film Theory*, trans. Jay Leyda (New York: Harcourt, Brace and World, 1949).

11. Paul C. Vitz and Arnold B. Glimcher in their *Modern Art and Modern Science: The Parallel Analysis of Vision* (New York: Praeger, 1983) explore the interdependence of developments in modern art with explorations in science and psychology done in the wake of the Kantian revolution (see esp. pp. 248–249).

12. Robert Motherwell, ed., *The Dada Painters and Poets* (Cambridge, Mass.: Harvard University Press, 1989), pp. 192, 306.

13. See, for example, V. Khlebnikov and A. Kruchënykh's "Slovo kak takovoye" (1913).

14. Marjorie Perloff, *The Futurist Moment: Avant Garde, Avant Guerre, and the Language of Rupture* (Chicago: University of Chicago Press, 1986), esp. Chapter 2.

15. André Breton, *Nadja* (Paris: Gallimard, 1964), pp. 71–73.

16. Margaret Cohen, *Profane Illumination: Walter Benjamin and the Paris of Surrealist Revolution* (Berkeley: University of California Press, 1993).

17. Benjamin, "Surrealism," p. 180.

18. Breton, *Nadja*, pp. 22, 19–20.

19. Ibid., p. 20.

20. Dragomanov in *Skandalist* is associated with the culture of the circuses (a central item in many of the agendas for theatrical reform; see Chapter 4), smokes opium, and also lives in such squalor that he is surrounded by rats—the creatures of the sewers. Arkhimedov in *Artist Unknown* is bohemian in a less colorful way but absolutely unable, by conventional standards, to care for himself or his infant child.

21. V. Kaverin, *Skandalist ili vechera na Vasil'yevskom ostrove* (Leningrad: Priboy, 1929), pp. 62–63.

22. V. Kaverin, *Khudozhnik neizvesten* (Leningrad: Izdatel'stvo pisateley v Leningrade, 1931), p. 149.

23. See Yu. Tynyanov, "O Khlebnikove," *Sobraniye proizvedeniy Velemira Khlebnikova,* vol. I (Leningrad: Izdatel'stvo pisateley v Leningrade, 1929), p. 20; Kaverin, *Khudozhnik neizvesten,* p. 61.

24. See Jeremy Howard, *The Union of Youth: The Artists' Society of Petersburg* (Manchester and New York: Manchester University Press, 1992), pp. 6, 202.

25. The Prologue was by Khlebnikov, the music by Matyushin, and the sets and costumes by Malevich.

26. Katherine Lahti has written an analysis of *Vladimir Mayakovsky: A Tragedy,* as a Nietzschean text ("Mayakovsky's Dithyrambs," a dissertation presented in the Slavic Department of Yale University, 1991).

27. This event is also a playful allusion to the Futurist V. Kamensky, who became an aviator and crashed.

28. Cited in Charlotte Douglas, *Swans of Other Worlds: Kasimir Malevich and the Origins of Abstraction in Russia* (Ann Arbor: University of Michigan Press, 1976), p. 37. Matyushin also defined it as "[conventional] beauty"; M. Matyushin, "Russkiye kubo-futuristy," *K istorii russkogo avangarda* (Stockholm: Hylaea Prints [Almqvist and Wiksell], 1976), p. 152.

29. *Pobeda nad solntsem,* opera by A. Kruchënykh, music by M. Matyushin (Lausanne: l'Age d'homme, 1976), p. 36.

30. Elizabeth Dalrymple Henderson, *The Fourth Dimension and Non-Euclidean Geometry in Modern Art* (Princeton: Princeton University Press, 1983), esp. Chapters 1, 2, and 5.

31. Note, for example, Kaverin's short story "The Eleventh Axiom" (Odinnadtsataya aksioma), which won a prize for fiction in Leningrad in 1920.

32. See *Die Geburt der Tragödie* (Munich: Wilhelm Goldmann Verlag, 1959), p. 37, Section 1.

33. Cited in R. Duganov, "'Mir pogibnet, a nam net kontsa!' ili teatr naiznanku," Foreword to *Pobeda nad solntsem* (Moscow and Vienna, 1983), pp. 3–4.

34. Kruchënykh, *Pobeda nad solntsem,* p. 8.

35. See V. I. Lenin's *Materialism and Empirio Criticism* (1908).

36. V. Kaverin, "E. T. A. Gofman: Rech' na zasedanii Serapionovykh brat'yev posv. pamyati E. T. A. Gofmana," *Kir,* no. 7 (1922), p. 24.

37. M. V. Matyushin, "Ne iskusstvo, a zhizn'," *Zi,* no. 20 (May 22, 1923), p. 15.

38. N. Punin, "Gosudarstvennaya vystavka," *Zi,* no. 22 (June 5, 1923), p. 5.

39. "O knige Metsanzhe i Gleza *Du cubisme,*" *Som,* no. 3 (Petrograd, 1913), pp. 25–34.

40. A. Kruchënykh, "Novye puti slova," *Troye* (Petersburg, 1913).

41. Yu. Annenkov, "Gibel' bogov," *Zi,* no. 14 (April 4, 1922), p. 3.

42. Since about 1919 Einstein had functioned in Russia as an emblem for the new science. The list of publications on him noted in a bibliography in *Kir* in 1922 was so long that it had to be continued in the next issue (no. 9–10, pp. 29–34; no. 11–12, pp. 26–32).

43. K. S. Malevich, "Pis'ma k M. V. Matyushinu," in Ye. F. Kovtun, *Yezhegodnik rukopisnogo otdela Pushkinskogo doma na 1974 god* (Leningrad: Nauka, 1976), pp. 192, 185 (letters of June 1916 and September 17, 1913).

44. For example, S. Gorodetsky, A. Remizov, A. Grin, and O. Mandelshtam.

45. "Chto videl slepoy zhurnalist. . . .," *As,* no. 8 (August 1913), pp. 25–27.

46. V. Shklovsky, "Ob iskusstve i revolyutsii," *Ik,* no. 17 (March 30, 1919), p. 2. See also his *Khod konya* (Moscow-Berlin: Gelikon, 1923), pp. 36–42.

47. Kruchënykh, *Pobeda nad solntsem,* p. 19.

48. Paul Carter, *The Road to Botany Bay: An Exploration of Landscape and History* (Chicago: University of Chicago Press, 1989); V. S. Naipaul, *The Enigma of Arrival* (New York: Knopf, 1987).

49. Breton, *Nadja,* p. 166.

50. Ibid., p. 179.

51. Ye. Zamyatin, "O literature, revolyutsii, entropii i prochem" (1923), published in *Pisateli ob iskusstve i o sebe* (Moscow: Krug, 1924).

52. The Russian title for this Commissariat, Prosveshcheniye, or "enlightenment," conflates its dual jurisdictions, Culture and Education.

53. D. P. Shterenberg, "Teoreticheskiye osnovy novoy programmy Svobodnykh gosudarstvennykh masterskikh," in "Otchët o deyatel'nosti Otdela Izobrazitel'nykh Iskusstv Narkomprosa," *Ii,* no. 1 (1919), p. 53.

54. Irving Howe, Introduction to *Literary Modernism* (London: Fawcett Publications, 1967), p. 15.

55. V. Mayakovsky, "Kaplya dëgti," in *Vzyal: Baraban futuristov* (Petrograd, December 1915).

56. When Malevich died of cancer in 1935, for example, he was buried in a coffin of his own Suprematist design. Note also that, even at the height of attacks on "Formalism" in 1931, Kaverin did not recant, as did Shklovsky, but avowed the principles of his set at a public debate. Compare V. Shklovsky, "Pamyatnik nauchnoy oshibki," *Lg,* no. 4 (January 27, 1930); "Diskussiya o 'Perestroyke pisateley poputchikov,' " *Nlp* (July 1931), p. 23.

57. In the 1920s Shklovsky drew closer to the Constructivist position and was satirized by Kaverin in 1929 as the eponymous *Troublemaker* for his failure to keep the ideals of their set.

58. Peter Alberg Jensen, *Nature as Code: The Achievement of Boris Pilnjak* (Copenhagen: Rosenkilde and Bagger, 1979), p. 65.

59. *The Naked Year* also has a specific association with Petersburg in that, though it was completed in 1920, it was only when Pilnyak went to Petrograd to stay with Gorky in 1921 that he was able to publish the novel, which first appeared in 1921 extracts in the journal of the House of Arts there and then in book form in 1922 in a publishing house where Gorky had influence; Gary Browning, *Boris Pilniak: Scythian at a Typewriter* (Ann Arbor: Ardis Press, 1983), pp. 17–21, 222–223.

60. R. Ivanov-Razumnik, *Skify,* no. I (Petersburg, 1917), pp. x, xi.

61. Note also the recurrent use of "I suddenly saw" ("Ya vdrug uvidel") in Zamyatin's *We,* which is in some respects an attack on avant-garde utopianism articulated in terms of a futuristic city-state that is drawn using many of the con-

ventions of the myth of Petersburg and with several key features reminiscent of Petersburg itself.

62. Boris Pilnyak, *Golyy god* (Berlin-Petersburg-Moscow: Izd-vo Z. I. Grzhebina, 1922), p. 68.

63. Ibid., p. 70.

2. Imperial Petersburg, 1913

1. The Russian calendar was, until the reform of 1918, thirteen days behind the Western calendar.

2. My account of the Jubilee ceremonial is, unless otherwise indicated, taken from "21-e yanvarya v Peterburge," *Bv,* February 21, 1913 (evening edition), pp. 2–4.

3. "Na ulitsakh," *R,* February 22, 1913, p. 4.

4. "Massovye aresty i obyski," *Bv,* April 19, 1913 (morning edition), p. 2; "K arestam sredi uchashchikhsya," *Bv,* April 23, 1913, p. 2; "Zabastovka 1-go maya i demonstratsiya rabochikh," *Bv,* May 1, 1913 (evening edition), p. 2.

5. Bresko-Boyanovskiy, "Russkiy sezon v Parizhe," *Bv,* May 12, 1913 (evening edition), pp. 7–8. In fact, the costumer Nikolai Roerich dressed them (inappropriately) in a combination of the Yakut and the Kirghiz national dress.

6. See I. M. Zdanevich, "Doklad o futurizme," *R,* no. 97 (April 9, 1913), p. 2.

7. "Uezzhayut," *Bv,* May 2, 1913 (evening edition), p. 5.

8. A. Rostislavov, "Madonna Benua," *A,* no. 4–5 (1916), p. 83.

9. See "Amerika-roller-rink," *R,* no. 44 (February 14, 1913), p. 6; "Nochnaya zhizn' v N'yu-iorke," *Bv,* April 12, 1913 (evening edition), p. 5.

10. Another possible term would be Retrospectivism. Here I regard Preservationism specifically as the movement for reviving "Old Petersburg" and as such a branch of the general Retrospectivist movement.

11. Richard Wortman, "Moscow and Petersburg: The Problem of Political Center in Tsarist Russia," in Sean Wilentz, ed., *Rites of Power: Symbolism, Ritual, and Politics since the Middle Ages* (Philadelphia: University of Pennsylvania Press, 1985), pp. 244–271.

12. See Alois Riehl, *Überbegriff der Philosophie* (1872), and Heinrich Wölfflin, *Kunstgeschichtliche Grundbegriffe* (1915).

13. A. Benois, "Zhivopisnyy Peterburg," *Mi,* no. 1 (1902), p. 3.

14. Ibid., p. 2.

15. Vladimir Gippius, "Dusha reaktsii," *R,* no. 60 (March 3, 1913), p. 3.

16. See "21-ye fevralya 1913 g.," *Bv,* February 21, 1913 (evening edition), p. 2. It is important to note that leading members of the lobby for a Neoclassical revival in Petersburg, Lanceray, Fomin, and Shchuko, originally submitted designs for the decorations to the Jubilee Commission but they were rejected as too costly; hence the decorations were designed by relative unknowns, though in the same style. A. R-v, "Khudozhestvennye vesti," *R,* no. 35 (February 5, 1913), p. 5.

17. Georgiy Lukomsky identifies *staticheskoye chut'yë* as a defining feature of Neoclassicism; see his "Novyy Peterburg [mysli o sovremennom stroitel'stve]," *A,* no. 2 (1913), p. 9.

18. "Russkaya khudozhestvennaya letopis' 1913 g.," *A*, no. 2 (1913), p. 62.

19. L. Rudnitsky, (lead article, untitled), *Istoricheskaya vystavka arkhitektury* (Petersburg, 1911), p. 32.

20. D. Filosof, "Iskusstvo nikomu ne nuzhno," *R*, no. 5 (January 6, 1913), p. 3.

21. Benois, "Zhivopisnyy Peterburg," pp. 1–2.

22. See Rudnitsky, *Istoricheskaya vystavka*, p. 34.

23. Ibid., pp. 32, 33.

24. Hugh Honor, *Neo-classicism* (Harmondsworth, Middlesex: Penguin Books, 1977), pp. 20, 40, 113, and 123.

25. Many of the clichés of Neoclassicism resurfaced later as clichés of Stalinist, socialist realist literature in identifying the positive hero as an emblem of political consciousness. See Katerina Clark, *The Soviet Novel: History as Ritual* (Chicago: University of Chicago Press, 1981), esp. pp. 57–63.

26. On *Apollo*, see "Phoebus, Apollo, or Mussagetes: The Position of *Apollon* in Russian Modernism," a dissertation presented by Dennis Mickiewicz at Yale University, 1967.

27. Lukomsky, "Novyy Peterburg," p. 37.

28. Immediately below this picture, the main article, by L. Rudnitsky, begins to discuss the *perelom* of Peter the Great (*Istoricheskaya vystavka*, p. 7).

29. Lukomsky, "Novyy Peterburg," p. 7.

30. Ibid., p. 37.

31. Sergey Gorodetskiy in one of these articles, "Nekotorye techeniya v sovremennoy russkoy poezii," adduces the architect as a metaphor for the Acmeist: *A*, no. 1 (1913), pp. 46, 50.

32. A. Rostislavov, "Disput o zhivopisi," *R*, no. 83 (March 26, 1913), p. 5.

33. Rudnitsky, *Istoricheskaya vystavka*, p. 34.

34. Akademiya nauk. Institut istorii, *Istoriya Leningrada,* vol. III, 1895–1917 (Moscow and Leningrad: Akademiya nauk, 1956), p. 916. Also see the illustration in Selim O. Khan-Magomedov, *Pioneers of Soviet Architecture*, trans. Alexander Lieven (New York: Rizzoli, 1987), p. 25.

35. Lukomsky, "Novyy Peterburg," p. 14.

36. For example, the Imperial family undertook to finance the *World of Art* when it seemed in danger of folding in 1900.

37. Rudnitsky, *Istoricheskaya vystavka*, p. 9.

38. Ibid., pp. 6, 8.

39. Others commonly involved include Count Zubov, who then headed what became the Institute for the History of the Arts (see Chapter 6), Prince S. Volkonsky, the leading exponent of the Dalcroze method (see Chapter 3), and P. P. Gaydeburov, the head of the Traveling Mass Theater (see Chapter 4). See Sergey Makovskiy, "Ministerstvo iskusstv," *A*, no. 2–3 (1917), pp. ix–vi; A. R-v, "Khudozhestvennaya letopis'," *A*, no. 2–3, pp. 65–69, no. 4–5, p. 73, no. 6–7, pp. 75–78 (1917).

40. Anita Brookner, *Jacques-Louis David* (London: Chatto and Windus, 1980), p. 117.

41. Benois, "Zhivopisnyy Peterburg," p. 2.

42. These characteristics are to be found among other Neoclassical movements, such as the Birmingham Lunar Society.

43. Kendall E. Bailles, *Science and Russian Culture in an Age of Revolutions: V. I. Vernadsky and His Scientific School, 1863–1945* (Bloomington: Indiana University Press, 1990), p. 106.

44. My account of Vernadsky and his circle is largely taken from Bailles, *Science and Russian Culture,* esp. pp. 10–12, 16, 18, 27–31, 49, 81, 84, 92, 99–100, 125, 139, and 140.

45. Actually, Sorokin was himself a fiery Socialist Revolutionary but his local mentors in sociology were, like Vernadsky, pillars of the Kadet Party (or of the Liberal Party).

46. "Chlen g. Soveta V. M. Andreevskiy o reforme kalendarya," *Bv,* March 1, 1913 (morning edition), p. 4.

47. See D. Ovsyaniko-Kulikovskiy's articles on "Nauka i demokratiya": *R,* January 1, 1913, p. 3; January 15, p. 5; March 10, p. 3.

48. A. Benois, "Chemu mogla byt' Akademiya Khudozhestv v nastoyashcheye vremya," *Trudy Vserossiyskogo s"yezda khudozhnikov v Petrograde dekabr' 1911-yanvar' 1912,* vol. III (Petrograd, 1915), p. 95.

49. These features come very close to the account A. Benois gave in 1913, writing in his weekly column for *Rech',* of what his group stands for: A. Benua, "Printsipy 'Mira iskusstva,' " *R,* no. 10 (January 11, 1913), p. 2.

50. Ernst Gellner, *Nations and Nationalism* (Ithaca, N.Y.: Cornell University Press, 1983), esp. pp. 35, 39, 54, 92, and 117.

51. See S. Rossiyev, "Paskha v starom Peterburge," *Bv,* August 13, 1913 (evening edition), p. 3; Ross, "Pervoye maya v starom Peterburge," *Bv,* March 6, 1913 (morning edition), p. 2.

52. See "V Pirogovskom obshchestve," *Bv,* February 22, 1913 (morning edition), p. 2.

53. V. I. Lenin, "Gosudarstvo i revolyutsiya," in N. Lenin (V. Ul'yanov), *Sobraniye sochineniy,* vol. VIX (Moscow and Petrograd, 1921), p. 354.

54. For examples of this, see A. Rostislavov's "Khudozhestvennaya letopis'," in *A:* no. 2 (1915), p. 63; no. 2–3 (1917), p. 64; no. 6–7 (1917), pp. 80, 84.

55. For example, Marius Petipa's production of *Sleeping Beauty* and M. Fokine's *Le Pavillion d'Armide* of 1907, for which Benois designed the sets.

56. I am grateful to Mark von Hagen for pointing this out.

57. Rostislavov, "Khudozhestvennaya letopis'," *A,* no. 6–7 (1917), p. 82.

58. See Sergey Makovskiy, "Ministerstvo iskusstv," *A,* no. 2–3 (1917), p. xi.

59. Mark Etkind, *A. N. Benua i russkaya khudozhestvennaya kul'tura* (Leningrad: Iskusstvo R.S.F.S.R., 1989), pp. 287–288.

60. See Rostislavov, "Khudozhestvennaya letopis'," *A,* no. 1, pp. 35–37, no. 2–3, p. 68 (1916).

61. See K. E., "Otkrytiye 'nashego teatra,' " *Bv,* February 20, 1913 (evening edition), p. 4.

3. *Masquerade*

1. B. Filippov, *Kak ya stal domovym* (Moscow: Iskusstvo, 1974), p. 41.

2. See R. Yurenev, *Sergey Eyzenshteyn: Zamysly, Fil'my, Metod,* Part 1, 1898–1929 (Moscow: Iskusstvo, 1985), p. 25.

3. Konstantin Rudnitsky, *Meyerhold the Director,* trans. George Petrov (Ann Arbor, Michigan: Ardis Press, 1981), p. 143.

4. V. Meyerhold, *O teatre* (Petersburg: Prosveshcheniye, 1913), p. 182.

5. See "Luna-Park," *Bv,* April 23, 1913 (evening edition), p. 4; "U rampy," *Bv,* May 24, 1913 (evening edition), p. 6.

6. N. N. Dolgov, "Razgadka trëkh yedinstv," *Yeit,* no. 5 (1913), p. 71.

7. "U rampy," *Bv,* May 11, 1913 (evening edition), p. 6.

8. See two anthologies of 1908 generally regarded as classic sources for this new orientation: *Kniga o novom teatre* (Petersburg: Shipovnik), and *Krizis teatra.*

9. There was, of course, a wide range of variations. Wagner, for instance, conceived the renovated theater as a transcendental space.

10. For example, Molière's *Don Juan* in 1910 (à la the court of Louis XIV) and Calderon's *The Constant Prince* in 1915 (à la seventeenth-century Spain).

11. Wagner's operas were also very much in vogue.

12. See Friedrich Nietzsche, *Die Geburt der Tragödie aus dem Geiste der Musik (Griechentum und Pessimismus)* (Munich: Wilhelm Goldmann Verlag, 1959), pp. 58–59, Section VIII.

13. See Bernice Glatzer Rosenthal's Introduction to *Nietzsche in Russia,* Bernice Glatzer Rosenthal, ed. (Princeton: Princeton University Press, 1982) pp. 11, 16.

14. V. I. Lenin, "Gosudarstvo i revolyutsiya," in N. Lenin (V. Ul'yanov), *Sobraniye sochineniy,* vol. XIV (Moscow and Petrograd: Gos. izd., 1921), p. 318.

15. Karl Marx, *Der 18te Brumaire des Louis Bonaparte* (New York: Deutsche Vereins-Buchhandlung von Schmidt und Helmich, 1852), p. 18, Section I; see also pp. 76, 100.

16. Nietzsche, *Die Geburt der Tragödie,* Section VIII.

17. A. Potëmkin, "U Aysedory Dunkan," *Bv,* January 5, 1913, p. 4.

18. Nietzsche, *Die Geburt der Tragödie,* p. 134, Section XX.

19. I. Rabinovich, "Na rekakh vavilonskikh," *Tii,* no. 1 (1917), p. 8.

20. Anastasiya Chebotarevskaya, "O teatral'nykh disputakh," *Lkta,* no. 2 (1914), p. 60.

21. Marx, *Der 18te Brumaire,* p. 71, Section V; for Louis Bonaparte as *Lumpenproletarian,* see p. 82, and for other intellectuals and literati as bourgeois or petty bourgeois hirelings, see pp. 46, 104.

22. See A. Bogdanov: *Elementy proletarskoy kul'tury* (Moscow: Gos. izd., 1919), pp. 38–39, 49; *Mir novyy (stat'i 1904–1905),* 3rd. ed. (Moscow: Giz, 1920), p. 28; and *Sotsializm nauki (nauchnye zadachi proletariata)* (Moscow: Proletarskaya kul'tura, 1918), esp. pp. 15–16, 26. See also A. V. Lunacharsky, "Pushkin," *I,* no. 34 (February 12, 1922); Fëdor Kalinin, "O metodakh raboty v Proletkul'takh," *G,* no. 4 (1920), pp. 10–13.

23. See Nietzsche, *Die Geburt der Tragödie,* p. 122, Section XVIII.

24. Ibid., Section IX.

25. A. Benois, "Zhivopisnyy Peterburg," *Mi,* no. 1 (1902), p. 2.

26. Georg Fuchs, "Zadachi nemetskogo teatra," *A,* no. 11 (1910), p. 50.

27. N. Evreinov, "Obshchestvennyy teatr na vzglyad poznavshego iskusstva i teatra dlya sebya," *Os,* no. 8 (1915), p. 21; A. A. Mgebrov, *Zhizn' v teatre,* vol. II (Moscow and Leningrad: Academia, 1932), p. 193.

28. Nietzsche, *Die Geburt der Tragödie,* Section VII.

29. See Mark B. Adams, "The Soviet Nature-Nurture Debate," in Loren R. Graham, ed., *Science and the Soviet Social Order* (Cambridge, Mass.: Harvard University Press, 1990), p. 98.

30. Cited in A. A. Gvozdev and Adr. Piotrovsky, "Petrogradskiye teatry i prazdnestva v epokhu voyennogo kommunizma," in *Istoriya sovetskogo teatra* (Leningrad, 1933), p. 96.

31. These latter groups in many respects defined themselves against Nietzschean Wagnerism. As the name "Apollon" imples, they generally opted for one side of the famous Nietzschean dichotomy and gave art and architecture priority.

32. Zigfrid Ashkinazi, "Bayreytskie vpechatleniya," *Yeit*, no. 5 (1912), pp. 75–78.

33. "Teatr i muzyka," *R*, December 6, 1913, p. 7.

34. See, for example, the caricature in *Tii*, no. 6 (1914), p. 137.

35. V. Soloviev, "'Maskarad' v Aleksandrinskom teatre," *A*, no. 2–3 (1917), p. 72.

36. Ibid., pp. 74–75; Friedrich Nietzsche, *Die Geburt der Tragödie, Nietzsches werke*, vol. I (Stuttgart: Alfred Kroner Verlag, 1921), p. 128, Section 14.

37. Soloviev, "'Maskarad' v Aleksandrinskom teatre," p. 75.

38. See, for example, "U Aysedory Dunkan," *Bv*, January 5, 1913, p. 4.

39. V. Soloviev, "K voprosu o teorii stsenicheskikh kompozitsiy," *Lkta*, no. 4–7 (1915), pp. 171–178.

40. See Nietzsche, *Die Geburt der Tragödie, Nietzsches werke*, vol. I, p. 90, Section 8, p. 179, Section 21; for music as a universal language, see p. 140, Section 16.

41. Litotes, "Obshchestvo revniteley khudozhestvennogo slova," *A*, no. 4–5 (1916), pp. 87–88. Note that neither of the two leading translators of classical Greek drama, I. F. Annensky or Radlov's mentor, F. F. Zelinsky, had attempted this.

42. See Yevgeniy Znosko-Borovskiy, "Teatr bez literatury," *A*, no. 7 (1912), pp. 22–33; and Z. Ashkinazi, "Teatr Vagnera," *Yeit*, no. 6 (1913), pp. 77–119.

43. Cited in Yu. Slonimskaya, "Novosti russkoy teatral'noy literatury," *Yeit*, no. 3 (1911), p. 96.

44. Aleks. St., "K istorii tipa P'yerro (O vozmozhnosti voskresheniya pantomimy)," *A*, no. 10 (1912), p. 50; Z. A. Stark [Zigfrid], "Renessans baleta," *Yeit*, no. 3 (1911), p. 109.

45. " '1914' Allegoricheskoye deystviye knyazya S. M. Volkonskogo," *A*, no. 1 (1915), p. 67.

46. Kn. Sergey Volkonsky, "Ritm v istorii chelovechestva," *Yeit*, no. 3 (1912), p. 6; "V zashchitu aktërskoy tekhniki," *A*, no. 1 (1911), esp. pp. 23–24.

47. Kn. Sergey Volkonsky, "Prazdnestva v Gellerau," *A*, no. 6 (1912), p. 6.

48. Kn. Sergey Volkonsky, "Iz knigi 'Vyrazitel'nyy chelovek stsenicheskogo zhesta (Po Del'sartu),' " *A*, no. 7 (1912), p. 35.

49. Volkonsky, "Prazdnestva v Gellerau," *A*, no. 6 (1912), p. 47.

50. Meyerhold, "Primechaniya," *O teatre*, p. 186.

51. Ibid., pp. 152, 154.

52. Ibid., p. 160.

53. Ibid., p. 149.

54. "Disput o teatre," *R*, December 23, 1913, p. 3.

55. Compare a series of reports (generally titled "Studiya: Klass Meyerkhol'da"): *Lkta*, no. 2, pp. 62–63, no. 4–5, pp. 12–97, no. 6–7, p. 122 (1914); no. 1–3, pp. 132–134 (1915); no. 1, p. 100, no. 2–3, pp. 144–146 (1916).

56. See Meyerhold, *O teatre*, p. 185.

57. Ibid., p. 183.

58. Ibid., pp. 148, 204.

59. "Teatry i muzyka," *R*, no. 337 (December 9, 1913), p. 6.

60. Meyerhold, *O teatre*, p. 162.

61. "Futurizm v teatre (Futuristicheskiy manifest. Perev. M. P.)," *Tii*, no. 5 (1914), pp. 108–110.

62. "Studiya: Klass Meyerkhol'da," *Lkta*, no. 2 (1914), p. 63.

63. See Meyerhold, *O teatre*, p. 159.

64. Ibid., p. 163; see also p. 162.

65. Ibid., p. 156.

66. See also "Po povodu 'Korolya Lira,' " *Zi*, no. 562–563 (September 20–21, 1920), p. 2; V. Shklovsky, "Tema, obraz i syuzhet Rozanova," *Zi*, no. 697699 (March 19–21, 1921), p. 1.

67. See V. Shklovsky, "Literatura i kinematograf," *Zi*, no. 142 (May 21, 1919), pp. 1–2; "Iskusstvo tsirka," *Zi*, no. 284–285 (November 4–5, 1919), p. 1; "Razvërtyvanie syuzheta (roman-drama)," *Zi*, no. 348 (January 21, 1920), p. 1.

68. For example, S. Radlov's "Osnovy teatra," appearing in *Zi*, nos. 361, 362, 363, 364 (1920), is sandwiched between two major texts by Shklovsky, "Razvërtyvanie syuzheta (roman-drama)" (nos. 348, 355) and "Kak sdelan 'Don Kikhot'" (nos. 373, 375, 376).

69. V. Shklovsky, "O psikhologicheskom rampe," *Zi*, no. 445 (May 7, 1920), p. 1.

70. For instance, B. Eikhenbaum's "Illusion of *skaz*" (Illyuziya skaza, 1918) analyzes this literary technique in terms of "improvisation," "mimicry," "gesture," sound play, and even the *komediant*, the actor in *commedia dell'arte*; V. Shklovsky, "Literatura i kinematograf," *Zi*, no. 142 (August 21, 1919), pp. 1–2, and "Iskusstvo tsirka," *Zi*, no. 284–285 (November 4–5, 1919), p. 1.

71. S. Volkonsky, "Ritm v stsenicheskom iskusstve (Doklad Vserossiyskomu s"yezdu khudozhnikov)," *A*, no. 3 (1912), p. 60; Soloviev, "'Maskarad' v Aleksandrinskom teatre," p. 75.

72. V. Shklovsky, "Iskusstvo kak priyëm," *Sborniki po teorii poeticheskogo yazyka*, II (Petrograd, 1917), pp. 3–14; S. Eisenstein, "Montazh attraktsionov," *L*, no. 3 (1923), pp. 70–75; Meyerhold, *O teatre*, pp. 166, 168–169.

73. Meyerhold, *O teatre*, pp. 156–157.

74. Ibid., p. 173. Compare Nietzsche, *Die Geburt der Tragödie* (Munich: Wilhelm Goldmann Verlag, 1959), pp. 155, 157, Section 24.

75. R. D. Timenchik, "Ob odnom pis'me Anny Akhmatovoy," *Z*, no. 9 (1991), pp. 165–167.

76. Meyerhold, *O teatre*, pp. 161, 162.

77. V. Kurbatov, "Teatral'nye prazdnestva i teatry Pavlovska," *Yeit*, no. 1 (1911), pp. 1–18.

78. Meyerhold, *O teatre,* pp. 158, 160; see the Epilogue to "Lyubov' k trëm apel'sinam," in *Lkta,* no. 1 (1914), p. 47; Vl. S., "Petrogradskiye teatry," *A,* no. 2 (1916), p. 45.

79. See S. Volkonsky, "Krasota i pravda na stsene," *A,* no. 4 (1911), pp. 64–66; Georg Fuchs, "Zadachi nemetskogo teatra," *A,* no. 11 (1910), p. 50.

80. Marcel Mauss, "A Category of the Human Mind: The Notion of the Person, the Notion of Self," trans. W. D. Halls, in Michael Carithers et al., eds., *The Category of the Person: Anthropology, Philosophy, History* (Cambridge: Cambridge University Press, 1985), pp. 4–23.

81. This was particularly true for the avant-garde. See Camilla Gray, *The Russian Experiment in Art, 1863–1922* (New York: Harry N. Abrams, 1970), p. 194; Wiktor Woroszylski, *The Life of Mayakovsky,* trans. Boleslaw Taborski (New York: Orion Press, 1970), pp. 88, 131.

4. Theater and Revolution in the New Republic

1. M. B. Keyrim-Markus, *Gosudarstvennoye rukovodstvo kul'tury: Stroitel'stvo Narkomprosa (noyabr' 1917–seredina 1918 gg.)* (Moscow: Nauka, 1980), pp. 115, 124, 131, 140, 147, 167.

2. Sheila Fitzpatrick, *The Commissariat of Enlightenment: Soviet Organization of Education and the Arts under Lunacharsky* (Cambridge: Cambridge University Press, 1970), pp. 129–130.

3. The House of Arts and the House of Literati are not covered here in the depth they deserve, partly because of such existing studies as Barry Scherr, "Notes on the Literary Life of Petrograd, 1918–1922: A Tale of Three Houses," *Slavic Review,* vol. 36 (June 1977), pp. 256–267, and Martha Hickey, "The Petrograd House of Arts, 1919–1922: Legacy of a Literary Community" (manuscript).

4. N. Altman, "Vospominaniya," extract reprinted in *Agitatsionno-massovoye iskusstvo. Oformleniye prazdnestv. Sovetskoye dekorativnoye iskusstvo. Materialy i dokumenty,* ed. V. P. Tolstoy, comp. I. M. Bibikova and N. I. Levchenko (Moscow: Iskusstvo, 1984), p. 65.

5. See L. Pumpyanskiy, "Oktyabr'skiye torzhestva i khudozhniki Petrograda," *Pl,* no. 35 (January 5, 1919), pp. 11–14. See also M. V. Dobuzhinskiy, "Bomba ili khlopushka: Beseda dvukh khudozhnikov," *Nz,* no. 83 (May 4, 1918).

6. See *Agitatsionno-massovoye iskusstvo,* pp. 80–96.

7. The Imperial theaters were renamed State theaters after the Revolution, and on January 1, 1920, they became Academic theaters.

8. See Vasiliy Bespalov, *Teatry v dni revolyutsii. 1917. Teatral'nye memuary* (Leningrad: Academia, 1927), pp. 111–119.

9. Actually, even the former Imperial theaters were liberalized somewhat. For instance, they mounted productions of Stravinsky's *Petrushka* and *Solvey* (originally to have been directed by Meyerhold), both unthinkable before the Revolution.

10. See O. Kameneva, "Na s"yezde po vneshkol'nomu obrazovaniyu: Zasedaniye teatra," *Vt,* no. 26 (May 14–16, 1919), p. 4.

326

11. Mark von Hagen, *Soldiers of the Revolution: Soldiers' Politics and State-Building in Soviet Russia, 1917–1930* (Ithaca, N.Y.: Cornell University Press, 1990).

12. Vl. V-skiy, "K istorii Krasnoy armii," *PP*, no. 248 (November 4, 1920), p. 3.

13. "Vserossiyskiy s"yezd po vneshkol'nomu obrazovaniyu: Rezolyutsiya s"yezda," *Vo*, no. 6–8 (1919), p. 18.

14. See "Pedagogicheskaya sektsiya," "Ob"yasnitel'nye zapiski k proyektu polozheniya o 'Vol'noy filosofskoy akademii,' " "Institut zhivogo slova," *Vtonkpp*, no. 1 (September 19, 1918), pp. 12–15.

15. See A. Polynin, "Ulichnyy teatr," *Vopzitil*, no. 1 (September 18, 1918), p. 3.

16. Christian J. Taylor, *Futurism: Politics, Painting, and Performance* (Ann Arbor: University of Michigan Research Press, 1974), p. 29.

17. A good example of the latter would be the Institute for the Living Word (Institut zhivogo slova), founded in Petrograd under the auspices of PTO on November 15, 1918, which organized classes in declamation and other oral skills and public readings by highbrow intellectuals; see "Otkrytiye Instituta zhivogo slova," *Ig*, no. 2 (1918), p. 59. For mass work see P. P. Gaydeburov, "Tvorcheskaya igra," *Vo*, no. 6–8 (1919), p. 35.

18. In 1918, 1,230 books were published in Petrograd, a considerable decline if compared with 8,420 in 1912, and there was a similar decline in book publishing in Moscow; see *Vl*, no. 4–5 (1920), p. 12.

19. N. Evreinov, *Teatr kak takovoy* (Spb.: Sovremennoye iskusstvo, 1913), pp. 27, 29.

20. Ibid., pp. 29, 34–36.

21. N. Evreinov, "Kazhdaya minuta—teatr," *Teatr dlya sebya*, vol. I (Spb., 1915), pp. 69–83.

22. Evreinov, *Teatr kak takovoy*, p. 29.

23. V. Shklovsky, "Drama i massovye predstavleniya," *Zi*, no. 688–690 (March 9–11, 1921), p. 1.

24. See A. A. Gvozdev and Adr. Piotrovsky, "Petrogradskiye teatry i prazdnestva v epokhu voyennogo kommunizma," in *Istoriya sovetskogo teatra*, vol. I (Leningrad: GIKhL, 1933), pp. 100–104, 106, 127–128.

25. A. Remizova, *Kul'turno-prosvetitel'naya rabota v RSFSR (1921–1925 g.)* (Moscow: Nauka, 1962), pp. 15–23, and Keyrim-Markus, *Gosudarstvennoye rukovodstvo kul'tury*, p. 81.

26. Lynn Mally, *Culture of the Future: The Proletkult Movement in Revolutionary Russia* (Berkeley: University of California Press, 1990).

27. See Fitzpatrick, *The Commissariat of Enlightenment*, p. 112.

28. Gorky and Andreeva emigrated in 1921, as did others active in TEO, such as F. Zelinsky. Other members of TEO associated with the Left Socialist Revolutionaries included K. Erberg and Ivanov-Razumnik.

29. See *Tii*, editorial, no. 1 (1918), p. 4.

30. A. Lunacharsky, "Sotsializm i iskusstvo," in the anthology *Teatr. Kniga o novom teatre. Sbornik statey* (Petersburg: Shipovnik, 1908), p. 37.

31. "Zasedaniye kollegii Otdela teatrov i zrelishch," *Zi*, no. 11 (November 12, 1918), pp. 4, 5; "Teatr v krasnoarmeyskoy srede," *Vt*, no. 44 (December 2–7, 1919), p. 12.

32. Gvozdev and Piotrovsky, "Petrogradskiye teatry i prazdnestva," p. 110; "K vvedeniyu besplatnykh zrelishch v Peterburge," *Vt*, no. 78–79 (January 4, 1921), p. 18; L. Nikulin, "Peterburgskiye pis'ma," *Vt*, no. 89–90 (May 1, 1921), p. 12.

33. See, for example, V. I. Lenin, "Iz doklada o partiynoy programme 19-ogo marta; VII s"yezd RKP(b) 18–23 marta 1919 g.," in N. I. Krutikova, ed., *Lenin o kul'ture i iskusstve* (Moscow: Iskusstvo, 1956), pp. 67–68.

34. See V. I. Lenin, "Gosudarstvo i revolyutsiya," in N. Lenin (V. Ul'yanov), *Sobranye sochineniy*, vol. XIV (Moscow and Petrograd: Gos. izd., 1921), pp. 311, 321, 327, 328, 332, 333, 339, 369, 370, 379, 393.

35. Romain Rolland, *Le Théâtre du peuple* (Paris: Libraire Hachette), pp. 54, 86–106; Cecil W. Davies, *Theatre for the People: The Study of the Volksbühne* (Austin: University of Texas Press, 1977); Eugene von Erven, *Radical Peoples' Theater* (Bloomington: Indiana University Press, 1988).

36. A. Polynin, "Ulichnyy teatr," *Vopzilil*, no. 1 (September 18, 1918), p. 3.

37. See, for example, K. A. Muratova, "M. Gor'kiy i sovetskiy teatr (1918–1921 gody)," in *Iz istorii russkikh literaturnykh otnosheniy, xviii–xxvv* (Moscow: Akademiya nauk, 1959), p. 300; "Khronika," *Zi*, no. 88 (February 28, 1919), p. 2; "Pto," *PP*, no. 70 (March 30, 1919); "Soobshcheniye: Pechal'nye rezul'taty konkursa (29 yanvarya–4 fevralya, 1920 g.," *Vt*, no. 50 (1920), p. 14; "Konkurs melodramy (Ot zhuri konkursa na melodramu)," *Zi*, no. 178 (July 2, 1919).

38. See S. Garin, "Geroicheskiy teatr," *Zi*, no. 417–418 (1920), p. 1.

39. See, for example, M., "O knige: Utrennik v malom zale Konservatorii," *Zi*, no. 589 (October 2, 1920), p. 1.

40. A. Lunacharsky, "Revolyutsiya i krizis teatra," *Vt*, no. 4 (1919), pp. 5–6; "M. Gor'kiy o kinematografe," *Vt*, no. 30 (June 3–8, 1919), p. 10.

41. Ibid.; "Instsenirovki istorii kul'tury," *Vt*, no. 36 (October 7–12, 1919), p. 14.

42. Of the two genres, Gorky favored tragedy, and Lunacharsky melodrama, although each supported both genres.

43. A. Blok, "Bolshoy dramaticheskiy teatr v predstoyashchem sezone," *Dela i dni Bol'shogo dramaticheskogo teatra* (Petrograd: Bol'shoy dramaticheskiy teatr, 1919), p. 10.

44. See A. Lunacharsky, "O repertuare," *Vt*, no. 33 (September 14–21, 1919), pp. 4–5.

45. Vyacheslav Ivanov, "K voprosu ob organizatsii tvorcheskikh sil narodnogo kollektiva v oblasti narodnogo deystva," *Vt*, no. 26 (May 14–16, 1919), p. 4; "O Vagnere," *Vt*, no. 31–32 (June 9–15, 1919), pp. 8–9.

46. Lunacharsky, "Sotsializm i iskusstvo," pp. 37, 30, 28, 26.

47. Note that he still cites Wagner as an authority in his *Teatr i revolyutsiya* (Moscow: Giz, 1924, p. 12); see also Fitzpatrick, *The Commissariat of Enlightenment*, pp. 152–157.

48. Quoted in P. P. Gaydeburov, *Literaturnoye naslediye. Vospominaniya, Stat'i, Rezhissërskiye eksplikatsii. Vystupleniya* (Moscow: Vserossiyskoye teatral'noye obshchestvo, 1977), p. 40.

49. See B. Filippov, *Kak ya stal "domovym"* (Moscow: Iskusstvo, 1974), pp. 80–82.

50. See A. A. Mgebrov, "Proletarskaya kul'tura," *G*, no. 2–3 (1919), pp. 23–24. See also Viktoriya Chekan (his wife and collaborator), "Poyezdka teatral'noy areny Proletkul'ta na Zapadniy front Krasnoy Armii," *G*, no. 2–3 (1919), p. 29, and N. G. Vinogradov-Mamont, *Krasnoarmeyskoye chudo: Povest' o teatral'no-dramaticheskoy masterskoy Krasnoy armii* (Leningrad: Iskusstvo, 1972), esp. pp. 31, 53, 78–79, 125.

51. "Teatr vol'noy komedii," *Zi*, no. 554–555 (September 11–12, 1920), p. 2; "Khronika," *Zi*, no. 557 (September 15, 1920), p. 1; "K godovshchine Oktyabr'skoy revolyutsii," *Zi*, no. 553 (September 10, 1920), p. 1 (here D. Tyomkin is listed as chief director of the re-enactment; compare Nik., "Vzyatiye zimnego dvortsa," *Zi*, no. 596–597 (October 30–31, 1920), p. 1).

52. V. Meyerhold, "Zadachi khudozhestvennogo prosveshcheniya," *Vt*, no. 80–81 (January 1921), p. 7.

53. For example, *Zori*: "Na kursakh masterstva stsenicheskikh postanovok," *Ig*, no. 2 (1918), pp. 58, 59; "Otchët o dvukhmesyachnom semestre Instruktorskikh kursov po obucheniyu masterstva stsenicheskikh postanovok (21 iunya–23 avgusta 1918)," *Vtonkpp*, no. 1 (1918), p. 23. Biomechanics: "Proyekt polozheniya o 'Shkole aktërskogo masterstva,' " compiled by L. S. Viv'yen and V. Meyerhold, *Vtonkpp*, no. 1 (1918), pp. 24–29. See also "Doklad V. V. Tikhonovicha" and "Rech' V. E. Meyerkhol'da," in "Na s"yezde po vneshkol'nomu obrazovaniyu. Zasedaniye teatral'noy sektsii," *Vt*, no. 28 (May 17–20, 1919), p. 5.

54. Valeriy Bebutov, "Vs. Em. Meyerkhol'd," *Vt*, no. 68 (September 21–26, 1920), p. 3.

55. "Petrograd," *Vt*, no. 7 (February 18–19, 1919), p. 5.

56. "Dramaticheskiye shkoly: Proyekt prepodavaniya dramaturgii na 'Kursakh Masterstva Stsenicheskikh Postanovok,' " *Vtonkpp*, no. 2 (1919), p. 47; "Primechaniya," in. A. Z. Yufit, ed., *Russkiy sovetskiy teatr 1917–1921: Dokumenty i materialy* (Leningrad: Iskusstvo, 1968), p. 356.

57. "Teatr studiya," *Zi*, no. 14 (Nov. 15, 1918), p. 4; no. 15 (Nov. 16, 1918), p. 4. S. Radlov, "Vospominaniya o teatre narodnoy komedii," publikatsiya P.V. Dmitriyeva, in *Minuvsheye: Istoricheskiy Al'manakh*, no. 16 (Moscow-Petersburg: Atheneum Feniks, 1994), pp. 80–101.

58. See Richard Schechner, *Drama, Script, Theater, and Performance: Essays on Performance Theory* (New York: Drama Book Specialists, 1977), pp. 36–39.

59. See N. Punin, "Vmesto predisloviya," in A. Lunacharsky, *Rech' proiznesënnaya na otkrytii Petrogradskikh gosudarstvennykh Svobodnykh khudozhestvenno-uchebnykh masterskikh 10-go oktyabrya, 1918 g.* (Petrograd: IZO, 1919), p. 6.

60. *Stenka Razin* (staged for the Baltic Fleet), *Zi*, no. 315 (December 11, 1919), p. 4; S. Radlov, *Stat'i o teatre*, p. 7; N. Punin, in "O forme i soderzhanii," *Ik*, no. 18 (April 1919), p. 1.

61. This position was even shared by Lunacharsky. See his "Vmesto vvedeniya" to the first issue of *Igra* in 1918, esp. p. 1.

62. "A. S. Aleksandrov: Po afishe Zhokey-nayezdniki pod upravleniyem Aleksandra Serzh," in Yevg. Kuznetsov, ed., *Sovetskiy tsirk, 1918–1938* (Leningrad and Moscow: Iskusstvo, 1938), pp. 92–101.

63. "Peterburg. Peterburgskiye pis'ma. VIII," *Vt*, no. 54 (February 24–29, 1920), p. 14.

64. Frantisek Deak in his article "Two Manifestoes: The Influence of Italian

Futurism in Russia," *Drama Review,* vol. XIX, no. 4 (December 1975), pp. 88–92, draws attention to the influence of Italian Futurism on the contemporary work in Petrograd of Yu. Annenkov in the Hermitage Theater, founded in July 1919 on Meyerhold's initiative. Since he describes Annenkov's work in some detail we will not discuss it here. It is worth noting, however, that Annenkov, who was also an artist, worked as either artistic director or director on three of the famous mass spectacles of 1920—*The Storming of the Winter Palace, The Mystery of Liberated Labor,* and *Toward a World Commune.*

65. "Dramaticheskiye shkoly," *Vtonkpp,* no. 2 (1919), p. 48; "Kursy Masterstva Stsenicheskikh Postanovok," *Vtonkpp,* no. 2 (1919), p. 59; Katerina Clark, "Aleksei Remizov in Petrograd, 1919–1921: The Bard of the Peoples' Theater," in Greta Slobin, ed., *Aleksei Remizov: Approaches to a Protean Writer,* U.C.L.A. Slavic Studies, vol. 16 (Columbus, Ohio: Slavica, 1987), pp. 261–276.

66. M. Pustynin, "Teatr shumnogo segodnya," *Vopzitil,* no. 9 (September 28, 1918), p. 3.

67. This is a well-known moment about which many have written. See A. Fevral'skiy, *Pervaya sovetskaya p'yesa: 'Misteriya-buff' V. V. Mayakovskogo* (Moscow: Sovetskiy pisatel', 1971), esp. pp. 52–88.

68. M. Gorky, "Trudnyy vopros," *Dela i dni Bol'shogo dramaticheskogo teatra,* pp. 7–9; A. Lunacharsky, "Kakaya nam nuzhna melodrama," *Zi,* no. 58 (January 14, 1919), pp. 2–3.

69. Compare Gorky, "Trudnyy vopros," p. 7; Lunacharsky, "Kakaya nam nuzhna melodrama," pp. 2–3.

70. Rolland, *Le Théâtre du peuple,* pp. 68, 113–116.

71. Gvozdev and Piotrovsky, "Petrogradskiye teatry i prazdnestva," p. 100.

72. See "Posledniy god," *Zi,* no. 57 (1919), p. 2.

73. "Raboty obshchegorodskoy kul't-prosvetitel'noy konferentsii," *PP,* no. 125 (June 16, 1918), p. 4.

74. See "Plany budushchego," *Tii,* no. 6–7 (1918), p. 74.

75. "Uluchsheniye sborov v teatrakh," *Zi,* no. 59 (January 13, 1919), p. 3.

76. See, for instance, the debate of 1918 over whether to nationalize the theaters (reported in *I,* no. 235 [1918]); P. Kerzhentsev called for their immediate nationalization, but his position represented an extreme—O. D. Kameneva, then head of TEO, was against it and Lunacharsky pointed out that it would strain the state budget.

77. See I. Vybra, "Svoboda i diktatura v iskusstve," *Ik,* no. 9 (February 16, 1919), p. 2.

78. Adr. Piotrovsky, "Diktatura," *Zi,* no. 584–585 (October 17–18, 1920), p. 2.

79. R. D. Timenchik, "Ob odnom pis'me Anne Akhmatovoy," *Z,* no. 9 (1991), pp. 165–167.

80. A case in point would be Radlov's translation of Plautus' "The Brothers Menaechmus" (Bliznetsy). See "Obshchestvo revniteley khudozhestvennogo slova," *A,* no. 4–5 (1916), p. 86; S. E. Radlov, "'Menekhmy' Plavta na stsene Zimnego Vodevilya i v Narodnom Dome v Petrograde," *Ge,* no. 1 (1918), pp. 116–117.

81. "Izucheniye teorii poeticheskogo yazyka," *Zi,* no. 273 (Oct. 21, 1919), p. 2.

82. "V petrogradskikh teatrakh," *Vt,* no. 26 (1919), p. 9; "Poyezdka v Kronshtadt v dni godovshchiny," *Vt,* no. 43 (November 25–30, 1919), p. 14.

330

83. N. N. Evreinov, *Teatral'nye inventsii* (Moscow: Vremya, 1922), p. 8; Adr. Piotrovsky, "Teatr vsego naroda," *Zi,* no. 456–457 (May 20–21, 1920), p. 1.

5. Petrograd: Ritual Capital of Revolutionary Russia

1. Evreinov was assisted by A. R. Kugel' and N. V. Petrov, the artistic director was Yu. P. Annenkov, and G. I. Varlikh was responsible for the music.

2. This is the version of the response presented in "Stat'ya neustanovlënnogo avtora 'Vzyatiye zimnego dvortsa' (vpechatleniya)" (November 9, 1920), reprinted in "Massovye prazdnestva," a section in A. Z. Yufit, ed., *Russkiy sovetskiy teatr 1917–1921: Dokumenty i materialy* (Leningrad: Iskusstvo, 1968), p. 273. There is some evidence that the event was not an unqualified success, however. For instance, although 100,000 sounds like an impressive audience, there was apparently seating for 170,000 on Palace Square, and an air show earlier in the day proved a much more popular event; see "Obshchiy plan torzhestv," *PP,* no. 249 (November 5, 1920), p. 2; "Vmestimost' mest zrelishch," *PP,* no. 250 (November 6, 1920), p. 2.

3. There are several different accounts of what happened in this mass spectacle. Compare "Libretto instsenirovki 'Vzyatie zimnego dvortsa'," in "Massovye prazdnestva," pp. 272–273 (also pp. 273–276), and Frantisek Deak, "Russian Mass Spectacles," *Drama Review,* vol. XIX, no. 2 (June 1975), pp. 7–22.

4. For a more comprehensive account of the mass spectacles of War Communism, see James von Geldern, *Bolshevik Festivals, 1917–1920* (Berkeley: University of California Press, 1993).

5. The same issue of *Vestnik teatra* that announced that Meyerhold was to head TEO also published an account of a meeting to discuss staging future mass spectacles in Moscow, suggesting that Meyerhold's earlier experience with them may have been a factor in his appointment; see "K priyezdu V. E. Meyerkhol'da: Naznacheniye V. E. Meyerkhol'da zaveduyushchim TEO," *Vt,* no. 68 (September 21–26, 1920), p. 3.

6. In addition to *The Storming of the Winter Palace,* these were *The Mystery of Liberated Labor,* performed for May Day, *The Blockade of Russia* (June 20), *For a World Commune* (staged for the delegates to a meeting of the Third Communist International on July 19), and an abridged version of the last mentioned staged on August 2. The major exception to the rule that the casts and audiences kept getting bigger would be *The Blockade of Russia,* which was staged in a specially constructed ampitheater that seated only 4,000; its cast was 750.

7. "K oktyabr'skim torzhestvam," *PP,* no. 240 (October 26, 1920), p. 1; N. Evreinov, "'Vzyatie zimnego dvortsa': Stat'ya glavnogo rezhissëra," *Km,* no. 4 (November 15, 1920), p. 5

8. V. Mayakovsky, "Prikaz po armii iskusstv," *Ik,* no. 1 (Petrograd, December 7, 1918), p. 1. These slogans were also used as banner headings for the journal.

9. Ibid.; V. Mayakovsky, V. Kamensky, and D. Burlyuk, "Dekret no. 1 o demokratizatsii iskusstv," *Gf* (March 1918); P. Kerzhentsev, *Tvorcheskiy teatr,* 3rd. ed. (Moscow: VTsIK, 1919), pp. 73–74; E. A. Speranskaya, ed., *Agitatsionnomassovoe iskusstvo pervykh let oktyabrya* (Moscow: Iskusstvo, 1971), p. 88.

10. Kerzhentsev, *Tvorcheskiy teatr,* p. 80.

11. Ibid., pp. 42, 45.

12. Ibid., pp. 35, 37, 40, 41, 42, 45, 49.

13. Ibid., p. 38.

14. *Tvorchestvo Fransua Rable i narodnaya kul'tura srednevokov'ya* (Moscow: Khudozhestvennaya literatura, 1965) is largely based on Bakhtin's dissertation, "Rable v istorii realizma," written in the early 1940s and defended in 1946.

15. M. Bakhtin, *Rabelais and His World*, trans. Hélène Iswolsky (Bloomington: Indiana University Press, 1984), p. 7.

16. Kerzhentsev, *Tvorcheskiy teatr*, p. 70.

17. Adr. Piotrovsky, "Khronika leningradskikh prazdnestv, 1919–22g.," in *Massovye prazdnestva* (Leningrad: Academia, 1926), pp. 75–76.

18. Adr. Piotrovsky, *Za sovetskiy teatr! Sbornik statey* (Leningrad: Academia, 1925), pp. 8, 21.

19. Ibid., p. 21.

20. "Teatr i revolyutsiya," *IPs*, no. 85 (April 21, 1920), p. 1.

21. "Misteriya osvobozhdënnogo truda," in *Russkiy sovetskiy teatr 1917–1921*, pp. 263–264. See also Deak, "Russian Mass Spectacles," pp. 7–10; "K prazdnovaniyu pervogo maya," *IPs*, no. 93 (April 30, 1920), p. 1; and "Pervomayskaya misteriya 'Gimn osvobozhdënnogo truda,' " *IPs*, no. 96 (May 3, 1920), p. 2.

22. Jean Jacques Rousseau, *Politics and the Arts: Letter to M. D'Alembert on the Theatre*, trans. Allan Bloom (Illinois: The Free Press of Glencoe, 1960), p. 126. For an example of a later invocation of the Rousseau model, see Romain Rolland, *Le Théâtre du peuple* (Paris: Libraire Hachette, 1933), pp. 154–155.

23. See, for example, Mona Ozouf, *Festivals and the French Revolution*, trans. Alan Sheridan (Cambridge, Mass.: Harvard University Press, 1988), esp. pp. 249–250.

24. Friedrich Nietzsche, *Die Geburt der Tragödie, Nietzsches Werke*, vol. I (Stuttgart: Alfred Kroner Verlag, 1921), p. 65, Section 4, p. 171, Section 20.

25. The first of these was *Sverzheniye samoderzhaviya* (The Overthrow of Autocracy), first staged under the direction of N. G. Vinogradov-Mamont in a riding manege in March 1919 and repeated many times; see N. G. Vinogradov-Mamont, *Krasnoarmeyskoye chudo: Povest' o teatral'no-dramaticheskoy masterskoy krasnoy armii* (Leningrad: Iskusstvo, 1972). Another was *Krovavoye voskreseniye* (Bloody Sunday), staged for the January 9 anniversary from January 9–22, 1920, and directed by Adrian Piotrovsky; see "9-oye yanvarya na petrogradskoy storone," *IPs*, no. 23 (January 15, 1920), p. 6.

26. In Moscow several spectacles were planned for a large field outside town but they never materialized. Some did, however, take place on Red Square—that is, most of those spectacles that took place were staged at the very heart of the old regime's symbolic geography.

27. Eisenstein made a study of some of the mass spectacles of Petrograd and also organized agitational theatrical work while in the Red Army; see R. Yurenev, *Sergey Eyzenshteyn: Zamysly, fil'my, metod*, Part I, 1898–1929 (Moscow: Iskusstvo, 1985), pp. 28–34.

28. Other obvious examples of the symbolic use of the stairs would include the parodic scene in Eisenstein's *October* (1927) when Kerensky ascends the marble staircase of the Winter Palace, and the ending of Vs. Pudovkin's *The End*

of Petersburg (also 1927), when, after the battle of revolution, a little old lady ascends them.

29. Specifically, K. Mardzhanov, N. Evreinov, N. V. Petrov, S. Radlov, A. Piotrovsky, and Yu. Annenkov.

30. For example, those playing the interventionists in *The Blockade of Russia.*

31. B. Smerala, "Pravda o sovetskoy Rossii: O prazdnestve 'Gimn osvobozhdënnogo truda' ('Misteriya osvobozhdënnogo truda')," in *Russkiy sovetskiy teatr 1917–1921,* p. 265.

32. René Fülöp-Miller, *Geist und Gesicht des Bolschewismus* (Zurich, Leipzig, Vienna, 1926).

33. Kerzhentsev, *Tvorcheskiy teatr,* p. 30.

34. See D., "Spektakl' na vode," *Bv,* August 12, 1913, p. 5; Anchar', D. V. and N. G. (successive articles), "Vzyatie Azova: Zrelishche pod otkrytym nebom," *Bv,* August 17, 1913 (morning edition), p. 6.

35. See A. L. Alekseyev-Yakovlev, *Russkiye narodnye gulyaniya* (Leningrad: Iskusstvo, 1948), esp. pp. 144, 166.

36. V. P. Lapshin, *Khudozhestvennaya zhizn' Moskvy i Petrograda v 1917 godu* (Moscow: Sovetskiy khudozhnik, 1983), p. 389.

37. Piotrovsky, *Za sovetskiy teatr!,* p. 21.

38. "V Politprosvetupravlenii," *IPs,* no. 85 (April 21, 1920), p. 1. *The Mystery of Liberated Labor,* for instance, was sponsored by the Political Department of the Petrograd Military District, and the Krasnoselsk version of *For a World Commune* by the Military Reserves, while the earlier version of that spectacle and *The Blockade of Russia* were sponsored by PTO.

39. Oliver M. Sayler, *Our American Theater* (New York: Benjamin Blair, Inc., 1971), p. 236.

40. S. Radlov, "Elektrofikatsiya teatra," *Stat'i o teatre 1918–1922* (Petrograd: Tsentral'noye kooperativnoye izdatel'stvo, 1923), pp. 15–23.

41. See Marx's *The Civil War in France* and Lenin's *State and Revolution* (1917).

42. Zhul'yen T'yerso, *Prazdniki i pesni frantsuzskoy revolyutsii,* trans. K. Zhikhareva (Petrograd: Parus, 1917; first edition, 1908); R. Rollan, *Narodnyy teatr,* introd. Vyacheslav Ivanov (Petrograd and Moscow: TEO, 1919; first Russian ed., 1910).

43. Piotrovsky, *Za sovetskiy teatr!,* pp. 21–22; Yevg. Kuznetsov, "Komissar teatrov," in *Mariya Fëdorovna Andreyeva: Perepiska, Vospominaniya, Stat'i* (Moscow: Gos. izd., 1961), pp. 418–420.

44. N. Evreinov, *Proiskhozhdeniye dramy. Pervobytnaya tragediya i rol' kozla v istorii yeyë vozniknoveniya. Fol'kloristicheskiy ocherk* (Petersburg: Petropolis, 1921).

45. Zelinsky himself played a minor administrative role in the early days of the Soviet theater (he sat on several TEO committees, including the Repertoire Committee) before emigrating in 1921.

46. Adr. Piotrovsky, "Chetvërtyy god," *Zi,* no. 602–604 (November 6–8, 1920), p. 1.

47. "Khronika," *Zi,* no. 85 (1919), p. 2.

48. "Salamanskiy boy," *Zi,* no. 114 (April 9, 1919), p. 3.

49. Piotrovsky, *Za sovetskiy teatr!,* p. 23.

50. Adr. Piotrovsky, "Teatr vsego naroda," *Zi,* no. 456–457 (May 20–21, 1920), p. 1.

51. Unless otherwise indicated, my information on the tower comes from Nikolay Punin, *Pamyatnik III Internatsionalu: Proyekt khud. V. Ye. Tatlina* (Petersburg: Izd. IZO v NKP, 1920). However, there are different versions of these glass forms. For example, V. Shklovsky in "Pamyatnik Tret'yemu Internatsionalu" (*Zi*, no. 650–652 [January 5–9, 1921], p. 1) describes the lowest glass volume as a cylinder housing the "International Sovnarkom," and the upper volume as a sphere housing ROSTA.

52. Punin, *Pamyatnik III Internatsionalu*, p. 2.

53. Ibid.

54. Ibid., p. 4.

55. Ibid., p. 3.

56. Ibid., p. 4.

57. In *Vladimir Tatlin and the Russian Avant-Garde* (New Haven: Yale University Press, 1983), John Milner has explored a number of ways this potential can be seen in the tower (pp. 151–180).

6. NEP and the "Art of Capitulation"

1. "Blokada Rossii konchayetsya," *V*, no. 1–2 (1922), pp. 1–3.

2. "Torzhestvuyushchiy oboz," *V*, no. 3 (May 1922), p. 2. The Piotrovsky remark comes from his article "Perelom," in *Zi*, no. 1 (January 3, 1922), p. 13.

3. See, for example, Stephen Cohen, *Rethinking the Soviet Experience: Politics and History since 1917* (New York: Oxford University Press, 1986), esp. pp. 75–76; Richard Stites, *Revolutionary Dreams: Utopian Dreams and Experimental Life in the Russian Revolution* (New York: Oxford University Press, 1989), p. 225.

4. See Michael Fox, "Glavlit, Censorship, and the Problem of Party Policy in Cultural Affairs," *Soviet Studies*, no. 6 (1922). See also Christopher Read, *Culture and Power in Revolutionary Russia: The Intelligentsia and the Transition from Tsarism to Communism* (London: Macmillan, 1990).

5. Karl Schlögel, *Jenseits des Grossen Oktober: Das Laboratorium der Moderne Petersburg 1909–1921* (Berlin: Siedler Verlag, 1988).

6. I. E. Barenbaum and N. A. Kostyleva, *Knizhnyy Peterburg-Leningrad* (Leningrad: Lenizdat, 1986), pp. 326–346.

7. "Rabota Gosudarstvennogo Izdatel'stva v Peterburge za 1920 god," *Kir*, no. 1 (1921), p. 26.

8. L. Meshcheryakov, "O chastnykh izdatel'stvakh," *Pir*, no. 2 (1922), pp. 129–131; Jeffrey Brooks, *When Russia Learned to Read* (Princeton: Princeton University Press, 1985), p. 156.

9. "Khronika," *Zi*, no. 28 (July 17, 1923), p. 26.

10. Katerina Clark, "The 'Quiet Revolution' in Soviet Intellectual Life," in Sheila Fitzpatrick, Alexander Rabinowitch, and Richard Stites, eds., *Russia in the Era of NEP: Explorations in Soviet Culture and Society* (Bloomington: Indiana University Press, 1991), pp. 210–230.

11. UNOVIS continued to exhibit but was a diminished presence. The Scythian movement folded in 1924. For other groups and institutions of War Communism that folded, see Ya. Lifshits, "Peterburgskiye pis'ma (7 iyunya 1922)," *Nrk*, no. 4 (1922), p. 25; Barry Scherr, "Notes on the Literary Life of Petrograd, 1918–22: A Tale of Three Houses," *Slavic Review* (June 1977), pp. 256–267.

12. For example, the emergence of the Constructivist movement.

13. See Katerina Clark, "The City Versus the Countryside in Soviet Peasant Literature of the Twenties: A Duel of Utopias," in Abbott Gleason, Peter Kenez, and Richard Stites, eds., *Bolshevik Culture* (Bloomington: Indiana University Press, 1985), pp. 175–189.

14. A. A. Mgebrov, *Zhizn' v teatre,* vol. II (Moscow and Leningrad: Academia, 1932), p. 386.

15. See, for example, "Iz instruktsii Vserossiyskoy tsentral'noy oktyabr'skoy kommissii o poryadke prazdnovaniya IV godovshchiny Oktyabrya," *I,* no. 33 (October 1921), p. 4.

16. See D. Shcheglov, "O Yedinom Khudozhestvennom Kruzhke, o metodakh i perspektivakh," *Zi,* no. 22 (June 5, 1923), p. 20; A. Zlat, "Iskusstvo i rabochiye kluby," *Zi,* no. 26 (June 26, 1923), p. 22; *Yedinyy khudozhestvennyy kruzhok: Metody klubno-khudozhestvennoy raboty* (Leningrad: Izdatel'stvo knizhnogo sektora GOBONO, 1924).

17. A prime example of this can be seen in Meyerhold's production of *The Trust D. E.* (see Chapter 7).

18. See, for example, D. Shcheglov, "Neskol'ko mysley o khudozhestvennoy rabote i o rabochikh klubakh'," and [unsigned], "Rabochiy repertuar," *Zi,* no. 21 (May 29, 1923), pp. 19–20.

19. Zlat, "Iskusstvo i rabochiye kluby," p. 22.

20. A. Piotrovsky, "Molodaya dramaturgiya," *Zi,* no. 12 (March 18, 1924), p. 3.

21. A. Lunacharsky, "Khudozhestvennaya politika sovetskogo gosudarstva," *Zi,* no. 9 (February 26, 1924), p. 2.

22. "Teatral'nyy god," editorial, *Zi,* no. 1 (January 3, 1922), p. 1; A. Piotrovsky, "Nashi katakomby," *Zi,* no. 4 (January 23, 1922), p. 2.

23. See Larissa A. Zhadova, *Malevich: Suprematism and Revolution in Russian Art, 1910–1930* (London: Thames and Hudson, 1982), p. 96.

24. *Istoriya Leningradskogo universiteta, 1819–1969: Ocherki* (Leningrad: Izdatel'stvo Leningradskogo universiteta, 1969), pp. 225–328.

25. See Sheila Fitzpatrick, *The Commissariat of Enlightenment* (Cambridge: Cambridge University Press, 1970), Chap. 5.

26. See Katerina Clark and Michael Holquist, *Mikhail Bakhtin* (Cambridge, Mass.: Harvard University Press, 1985), Chaps. 4 and 5.

27. Even after the Institute was nationalized, Zubov continued to play some role in running its affairs until he was arrested in 1924. He was released and emigrated in 1925.

28. The formation of the Division in some senses represented the realization of the agenda of left art presented in a slogan of its mouthpiece *Iskusstvo kommuny* as "Let Us Organize a Division of the Verbal Arts!" (December 7, 1918), p. 2. See Halina Stephan, *"Lef" and the Left Front of the Arts, Slavistische Beitrage,* vol. 142 (Munich: Verlag Otto Sagner, 1981), pp. 9–10.

29. N. Strel'nikov, "Pozdno—luchshe, chem nikogda," *Zi,* no. 20 (May 13, 1924), pp. 7–8.

30. It seems probable that Bakhtin gave one of the public lectures there, as is indicated in his Work Book. Although Michael Holquist and I state in our book *Mikhail Bakhtin* that this entry in the Work Book is false, I have come to recon-

sider this position and entertain the possibility that a lecture of June 28, 1924, listed in GIII's report as having been given by N. N. Bakhtin, was actually given by Mikhail, since its topic, "Problema 'geroya' v literaturnom proizvedenii," seems close to what he had been working on in recent years. N. N. Bakhtin gave other lectures at GIII, on the childrens' theater, his area of expertise.

31. Compare the activities, subjects broached, and lectures given in GIII with those of GAKhN, reported, for example, in *BG*, no. 1 (1925), pp. 46–62; no. 2–3 (1926), pp. 57–60; and no. 4–5 (1926), p. 91.

32. One famous, though short-lived, example would be the *Economist* (Ekonomist), to which the sociologist Pitirim Sorokin contributed.

33. See, for example, the attacks on *Mysl'*, "idealists," F. F. Zelinsky, and others in virtually every issue of *Kniga i revolyutsiya* from 1922.

34. "V Petrogradskom teatral'nom otdelenii," *Zi*, no. 4 (January 22, 1924), p. 27.

35. N. Punin, "Zangezi," *Zi*, no. 19 (May 15, 1923), p. 10; V. Tatlin, "O 'Zangezi,' " *Zi*, no. 17 (May 8, 1923), p. 15.

36. In Western historiography, this position is generally associated with the Serapion Brothers, discussed in the next chapter; "Serapionovye brat'ya o sebe," *Lz*, no. 3 (1922), pp. 25–31. What is less generally recognized is that their position was far from unique for early NEP. See P. Medvedev, "O 'Sodruzhestve' (k 4-letiyu gruppy)," in *Sodruzhestvo: Literaturnyy al'manakh* (Leningrad: Priboy, 1927), pp. 286–296.

37. Sergey Radlov, "Sud'by teatra za vremya revolyutsii," *Zi*, no. 42 (October 24, 1922), p. 2.

38. A. Lunacharsky, "Khudozhestvennaya politika sovetskogo gosudarstva," *Zi*, no. 9 (February 26, 1924), p. 3. See also N. Bukharin, "O khudozhestvennoy literature i politike RKP (Rech' na soveshchanii TsK RKP o literature)," *Zi*, no. 36 (September 2, 1924), pp. 2–3.

39. For material on the new universities, see Akademiya obshchestvennykh nauk pri TsK KPSS, *Sovetskaya intelligentsiya (istoriya formirovaniya i rosta 1917–1965 gg.)* (Moscow: Mysl', 1968), p. 104, and D. P. Konchalovskiy, *Vospominaniya i pis'ma (ot gumanizma k Khristu)* (Paris: Libraire du cinq continents, 1971), pp. 158–161.

40. Figures such as A. Volynsky, Ye. Zamyatin, and K. Chukovsky took prominent roles in running the Petrograd branch of VSP.

41. This circumstance is quite clear in the many articles about the situation of Soviet publishing that appeared in *Pechat' i revolyutsiya* in these years. See, for example, no. 1 (1921), pp. 9–42.

42. An exception to the rule that the cultural journals of NEP came out of the two capitals would be *Sibirskiye ogni*, founded in 1922, which helped launch the careers of several young writers.

43. *Krasnaya nov'*, for instance, had a hitherto unprecedented circulation of fifteen to twenty thousand in its first year, although this declined to eight thousand during 1922, before settling down to ten to twelve thousand for some years.

44. Petrograd was still the capital for scholarship and research, particularly in the natural sciences, and an overwhelming majority of works in this field came out of that city, as can be sensed by looking at the sections reviewing scientific literature in *Pechat' i revolyutsiya*.

45. *Zvezda*'s circulation was around three thousand, increasing by the end of 1926 to five thousand, but that could not compete with *Novyy mir,* with a circulation of fifteen thousand.

46. El. "Itogi IV-ogo Vserossiyskogo s"yezda rabotnikov iskusstv," *Zi,* no. 20 (May 22, 1923), p. 16.

47. "Ekran," *Zi,* no. 31 (August 5, 1923), p. 5.

48. "Khronika i ruchnye zametki," *Nrk,* no. 1 (1922), p. 35.

49. For music, see Igor' Glebov (pseud. of B. Asaf'yev), "Russkaya muzykal'-naya zhizn' v 1921 godu," *Zi,* no. 1 (January 3, 1922), p. 3. In theater, Meyerhold's Moscow productions dominated the horizon.

50. B. Eikhenbaum, "Retsenziya na sborniki V. Rozhdestvenskogo i Ye. Polonskoy," *Ku,* no. 7 (1921), p. 42.

51. Mikh. Spassovskiy, "Akademiya khudozhestv: Yeyë proshloye i nastoyashcheye," *Ar,* no. 1 (1923), pp. 72–76.

52. Victor Turner, *The Ritual Process: Structure and Anti-Structure* (Chicago: The Aldine Press, 1969), esp. pp. 112–113, 128–133.

53. Sergey Radlov, "Sud'by teatra za vremya revolyutsii," *Zi,* no. 42 (October 24, 1922), p. 2.

54. For a fuller account of the "Pushkin Days" see John Malmstad, "Mikhail Kuzmin: A Chronicle of His Life and Times," in M. A. Kuzmin, *Sobraniye sochineniy,* vol. I (Munich: Wilhelm Fink Verlag, 1977), pp. 256–257.

55. See also D. Segal's account of Akhmatova's role immediately after the Revolution in his " 'Sumerki svobody': O nekotorykh temakh russkoy yezhednevnoy pechati 1917–1918 gg.," *Minuvsheye: Istoricheskiy al'manakh,* no. 3 (Paris: Atheneum, 1987), pp. 131–195.

56. V. N. Sazhin, "Neudavshiysya proryv nemoty (o nevyshedshem nomere 'Literaturnoy gazete' 1921 goda)," in *Pyatye Tynyanovskiye chteniya* (Riga: Zinatne, 1990), pp. 162–167. See also *Lo,* no. 2 (1992).

57. See, respectively, V. Khodasevich, "Pamyati predka," Ye. Zamyatin, "Pora," and N. I., "Iz Moskvy," articles summarized in V. N. Sazhin, "Neudavshiysya proryv nemoty."

58. B. Eikhenbaum, "Mig soznaniya," *Ku,* no. 7 (1921), pp. 10, 17.

59. Ye. Zamyatin's dystopic novel *We* (*My,* 1920) is a cousin of *Brave New World* and *1984,* but in this instance the critique of the utopian society with its overbearing state is refracted through clichés from the myth of Petersburg, and the novel has a Pushkin figure as its martyred hero (R-13).

60. See, for example, A. Bogdanov, *Elementy proletarskoy kul'tury* (Moscow: Gos. izd., 1920), p. 49; P. Bessal'ko, "O forme i soderzhanii," *G,* no. 4 (1918), p. 4; V. Mayakovsky, "Radovat'sya rano," and O. M. Brik, "Khudozhnik-proletariy," *Ik,* no. 2 (December 15, 1918), p. 1; A. Lunacharsky, "Lozhka protivoyadiya," *Ik,* no. 4 (December 29, 1918), p. 1.

61. Cited in Edward J. Brown, *Russian Literature since the Revolution* (Cambridge: Harvard University Press, 1982), p. 31.

62. Pushkinskiy dom acquired a permanent home only in the postrevolutionary years and also expanded its purview to all of Russian literature; see "Pushkinskiy dom pri Rossiyskoy akademii nauk," *Kir,* no. 1 (1920), p. 61; M. G., "Pushkinskiy dom," *Niyer,* no. 2 (1921), pp. 23–25.

63. Igor' Glebov, "Kamernye kontserty starogo Peterburga," *Zi*, no. 14 (April 4, 1922), p. 1; Professor Mikhaylovskiy, "Staryy Peterburg," *Kp*, no. 7 (1923), p. 6; *Obshchestvo 'Staryy Peterburg' 1921–1923* (Petersburg, 1923), esp. pp. 11–16.

64. Rusticus, "Poeziya starogo Peterburga," *Zi*, no. 17 (May 2, 1922), p. 5.

65. See *Peterburg: Avtobiografiya A. P. Ostroumovoy*, Vstupitel'naya stat'ya Al. Benua (Petersburg: Komitet populyarizatsii khudozhestvennykh izdaniy pri Rossiyskoy akademii istorii material'noy kul'tury, 1922).

66. Lit, "Vnimaniye 'okhrany' pamyatnikov iskusstva i stariny," *Zi*, no. 19 (May 15, 1923), p. 18.

67. "Khronika," *Zi*, no. 4 (January 30, 1923), p. 15.

68. N. Punin, "Ot svyashchennykh mogil ruki proch'!" *Zi*, no. 12 (March 27, 1923), p. 8.

69. "Obshchenatsional'nye Pushkinskiye pominki," *Vl*, no. 2 (1921), p. 15.

70. "Khronika," *Pir*, no. 3 (May–June, 1924), pp. 286–287; "Khronika," *Nk*, no. 3–4 (1924), p. 5. Vyacheslav Ivanov was brought up from Baku to be one of those presiding over the celebrations, a service that apparently enabled him to emigrate afterwards.

71. N. Punin, "Vystavka pamyati Khlebnikova," *Zi*, no. 26 (July 3, 1923), p. 14; I, "Vystavka . . .," *Zi*, no. 27 (July 10, 1923), p. 19; "Khronika," *Zi*, no. 25 (June 26, 1923), p. 24. Note the hagiographic elements in N. L., "Poet vremeni," *Zi*, no. 37 (September 19, 1922), p. 7.

72. "Khronika," *Zi*, no. 39 (October 3, 1922), p. 3. Radlov was closer to the Tatlin / Altman / Punin camp at the Myatlev House than to the opposing Malevich camp. See Sergey Radlov, "Sud'by teatra za vremya revolyutsii," *Zi*, no. 42 (October 24, 1922), pp. 1–2.

73. Pavel Filonov, "Deklaratsiya 'mirovogo rassveta,' "; P. Mansurov, "Deklaratsiya,"; M. V. Matyushin, "Ne iskusstvo, a zhizn',"; K. Malevich, "Suprematicheskoye zerkalo," *Zi*, no. 20 (August 26, 1923), pp. 13–16.

74. N. Punin, "Zangezi," *Zi*, no. 20 (May 15, 1923), p. 10.

75. See O. Brik, "T. n. 'formal'nyy metod,' " *L*, no. 1 (1923), pp. 213–215.

76. S. Radlov, "Slovesnaya improvizatsiya v teatre," *Zi*, no. 9 (March 1, 1922), p. 4; V. Tatlin, "O 'Zangezi,' " *Zi*, no. 17 (May 8, 1923), p. 15.

77. B. Eikhenbaum, "O Shatobriane, o chervontsakh i o russkoy literature," *Zi*, no. 1 (1924), p. 3.

78. D. Vygodskiy, "Stikhi 1923 goda," *Zi*, no. 1 (1924), p. 5.

79. See Katerina Clark, *The Soviet Novel: History as Ritual* (Chicago: University of Chicago Press, 1981).

80. N. N., "Radostnoye barokko," *Zi*, no. 18 (May 9, 1922), p. 4.

81. N. L., "Poet vremeni," *Zi*, no. 37 (September 19, 1922), p. 7, and N. Punin, "Zangezi," *Zi*, no. 20 (May 22, 1923), p. 11.

7. Revolutionary Culture Meets the Jazz Age

1. The city was renamed Leningrad after Lenin's death in January 1924, and hence was called Leningrad at the time of this premiere. However, because this chapter covers primarily the period before the city was renamed, for consistency's sake, I will refer to it throughout as Petrograd.

2. Actually, Ehrenburg had refused to adapt his novel *The D. E. Trust* (Trest D. Ye. Istoriya gibeli Yevropy, 1923) for Meyerhold, and the play combines elements from not only the Ehrenburg novel but also Bernhard Kellermann's story "The Tunnel."

3. This was not the first time Meyerhold used jazz on stage; he had already used it for *The Magnanimous Cuckold* in 1922.

4. See S. Frederick Starr, *Red and Hot: The Fate of Jazz in the Soviet Union, 1917–1980* (New York and Oxford: Oxford University Press, 1983), pp. 45–46.

5. Gayk Adonts, "Novyy vid pornografii," *Zi,* no. 37 (1923), pp. 1–2.

6. A. Gvozdev, "Postanovka 'D. Ye.' v 'Teatre imeni Vs. Meyerkhol'da,' " *Zi,* no. 26 (June 24, 1924), p. 6.

7. Starr, *Red and Hot,* pp. 51, 52.

8. Gvozdev, "Postanovka 'D. Ye.,' " p. 5.

9. M., "Meyerkhol'd o proshlom i budushchem russkogo teatra," *Zi,* no. 27 (July 1, 1924), pp. 11–12.

10. Valentin Parnakh, "Novye tantsy," "Dzhaz-band," *V,* no. 4 (1922), p. 25.

11. S. Mokul'skiy, "Novaya postanovka Meyerkhol'da ('D. Ye.' Podgayetskogo)," *Zi,* no. 27 (1924), p. 11.

12. "Obshchestvo izucheniya zapadnoy kul'tury," *Zi,* no. 577 (October 8, 1920), p. 1.

13. For instance, A. Tolstoy's play *The Revolt of the Machines* (Bunt mashin) is from K. Capek's *R.U.R.* Piotrovsky's *Padeniye Yeleny Ley* is in fact from Kaiser's *Gas,* though Piotrovsky has given his protagonists Greek names.

14. B. Eikhenbaum, "O Shatobriane, o chervontsakh i russkoy literature," *Zi,* no. 1 (January 1, 1924), p. 3.

15. "Ob izdatel'skoy strategii," *Zi,* no. 38 (September 16, 1923), p. 26.

16. "Sevzapkino v 1923 godu," *Zi,* no. 1 (January 2, 1923), p. 23.

17. Richard Taylor, *The Politics of the Soviet Cinema, 1917–1929* (Cambridge, England: Cambridge University Press, 1979), p. 75.

18. [unsigned], "Okno v Yevropu," *Zi,* no. 1 (January 1, 1920), p. 2; "Meri Pikford, Duglas Ferbenks i Charli Chaplin yedut v Moskvu," *Zi,* no. 23 (1924), p. 3; "Khronika," *Zi,* no. 8 (February 21, 1922), p. 7.

19. "Khronika," *Zi,* no. 37 (September 9, 1924), no. 31, (July 29, 1924), p. 23.

20. "Pis'mo Romanu Yakobsonu," *V,* no. 1–2 (1922), p. 5. Shklovsky himself was soon obliged to flee the Soviet Union for Berlin (in March 1922) but negotiated to return in 1923.

21. A. S. Oslinovskiy and A. F. Kononkov, *D. S. Rozhdestvenskiy* (Moscow: Prosveshcheniye, 1974), pp. 95–96; Akad. A. I. Yoffe, *Moya zhizn' i rabota: Avtobiograficheskiy ocherk* (Moscow and Leningrad: Tekhniko-teoreticheskoye izdatel'stvo, 1933), p. 24; *Erenfest-Yoffe: Nauchnaya perepiska (1907–1933 gg.)* (Leningrad: Nauka, 1973), pp. 150–175, 184–186, 203.

22. See, for example, S. Efis, "D. S. Rozhdestvenskiy—uchënyy i organizator," in *Vospominaniya ob akademike D. S. Rozhdestvenskom: K 100-letiyu so dnya rozhdeniya* (Leningrad: Nauka, 1976), p. 69; Oslinovskiy and Kononkov, *D. S. Rozhdestvenskiy,* p. 95.

23. G. Ertsikovskiy, "Sovremennaya aviatsiya," *Sz,* no. 1 (1922), pp. 180–182; "Sovremennyy kontsert," *Sz,* no. 1 (1922), p. 187.

24. "Institut istorii iskusstv," *ZptGiS,* no. 51 (February 23, 1924), pp. 6–7; A. Gvozdev, "Nechto o zritele, prospavshem 7 let," *Zi,* no. 28 (July 8, 1924), p. 6.

25. See Chapter 6. In Marietta Shaginyan's novel *Mess-Mend* to be discussed later in this chapter, such Russophile trends are parodied as the "Society for Russia and the Samovar," issue I (Moscow: Giz, 1924), p. 28.

26. See Gvozdev, "Postanovka 'D. Ye.,' " pp. 5–6.

27. Marietta Shaginyan, for instance, felt this when she wrote *Mess-Mend* between October 6 and December 23, 1923; see L. Skorino, "Obgonyaya vremya," in Marietta Shaginyan, *Mess-Mend* (Moscow: Pravda, 1988), p. 430.

28. See A. Piotrovsky, "Mysli avtora," *Kp,* no. 1 (1923), p. 14; Ye. R. D. R., "Kino shagayet," *Zi,* no. 14 (April 1, 1924), pp. 10–11.

29. F. Scott Fitzgerald, "Echoes of the Jazz Age," reprinted in Arthur Mizener, ed., *The Fitzgerald Reader* (New York: Charles Scribner's Sons, 1963), pp. 323–331.

30. Ibid.

31. See Viktor Shklovsky, "Drama i massovoye predstavleniye," *Zi,* nos. 688–690 (March 9, 10, 11, 1921), p. 1.

32. See, for example, Ye. Zamyatin, "O literature, revolyutsii, entropii i prochem" (1923), published in *Pisateli ob iskusstve i o sebe* (Leningrad: Krug, 1925).

33. Other members were Ye. Polonskaya, I. Gruzdev, L. Lunts, M. Slonimsky, N. Nikitin, N. Tikhonov, and V. Pozner. Their mentors were Gorky, Shklovsky, and Ye. Zamyatin, a list that in itself bespeaks the heterogeneous nature of their literary orientations.

34. Lev Lunts, "Na zapad!" *B,* no. 4 (1923), p. 262.

35. Ibid., p. 259.

36. V. Kaverin, *Ocherk raboty* (Moscow: Sovetskaya Rossiya, 1964), p. 19.

37. Lunts, "Na zapad!" pp. 267–269.

38. Others include a rather precious literary group known as "the Islanders" *(Ostrovityane)* whose members included K. Vaginov, S. Kolbas'yev, and N. Tikhonov. See also Boris Lavrenev, "Vmesto predisloviya," *Krusheniye respubliki Itl'* (1925).

39. I. Oksënov, "Proza 1923 goda," *Zi,* no. 1 (January 1, 1924), pp. 6 7.

40. B. Eikhenbaum, "O Shatobriane, o chervontsakh i russkoy literature," *Zi,* no. 1 (January 1, 1924), p. 4.

41. It should be noted that in Shklovsky's "Art as Technique" though the message is radical, the examples come principally from Russian literature of the nineteenth century.

42. "Gotovitsya k pechati," *N,* no. 1 (1921), p. 267.

43. Viktor Shklovsky, "Razvërtyvaniye syuzheta," *Sborniki po teorii poeticheskogo yazyka* (Petrograd, 1921), p. 56; B. Eikhenbaum, "O'Genri i teoriya novelly," *Z,* no. 6 (1925).

44. "Otdel slovesnykh iskusstv," in *Gosudarstvennyy institut istorii iskusstv, 1912–1927* (Leningrad: GIII, 1927), p. 24.

45. V. Kaverin, "Vstrechi v krasnoy gostinoy," *Sobesednik: Vospominaniya i portrety* (Moscow: Sovetskiy pisatel', 1973), p. 58.

46. See V. Kaverin, *The End of the Gang* (Konets khazy, 1925), and V. Shklovsky and Vs. Ivanov, *Mustard Gas* (Iprit, 1925—also called *Iperit* when published in *Lef*).

340

47. D. S. Likhachëv, "Zametki k intellektual'noy topografii Peterburga pervoy poloviny dvadtsatogo veka (po vospominaniyam)," in *Semiotika goroda i gorodskoy kul'tury: Peterburg, Trudy po znakovym sistemam*, XVIII (Tartu, 1984), pp. 76–77.

48. "Literaturnaya khronika," *Zi*, no. 8 (February 21, 1922), p. 7.

49. Ye. Shamurin, "Obshchiye kontury knizhnoy produktsii 1924 g.," in I. F. Yanitskiy, ed., *Kniga v 1924 g. v SSSR* (Moscow: Seyatel', 1925), pp. 124–125.

50. B. Eikhenbaum, "V poiskakh zhanra," *Rs*, no. 3 (1924), p. 229.

51. Lunts, "Na zapad!," p. 259.

52. "Bazarnaya literatura," editorial, *Zi*, no. 4 (January 22, 1924), p. 1; Dukh Bankvo, "Velikiy glukhonemoy," *Zi*, no. 2 (January 8, 1924), pp. 21–22.

53. "Zapreshcheniye ektsentricheskikh tantsev," *Zi*, no. 34 (August 19, 1924), p. 24.

54. See Paul Josephson, "Scientific Contacts between Germany and the Soviet Union in the Twenties," a paper presented to the Annual Convention of A.A.A.S.S. in Boston, November 1987.

55. See the open letter the group (also led by M. Kuzmin, K. Vaginov, and A. Radlova) sent to the German Expressionists: "Privetstviye khudozhnikam molodoy Germanii ot gruppy emotsionalistov," *Zi*, no. 10 (March 13, 1923), p. 8.

56. Viktor Shklovsky, "Aktsiz na Tarzana," *Zi*, no. 13 (March 25, 1924), p. 18.

57. A. F. Britikov, "Detektivnaya povest' v kontekste priklyuchencheskikh zhanrov," in V. A. Kovalëv, ed., *Russkaya sovetskaya povest' 20–30-kh godov* (Leningrad: Nauka, 1976).

58. A., "Revolyutsionnaya opera," *Zi*, no. 37 (September 9, 1924), p. 23; N. Mal'kov, " 'V bor'be za kommunu' ili 'Vzorvavshayasya bomba,' " *Zi*, no. 40 (September 30, 1924), pp. 5–6.

59. See B. Eikhenbaum, "O. Genri i teoriya novelly," *Z*, no. 6 (1925); see also K. Fedin's review of A. Piotrovsky's *Padeniye Yeleny Ley*—"Gaz," *Zi*, no. 46 (November 21, 1922), p. 3.

60. Yuri Tynyanov, "O literaturnom fakte," *L*, no. 2 (1924), pp. 101–116, esp. p. 103; Eikhenbaum, "O. Genri i teoriya novelly."

61. Carol Avins, *Border Crossings: The West and Russian Identity in Soviet Literature, 1917–1934* (Berkeley: University of California Press, 1983), p. 55.

62. A good example would be A. Tolstoy's novel *Aelita*.

63. M. Shaginyan, "Kak ya pisala 'Mess-Mend,' " in *Sobraniye sochineniy* (1935), p. 377.

64. N. Meshcheryakov, "Yanki v Petrograde," *Zi*, no. 7 (February 12, 1924), p. 14.

65. Shklovsky and Ivanov, *Mustard Gas* (see "Literaturnaya khronika," *Zi*, no. 43 [October 21, 1924], p. 19).

66. Skorino, "Obgonyaya vremya," p. 436.

67. F. Britikov, "Detektivnaya povest'," p. 434.

68. Jeffrey Brooks, *When Russia Learned to Read: Literacy and Popular Literature, 1861–1917* (Princeton: Princeton University Press, 1985), p. xvii.

69. Jim Dollar [Marietta Shaginyan], *Mess-Mend ili yanki v Petrograde*, issue V (Moscow: Gos. izd., 1924), pp. 179–180.

70. Ibid., p. 179.

71. Ibid., p. 181.

72. As we will see in the account of the linguistic theories of N. Ya. Marr in Chapter 9, the term *yedinyy* was not at this time an innocent one.

73. *Mess-Mend*, issue V, p. 183.

74. See Shaginyan's account of this in M. Sh., "Dollar: Yego zhizn' i tvorchestvo," in *Mess-Mend*, issue I, pp. 7–10.

75. *Mess-Mend*, issue III, p. 222.

76. Films were more likely to be centered in Moscow; in fact when A. Tolstoy's *Aelita* was made into a film (directed by Ya. Protozanov), the setting was changed from Petrograd to Moscow.

77. Thomas S. Kuhn, *The Structure of Scientific Revolutions*, 2nd ed., enlarged (Chicago: University of Chicago Press, 1970), esp. pp. 3–22.

78. This position is most cogently formulated in Tynyanov's introduction "O Khlebnikove" to *Sobraniye proizvedeniy Velemira Khlebnikova*, vol. I (Leningrad: Izdatel'stvo pisateley v Leningrade).

79. Eikhenbaum in his article on O. Henry discusses how O. Henry parodied the clichés of the adventure story as a first step in developing new narrative techniques; see "O. Genri i teoriya novelly."

80. See Shaginyan's preface to her revised edition: *Mess-Mend, ili yanki v Petrograde. Roman-skazka* (Moscow, 1960), p. 340.

81. G. Kozintsev and L. Trauberg, "Yeshchë odno D. Ye.," *T*, no. 7 (1923), p. 13.

82. Ibid., p. 13; Grigoriy Kozintsev, Leonid Trauberg, "Vneshtorg na Eyfelovoy bashne, ili printsip sego dnya (ektsentriki o sebe)," *Kp*, no. 4 (1923), p. 15; G. Kozintsev, "Glubokiy ekran," *Sobraniye sochineniy v pyati tomakh*, vol. I (Leningrad: Iskusstvo, 1982), pp. 52, 54–56; V. Shklovsky, "O rozhdenii i zhizni FEKSov," in V. Nedobrovo, *FEKS: Grigoriy Kozintsev, Leonid Trauberg* (Moscow-Leningrad, 1928).

83. Grigoriy Kozintsev, "A. B.! Parad ekstsentrikov," in Grigoriy Kozintsev et al., *Ekstsentrizm* (Ekstsentropolis [byvsh. Petrograd], 1922), pp. 3–5.

84. Ibid.

85. Ibid.; Kozintsev and Trauberg, "Vneshtorg na Eyfelevoy bashne, ili printsip sego dnya," p. 15.

86. This can be seen in their early play *Vneshtorg on the Eiffel Tower*, the title of which invokes Cocteau's *Wedding Party on the Eiffel Tower*, although the play is less a self-reflexive piece about the nature of art and its relation to reality (as was Cocteau's play) than a zany version of the standard plot about how the Soviet Union saves Europe and wins the world for a greater tomorrow.

87. Kozintsev, "Glubokiy ekran," p. 55; "Pis'mo k L. M. Kozintsevoy-Erenburg [1922]," in Grigoriy Kozintsev, *Sobraniye sochineniy v pyati tomakh*, vol. III (Leningrad: Iskusstvo, 1983), p. 170.

88. L. Trauberg, "Otdel'nyy vzglyad na Lopukhovu," *Izbrannye prizvedeniya*, vol. I (Moscow: Iskusstvo, 1988), pp. 308–400.

89. M., "Meyerkhol'd o proshlom i budushchem russkogo teatra," pp. 11–12.

90. V. Shklovsky, "Tema, obraz i syuzhet Rozanova," *Zi*, nos. 697–699 (March 19, 20, 22, 1921), p. 1; V. Shklovsky, *Khod konya* (Moscow and Berlin: Gelikon, 1923), p. 38. V. Erlich suggests in *Russian Formalism: History-Doctrine*, 2nd revised ed. (The Hague: Mouton and Co., 1965), p. 55, that the Formalists tended to over-

state their ideas for the purposes of polemic, and in keeping with the "timbre" of their generation.

91. F. Starr in *Red and Hot* chronicles the radical shifts as Soviet officialdom and critics tried to negotiate this particular dilemma.

92. V. Shklovsky, "Iperit (otryvok iz romana)," *L*, no. 3 (1925), p. 70.

93. See Eikhenbaum, "V poiskakh zhanra."

94. Here I have in mind particularly the Vengerov Circle at Petersburg University (see Chapter 8).

8. The Establishment of Soviet Culture

1. See, for example, "V Leningradskom teatral'nom upravlenii," *Zi*, no. 40 (September 30, 1924), p. 20; "Na pomosch'!" *Zi*, no. 41 (October 7, 1924), p. 2.

2. "Istoricheskaya doska" and "Navodneniye v 1824 godu," *Kg*, no. 217 (September 24, 1924), p. 1, p. 2, respectively.

3. N. Yevreinov, "Kommuna pravednykh," *Zi*, no. 41 (October 7, 1924), pp. 3–5. The play was subsequently renamed *Korabl' pravednykh* (The Ship of the Righteous), a title more closely echoed in Olga Forsh's thinly fictionalized account of the House of Arts during War Communism, *Sumasshedshiy korabl': Povest'* (Leningrad: Izdatel'stvo pisateley v Leningrade, 1931), which also uses the "Noah's ark" metaphor. Another institution in the play, the Society for the Protection of Animals, appears to have been a dig at another Gorky-founded intellectual institution, Kubuch (the Committee for the Improvement of Conditions for Scholars).

4. A case in point would be the formation of the Federation of Soviet Writers (FOSP) in 1925–1926, which in many respects anticipates the formation of the Writers Union in 1932–1934 (for example, incorporating most factions but excluding the extreme "left" and "right," and a platform for ameliorating writers' living conditions).

5. This was not true in all fields. Popular music was a particular exception.

6. V. S., "Knizhnyy rynok v 1925 godu," *Nk*, no. 3–4, (1925), pp. 24–25.

7. "Pisateli privetstvuyut oktyabr': Sodruzhestvo," *Zi*, no. 45 (November 7–10, 1925), p. 7.

8. See K. Fedin's letter to Gorky in *Gor'kiy i sovetskiye pisateli, Literaturnoye nasledstvo*, no. XXV (Moscow: Akademiya nauk, 1963), p. 474.

9. "Ne Piter, A Leningrad. Pis'mo tov. Zinov'yeva Petrosovetu" and "Traurnyy plenum Petrosoveta," *Kg*, no. 18, January 24, 1924 (evening edition), p. 1, p. 2, respectively.

10. S. Sheshukov, *Neistovye revniteli: Iz istorii literaturnoy bor'by 20-kh godov* (Moscow: Moskovskiy rabochiy, 1970). See also E. Brown, *The Proletarian Episode in Russian Literature, 1928–1932* (New York: Columbia University Press, 1953), and H. Ermolaev, *Soviet Literary Theories, 1917–1934: The Genesis of Socialist Realism* (Berkeley: University of California Press, 1963).

11. See "Klassiki-poputchiki—proletpisateli," editorial, *Nlp*, no. 5–6 (March 20, 1927), p. 5.

12. Ye. Yefremov, "Tvorcheskiy byt LAPPa," *Zi*, no. 15 (April 7, 1929), p. 7.

13. Ye. Ye. Essen, "Oktyabr' i rabotnik iskusstva," *Zi*, no. 45 (November 7–10, 1925), p. 19.

14. K. Malevich, "Otkrytoye pis'mo gollandskim khudozhnikam Van-Gofu i Bekmanu," *Zi*, no. 50 (December 9, 1924), p. 13.

15. See Il'ya Ionov, "Regalii Peredvizhnogo teatra," *Zi*, no. 6 (February 5, 1924), p. 5. (It later reopened before closing for good in 1927.) The case of art is more complicated. AKhRR's activists were almost all young, however, many of them being art students in the Komsomol movement, a pattern that was particularly marked in its Leningrad branches; see V. S. Ginger, "Yacheyka AKhRR v Akademii Khudozhestv," in *AKhRR. Assotsiatsiya khudozhnikov revolyutsionnoy Rossii. Sbornik vspominaniy, statey, dokumentov,* comp. I. A. Gronskiy (Moscow: Izobrazitel'noye iskusstvo, 1973), pp. 136–151.

16. See, for example, L. Trotsky, *Voprosy byta: Epokha kul'turnichestva i yeyë zadachi,* 2nd ed. (Moscow: Krasnaya nov', 1923), pp. 3–4.

17. "V Narkomprose," *Zi,* no. 26 (June 30, 1925), p. 22.

18. G. Lelevich, "Attestat zrelosti," *Zi,* no. 52 (December 21, 1926), p. 8.

19. An entire issue of *Pechat' i revolyutsiya* (no. 5) was devoted to the debate. See also L. Trotsky, *Literatura i revolyutsiya* (Moscow: Krasnaya nov', 1923), Chapter 5.

20. See, for example, S. Isakov, "Krivaya trëkh I," *Zi,* no. 30 (July 22, 1924), pp. 5–6.

21. "V Insitute istorii iskusstv," *Zi,* no. 10 (March 4, 1924), p. 21.

22. "Sotsiologicheskoe izucheniye iskusstva," *Zi,* no. 8 (February 24, 1925), p. 23.

23. F. I. Shmidt, "Rossiyskiy institut istorii iskusstv," *Zi,* no. 6 (February 10, 1925), p. 5.

24. "Institut istorii iskusstv," *Zi,* no. 45 (November 7–10, 1925), p. 35.

25. This position is set out most cogently in his book *West and East* (Zapad i Vostok: Voprosy mirovoy politiki i mirovoy revolyutsii) (Moscow: Krasnaya nov', 1924).

26. V. Vsevolodskiy, "'Levyy' teatr sego dnya," *Zi,* no. 6 (February 5, 1924), p. 6.

27. Shmidt, "Rossiyskiy institut istorii iskusstv," p. 4; "Ocheredniye zadachi AKhRR," *Zi,* no. 22 (May 27, 1924), p. 5.

28. See L. Trotsky, "O khudozhestvennoy literature i politike RKP (Rech' na soveshchanii pri TsK RKP o literature)," *Zi,* no. 34 (August 19, 1924), p. 4.

29. For an account of this, see Robert C. Tucker, *Stalin as Revolutionary, 1879–1929: A Study in History and Personality* (New York: W. W. Norton and Co., 1973), esp. pp. 373–392.

30. See the account of "Tri dnya" in Adr. Piotrovsky, "Khronika leningradskikh prazdnestv 1919–22 g.," in Gosudarstvennyy institut istorii iskusstv, *Massovye prazdnestva: Sbornik Komiteta sotsiologicheskogo izucheniya iskusstva* (Leningrad: Academia, 1926), pp. 58–60, 78–79, 84; "Rabochiy repertuar," *Zi,* no. 21 (May 29, 1923), p. 20; and "Oktyabr' v rabochikh klubakh," *Zi,* no. 43 (October 30, 1923), pp. 13–16.

31. N., "Novaya postanovka Akdramy," *Zi,* no. 37 (1924), p. 23; Gr. Avlov, "'Lyzistrata,' " *Zi,* no. 42 (October 14, 1924), p. 11.

32. "ORIS (Obshchestvo revniteley istorii)," *Zi,* no. 4 (January 26, 1926), p. 21; V. B., [review of] "D. Shcheglov, 'Spektakl' v klube,' " *Zi,* no. 4 (January 26, 1926), p. 22.

33. "Revolyutsionnaya data. 1905," editorial, *Zi,* no. 51 (December 22, 1925), p. 1.

34. Gayk Adonts, "Istoriya ili balagan," *Zi,* no. 23 (June 9, 1925), p. 2.

35. *Voprosy kul'tury pri diktature proletariata* (Moscow and Leningrad: Giz, 1925), p. 137.

36. Two of them, Gorky's *Mother* (Mat', 1906) and D. Furmanov's *Chapaev* (1923), had been published earlier; Gladkov's *Cement* appeared in 1925, and although A. Fadeyev's *The Rout* (Razgrom) did not appear until 1927, some chapters were published in 1925.

37. Lunacharsky, "Dostizheniya nashego iskusstva," *Zi,* no. 19 (May 11, 1926), p. 4.

38. See Katerina Clark, *The Soviet Novel: History as Ritual,* Appendix (Chicago: University of Chicago Press, 1981).

39. Adr. Piotrovsky, "O novykh dramaturgakh," *Zi,* no. 4 (January 20, 1925), p. 12.

40. "Khudozhnik I. I. Brodskiy," *Zi,* no. 52 (December 23, 1924), p. 21. Unless otherwise stated, my information on Brodsky comes from *Isaak Izraylevich Brodskiy: Stat'i, pis'ma, dokumenty* (Moscow: Sovetskiy khudozhnik, 1956), pp. 100–118.

41. "Izo Gubpolitprosveta," *Zi,* no. 15 (April 14, 1925), p. 29.

42. *Isaak Izraylevich Brodskiy,* pp. 313–318.

43. See the attacks on AKHRR of Filonov, Punin, and even Petrov-Vodkin in "Disput ob AKhRR'e v Dome Iskusstv," *Zi,* no. 45 (1926), pp. 4–5, or K. Malevich's "Otkrytoye pis'mo gollandskim khudozhnikam Van Gofu i Bekmenu," *Zi,* no. 50 (December 9, 1924), p. 13.

44. The Biocosmists were influenced by N. N. Fëdorov. For the centrality of the Cosmists, see "Literaturnaya khronika," *Zi,* no. 8 (February 21, 1922), p. 7.

45. See V. Blyumenfel'd, "Proletpoety LAPP," *Zi,* no. 50 (December 15, 1925), p. 4; G. Gor, "Zamedleniye vremeni," *Z,* no. 4 (1962), esp. pp. 175–176, 182, 188.

46. Compare the coverage accorded the two in the same commemorative issue of *Zhizn' iskusstva* for 1925, no. 51 (December 14–17); Adr. Piotrovsky, "1905 god v sovetskoy dramaturgii," *Zi,* no. 51 (December 14–17, 1925), p. 7.

47. See, for example, two films made by Kozintsev and Trauberg with Tynyanov as the scenario writer, *The Overcoat* (Shinel', 1926) and *SVD* (The Club of the Big Deed, or Soyuz velikogo dela, 1927).

48. See B. Brodyanskiy's account of the October Revolution celebrations in Leningrad in 1925, "Shagi tysyach," *LP,* no. 257 (November 10, 1925).

49. See V. Zil'ber [Kaverin], "Sen'kovskiy (Baron Brambeus)," in *Russkaya proza* (Leningrad, 1926); and V. Kaverin, *Baron Brambeus* (Leningrad: Izdatel'stvo pisateley v Leningrade, 1929).

50. B. Kostelyanets, "Primechaniya" to Yuri Tynyanov, *Sochineniya v dvukh tomakh,* vol. I (Leningrad: Khudozhestvennaya literatura, 1985), p. 506.

51. Here I am disagreeing with the position taken by A. Belinkov in his book *Yuriy Tynyanov,* 2nd ed. (Moscow: Sovetskiy pisatel', 1965). See Yuriy Tynyanov, *Kyukhlya,* in *Sochineniya v dvukh tomakh,* vol. I (Leningrad: Khudozhestvennaya literatura, 1985), pp. 76, 138–139, 185, 200.

52. Tynyanov, *Kyukhlya,* pp. 138–139, 171.

53. One could even view the celebrated shift in the Formalists' work from totally disregarding extraliterary factors to writing about the historical and social context of literature *(literaturnyy byt)* in this broader context, rather than explaining it purely in terms of political persecution (this shift is usually placed in 1927, but actually occurred slightly earlier, as can be seen, for instance, in the announcement of September 1925 that Eikhenbaum was "working on essays about the history of the formation of the naturalist novel to be called *[Byt] in Literature*" ("Leningrad. B. Eykhenbaum," *Zi,* no. 36 [September 8, 1925], p. 31).

54. *Voprosy kul'tury pri diktature proletariata* (Moscow and Leningrad, GIZ, 1925), p. 137.

55. See Trotsky, "O khudozhestvennoy literature i politike RKP," pp. 2–5; L. Trotsky, *Problems of Life,* trans. Z. Vengerova (London: Methuen and Co., 1924), p. 24.

56. Lunacharsky, "Dostizheniya nashego iskusstva," p. 4; no. 20 (May 18, 1926), p. 12.

57. See V. S. Ginger, "Yacheyka AKhRR v Akademii khudozhestv," in *AKhRR,* pp. 136–151.

58. "Khronika," *Rit,* no. 3 (October 2, 1924), p. 20; A. Bek, "Litso rabochego chitatelya," *Rit,* no. 6 (1925), p. 16 (literature); *Zi,* no. 7 (1924), p. 22 (theaters).

59. *The Thief of Baghdad* came to Leningrad for a three-week season, starting March 31; see "Leningrad," *Zi,* no. 10 (March 10, 1925), p. 28. *Robin Hood* came in September and was shown simultaneously at two of the main Leningrad theaters, the Picadilly and the Parisiana; see "Sevzapkino," *Zi,* no. 37 (September 15, 1925).

60. An article in the *Life of Art* of July 1925 reports that, over the preceding nine-month period, of the 183 new films shown in Leningrad, 103 were from the United States, and only 25 from the Soviet Union; see Vlad. Nedobrovo, "Devyatimesyachnyy balans kinoekrana," *Zi,* no. 27 (July 7, 1926), pp. 10–11.

61. Vl. N[edobrogo], "Robin Gud'," *Zi,* no. 38 (September 22, 1925), p. 23.

62. A. Slivkin, "Tov. Krasin i kino," *Zi,* no. 49 (December 7, 1926), pp. 2–3.

63. See the advertisement for the journal in *Zi,* no. 19 (May 11, 1926).

64. "Literaturnaya khronika," *Zi,* no. 48 (December 1, 1925), p. 18.

65. I. Traynin, "Kolichestvo i kachestvo kino," *Zi,* no. 44 (November 3, 1925), p. 14.

66. A. V. Lunacharsky, "Kino—velichaysheye iz iskusstv," *KP* (December 15, 1926).

67. See A. Belogorskiy, "Sila Feyerbenksa," *Rit,* no. 29 (July 21, 1925), pp. 18–19.

68. Larry L. May, *Screening out the Past: The Birth of Mass Culture and the Motion Picture Industry* (New York: Oxford University Press, 1980).

69. It should be noted that at the First Writers Congress of 1934 the official speech by S. Marshak (who was not a Party member and had even acted as patron of the OBERYu (see Chapter 10) and other less-conformist writers), presented (authoritatively), immediately after Gorky's opening address, although ostensibly on children's literature, essentially defined socialist realism as travel and adventure literature, a formula that he said he derived from readers' letters about the literature they preferred. This account anticipates much of the fiction

346

of the 1930s; see "Sodoklad S. Ya. Marshaka o detskoy literature," *Perviy s"yezd pisateley: Stenograficheskiy otchët* (Moscow: Ogiz, 1934), pp. 20, 33. See also V. Kirpotin's address on drama, in which he makes a similar recommendation (on p. 378).

70. O. M. Brik, "Pochemu ponravilsya 'Tsement,' " *Nlp,* no. 2 (1926), pp. 31–32.

71. Fedor Gladkov, *Tsement, Kn,* no. 1 (1925), p. 18.

72. For example, in B. Pilnyak's *Golyy god* (1922).

9. Promethean Linguistics

1. See the photo and poem in *Kp,* no. 1 (1927), p. 1. Gennady Fish graduated from GIII in 1924.

2. See "Rabochiye delavshiye Aelitu," *K-n* (Leningrad), no. 35 (September 30, 1924), p. 14; cover photo, *Lg,* no. 23 (December 15, 1924).

3. Il'ya Ionov, "Rabochiye, bud'te agitatorami za kino," *Zi,* no. 45 (November 7–10, 1925), p. 10.

4. Grigoriy Kozintsev, *Sobraniye sochineniy v pyati tomakh,* vol. III (Leningrad: Iskusstvo, 1984), pp. 178–189.

5. L. Stepanov [Skvortsov-Stepanov], *Elektrofikatsiya RSFSR v svyazi s perekhodnoy fazoy mirovogo khozyaystva* (Moscow: Gos. izd., 1922), pp. 288–304; G. Tsiperovich, *Budushcheye Petrograda,* Eko ocherk s predisloviyem G. Zinov'yeva (Petrograd: Gos. izd., 1922).

6. See, for example, "Nauke—na pomoshch' industrializatsii strany (Ob"yedinenie Leningradskikh uchenykh)." Report of a larger than usual meeting of KEPS, *Kg,* no. 50 (February 22, 1927), p. 3; "Nauchno-proizvodstvennye konferentsii," *Kg,* no. 97 (April 12, 1927), p. 2.

7. Mak, "Laboratoriya budushchego," *Kg,* no. 74 (March 20, 1927), p. 3.

8. Information provided by Stephen Kotkin and R. W. Davies in conversation with Katerina Clark at the conference entitled "Industrialization and Change in Soviet Society," held at Ann Arbor, Michigan, April 22–24, 1988. See also Edward Hallett Carr and R. W. Davies, *Foundations of a Planned Economy, 1926–1929,* vol. I (London: Macmillan, 1969), pp. 405, 411.

9. See "Dve iz shesti," *Kg,* no. 49 (February 21, 1927), p. 3.

10. It was designed by O. Munts. See V. E. Khazanova, *Sovetskaya arkhitektura pervykh let oktyabrya* (Moscow: Nauka, 1970), p. 15.

11. There had long been tensions between Malevich and Tatlin, and Tatlin left in October 1925.

12. L. Leonov, "Konets melkogo cheloveka," *Kn,* no. 3 (1924).

13. "Itogi vsesoyuznogo soveshchaniya pri Glavpolitprosvete 10–13 dekabrya v Moskve: Doklad t. Pel'she," *Zi,* no. 1 (January 5, 1926), p. 1.

14. Pavel Novitskiy, "Nauchnaya konferentsiya po sotsiologii iskusstva," *Zi,* no. 37 (September 14, 1926), pp. 4–7.

15. It was during this phase that A. Luria and L. Vygotsky joined forces in Moscow in "a small group of scholars who were charged with reconstructing Russian psychology in order to bring it into line with the goals of the Revolution." A. R. Luria, *The Making of Mind: A Personal Account of Soviet Psychology,*

trans. Michael Cole and Sheila Cole (Cambridge, Mass.: Harvard University Press, 1979), pp. 28, 39–40.

16. "Khronika," *Pir,* no. 2 (1927), p. 225.

17. RANION was originally formed in 1921–1922 in a coalition of social science and humanities institutes at Moscow University. For its convoluted subsequent history see G. D. Alekseyeva, "Rossiyskaya assotsiatsiya nauchno-issledovatel'skikh institutov obshchestvennykh nauk (RANION)," in M. V. Nechkina et al., eds., *Ocherki istorii istoricheskoy nauki v SSSR* (Moscow: Nauka, 1966), pp. 233–237.

18. Its faculty and graduate students included V. V. Vinogradov, B. M. Eikhenbaum, Yu. Tynyanov, V. A. Zil'ber [Kaverin], and L. Ya. Ginzburg. See "Kratkiy otchët o rabote Nauchno-issledovatel'skogo Instituta sravnitel'nogo izucheniya literatur i yazykov Zapada i Vostoka pri Leningradskom Gosudarstvennom Universitete za 1925–1926 g.," *Yail,* vol. I, no. 1–2 (Leningrad, 1926), pp. i–xx.

19. See N. V. Yakovlev, "Leningradskiy institut yazyka i literatury," *Nr,* no. 4 (1927), pp. 17–25.

20. "Usloviya priyëma v aspiranty nauchno-issledovatel'skikh institutov (RANION)," *Pzm,* no. 5 (1927), p. 235.

21. See, for example, S. M. Dorogayev (head of the Kruzhok yazykovedov-biomekhanistov and of Laboratoriya fiziologii rechi at ILYaZV), "Fiziologicheskiye i sotsiologicheskiye elementy v uchenii o rechi cheloveka," *Yail,* vol. III (1929), pp. 259–309; "Khronika," *Lim,* book 2, (1928), pp. 148–149.

22. This group included the Taylorist A. Gastev, the original Constructivist theoretician A. Gan, Osip Brik, and N. Chuzhak.

23. L. Trotsky, *Voprosy byta: Epokha kul'turnichestva i yeyë zadachi,* 2nd, enlarged ed. (Moscow: Krasnaya nov', 1923), p. 71; B. Arvatov, "K iskusstvu yazyka (v poryadke diskussii)," *Zi,* no. 40 (October 6, 1925), p. 4.

24. Carmen Claudin-Urondo, *Lenin and the Cultural Revolution,* trans. Brian Pearce (New Jersey: Humanities Press, 1977), p. 16.

25. Trotsky, *Voprosy byta,* p. 69. Compare Karl Marx and Friedrich Engels, "Manifesto of the Communist Party," *Selected Works in One Volume* (New York: International Publishers, 1984), p. 43, and Lenin's remarks about the need for overcoming the "trackless roads" of Russia, "an area of wholesale patriarchalism and semi-barbarism"; Claudin-Urondo, *Lenin and the Cultural Revolution,* p. 16.

26. See Introduction.

27. B. Arvatov, "O rabkorakh, khudozhestvennoy literature i proch.," *Zi,* no. 38 (September 22, 1925), p. 2. He also called it "literary Americanism," which of course meant that he, like FEKS and many other groups, sought to achieve the fast pace of American culture.

28. This position, which was often presented as an attack on *Pilnyakovshchina,* was also adopted by the Smena faction within LAPP.

29. Trotsky, *Voprosy byta,* p. 63.

30. Ibid. See also pp. 67, 70.

31. Ibid., p. 71.

32. See Chapter 10; also, see L. Trotsky, "Vodka, tserkov' i kino," *Voprosy byta,* p. 36.

33. Ibid., p. 67. See also p. 72.

348

34. See, for example, Ionov, "Rabochie, bud'te agitatorami za kino!," pp. 8–10; G. Boytyanskiy, "Kino i sovetskaya obshchestvennost'," *Zi*, no. 45 (no. 7–10) (1925), p. 13.

35. Originally, two other films were projected as well, *The Scourge of Mankind* (Bich chelovechestva), about tuberculosis, and *The Truth about Gonorrhea* (Pravda o gonoreye); see N. Abay, "Novyy kurs v sovetskoy kinematografii," *K-n*, no. 40–41 (November 7, 1924), p. 11.

36. "Novosti kino," *Zi*, no. 38 (September 22, 1925), p. 21.

37. They were: Panteleymon Romanov, "Bez cherëmukhi," *Mg*, no. 6 (1926), and "Pis'ma zhenshchin," in *KP* (April 11, 18, 1926), and *Kg* (July 14–17, 1926); Sergey Malashkin, *Luna s pravoy storony*, *Mg*, no. 9 (1926); and Lev Gumilëvskiy, *Sobachiy pereulok* (Leningrad: Izdaniye avtora, 1927).

38. See V. Petrochenkov, *Tvorcheskaya sud'ba Panteleymona Romanova* (Tenafly, N.J.: Hermitage Press, 1988), pp. 28–31.

39. See also Eric Naiman, "The Case of Chubarov Alley: Collective Rape, Utopian Desire and the Mentality of NEP," *Russian History* / Histoire Russe, *vol. XVII, no. 1 (Spring 1990)*, pp. 1–30.

40. Peter Stallybrass and Allon White, *The Politics and Poetics of Transgression* (Ithaca, N.Y.: Cornell University Press, 1986), pp. 22–23.

41. Unless otherwise stated, biographical information on Marr is from Lawrence L. Thomas, *The Linguistic Theories of N. Ja. Marr*, The University of California Publications in Linguistics, vol. XIV (Berkeley and Los Angeles: University of California Press, 1957), and V. M. Alpatov, *Istoriya odnogo mifa: Marr i marrizm* (Moscow: Nauka, 1991).

42. "Basic Tables for the Grammar of Old Georgian with a Preliminary Communication on the Georgian Relationship to Semitic" (Osnovnye tablitsy k grammatike drevnegruzinskogo yazyka s predvaritel'nym soobshcheniyem o rodstve gruzinskogo yazyka s semiticheskimi) (Spb., 1908). Marr had been working on this theory since 1886.

43. An account of the many language groups that fall within the purview of his theory is given by Marr in his "Pochemu tak trudno stat' lingvistom teoretikom" (1928), in N. Ya. Marr, ed., *Yazykovedeniye i materializm* (Leningrad: ILYaZV RANION, 1929), pp. 25–26.

44. These two collections more or less correspond to volumes I and II, respectively, of his *Izbrannye raboty* (Leningrad: izd-vo GAIMK, 1933, 1937).

45. See, for example, his invocation of Saussure in "Ob yafeticheskoy teorii," *Yafeticheskaya teoriya* (Moscow: Nauchnaya assotsiatsiya vostokovedeniya pri TsIK, 1924), p. 8.

46. See N. Ya. Marr, *Yafeticheskaya teoriya: Programma obshchego kursa ob yazyke* (Baku, 1927), p. 19.

47. See "K proiskhozhdeniyu yazykov," *Kg*, no. 247 (October 2, 1925).

48. N. Ya. Marr, "Avtobiografiya," *O*, no. 27 (1927); Marr, *Yafeticheskaya teoriya: Programma obshchego kursa ob yazyke*, pp. 2–3.

49. Marr, "K proiskhozhdeniyu yazykov."

50. Ibid.

51. Marr, "Pochemu tak trudno stat' lingvistom teoretikom," p. 33.

52. Marr, "Ob yafeticheskoy teorii," p. 4.

53. Marr, *Yafeticheskaya teoriya: Programma obshchego kursa ob yazyke*, p. 64.

54. Marr, "Pochemu tak trudno stat' lingvistom teoretikom," p. 33.

55. Katerina Clark, *The Soviet Novel: History as Ritual* (Chicago: University of Chicago Press, 1981), Chapter 5.

56. Marr, "K proiskhozhdeniyu yazykov."

57. Marr, *Yafeticheskaya teoriya: Programma obshchego kursa ob yazyke*, p. 30.

58. Marr, "Ob yafeticheskoy teorii," p. 2.

59. Marr, *Yafeticheskaya teoriya: Programma obshchego kursa ob yazyke*, p. 32; Marr, "Ob yafeticheskoy teorii," p. 12.

60. Marr, "Ob yafeticheskoy teorii," p. 2.

61. Ibid., p. 30.

62. N. Ya. Marr, "Termin skif," *Yafeticheskiy sbornik*, no. 1 (Moscow, 1922), pp. 67–122; "K proiskhozhdeniyu yazykov"; "Ob yafeticheskoy teorii," p. 30; *Yafeticheskaya teoriya: Programma obshchego kursa ob yazyke*, p. 29.

63. E. D. Polivanov, his chief rival in the late 1920s, shared this contempt for Greek and Sanskrit and advocated that instead linguists become involved in the practical work of giving alphabets to the minority peoples. See E. D. Polivanov, "Spetsificheskiye osobennosti poslednego desyatiletiya 1917–1927 v istorii nashey lingvisticheskoy mysli (vmesto predisloviya)," *Stat'i po obshchemu yazykoznaniyu* (Moscow: Glavnaya redaktsiya vostochnoy literatury, 1968), p. 53.

64. Marr, "Pochemu tak trudno stat' lingvistom teoretikom," pp. 12–13.

65. Marr, *Yafeticheskaya teoriya: Programma obshchego kursa ob yazyke*, p. 34.

66. The Scythian movement in Russia was at its height from 1918 to 1922 (when Marr published "Termin skif").

67. Marr, "K proiskhozhdeniyu yazykov."

68. Marr, *Yafeticheskaya teoriya: Programma obshchego kursa ob yazyke*, p. 88; "Pochemu tak trudno stat' lingvistom teoretikom," p. 39.

69. Marr, *Yafeticheskaya teoriya: Programma obshchego kursa ob yazyke*, p. 89.

70. Ibid., pp. 90–92, 94, 97.

71. Thomas, *The Linguistic Theories of N. Ja. Marr.*

72. Cited in A. P. Andreev, *Revolyutsiya yazykoznaniya: Yafeticheskaya teoriya akademika N. Ya. Marra* (Moscow: Izd. TsK SESR, 1929), p. 3.

73. Polivanov, "Spetsificheskiye osobennosti poslednego desyatiletiya," pp. 53–54.

74. For an account of these events see A. A. Leont'yev, L. I. Royzenzonin, and A. D. Khayutin, "Zhizn' i deyatel'nost' Ye. D. Polivanova," in Polivanov, *Stat'i po obshchemu yazykoznaniyu*, pp. 21–22; A. A. Leont'yev, *Yevgeniy Dmitriyevich Polivanov i yego vklad v obshcheye yazykoznaniye* (Moscow: Nauka, 1983), p. 17; V. Lartsev, *Yevgeniy Dmitriyevich Polivanov: Stranitsy zhizni i deyatel'nosti* (Moscow: Nauka, 1986), p. 16.

75. See Dragomanov (Polivanov), in V. Kaverin, *Skandalist ili vechera na Vasil'yevskom ostrove* (Leningrad: Priboy, 1929), esp. pp. 142–143, 234–255; Lartsev, *Yevgeniy Dmitriyevich Polivanov*, pp. 127–187.

76. Leont'yev, *Yevgeniy Dmitriyevich Polivanov*, p. 11.

77. Elena Luriya, *Moy otets A. R. Luriya* (Moscow: Gnosis, 1994), p. 124.

78. Oksana Bulgakova, "Sergey Eizenshteyn i psikhologicheskiy Berlin—mezhdu psikhoanalizom i strukturnoy psikhologii," *Kz*, no. 13 (1992).

79. V. V. Ivanov, *Ocherki po istorii semiotiki v SSSR* (Moscow: Nauka, 1976), p. 188.

80. See "Vertikal'nyi kino," *Iko,* no. 9 (1940), pp. 16–25; no. 1 (1941), pp. 29–38.

81. Some believe that these essays were ghost written by V. V. Vinogradov, an associate of the Formalists who had himself been persecuted in the most recent round of pro-Marrist assaults, or by the Georgian linguist A. S. Chikobava, another—and initial—contributor to the *Pravda* debate. But the scholarly consensus is that Stalin was the principal author; see M. V. Gorbanevskiy, *V nachale bylo slovo . . .: Maloizvestnye strannitsy istorii sovetskoy lingvistiki* (Moscow: Izd. Universiteta druzhby narodov, 1991), p. 114.

10. Straight Talk and the Campaign against Wagner

1. Ye. Polivanov, "Russkiy yazyk segodnyashnego dnya," *Lim,* no. 4 (1928), p. 167.

2. M. Bakhtin, "Slovo v romane" (Discourse in the Novel; 1934–1935), *Voprosy literatury i estetiki* (Moscow: Khudozhestvennaya literatura, 1975), see pp. 168–170.

3. *Puti razvitiya sovetskogo teatra: Stenograficheskiy otchёt resheniy partiynogo soveshchaniya po voprosam teatra pri Agitprope TsK VKP(b) v maye 1927 g.,* ed. S. M. Krylov (Moscow and Leningrad: Teakinopechat', 1927), pp. 267–268, 302, 498.

4. Igor' Glebov [B. Asafiev], "Dva opernykh prem'yera," *Zi,* no. 21 (May 24, 1927), pp. 8–9.

5. N. Malko, "Pryzhok cherez ten'," *Zi,* no. 22 (May 31, 1927), pp. 11–12.

6. I. Sollertinsky, "'Nos'—orudiye dal'noboynoye," *Rit,* no. 3 (1930), p. 11.

7. S. M. Khentova, *Shostakovich v Petrograde-Leningrade* (Leningrad: Lenizdat, 1979), p. 58.

8. D. Shostakovich, "Pochemu 'Nos,' " *Nos: Polnyy tekst opery* (Leningrad: Teakinopechat', 1930), p. 4.

9. Khentova, *Shostakovich v Petrograde-Leningrade,* pp. 72, 99.

10. B. M. Bogdanov-Berezovskiy, *Sovetskaya opera* (Leningrad: Leningradskoye otdeleniye VTO, 1940), pp. 81, 97.

11. S. E. Radlov, "Teatr i opera Deshevova," printed in a manifesto-like brochure produced by the directors of the State Opera on the occasion of the premiere of Deshevov's *Ice and Steel,* discussed below (cited in Bogdanov-Berezovskiy, *Sovetskaya opera,* p. 105).

12. Nick Worrall, "Meyerhold Directs Gogol's 'Government Inspector,' " *Theater Quarterly,* vol. II, no. 7 (July-September 1972), pp. 75–95.

13. In the scholarship there is a controversy over whether Shostakovich's interpretation was influenced by Meyerhold's production of *The Inspector General* (the view of Laurel Fay) or that of I. Terentiev in the Press House in Leningrad; see G. Fёdorov, "Vokrug i posle 'Nosa,' " *Sm,* no. 9 (1976), pp. 41–50, esp. p. 46.

14. "Novaya postanovka 'Shchelkunchika,' " *Pir,* no. 10 (1929), p. 127.

15. Incidentally, many of its members had previously belonged to the group of A. Tufanov, an epigone of the prerevolutionary *zaumniki.*

16. "OBERIU," an appendix to R. R. Milner-Gulland, "'Left Art' in Leningrad: The OBERIU Declaration," Oxford Slavonic Papers, New Series, III, p. 70. This statement rides roughshod over the complexity of what OBERYu attempted in its appropriation of everyday speech. See Robin Milner-Gulland, "Beyond the Turning Point: An Afterword," in Neil Cornwall, ed., Daniil Kharms and the Poetics of the Absurd (New York: St. Martins Press, 1991), pp.243–267.

17. "Leningrad," Zi, no. 38 (September 22, 1929), p. 14 (Kharms); "Novaya sovetskaya opera," Pir, no. 9 (1929), p. 123 (Oleinikov's "Karas'," on which Shostakovich worked).

18. See, for example, N. V. Yakovlev, "Leningradskiy institut yazyka i literatury," Nr (1927), pp. 17–18; "Khronika," Lim, no. 6 (1930), pp. 85–86.

19. Yakovlev, "Leningradskiy institut yazyka i literatury," p. 19.

20. N. Bukharin, "O formal'nom metode v iskusstve," Kn, no. 3 (1925), pp. 248–257, esp. pp. 250–252.

21. See S. M. Dorogayev, "Fiziologicheskiye i sotsiologicheskiye elementy v uchenii o rechi cheloveka," Yil [ILYaZV], vol. III (1929), pp. 259–309; "Khronika," Lim (1928), book 2, pp. 148–149.

22. We might also note in this connection L. S. Vygotsky's pioneering work done in Moscow at this time.

23. My formulation here is ambiguous because the question of authorship of certain texts key to the concerns of this chapter and published under the name of V. N. Voloshinov but widely attributed to M. M. Bakhtin (such as Freudianism: A Critical Sketch and Marxism and the Philosophy of Language) continues to be disputed. My research for this book has made me more convinced that Bakhtin was the author of the disputed texts than I was when I addressed this question in Mikhail Bakhtin. This can probably never be established with any finality, and the claim that Bakhtin was the principal author is stronger for the other disputed texts published under the name of P. N. Medvedev for the simple reason that Medvedev published prolifically in the second half of the 1920s (while Voloshinov published scarcely anything besides the disputed texts) and it is possible to compare the undisputed texts published under Medvedev's name with the disputed texts.

24. R. Shor, Yazyk i obshchestvo, Dopushcheno Nauchno-pedagagogicheskoy sektsiyey Gosudarstvennogo uchënogo soveta, 2nd ed. (Moscow: Rabotnik prosveshcheniya, 1926); V. Voloshinov, "Slovo v zhizni i slovo v iskusstve," Z, no. 6 (1926), pp. 244–267.

25. Khentova, Shostakovich v Petrograde-Leningrade, p. 58.

26. Yakovlev, "Leningradskiy institut yazyka i literatury," p. 19.

27. Ibid., p. 18.

28. "Po literaturnym institutam i organizatsiyam," Pir, no. 1 (1930), p. 85.

29. This was especially true of writers in Leningrad's Smena. See, for example, their anthology Kadry, especially the stories by M. Ostanin and Vissarion Sayanov; Kadry (Leningrad: Assotsiatsiya proletarskikh pisateley, 1928), pp. 57–58 and 78–81, respectively.

30. Khentova, Shostakovich v Petrograde-Leningrade, p. 67.

31. The libretto for the opera was written by V. Lavrenëv.

32. Gennadiy Gor, "Zamedleniye vremeni," *Z*, no. 4 (1968), p. 177.

33. B. Eikhenbaum, "Illyuziya skaza," *Skvoz' literaturu, Voprosy poetiki*, no. IV (Leningrad, 1924), pp. 152, 154 (see also p. 175).

34. See V. V. Vinogradov, "Problema skaza v stilistike" (1925), "Yazyk Zoshchenki (zametki o leksiki)" (1929), and "Literatura i ustnaya slovesnost'" (prepared for publication in 1929 but not published); and M. M. Bakhtin, "Tipy prozaicheskogo slova: Slovo u Dostoevskogo," in *Problemy poetiki Dostoevskogo* (1929, see fourth ed., Moscow, 1979, pp. 210–236).

35. Yu. Tomashevskiy, "Rasskazy i povesti Mikhaila Zoshchenko" and "Primechaniya," in M. Zoshchenko, *Sobraniye sochineniy*, vol. I (Leningrad: Khudozhestvennaya literatura, 1986), pp. 5, 540.

36. V. Bogdanov-Berezovskiy, "Novinki budushchego sezona," *Rit*, no. 33 (August 12, 1928), p. 4.

37. D. Shostakovich, "Pered prem'yeroy," *Rit*, no. 7 (1930), p. 7.

38. V. Bogdanov-Berezovskiy wrote at the time, in describing what Shostakovich sought to do in *The Nose*, that he used "intonational speech" and "conversational speech" to bring out "all the very subtle nuances of Gogolian language"; see "Sovetskaya opera v predstoyashchem sezone," *Rit*, no. 36 (September 8, 1929), p. 9.

39. Quoted in Khentova, *Shostakovich v Petrograde-Leningrade*, p. 61.

40. S. Tretyakov, "Kino k yubileyu," *Nl*, no. 10 (1927), p. 29.

41. Eisenstein was far from the only creative intellectual in this period who focused on the bodily functions of authority figures. Compare N. Erdman's play *The Mandate* (Mandat, 1925) and Yu. Olesha's novel *Envy* (Zavist', 1926). I. Terentiev in his 1927 production of *The Inspector General* in Leningrad's Press House also gave prominence to the chamber pot and water closet.

42. M. M. Bakhtin, *Tvorchestvo Fransua Rable i narodnaya kul'tura srednevekov'ya i renessansa* (Moscow: Khudozhestvennaya literatura, 1965).

43. The erotic and Freudian were important elements in many of the new German operas, such as Krenek's *Johnny spielt auf*.

44. See, for example, the articles by Iakov Druskin, Robin Milner-Gulland, and others, in Cornwall, ed., *Daniil Kharms and the Poetics of the Absurd*.

45. "Novosti iskusstva," *Rit*, no. 31 (June 5, 1930), p. 15; also "Khronika," *Rit*, no. 30 (July 22, 1928), p. 15; and "Kontsertnaya nedelya," *Rit*, no. 49 (December 8, 1929), p. 9.

46. N. Malko, "Iz zagranichnykh vpechatleniy," *Zi*, no. 17 (April 21, 1929), p. 17; "Khronika," *Zi*, no. 28 (1928).

47. The wreckers put a bolt in the factory's machinery, thus destroying it (note the weight given the small part, typical of the symbolic system of the Plan years).

48. Gregory Freidin, *A Coat of Many Colors: Osip Mandelstam and His Mythologies of Self-Presentation* (Berkeley: University of California Press, 1987), p. 228.

49. See, for example, M. Slonimsky's *Lavrovy* (1927), critiquing members of his own family dynasty, which includes the Formalists' former teacher at the University, S. A. Vengerov; Kaverin's two novels (see Chapter 1); and K. Vaginov, *Kozlinaya pesn'* (1927), which includes a representation of M. M. Bakhtin as "the philosopher."

50. See O. Mandelshtam's *Egyptian Stamp* (Yegipetskaya marka, *Z*, May 1928), which draws on the Petersburg literary tradition and facts of the author's own biography.

51. "K. S. Malevich: Pis'ma k M. V. Matyushinu," a publication of Ye. F. Kovtun in *Yezhegodnik rukopisnogo otdela Pushkinskogo doma na 1974 god* (Leningrad: Nauka, 1976), p. 194.

52. Nikoletta Misler, "Filonov, master metamorfozy," in Nikoletta Misler and Dzhon E. Boult, *Filonov: Analiticheskoye iskusstvo* (Moscow: Sovetskiy khudozhnik, 1990), pp. 131–151.

11. The Sacralization of Everyday Life

1. See I. Stalin, "God velikogo pereloma," *Kg*, no. 257 (November 7, 1929), pp. 2–3.

2. B. Filippov, "Za proverku!" *Rit*, no. 17 (April 22, 1928), p. 3.

3. Space does not permit me to cover most of the major political and institutional changes affecting culture, such as the founding of Glaviskusstvo in 1928 or the All-Union Conference on Agitation and Propaganda of the summer of 1928 leading to a Central Commitee Resolution on the press in December of that year.

4. Valentina Khodasevich, *Portrety slovami: Ocherki* (Moscow: Sovteskiy pisatel', 1987), p. 219.

5. Ibid., p. 248.

6. For a fuller description of the spectacle, see Nikolay Petrov, *50 i 500* (Moscow: Vserossiyskoye teatral'noye obshchestvo, 1960), pp. 195–207.

7. "Leningrad: Massovye prazdnestva," *Zi*, no. 45 (November 6, 1927), p. 38.

8. Sergey Radlov, "Oktyabr'skaya instsenirovka na Neve," *Zi*, no. 42 (October 18, 1927), p. 5.

9. A. Gvozdev, "Massovoye prazdnestvo na Neve," *Zi*, no. 47 (November 22, 1927), p. 5.

10. D. T., "Rezhissërskiye vyvody," *Zi*, no. 47 (November 22, 1927), p. 7.

11. See, for example, A. Piotrovsky, "Torzhestvo rebyat," *Kg*, no. 124 (May 28, 1930), p. 4; Khodasevich, *Portrety slovami*, pp. 226–231.

12. See Katerina Clark, "Little Heroes and Big Deeds: Literature Responds to the First Five-Year Plan," in Sheila Fitzpatrick, ed., *Cultural Revolution in Russia, 1928–1931* (Bloomington: Indiana University Press, 1978), pp. 189–206.

13. See especially Fëdor Gladkov's novel *Energiya* (*Nm*, 1932–1937).

14. One can detect this shift already in 1927. See G. A., "Rayonnye instsenirovki k desyatiletiyu oktyabrya," *Zi*, no. 44 (November 1, 1927), p. 5.

15. Other examples include *War to War*; see L. T., "Voyna-voyne," *Kg*, no. 176 (August 3, 1929), p. 6.

16. Gvozdev, "Massovoye prazdnestvo na Neve," p. 5; A. Piotrovsky, "Torzhestvo 10-ogo noyabrya," *Zi*, no. 46 (November 15, 1927), pp. 1–2.

17. See L. T., "Voyna-voyne," p. 6.

18. "Pervomayskaya instsenirovka u Fondovoy birzhi," *Kg*, no. 96 (April 26, 1929), p. 6; "Staryy byt sdayët pozitsii," *Kg*, no. 102 (May 8, 1929), p. 3.

19. "Na tekh zhe pozitsiyakh (Na tea-soveshchanii v Narkomprose)," "Orlinskiy," *Zi*, no. 14 (April 5, 1927), p. 13.

20. S. Gres, "'Plan velikikh rabot': Fil'm A. Rooma," *Rit*, no. 19 (April 6, 1930), p. 12.

21. "Shchastlivaya ultitsa: Fil'm o 'Krasnom Putilovtse,' " *Rit*, no. 15 (March 16, 1930), p. 13. This rebuilding was actually done (in 1925–1927); see Selim O. Khan-Magomedov, *Pioneers in Soviet Architecture: The Search for New Solutions in the 1920s and 1930s*, trans. Alexander Lieven (New York: Rizzoli, 1987), p. 276.

22. See N. Spoluchnyy, "Iskusstvo—sotsialisticheskim gorodam," *Rit*, no. 27 (May 16, 1930), p. 2.

23. Gres, "'Plan velikikh rabot,' " p. 12.

24. For example, for Christmas see "'Den' sotsialisticheskogo truda," *Kg*, no. 296 (December 25, 1929), p. 3.

25. "'Den' industrializatsii' dolzhen byt' dnëm kul'tury truda," and Artemenko, "Bez progulov i opozdaniy," "Prazdnovaniye 'Dnya industrializatsii,'" *Kg*, no. 177 (August 4, 1929); "'Den' industrializatsii' proshël," *Kg*, no. 178 (August 7, 1929), p. 1.

26. Khan-Magomedov, *Pioneers of Soviet Architecture*, pp. 40–42, 77–93.

27. Katerina Clark, *The Soviet Novel: History as Ritual* (Chicago: University of Chicago Press, 1981), pp. 93–100, 109–110.

28. Mosey Ginzburg, "Tselevaya ustanovka v sovremennoy arkhitekture," *Sa*, no. 1 (1927), pp. 4–10.

29. Aleksei Gan, *Konstruktivizm* (Tver': Tverskoye izdatel'stvo, 1922), p. 63.

30. Khan-Magomedov, *Pioneers of Soviet Architecture*, p. 389.

31. Ginzburg, "Tselevaya ustanovka v sovremennoy arkhitekture," pp. 4–10.

32. See Richard Stites, *Revolutionary Dreams: Utopian Visions and Revolutionary Life in the Russian Revolution* (New York: Oxford University Press, 1989), pp. 145–155, 214–215.

33. Gr. Avlov, "Pereustroystvo byta i klub," *Rit*, no. 3 (1930), p. 7.

34. Khan-Magomedov, *Pioneers of Soviet Architecture*, p. 343; "Pervyy dom-kommuna v Leningrade," *Kg*, no. 284 (December 11, 1929), p. 4.

35. S. Ts., "Pereustroystvo byta i iskusstva: Na doklade A. V. Lunacharskogo," *Rit*, no. 3 (January 15, 1930), p. 2.

36. "Bez kukhonnogo chada," *Kg*, no. 284 (December 11, 1929), p. 4.

37. "Zhizn' v sotsialisticheskom gorode," *Kg*, no. 77 (April 2, 1930), p. 3.

38. S. Ts., "Pereustroystvo byta i iskusstva," p. 3.

39. N. Spoluchnyy, "Iskusstvo—sots. gorodam," *Rit*, no. 27 (May 16, 1930), p. 2.

40. See, for example, the remarks about the "velichayshaya tyaga k kul'ture, k nauke," which is especially marked among worker youth in V. Leyzerovich, ed., *Kommuna molodëzhi* (Moscow: Molodaya gvardiya, 1929), p. 3.

41. "Vs. Meyerkhol'd o kinofikatsii teatra," *Zi*, no. 28 (July 14, 1929), p. 4.

42. A. Gvozdev, "Teatr budushchego," *Zi*, no. 45 (November 6, 1927), p. 21.

43. Ibid.

44. Siegfried Kracauer, "Das Ornament der Masse" (1927), in *Das Ornament der Masse* (Frankfurt am Main: Suhrkamf Verlag, 1965).

45. Walter Benjamin's Afterword to "Das Kunstwerk im Zeitalter seiner technischen Reproduzierbarkeit," *Illuminationen* (Frankfurt, 1961), p. 175.

46. "Moskva: Otkrytiye obshchestva 'Muzyka-massam,' " *Zi*, no. 22 (June 14, 1929), p. 14.

47. "Programma chetvërtoy muzykal'noy olimpiady," *Rit*, no. 33 (June 15, 1930), pp. 10–11.

48. See also Dziga Vertov's *The Man with a Movie Camera*, discussed below.

49. A. Lunacharsky, "Muzyka i sovremennost'," *Zi*, no. 25 (June 23, 1929), p. 2.

50. In the mid-1920s intellectuals carried away by a collectivist zeal had instituted a conductorless orchestra known as Persimfans, which spawned several imitations.

51. "Klassovyy vrag v bulochnykh," *Kg*, no. 290 (December 17, 1929), p. 4.

52. V. I. Lenin, "Iz doklada Vserossiyskogo tsentral'nogo komiteta i Soveta narodnykh komissarov o vneshney i vnutrenney politike 22 dekabrya," *Polnoye sobraniye sochineniy*, vol. XLII, pp. 145–157.

53. The writers who contributed to this book, *Belomorsko-Baltiyskiy kanal imeni Stalina*, included M. Zoshchenko and V. Shklovsky. The leading Constructivist artist Rodchenko did many of the photographs. It is to be noted that Shklovsky at any rate seems to have been motivated to participate because his older brother, V. B. Shklovsky, was among the prisoners working on the canal (he was released in 1933 and Shklovsky made his visit there in 1932). See Aleksandr Galushkin, "Chetyre pis'ma Viktora Shklovskogo," *Strannik*, no. 2 (Moscow, 1991), p. 77.

54. *Belomorsko-Baltiyskiy kanal imeni Stalina* (Moscow, 1934), p. 356.

55. P. Mordvinov, "Stroitel'stvo novykh gorodov," *Lii*, no. 1 (1930), p. 140.

56. Khan-Magomedov accounts in these terms for the demise of a communal house in Leningrad for engineers and writers, designed by Ol' and built on Rubinstein Street in 1930; see *Pioneers of Soviet Architecture*, p. 392.

57. Jean-Louis Cohen, *Le Corbusier and the Mystique of the U.S.S.R.: Theories and Projects for Moscow, 1928–1936*, trans. Kenneth Hylton (Princeton: Princeton University Press, 1992).

58. A. Movshenson, "Mebel' novogo byta," *Rit*, no. 42 (July 30, 1930), pp. 4–5.

12. The Ultimate Cultural Revolution

1. Compare "S"yezd rabotnikov nauki," *Kg*, no. 61 (February 23, 1927), p. 2; Ye. Kaganskaya, "Leningradtsy na Sel'mashstroye: Opyt udarnoy brigady," *Lg*, no. 25 (June 30, 1930), p. 1.

2. "Pisateli na bol'shevistskiy sev," *Lg*, no. 8 (February 9, 1930), p. 1; "Leningradskiye teatry na fronte krasnogo seva," *Pir*, no. 3 (1930), p. 90.

3. "Nam predstoit slomat' pisatel'skiy individualizm," *Lg*, no. 16 (August 6, 1929), p. 1.

4. See D. Kal'm, "Zavodskaya gazeta zhdët pisatelya," *Lg*, no. 3 (1930), p. 2.

5. "Rabochiye berut shefstvo nad VOSP," L. I. Div, "Signal rabochim uslyshan," *Lg*, no. 33 (August 5, 1930), p. 11; "Za rabocheye shefstvo nad pis-

atel'skimi organizatsiyami," *Lg,* no. 34 (August 10, 1930), p. 11. For more specific details about which factory was to undertake *shefstvo* over which writers' organization, see *Lg,* nos. 50–51 (1930).

6. "Khronika," *Pir,* no. 1 (1930), p. 89.

7. "Leningrad: Prem'yery," *Pir,* no. 3 (1930), p. 89.

8. "Muzykal'naya olimpiada," editorial, *Rit,* no. 23 (June 3, 1928), p. 3.

9. See M. Chumandrin, "Yeshchë i yeshchë raz ob etom," *Nlp,* no. 17 (1930), p. 60.

10. "Pisateli—na krusheniye stroyki SSSR, po-boyevomu vklyuchit'sya v bor'bu za vtoruyu metallicheskuyu bazu Ural-Kuzbass," *Lg,* no. 22 (April 24, 1931).

11. Vl. Mayakovsky, "Nashemu yunoshestvu," *Nl,* no. 2 (1927), pp. 6–9, "Iz poemy 'Oktyabr,' " *Nl,* no. 6 (1927), p. 3; O. Brik, "Za novatorstvo!" *Nl,* no. 1 (1927), p. 26.

12. Vl. Korobinov, "Proyetza," *Nl,* no. 7 (1927), pp. 33–55; Lef, "Tsitadel'," editorial, *Nl,* no. 1 (1927), p. 1.

13. See N. M. Lary, *Dostoevsky and Soviet Film* (Ithaca, N.Y.: Cornell University Press, 1986), Chapter 1.

14. Robert B. McKean, *St. Petersburg between the Revolutions: Workers and Revolutionaries, June 1907–February 1917* (New Haven: Yale University Press, 1990), p. 2 and map no. 1 on p. xvi.

15. Orest Tsekhnovitser, "Nuzhen tsentr," *Zi,* no. 31 (August 4, 1929), p. 4; "Khronika," *Pir,* no. 2 (1930), p. 82; "Khronika. Prostranstvennye iskusstva. Likvidatsiya Vkhuteina," *Pir,* no. 5–6 (1930), p. 130.

16. See, for example, A. Room's *Plan velikikh rabot* and Kozintsev and Trauberg's *Odna,* respectively.

17. I. V. Stalin, *Sochineniya* (Moscow: Institut Marksa-Engelsa-Lenina), vol. XI, pp. 246–249, 256–257, 276.

18. Anatole Kopp, *Constructivist Architecture in the U.S.S.R.* (New York and London: St. Martins Press, 1985), pp. 142–143.

19. V. Shklovsky, "60 dney bez sluzhby," *Nl,* no. 6 (1927), p. 18.

20. This was also advocated by highbrow musicians. See N. Malko, "V zashchitu garmoniki," *Zi,* no. 2 (January 11, 1927), p. 4.

21. See Katerina Clark, "Little Heroes and Big Deeds: Literature Responds to the First Five-Year Plan," in Sheila Fitzpatrick, ed., *Cultural Revolution in Russia* (Bloomington: Indiana University Press, 1978), esp. pp. 194–201.

22. "Leningrad: Kvalifikatsiya chlenov khudsovetov," *Pir,* no. 2 (1930), p. 79.

23. For more information on TRAM, see Katerina Clark, "The Russian Avant-Garde Theater in the Late Twenties," in Sheelagh Graham, ed., *New Directions in Soviet Literature* (London: Macmillan, 1992), and Lynn Mally, "The Soviet Youth Theater TRAM," *Slavic Review,* vol. 54, no. 3 (Fall 1992), pp. 411–430.

24. Ivan Chicherov, "TRAM—eto rabota po-novomu," *Zi,* no. 21 (May 6, 1929), p. 2.

25. A. Piotrovsky, "TRAM (Stranitsa teatral'noy sovremennosti)," *Z,* no. 4 (1929), p. 143; P. Sokolov, "O vikhrastom yunoshe i mage komsomol'skogo teatra" [a foreword to the TRAM play], *Druzhnaya gorka* (Leningrad: Tea-kino-

pechat', 1929), p. 3; N. Radyants, "Teatry rozhdënnye revolyutsii," in *Teatr i zhizn'* (Leningrad and Moscow: Iskusstvo, 1957), p. 145.

26. Mikh. D., "Idut novye lyudi (Na dispute o teatre rabochey molodëzhi)," *KP,* no. 138 (June 16, 1928), p. 5; A. V. Lunacharsky, "Tram," *P,* July 8, 1928.

27. "Za druzhnuyu stroyku komsomol'skogo teatra!" *Kg,* no. 91 (April 20, 1929), p. 4.

28. V. Mironova, *TRAM: Agitatsionno-molodëzhnyy teatr 1920–1930-kh godov* (Leningrad: Iskusstvo, Leningradskoye otdeleniye, 1977), p. 6.

29. "V nogu s zhizn'yu!" *Kg,* no. 224 (September 29, 1929), p. 6.

30. S. R., "TRAM na zavtra," *Rit,* no. 11 (February 26, 1930), p. 4.

31. Revfront also includes the Krasnyy teatr, Leningradskiy rabochiy teatr Komsomola, and Gosagitteatr (also known as the Kolkhoznyy teatr—this last theater's lineage goes back via its one-time director Shimanovsky and other members to the Traveling Mass Theater of Gaydeburov and Skarskaya). See D., "Krasnyy front teatrov," *LP,* no. 239 (November 5, 1929), p. 5.

32. "Yedinyy front revolyutsionnykh teatrov," *Kg,* no. 255 (November 5, 1929), p. 6. See also the account by N. V. Petrov, then director of the State Theater, in his *50 i 500* (Moscow: Vserossiyskoye teatral'noye obshchestvo, 1960), pp. 288–293.

33. Pavel Marinchik, *Rozhdeniye komsomol'skogo teatra* (Moscow and Leningrad: Iskusstvo, 1963), p. 35.

34. D. Tolmachëv, "Teatr rabochey molodëzhi," *Rit,* no. 40 (October 6, 1925), p. 4; "Teatr rabochey molodëzhi," *Rit,* no. 33 (August 15, 1926).

35. M. Sokolovsky, "TRAM," *St,* no. 28–29 (1929), pp. 396–397.

36. "Za druzhnuyu stroyku komsomol'skogo teatra!" p. 4; V. G-v, "V bor'be za tramovskogo dvizheniya," *Zi,* no. 19 (May 12, 1929), p. 11.

37. [M. Sokolovsky's speech], "Pervaya vsesoyuznaya konferentsiya TRAMov," *Pir,* no. 8 (1929), p. 120.

38. TRAM et al., "Ko vsem rabotnikam klubnykh khudozhestvennykh organizatsii. . . .," *Zi,* no. 46 (November 18, 1929), p. 12; A. Piotrovsky, "Puti i pereput'ya samodeyatel'nogo teatra," *Rit,* no. 39 (July 15, 1930), pp. 4–5.

39. Mironova, *TRAM,* p. 6.

40. See "TRAM gotov k nastupleniyu" and "Leningrad," *Zi,* no. 38 (September 16, 1928), pp. 11, 14.

41. See, for example, "Pod znakom peregruppirovki," *Zi,* no. 20 (May 19, 1929), p. 1; Veg, "Revolyutsionnyy-proletarskiy front teatra pod ugrozoy," *Zi,* no. 38 (September 22, 1929), p. 2.

42. Marinchik, *Rozhdeniye komsomol'skogo teatra,* pp. 35, 67; Sokolov, "O vikhrastom yunoshe," p. 3.

43. D. Shen, *Vladimir Mikhaylovich Deshevov: Ocherk zhizni i tvorchestva* (Moscow: Sovetskiy kompozitor, 1961), pp. 5–15; S. M. Khentova, *Shostakovich v Petrograde-Leningrade* (Leningrad: Lenizdat, 1979); "Novosti iskusstva: TRAM," *Rit,* no. 15 (March 16, 1930), p. 15.

44. L. Zhadova, "Iz istorii sovetskoy polikhromii," *Tekhnicheskaya estetika,* no. 7 (1975).

45. N. Radyants, "Teatry rozhdënnye revolyutsii," *Teatr i zhizn'* (Leningrad and Moscow: Iskusstvo, 1957), p. 308; V. Rafalovich, *Vesna teatral'naya* (Leningrad: Iskusstvo, 1971), p. 44.

46. "Khronika. Ak. opera," *Rit,* no. 7 (February 12, 1928), p. 15.

47. Vs. Meyerhold, "O kinofikatsii teatra," *Zi,* no. 28 (July 14, 1929), p. 4.

48. N. Malko, "Neobkhodimye dopolneniya," *Zi,* no. 15 (April 7, 1929), p. 33.

49. I. Sollertinsky, "Problema 'opernogo naslediya,' " *Zi,* no. 18 (May 1, 1929), p. 10, and "Vozmozhnye printsipy sovetskoy opery," *Zi,* no. 31 (August 4, 1929), p. 3.

50. Piotrovsky, "TRAM," esp. pp. 142, 144.

51. This was mostly achieved through extensive use of *naplyv* (the cinematic technique of the "lap dissolve"). See esp. N. Lvov, *Kleshch zadumchivyy* (Leningrad: Tea-kino-pechat', 1930).

52. Piotrovsky, "TRAM," pp. 147–148, and "Aktëry v TRAMe," *Rit,* no. 43 (August 4, 1930), pp. 2–3.

53. Piotrovsky, "TRAM," pp. 147, 151.

54. S. Radlov, "Dramaturgi—v laboratoriyu!" *Zi,* no. 14 (April 1, 1929), p. 3.

55. S. Mokul'skiy, "Kleshch zadumchivyy i lngr. TRAM," *Zi,* no. 20 (May 19, 1929), p. 6.

56. A. Piotrovsky, "My eto peresmotrim," *Zi,* no. 39 (September 29, 1929), p. 4.

57. For family melodrama, see N. L'vov, *Plavyatsya dni. Dialekticheskoye predstavleniye v 3-kh krugakh,* redaktsiya i vstupitel'naya stat'ya A. Piotrovskogo i M. Sokolovskogo (Leningrad: Tea-kino-pechat', 1929); for the comedy of errors, see *Druzhnaya gorka: Komsomol'skaya operetta v 3-kh deystviyakh,* tekst P. Maksimova i N. L'vova, muzyka N. Dvorikova i V. Deshevova, obshcheye rukovodstvo M. Sokoloskogo (Leningrad: Tea-kino-pechat', 1929).

58. It should be noted that TRAM's demise was not immediate and the Komsomol and cultural bureaucracy continued to bestow honors and subsidies upon it; see "O podgotovke kadrov v teatre: Postanovleniye Lenobkoma VLKSM," *Rit,* no. 66–67 (December 11, 1930), p. 1; "Khronika," *Pir,* no. 2 (1930), p. 79.

59. "Leningradskiy diskussionnyy klub," *Zi,* no. 16 (April 14, 1929), p. 14.

60. "Konsolidatsiya sil—pervoocherednyaya zadacha," *Rit,* no. 54–55 (October 16, 1930), p. 1.

61. Gail Warshofsky Lapidus, "Educational Strategies and Cultural Revolution," in Fitzpatrick, ed., *Cultural Revolution in Russia, 1928–1931,* p. 93.

62. Radyants, "Teatry rozhdënnye revolyutsii," p. 321; A. Fadeyev, "Za TRAM i protiv tramchvanstvo," *Nlp,* no. 20 (1929).

63. V. Druzgin, "Uchëba u zapada," *Zi,* no. 21 (May 26, 1929), pp. 3–4.

64. See articles by Milka Bliznakov and Anatole Kopp in William C. Brumfield, ed., *Reshaping Russian Architecture: Western Technology, Utopian Dreams* (New York: Cambridge University Press, 1990), pp. 145–175, 176–214.

65. "TRAM-Krasnyy rupor," *Rit,* no. 40 (October 5, 1929), p. 14. Another important aspect of the links was journals featuring industrial photography of the new Soviet Union, such as *Arbeiter-Illustrierte-Zeitung* and *SSSR na stroyke.*

66. See "Khronika," *Pir* (1929), no. 10, p. 129, no. 11, p. 117.

67. "Teatr revolyutsii," *Rit,* no. 7 (February 12, 1928), p. 16 (Brecht); "Anketa sredi pisateley: Ervin Piskator," *Kg,* no. 146 (June 23, 1930), p. 2.

68. I have in mind here the campaign in the fall of 1929 against the writers Zamyatin and Pilnyak (not coincidentally they were heads of the Leningrad and

Moscow branches of VSP, a writers' organization representing the right and center) for publishing works in the West. Space does not permit me to cover here this well-known incident.

69. "Ob"yedinim proletarskiye sily na teatral'nom fronte: Na teatral'nom soveshchanii RAPP," *Rit*, no. 6 (March 1, 1931), p. 14.

70. "GIII reorganizovan," *Rit*, no. 62–63 (November 20, 1930), p. 5. In that year Moscow's GAKhN was renamed GAIS and transferred to Leningrad to be incorporated into GIII.

71. S. R., "Slët 70 TRAMov," *Rit*, no. 10 (February 21, 1930), p. 5.

72. "Oblastnoye tramovskoye soveshchaniye," *Rit*, no. 13–14 (May 21, 1931), p. 5; "Nashi osnovnye zadachi na segodnyashniy den': Beseda s predsedatelem Teasektsii Leningradskogo otdela Komakademii tovarishchem Libedinskim," *Rit*, no. 29–30 (December 7, 1931), pp. 5–6.

73. Erde, "Fabrika marksizma," *S*, no. 21 (1929), pp. 10–11.

74. "Gvozdev i 'Gvodevshchina,' " *Rit*, no. 11 (April 21, 1931), p. 2.

75. See "Burzhuaznaya teatrovedeniye pod sudom istorii: Gvozdev govorit," *Rit*, no. 10 (April 11, 1931), p. 6; I. Sollertinsky, "Ideologicheskiye predposylki gvozdevskoy shkoly," *Rit*, no. 12 (April 30, 1931), pp. 5–6.

76. Sollertinsky, "Vozmozhnye printsipy sovetskoy opery," p. 3.

77. Ye. G., "Shkola Filonova (Vystavka v Dome pechati)," *Kg*, no. 118 (May 5, 1927), p. 4.

78. "Formalizmu, beskusovshchine, bessistemnosti—konets!" editorial, *Rit*, no. 7 (February 5, 1930), p. 1.

79. Compare ibid., p. 3; I. Sollertinsky, " 'Nos'—orudiye dal'noboynoye," ibid., pp. 6–7.

80. "VI plenum TsK Rabisa," *Rit*, no. 28 (October 28, 1931), pp. 6–7.

81. D. Shostakovich, "Deklaratsiya obyazannostey kompozitora," *Rit*, no. 31 (November 20, 1931), p. 6. It is always tricky to pinpoint motives for individuals' involvement in an enterprise like TRAM. It could be that Shostakovich sat out the storm of the cultural revolution in that relatively safe haven and abandoned it when it was over (reported in Solomon Volkov's not entirely reliable *Testimony: The Memoirs of Dmitri Shostakovich*, trans. Antonina W. Bouis [New York, 1980], p. 112). But it could also be that Shostakovich, himself from a family with a tradition of revolutionary leftism, joined TRAM at least in part out of idealism.

82. I. Stalin, "Novaya obstanovka—novye zadachi khozyaystvennogo stroitel'stva (rech' na soveshchanii khozyaystvennikov 23 iyunya 1931 goda)," *P*, July 5, 1931, p. 1.

83. I. Stalin, "O nekotorykh voprosakh istorii bol'shevizma: Pis'mo k redaktsii zhurnala 'Proletarskaya revolyutsiya,' " *Proletarskaya revolyutsiya* (1931), no. 6 (113), pp. 3–12 (the quotation is from p. 12).

84. I. Stalin, "O nekotorykh voprosakh istorii bol'shevizma," p. 6.

85. Sheila Fitzpatrick, *The Cultural Front: Power and Culture in Revolutionary Russia* (Ithaca, N.Y.: Cornell University Press, 1992), pp. 165–167.

86. Victor Turner, *The Ritual Process: Structure and Anti-Structure* (Chicago: Aldine, 1969).

87. "Khronika," *Pir*, no. 11 (1929), p. 117.

88. "Za pyat' dney," *Rit*, no. 47 (August 24, 1930), p. 15.

89. Katerina Clark, "Political History and Literary Chronotope: Some Soviet Case Studies," in Gary Saul Morson, ed., *Literature and History: Theoretical Problems and Russian Case Studies* (Stanford: Stanford University Press, 1986), pp. 230–246.

90. "Khronika: Po literaturnym institutam i organizatsiyam," *Pir,* no. 1 (1930), p. 85.

91. Mikhail Bakhtin, "Forms of Time and the Chronotope in the Novel," *The Dialogic Imagination,* trans. Caryl Emerson and Michael Holquist (Austin: University of Texas Press, 1981), p. 85.

92. "Khronika," *Pir,* no. 12 (1928), p. 111.

93. His *Khudozhnik neizvesten* of 1931 represents a shift from his *Skandalist* of 1929, where he satirized his own set.

94. See V. Pudovkin's *Potomok Chingiz Khana* of 1928 and *Krasnyy partizan, Turkmeniya,* and *Put' entuziastov* of 1929.

95. A. Karaganov, *Vsevolod Pudovkin* (Moscow: Iskusstvo, 1973), p. 95.

Epilogue: The Thirties

1. Niles Eldredge and Stephen J. Gould, "Punctuated Equilibrium: An Alternative to Phyletic Gradualism," in T. J. M. Schopf and J. M. Thomas, eds., *Models in Paleontology* (San Francisco: Freeman, Cooper, 1972), pp. 82–115.

2. Sheila Fitzpatrick in *The Russian Revolution, 1917–1932,* dates the Great Purge as 1937–1938 but also discusses a series of sweeping purges that began early in 1935. My dates, which encompass the "show trials" of 1936, 1937, and 1938, are the approximate parameters used by Robert Conquest in *The Great Terror.*

3. M. Gorky, "O rabote nad yazykom," *Lg,* no. 26 (May 15, 1931).

4. "Knigi na stole delegatov s"yezda," *Lg,* no. 9 (January 28, 1934).

5. M. Gorky, "Po povodu odnoy diskussii," *Lg,* no. 10 (January 30, 1934); A. Serafimovich, "O pisatel'yakh 'oblizannykh' i 'neoblizannykh,' " *Lg,* no. 13 (February 6, 1934); M. Gorky, "Otkrytoye pis'mo A. S. Serafimovichu," *Lg,* no. 17 (February 14, 1934); M. Gorky, "O boykosti," *Lg,* no. 24 (February 28, 1934); A. S. Serafimovich, "Otvet A. M. Gor'komu," *Lg,* no. 25 (March 1, 1934).

6. "Vchera otkrylsya Plenum Orgkomiteta" and "XVII s"yezd partii i zadachi pisateley: Sokrashchënnaya stenogramma doklada zav. kul'tpropom TsK VKP (b) t. A. Stetskogo na sobraniye pisateley 3 marta," *Lg,* no. 28 (March 8, 1934).

7. "Za kul'turu yazyka," editorial, *Lg,* no. 34 (March 20, 1934), p. 1.

8. "Rech' sekretarya TsK VKP (b) A. A. Zhdanova," *Pervyy s"yezd pisateley: Stenograficheskiy otchët* (Moscow: Ogiz, 1934), p. 5.

9. M. Gorky, "Otkrytoye pis'mo A. Serafimovichu," *Lg,* no. 17 (February 14, 1934).

10. See Katerina Clark, *The Soviet Novel: History as Ritual* (Chicago: University of Chicago Press, 1981).

11. This function of the Writers Union was apparent from the very first meeting of its organizational committee. See, for example, "V Orgkomitete soyuza pisateley RSFSR," *Lg,* no. 27 (June 17, 1932), p. 1; "Uluchshit' materi-

al'no-bytovoye obsluzhivaniye pisateley!" *Lg,* no. 31 (July 11, 1932), p. 1; "Uluchshit' byt," *Lg,* no. 45 (October 5, 1932).

12. See Katerina Clark, "Little Heroes and Big Deeds: Literature Responds to the First Five-Year Plan," in Sheila Fitzpatrick, ed., *Cultural Revolution in Russia, 1928–1931* (Bloomington: Indiana University Press, 1978), pp. 191, 205–206.

13. M. Gorky, "O 'karamazovshchine' " (on a staged version of *The Possessed* at MKhAT), *Rso,* no. 219 (September 22, 1913); "Yeshchë o 'karamazovshchine,'" *Rso,* no. 248 (October 27, 1913).

14. See, for example, *Sto let so dnya smerti A. S. Pushkina: Trudy Pushkinskoy sessii Akademii nauk SSSR* (Moscow and Leningrad: Akademiya nauk, 1938): "Pushkin vkhodit v kommunisticheskoye segodnya" (Nechkina, p. 55); "Zhivoy uchastnik nashey literaturnoy sovremennosti" (Desnitskiy, p. 137).

15. See the concluding sentence of B. Meylakh in *Pushkin i russkiy romantizm* (Moscow-Leningrad: Akademiya nauk, 1937): "V tvorchestve Pushkina genial'no osushchestvlën tot splav realizma i ustremlënnogo *vperëd* romantizma, kotoryy tak dorog nam"; compare Zhdanov's account of socialist realism in his speech to the First Writers Congress. See also "Nasha gordost', nasha slava," editorial, *I,* February 10, 1937, p. 1; "Torzhestvennoye zasedaniye v Bol'shom teatre posvyashchënnoe stoletiyu so dnya smerti A. S. Pushkina," *P,* February 11, 1937, p. 2 (esp. P. Luppol: "Vsya russkaya literatura, rodonachal'nikom kotoroy byl Pushkin, stala sovetskoy literaturoy").

16. Evgeniya Ginzburg, *Krutoy marshrut,* published in English as *Journey into the Whirlwind,* trans. Paul Stevenson and Max Hayward (New York: Harcourt, Brace and World, 1967).

17. In the 1991 putsch one finds similar ambiguity in the appropriation of Pushkin: the ideologues of the putsch frequently claimed that Pushkin was "theirs" ("ours") by citing from his verse and alleged beliefs in support of their calls for resistance to Gorbachev. Those who resisted the putsch also recited from Pushkin in, for example, the speeches made on a tank outside the R.S.F.S.R. "White House."

18. "Slava russkogo naroda," editorial, *P,* February 10, 1937, p. 1.

19. See, for example, the materials on the reception of Andrei Sinyavsky's *Strolls with Pushkin* (Progulki s Pushkinym), in Catherine Nepomnyashchy, ed., *The Return of Abram Tertz: Siniavskii's Reception in Gorbachev's Russia,* a special issue of *Studies in Russian Literature.*

20. "Torzhestvuyushchiy oboz," editorial, *V,* no. 3 (May 1922), p. 2 (cited in Chapter 5).

21. L. S. Viv'yen, "Nashi spektakli," *Leningradskiy gosudarstvennyy Ordena Trudovogo Krasnogo Znameni Akademicheskiy teatr dramy im. A. S. Pushkina* (Leningrad, 1940), p. 43.

22. N. V. Petrov, *50 i 500* (Moscow: Vserossiyskoye teatral'noye obshchestvo, 1960), pp. 275, 285–288.

23. Sergey Radlov, "Teatr opery i baleta," *Rit,* no. 23 (September 10, 1931), p. 8.

24. Of course the meaning of Shakespeare is not self-evident since his theater had been a model for the people's theater. Although Radlov now directed Shakespeare as high culture, still he tried to make his productions less pious and grim than those of other contemporary directors.

25. "Sumbur vmesto muzyki," *P,* January 28, 1936, p. 3.

26. "Baletnaya fal'sh," *P,* February 6, 1936.

27. "Soveshchaniye v Komitete po delam iskusstv," *P,* March 15, 1936, p. 4.

28. For a fuller account of these events see Konstantin Rudnitsky, "Krusheniye teatra," in *Meyerkhol'dovskiy sbornik,* issue I, part II, ed. A. A. Sherel' (Moscow: Tvorcheskiy tsentr im. Vs. Meyerkhol'da, 1992), pp. 7–29.

29. See the documents and memoir materials relating to Meyerhold's arrest and execution in two issues of *Teatral'naya zhizn'* for 1989: "K 50-letiyu gibeli Vs. Meyerkhol'da," no. 2, and "Meyerkhol'd: Posledniy akt tragedii," no. 5.

30. A glossy book on the history and achievements of the theater produced that year discusses the production in some detail but does not mention Meyerhold's name and lists Yuriev as the director: *Leningradskiy Gosudarstvennyy Ordena Trudovogo Znameni Akademicheskiy Teatr Drama im. A. S. Pushkina,* pp. 30–31, 43, 46.

31. N. A. Zabolotsky, "Istoriya moego zaklyucheniya," *Minuvsheye: Istoricheskiy al'manakh,* no. 2 (Paris: Atheneum, 1986), p. 322.

32. V. Gaydebura, "Tak rasskazat' pravdivo," *Sk* (1989), p. 6.

33. Others include L. S. Viven, who in Petrograd in 1918 had co-authored with Meyerhold a theoretical article on body movement that anticipated his later theories of Biomechanics, and K. S. Derzhavin, who during War Communism had doubled for the circus acrobat Serge on occasion at Radlov's Peoples Comedy Theater.

34. See, for instance, *Lo,* no. 11 (1991), an "issue devoted to the erotic tradition in Russian literature."

35. Richard Stites, *Russian Popular Culture: Entertainment and Society since 1900* (Cambridge: Cambridge University Press, 1992), pp. 72–78.

36. This account comes from my interview with Leonid Trauberg in Moscow in June of 1989.

37. Katerina Clark, "Aural Hieroglyphics? Some Reflections on the Role of Sound in Recent Russian Film and Its Historical Context," in Nancy Condee, ed., *Russian/Soviet Hieroglyphics (British Film Institute/Indiana University Press,* 1995).

38. S. Eisenstein, "Vertikal'noye kino," *Iko,* no. 9 (1940), pp. 16–25.

39. Many of the principals involved came originally not from Leningrad but from Jewish enclaves in the Ukraine (especially Odessa), as was also true of many of the pioneering names in Tin Pan Alley.

40. A. Badulin, "'Uslovno ubityy': Prem'yera v myuzik-kholl," *Rit,* no. 28 (October 28, 1931), p. 9; Lorel E. Fey, "Mitya v myuzik-kholle: Yeshchë odin vzglyad na *Uslovno ubitogo,*" unpublished paper presented in Petersburg on April 12, 1993, to the conference "Otechestvennaya muzyka XX veka: Novoye ob izvestnom."

41. E. D. Uvarova, ed., *Russkaya sovetskaya estrada, 1930–1945: Ocherki istorii* (Moscow: Iskusstvo, 1977), p. 240; A. Razumovskiy, "Dzhaz na estrade: Mozhet li on stat' sovetskim?" *Rit,* no. 43 (August 4, 1930), p. 7; "Myuzik-kholl," *Rit,* no. 50 (September 11, 1930), p. 19.

42. "K. Ye. Voroshilov na IX s"yezde VLKSM," *P,* January 22, 1931, p. 2.

43. "Prakticheskiye meropriyatiya po uluchsheniyu i razvitiyu moskovskogo gorodskogo khozyastva: Postanovleniye Moskovskogo oblastnogo i gorodskogo sovetov VKP (b) . . .," *P,* June 25, 1931, p. 3.

44. See "Obraztsy bol'shevistskoy bor'by za finplan" and "Smotreniye bol'- shevistkikh pobed" as headings for *Pravda* reports on production achievements (September 22 and October 1, 1931, respectively).

45. The importance of precedents from Petersburg in the designs for the new monumental buildings is particularly apparent in the illustrations (most of them for plans never executed) in Alexei Tarkhanov and Sergei Kavtaradze, *Architecture of the Stalin Era* (New York: Rizzoli, 1992).

46. "Prakticheskiye meropryatiya," p. 3; "O Moskovskom gorodskom khozyaystve i o razvitii gorodskogo khozyaystva SSSR: Dokald tov. Kaganovicha L. L. na iyunskom plenume TsK VKP(b)," *P,* July 4, 1931, p. 4.

47. See, for example, Alex Scobie, *Hitler's State Architecture: The Impact of Classical Antiquity* (University Park and London: University of Pennsylvania Press, 1990); Alan Balfour, *Berlin: The Politics of Order, 1757–1989* (New York: Rizzoli, 1991); Robert A. M. Stern, *Modern Classicism* (New York: Rizzoli, 1988).

48. "Net takikh krepostey, kotorykh bol'sheviki ne mogli by vzyat': Rech' tov. Stalina na vsesoyuznoy konferentsii rabotnikov promyshlennosti," *P,* February 5, 1931, p. 2.

49. Even in 1926 when the Alexandrinsky staged a revival of the Meyerhold production it was attacked as "untimely," "aestheticism," and "apoliticism"; Sadko, "'Maskarad'. . .," *Zi,* no. 21 (May 25, 1926), p. 17.

50. Vladimir Papernyy argues that in the 1930s first Neoclassical models dominated as the official inspiration for Soviet architecture and then models from more strictly "native traditions"; see *Kul'tura "dva"* (Ann Arbor: Ardis, 1985), pp. 36–40. In the account of the 1930s in Tarkhanov and Kavtaradze's *Architecture of the Stalin Era,* however, indebtedness to classical models is emphasized. It is worth noting that avant-garde designs were also prominent in some of the competitions of that decade.

ACKNOWLEDGMENTS

I would like to express my deep gratitude to the Guggenheim Foundation and also to the Humanities Research Centre of the Australian National University, who at different times enabled me to devote a year or a semester to research and writing; without their support the project would have been unrealizable. I am also grateful to the Fox Fellowship Exchange Program between Moscow State University and Yale University, which enabled me to do some crucial research in Moscow.

I would also like to thank many individuals who helped me research or conceptualize this book: my tremendously rewarding undergraduate and graduate students at Yale University; Edward Kasinec in the Slavic Reading Room at the New York Public Library; colleagues in the field such as Svetlana Boym, Jeffrey Brooks, Evgeny Dobrenko, Caryl Emerson, Laurel Fay, Gregory Freidin, Nina Perlina, Svetlana Semyonova, Vladimir Skorodenko, Mark Steinberg, Mark von Hagen, Richard Wortman, Lazar Fleischman, and John Malmstad; and my dear friend Heather Sutherland. Thanks are also due members of my own family: my late father, Manning Clark, and also Dymphna and Sebastian Clark, who read the manuscript while it was still a very baggy monster and made useful suggestions; Nicholas and Sebastian Holquist, my two staunchest supporters; and lastly Michael Holquist, the best cure for the loneliness of the long-distance writer.

INDEX

Academy of Sciences, 67, 205, 218, 294, 298, 302. *See also* KEPS

Academy of the Arts, 68, 100, 103, 154, 187, 269

Acmeism, 63, 65, 86, 96

Aeschylus, 80, 111, 137, 292

Agitprop (Department of Agitation and Propaganda), 225, 243, 266, 271; TRAM as, 268

Aida. See Verdi

Akhmatova, Anna, 7–8, 96, 98, 155, 182, 300

AKhRR (Association of Artists of Revolutionary Russia), 185–186, 188, 191, 194

Akimov, Nikolai, 296

Alekseyev-Yakovlev, A. Ya., 132

Alexander I, 57, 64, 66, 96, 221–222

Alexander III, 57–58

Alexandrinsky (renamed State, then Academic) Theater, 74, 77, 101, 267–268, 290, 292

Alexandrov, Grigory, 294–296, 302

Alienation, 16–17, 80, 98

All-Russian Association of Proletarian Writers. *See* VAPP

All-Union Society for Overseas Cultural Links. *See* VOKS

Altman, Natan, 100, 103, 154–155, 261

America, 1, 5, 56, 132, 136, 162; "americanization," 165

Anarchism, 30, 79

Andreeva, M. F., 101, 103, 107, 110–111, 116, 117

Annenkov, Yury, 45–46, 116n64, 184; and mass spectacle, 126, 132, 136

Anthroposophy, 9

Antsiferov, N. F., 158

Apollo (Apollon), 17, 62–65, 71, 72, 86, 86n31, 88, 89, 95

Appia, Adolphe, 76

Architecture, 23, 51, 57–64, 76, 139–141, 145; role in Soviet mythology, 302. See also *Dom-kommuna; Sotsgorod*

Argus, 47, 197

Aristophanes, 111

Arkhplan, 298, 304

Arvatov, Boris, 207 209, 211–212, 216, 286

Asafiev, B., 150, 227, 228

Avant-garde, 14, 25–27, 28–53, 93–94, 98, 102, 112. *See also* Dada; Expressionism; Futurism; Left art; OBERYu; Surrealism

Averbakh, Leopold, 292

Babel, Isaak, 153

Bacon, Francis, 68

Bakhtin, Mikhail, 24, 25, 150n30, 169, 238, 257; and carnival, 19, 96–97, 125, 128; circle of, 149, 205, 233, 281, 282; and language, 224–225, 231, 233–234, 236

Bakunin, Mikhail, 79

Balagan (fairground theater), 82, 87, 92–93, 96

Ballet, 55, 56, 71, 103, 230

Ballets Russes, 54, 56, 103

Baltic Fleet. *See* Navy

Baltic-White Sea Canal. *See* Belomor Canal

Balzac, Honoré de, 6, 9

Baudelaire, Charles, 35, 49, 192

Bauhaus, 22, 36, 140, 274

Beethoven, Ludwig von, 83